SEX CHANGES

The Politics of Transgenderism

SEX CHANGES

The Politics of Transgenderism

Pat Califia

CLEIS
PRESS

Published in the United States by Cleis Press Inc., P.O. Box 14684, San Francisco, California 94114.

Printed in the United States.
Cover design: Scott Idleman/Blink
Cover photo: Phyllis Christopher
Text design: Karen Huff
Logo art: Juana Alicia
First Edition.
10 9 8 7 6 5 4 3 2 1

Library of Congress Cataloging-in-Publication Data

Califia, Pat
    Sex changes: the politics of transgenderism/Pat Califia.
        p. cm.
    Includes bibliographical references and index.
    ISDN 1-57344-072-8 (pbk.)
    1. Transsexualism.   2. Transvestism.   3. Sex change.   4. Gender identity.   I. Title.
HQ77.9.C35   1997
305.9'066—dc21   97-19966
                                                        CIP

This book is dedicated to the memory of Lou Sullivan
and to differently-gendered young people,
with the hope that they will not allow
this culture's gender insanity
to drive them crazy.

Acknowledgments

Without the help of many people, some of whom were kind enough to assist me even though we have never met, this book would not have been possible.

Felice Newman and Frédérique Delacoste took a risk on me personally and on this book, which I will always remember. Their patience (albeit sometimes strained) during the many health problems and personal crises that delayed completion of this manuscript is a rare commodity in the publishing business. As friends and as professionals who have dedicated their lives to enriching queer and feminist literature, they have no peers.

I would like to thank Susan Stryker, Ph.D. and Jill Enquist for their patience and assistance with locating reference materials. I'd also like to thank Warren J. Blumenfeld, editor of the *Journal of Gay, Lesbian and Bisexual Identity*, for putting me in touch with a key informant. Margaret Deirdre O'Hartigan provided crucial documentation for chapter three and other key points in the manuscript. Joanne Meyerowitz shared primary sources uncovered during her research on Christine Jorgensen. Shadow Morton of the San Francisco Human Rights Commission generously gave of his time and resources. Linda Suzuki of the Interlibrary Loan Department, San Francisco Public Library, rescued me from that special hell researchers are sent to when their paperwork is lost, and located journal articles from other libraries for me in record time. Davina Anne Gabriel put me in touch with original sources regarding the Brandon Teena murder case. And the ever-helpful staff at A Different Light bookstore, San Francisco, supplied last-minute information necessary to complete my footnotes.

The manuscript was reviewed and greatly benefited from the critical comments of Ian Philips and Val Langmuir. Special thanks are due to Val Langmuir for many hot suppers, neck rubs, and chauffeured jaunts to this and that bookstore and copy center. Portions of the manuscript were reviewed by Riki Anne Wilchins and James Green. Their remarks and corrections were invaluable.

The following editorial interns were of great help in organizing the interview data: Anne Bevilacqua, Bree Coven, and Rachel Lanzerotti. Their selfless contribution of time, energy, and intelligence is much appreciated. I am also indebted to the people who took time out of their busy lives to be interviewed. I hope I have merited the trust vested in me by the people who allowed me to glimpse some of the most intimate and vulnerable parts of their lives.

As always, any errors or omissions herein are my own responsibility.

Table of Contents

An Introduction

Spare Changes: Why and How This Book Came into Being

Sex Changes: The Politics of Transgenderism is an examination of trans-sexuality, gender dysphoria, and transgenderism in the twentieth century. It combines history, interviews, cultural analysis, and personal anecdotes in an attempt to give the reader some idea of the way differ-ently-gendered people's perceptions of themselves and the perceptions of those outside the gender community have evolved, and some of the complex medical, sexual, political, and social issues these phenomena present.

But before beginning this process of teasing out meaning and fram-ing new questions, it is important for me to clarify my position in rela-tion to my subject. Most of the literature about transsexuals has been written by self-proclaimed experts, from a position that claims to be academic or scientific, and therefore objective. (One exception to this is anti-transsexual pundit Janice Raymond, author of *The Transsexual Empire*, who claims expert status because of her feminism.)

I am uncomfortable with the stance of the objective outsider who, because of a sheaf of credentials, purports to have a point of view that is more important or powerful than that of transgendered people themselves. In medical and feminist discourses, transsexuals are stereo-typed as patients undergoing sex reassignment, the troubled clients of psychotherapists, or faux, man-made "women" created by the patri-archy to act as moles in the war between the sexes. This gives the experts a privileged voice and disenfranchises differently-gendered people. In autobiographical or fictional accounts, they may set down what they perceive to be true about themselves and the world around them, but it is the medical doctor, therapist, academic, and feminist theoretician who interpret "them" for the rest of "us," and thus claim to be the voice of reality.

There is a powerful assumption here about the audience, as well, that it is constituted for the most part of "normally" gendered people. The setting-aside or excommunication of the transsexual from the main body of society is a vital, and easy to miss, part of this conceptual process. I suspect this is a strategy for reducing the anxiety of a reader who might otherwise be forced to confront his or her own failures at living up to gender stereotypes. It makes it easier to disavow or avoid imagining altogether the guilty pleasures that potentially may be taken in deliberately violating these norms. In industrialized Western societies, it is a thought crime to imagine oneself in the body of the other (always opposite) sex, or appropriate any of the artifacts of the other gender's role. To be differently-gendered is to live within a discourse where other people are always investigating you, describing you, and speaking for you; and putting as much distance as possible between the expert speaker and the deviant and therefore deficient subject.

I have tried in this book to examine the claims of medical professionals and scientists with all the tools of rational intelligence and objectivity. Despite the academic format of this book and my work as a therapist, I am not comfortable allying myself with supposedly objective experts or positioning myself as one of their colleagues. The claim that anybody is objective about transgenderism should be met with profound skepticism. Anyone who confronts gender variation has a highly personal and emotional response. Transsexuals challenge our ideas of right and wrong, politically correct and politically incorrect, mental health and mental dysfunction. If we have a sense of "rightness" about ourselves as men or women, gender outlaws scramble it. Gender dysphoria—even someone else's—literally gets us by the short hairs, where we live, between our legs. When such visceral responses are ignored, they surface in other ways. I trust the investigator who outlines his or her own biases much more than the expert who compulsively excludes the personal element from his or her prescriptions and explanations. In matters of sexuality, we understand so very little that any claim to authority is premature. The best we can do is speak our own truth, make it safe for others to speak theirs, and respect our differences.

This work springs from my own profound discomfort with social sex-role conditioning. As a small child, I rarely wanted to wear dresses, unless they were glamorous or slinky. My family still tells a funny (?) story about a confrontation I had with my father one Christmas day, when I was upset about being given girls' toys. He told me that if I wanted to have boys' toys, I would have to have a penis, and I informed him that I had once had one, but he had removed it with a clothespin. So much for feminist claims that penis envy does not exist. It was alive and well in my little psyche!

When I got a little older, I found out that Barbie could wear Ken's clothes, and vice versa, so I put Ken in Barbie's prettiest formal, tied him up with some coarse, scratchy twine, and stuck him back in his box. He had been kidnapped, I decided. Barbie got to wear Ken's suit and had a series of mad adventures with her sidekick, trying to rescue Ken. For reasons that are obvious to me now, my mother would not invest in a second Barbie doll to accompany my cross-dressed heroine on her mission of derring-do. So the sidekick (who could be seen as Barbie's femme, looking back through grown-up lesbian eyes) was a troll doll with bright green hair. I don't think Ken was ever rescued. And my fondness for girls with punk haircuts in primary colors now has its exegesis. Not to mention well-restrained boys in dresses.

My lesbianism is largely a product of my profound emotional and erotic involvement with other women. But it was also a strategy for reducing gender dysphoria, part of a search for a place where I could be more of a man, or at least a different sort of woman. Historically, dykes have been defined as "not-women." This part of our identity has been submerged today, in part as a result of our struggle to participate in the feminist movement of the seventies. This made it necessary for us to aggressively claim an identity as women. Few dykes, even lesbian feminists, remember today that the first negative response to lesbian participation in the women's movement was the idea that we would contaminate consciousness-raising groups with male behavior— specifically, sexual predation. Straight feminists assumed that lesbians had the equivalent of male identities.

A straightforward equation of dykes with men is obviously homophobic. But the lesbian-feminist vision of dykes as ultrafeminists and ultrawomen left a lot of us in the dust. Butch-femme role-playing certainly didn't stop, but within lesbian feminism it became a subterranean game, doubly suppressed by straight society and by lesbian feminists. Some segments of the lesbian community became deeply alienated from others. Dykes still wrestle with these questions of identity. Do we affiliate with straight women who are also feminists, even if they are not vulnerable to some of the persecution that lesbians face? Do we affiliate with other lesbians, despite sexual, cultural, political, racial, or class differences? Do we insist on being seen as women and try to better our lot by improving the lot of women in general? Or do we acknowledge the ways that many of us have "unwomaned" ourselves by rejecting the traditional roles for females in this society?

During the time when I came out as a sadomasochist, the lesbian-feminist movement was not a safe place to bring up any of these issues. Fortunately, the S/M community offered me a comparatively secure haven for cross-dressing and gender play. Unfortunately, the male/female paradigm is a powerful one, and it is difficult even for polymorphous perverts to create top/bottom roles that do not share the worst characteristics of polarized, dichotomous genders. To put it in less academic terms, my first long-term S/M relationship was with a bottom who equated masculinity with maleness with being a "real top." She perceived any sexual pleasure that was experienced by a woman's body or any stimulation of the female genitals, especially penetration, to be submissive and degrading. Her fantasy was to find a "real top" who would be sexually satisfied by the act of dominating her. She told me many times that if I were a man, I would come from fucking her, and she would not have to leave bottom space to cope with my annoying requests for an orgasm.

Well, we put up with a lot of crap when we are in love. I was hooked into this weird belief system because I still had a significant amount of shame about being a sexually-active woman and more than a little cognitive dissonance when I tried to associate the body I actually had with the person I felt myself to really be. There was a part of me that agreed with the negative value she placed on a woman's pleasure. When she hinted that her desires would be more completely satisfied by a man, I wanted to be that man. Being a young butch dyke top with no role models, I wanted very much to be real, to succeed at this erotic task of being recognized by her and by other sadomasochists as a master.

So, without discussing the matter much with my girlfriend, I investigated the process of sex reassignment. It seemed to me that I had enough of the right sort of stories from childhood and adolescence to convince a psychiatrist that I ought to be given hormones and, eventually, surgery. The idea of having a beard and the upper-body musculature of a man was very appealing. But testosterone would not make me taller, and I did not want to become a bantam rooster of a man. I couldn't imagine living with a reconstructed body. I was unable to think of a mastectomy as anything other than mutilation. Much as I would have enjoyed having a penis, it was very clear that surgical techniques did not exist that would create a functional and attractive male sex organ. At least I could take a strap-on dildo off when I wanted to be more comfortable. The pleasure that I got from my cunt might be problematic, but the physiological changes that testosterone produced (clitoral enlargement and vaginal atrophy) didn't seem to be much of an improvement.

In the end, I decided that I could not separate my personal ambivalence about being female from the misogyny and homophobia of the surrounding culture. I could not tell if I wanted to have a cock because I wanted to be a man, or because I had been told all my life that any real sex had to involve a penis and a vagina. Did I hate my tits because I was transsexual, or did I hate them because I was sick to death of being leered at, grabbed, and ridiculed? I went around and around with this question for months, and could not come to any honest answer.

And so I became a sort of psychic hermaphrodite. If I was going to live in a female body, I decided that I had to embrace (as much as this was possible for me) my tits, my cunt, and my femininity. Sometimes, I have to admit, I am only able to channel that girly-girl stuff by becoming an aggressive and bitchy drag queen. (You can't assume just because you see somebody wearing a little black dress and high heels that they are in femme or female mode.) I did not want to give up male apparel or the sexual fantasy of sometimes being a man. But I knew that if I went too far in that direction, it would drive me crazy. It's wonderful to fuck someone in male persona. I have a strong psychic connection to my phallus, but I also have to get away from the male mode sometimes because it's not real, I don't have a cock, and I have to be able to love and cherish my own body if I am going to have any sort of a happy life. I rejected the fifties' solution to gender dysphoria, becoming a stone butch, because I had slept with enough stone butches to know how miserable and resentful they were.

S/M interested me because it made it possible to assign power and meaning on a voluntary basis, according to one's desire or whim. I wanted to challenge the correlation of maleness with masculinity and running the fuck; the correlation of femaleness with femininity and getting run over in bed. Where was the challenge or the power in being an ostensibly dominant woman who serviced other people's fantasies and refused to let anyone touch her?

I mean no disrespect to lesbian culture and history when I ask this question. There are reasons why stone butches existed and continue to exist, and those women are among my most cherished heroes. But I don't want anybody to be shamed out of enjoying human touch or sexual stimulation, especially not women who share my queasiness with the messages we inherited about our bodies being inferior, weak, and dirty.

The only thing that worked for me, in the crazy context I found myself in, was to build strong personas as both male and female, so I could access and enjoy any part of my own nature. It sometimes gets a little crowded in the control room, and I continue to be sad about the limits biology has placed on my ability to manifest as a man, but most of the time I am pretty comfortable in my own skin and up against other people's bodies. The hardest part is getting others to recognize the kaleidoscopic nature of my identity. It's amazing what people will infer from a haircut—or a hemline.

These autobiographical musings are not meant to be a condemnation of sex reassignment. That process looks very different to people who change their sex. I was most aware of its drawbacks. Transsexuals see its most positive aspects. They are willing to take a lot of risks in exchange for the chance to acquire a body image that will match their self image. I do not advocate my personal solution for anyone who is experiencing severe gender dysphoria. Nor do I tell this story to make myself out to be a transsexual. Certainly I was in great distress when I considered a sex change. I couldn't imagine being more unhappy. But I think the distress that motivates someone to take hormones or get surgery is of a different magnitude. I tell it only to place myself on the gender continuum, and to encourage readers to think about how the tyranny of the male/female dichotomy affects their own body image, clothing, sexuality, mannerisms, career choice, speech, eating habits, and every other aspect of human existence. Consider the possibility that one of the purposes a transsexual identity serves is to make the rest of us look contented and well-adjusted by comparison. There are many levels of gender dysphoria, many aberrant accommodations other than a sex change. Feminism, for example.

The topic of gender is relevant to everyone. But lesbians and gay men should be especially sensitive to the way transsexuality has been positioned as the property of medical and psychiatric experts. It was not so very long ago that a similar condition existed for us. Through cultural and legal activism, we have very nearly managed to extricate ourselves from the grip of scientists. Unlike the transgendered person who seeks hormonal therapy or surgery to facilitate living in his or her gender of preference, homosexuals do not need to seek out doctors or therapists to obtain prescriptions or letters of approval before we can go out into the world and try to mold it a little closer to our heart's desire. But we do share a common history with them of being viewed as mentally ill people who require treatment.

And we've often shared public space with one another, freaks of all sorts thrown together and crowded away from the mainstream, into the margins. The oppression of gay men and lesbians overlaps that of transsexuals. To the extent that homosexuals are viewed as men and women who do not conform to social sex-role stereotypes, we are also gender outlaws. And, of course, there are many transsexuals who are gay men, lesbians, or bisexuals. This book was written in part to bolster an alliance between gay and transgender activists and community organizers.

Sex Changes begins with the first generation of transsexual writing—autobiographical testimony about the benefits of medically-mediated sex reassignment. Chapter one examines three of these pioneering works: *Christine Jorgensen: A Personal Autobiography*, Jan Morris's *Conundrum*, and *Emergence*, a lesser-known life story by female-to-male (FTM) transsexual Mario Martino. Even at this early date, key differences between transgendered men and women can be seen.

Most of these early autobiographies are dedicated to the doctors and sex researchers who first advocated that sex reassignment be used as a treatment for gender dysphoria. Chapter two is an exploration of the work published by this premiere generation of gender experts, which dominated the public's understanding of transsexuality and for all intents and purposes dictated public policy about "treatment" for this "dysfunction." Chief among these experts were Harry Benjamin, John Money, and Richard Green.

The third chapter outlines the feminist backlash against the concept of gender dysphoria, the therapy of sex reassignment, and the first transsexual activists. This backlash was informed by two separate theoretical currents, the New Christian Right, which condemned transsexuals as violating God's divine plan for life on earth, and an essentialist sort of feminism that relied on biologically-determined differences between men and women to fuel its call for social change. The spokeswoman for this latter trend was Janice Raymond, of course, whose passionate work *The Transsexual Empire* has become a classic in the debate about whether or not male-to-female transsexuals (MTFs) should be accepted as women, much less as feminists or lesbians. This chapter also includes a look at *Horsexe*, an essay on transsexuality by Lacanian devotee Catherine Millot. Since Millot's perspective owes much to psychoanalysis and the research of Robert J. Stoller, M.D., author of *Perversion: The Erotic Form of Hatred*, Stoller's work is also examined here.

Meanwhile, within gay academia, anthropological data about the roles available to those who cannot conform to gender stereotypes in non-Western or preindustrial societies was being used to bolster an argument that homosexuality was a natural part of human sexuality and has existed in all human cultures. The fourth chapter deals with gay academics' research on the Native American berdaches, the hijra of India, and "passing women." The work of Jonathan Katz, Walter L. Williams, Will Roscoe, Ramón A. Gutiérrez, and other gay male academics is examined.

Chapter five evaluates a second wave of transsexual autobiography, to see what changes took place in the post-Jorgensen decades. Renée Richards' narrative and work by English FTM transgender activist Mark Rees are the central works analyzed here. Although gay male FTM Lou Sullivan left no autobiography, because of his important role as the founder of the first support group for transsexual men, his life is examined using other sources. Leslie Feinberg's novel *Stone Butch Blues* is also included, to complete the reader's picture of new connections that transsexuals are making with gay and lesbian communities. Kate Bornstein, author of *Gender Outlaw*, an important book that breaks the autobiographical frame of transsexual narrative, is also featured.

When the notion of transsexuality first entered American popular culture, the idea that anyone would connect sexually or romantically with a transsexual seemed freakish and ridiculous. Later on, since it was the goal of medical science to turn transsexuals into masculine heterosexual men and feminine heterosexual females, the notion evolved that the partners of transsexual people would be "normal," and the identity of the transsexual would somehow be lifted or erased by marriage. Today, it has become clear that this is a limited view of the allies, lovers, spouses, and families of transgendered individuals. Chapter six addresses these people, "invisible gender outlaws." To give the reader a sense of how the concepts of differently-gendered people's partners have altered over time, Virginia Prince's *The Transvestite and His Wife*, Minnie Bruce Pratt's groundbreaking work *S/he*, and other works are examined.

The single most important factor impacting on transgender identity in the nineties is a new wave of radical activism. Chapter seven sketches the outlines of a history of political efforts by transsexuals to improve the quality of their lives and change deeply entrenched, negative attitudes about them. Direct-action campaigns to draw public attention to violence against transsexuals are highlighted, as well as other issues.

Sex Changes concludes with a chapter on the future of gender and the new generation of transgender activists. Enfant terrible Kate Bornstein makes a sweeping claim in *Gender Outlaw* that gender does not exist; it is nothing but a social construct. How does this notion play in the transgender community? And does it not imply that transsexuality, along with sexual orientation as we know it, is an artifact of patriarchy that will wither away along with gender oppression and discrimination against homosexuals? If this is true, what might replace our binary and polarized system of gender?

The book concludes with a bibliography and resource list, because it is my experience that books go many more places than their authors can hope to travel in one lifetime. The debate about the many facets of gender politics is vital to our ability to understand ourselves, form healthy relationships with others, and create institutions that will foster human happiness rather than blindly enforce conformity.

While the debate about transsexual rights rages, people (some of them quite young) are going to be realizing, to their confusion and dismay, that they want to dress up in clothing that they are told is not appropriate for them. Children, teenagers, and adults will have to confront the devastating fact that they do not want to perform in the gender roles that their families, churches, and schools tell them they must fulfill. Speculation about genetics, conditioning, the long-term effects of hormones, and whether or not to allow transsexual lesbians to attend women's music festivals is fascinating. But these people must also find short-term, practical solutions that will allow them to go on with their lives with a minimum of suffering and a maximum potential to experience intimacy, sexual pleasure, self-love, and joy.

I hope the resource list will be of use to those who are struggling to find their place on the gender continuum. It includes ways to find support via the Internet, which is quickly becoming a way for members of all sexual minorities to end their isolation and find community.

As should be obvious from the foregoing, another powerful motive for putting this book together was a simple distaste for injustice. When well-meaning physicians perform surgery on infants with ambiguous genitalia, surgery that may make their families more comfortable with the gender the doctor assigns to the baby, but will also impair that child's sexual functioning as an adult, it isn't right. When a young boy is forced to receive punitive psychiatric treatment because his mannerisms are judged to be effeminate, it isn't right. When a teenage girl is incarcerated in a mental institution for refusing to wear dresses, or for having a sexual relationship with another girl, it isn't right. When a man loses custody of his children in a divorce case because his wife reveals he dresses up in her undergarments, it isn't right. When someone who needs sex-reassignment surgery can't obtain it, either because it's not locally available, or because insurance companies and government programs won't foot the bill, it isn't right.

The violence, discrimination and hatred heaped upon differently-gendered people is an enormous wrong. This bigotry will stop only when the rest of "us" are able to accept our own gender conflicts and pinpoint our own prejudices about biological sex and social sex-roles. This book was written with the hope that someday gender will be a voluntary system for self-expression, used chiefly to enhance the pleasure we take in one another's unique realities.

CHAPTER 1

Transsexual Autobiography: The First Wave

The history of transgenderism in the latter half of this century begins with autobiographical accounts written by male-to-female transsexuals. Certainly there was an awareness before these books appeared that there were people who were born male who longed to live as women; or females who appropriated certain aspects of male attire and sexuality. A complete history of such a wide-ranging and complex phenomenon is impossible to include here, but some of the highlights appear below.

In the late nineteenth and early twentieth centuries, a few celebrated, differently-gendered individuals were known to doctors and sexologists. One of the most prominent of these was the Chevalier d'Eon de Beaumont, whose name provided Havelock Ellis with his own term for transvestism, *eonism*.[1] This eighteenth-century nobleman served his country as a diplomat and spy, first in Russia, and later in England. Questions and gossip about his (or her) true gender were rampant. The Chevalier reportedly feared being kidnapped by gamblers who had placed high-stakes bets upon his sex. Louis XVI eventually sent his envoy Beaumarchais to England to persuade the Chevalier to return to France. The condition for this was that he sign an agreement promising to don, forevermore, women's attire and live in the female gender, without any ambiguity.

The "Chevalière"[2] expressed considerable frustration with being forced to give up military uniform and adopt confining and awkward women's clothing, as well as the inactivity and trivial pursuits of court ladies. Eventually he returned to England to perform as a female fencer, to pay off his always pressing debts. It is difficult to know what the Chevalier himself thought of his gender identity, given that he sometimes spoke of himself as a man, and sometimes as a woman. In correspondence with a friend, he said simply, "I am what the hands of God have made me."[3] It seems that it was more important for other people to remove ambiguity from his identity than it was for d'Eon. Renowned for his cold temperament as much as he was for his transvestism, d'Eon is not known to have had any love affairs or seductions.

During the last years of his life, he kept a journal in which he referred to himself by feminine pronouns. He lived for many years with a companion, Mrs. Cole, and when he died in 1810, that gentlewoman was astonished to learn that his biological sex was male. This medical testimony is not as definitive as it might sound, since during the height of the betting frenzy in England about his gender, experts appointed by a British court had announced that d'Eon was a woman.[4]

The mid-nineteenth century case of the hermaphrodite Herculine Barbin was known to sexologists since the Victorian era, and the fact that some people possessed ambiguous genitalia or had both male and female sexual characteristics was well-established in folklore.[5] This focus on a few "celebrity transsexuals" reinforced the public's impression that gender disorders were very rare. It also gave the syndrome a vague air of glamour, heroism, and eroticism. To be differently-gendered was to be a freak and a moral monstrosity, certainly, but it was also associated with the mysticism and heroism of Joan of Arc, the romance of the double-agent d'Eon, the flamboyance of Abbe d'Choissy. Thus, the general public did not have to worry about their spouses or children or close friends being transgendered—this was not something that ordinary people experienced, it was of another realm, whether that realm was the French aristocracy or the stuff of Greek mythology.

Early research on transsexuality among ordinary people was undertaken in tandem with a scientific examination of homosexuality. Karl Heinrich Ulrichs was one of the first self-declared homosexuals, although Ulrichs coined and preferred the term *urnings*. Ulrichs thought that urnings were a third sex. His first published work was the 1864 booklet *Vindex*, published under the pseudonym Numa Numinantius. By 1879 he had produced a dozen books about the phenomena we now call homosexuality and transsexuality. Later works appeared under his own name, a courageous act in that era. Ulrichs is remembered for alerting the medical community to the existence of people who would come to be called homosexuals. He also set up a paradigm of sexual deviance in which sexual desire for a member of one's own sex is paired with a desire to be a sex other than the one that was received at birth.[6]

This conflation of homosexuality and gender dysphoria continued to be a theme in the work of Magnus Hirschfeld. Hirschfeld was a self-avowed homosexual, a sex researcher, and a legal reformer. In 1897 he founded the Scientific Humanitarian Committee, an organization aimed at helping homosexuals and other people whose sexual differences were considered pathological. Hirschfeld coined the term *transvestism* and published a key work about that topic in 1910 (its English title was *The Transvestites: An Investigation of the Erotic Drive to Cross Dress*). This work is notable for Hirschfeld's report that the majority of transvestites he interviewed were heterosexual. He also included a woman in this early sample of seventeen.

However, Hirschfeld followed the tradition established by Ulrichs when he created a theory to explain homosexuality. His "theory of intermediaries" recognized the two sexes and several departures from that norm. These "departures" included hermaphrodites, people whose secondary sexual characteristics were anomalous, and homosexuals. Hirschfeld placed men who wished to be passive during sex and women who wished to be sexually aggressive in the same category as homosexuals. There was also a fourth category for cross-dressers and for people who wished to become members of the opposite sex.[7] This classification system continued the tradition of associating disturbances in gender identity with homosexuality.

Victorian physician and sexologist Richard von Krafft-Ebing had an even greater impact than Ulrichs or Hirschfeld on the medical profession's view of sexual deviance. His work also affected popular notions of what caused people to be sexually different and the catastrophic effects of deviance on the lives of such misfits. His major work, *Psychopathia Sexualis*, was first published in 1887 and went through many revisions. It was to his era what the Kinsey reports have been to us. A few of the cases Krafft-Ebing reported in this book involved behavior that we would call cross-dressing today. Most of the people Krafft-Ebing studied came to his attention when they fell into the hands of law enforcement or were confined in mental institutions. So the picture of the typical transvestite that one obtains from reading *Psychopathia Sexualis* is one of a compulsive thief who may injure someone who possesses an item of apparel that he feels driven to obtain, who is also an obsessive masturbator, and a danger to himself and others.[8]

In the world of Krafft-Ebing, there is no such thing as benign sexual variation. Everyone who departs from reproductive, monogamous, male-dominant heterosexuality is described as criminally insane. He bears an enormous responsibility for much of the sex negativity that continues to flourish in the West today. We still tend to see masturbation as a debilitating and shameful act that is dangerous if done to excess, and we still view fetishes as dangerous symptoms of a tendency to objectify or damage women, rather than simple cues for sexual arousal, which most of us (both men and women) possess. It should also be noted that Krafft-Ebing made very little space in his observations for the female deviate. Given how poisonous his analyses were, perhaps this was a blessing, but even today, lesbians, women with an interest in sado-masochism, biological females who cross-dress and female-to-male transsexuals have to fight a cultural blackout that renders them invisible.

Havelock Ellis's humanitarian, curious, and compassionate response to human sexual variation stands in stark contrast to the Puritan black-and-white thinking of Krafft-Ebing. Ellis supported the attempts of reformers like Hirschfeld who sought the decriminalization of sodomy and other sexual-minority conduct. Ellis did not like the term *transvestism,* which he felt placed too much emphasis upon garments. He coined the term *sexo-aesthetic inversion,* and described four cases of this anomaly. He felt that the people he studied cared as much about empathizing with or assuming the role of the opposite sex as they did about acquiring or wearing fetishized clothing. Eventually he came to feel that the term *inversion* was problematic because of its association with homosexuality, and substituted the term *eonism.* According to Ellis, most cross-dressers were leading satisfactory lives and were not harming others, so he saw no point in trying to change their sexual behavior.[9]

Before the nineteen-fifties, people who were not comfortable in their birth-genders were forced to resolve their gender conflicts without the benefit of the combination of hormone therapy and surgery that would come to be called sex reassignment. It was also generally assumed, prior to the fifties, that the identities and behaviors we now call cross-dressing or transvestism, transsexuality, and homosexuality were all of one piece, that the desire to love or experience erotic pleasure with a member of one's own sex also involved the desire to defeat or deny one's own sex chromosomes. The hope to change one's gender or to create a same-sex relationship was seen as a pathetic, doomed, neurotic, and criminal impulse. The people who were unfortunate enough to be identified as sex deviates were also seen as ridiculous for engaging in a vain parody of healthy, normal heterosexuality. Erotic activity between masculine men and feminine women was a sort of "gold standard" of human sexuality.

This popular wisdom was overturned forever by a brave transsexual woman named Christine Jorgensen who in 1967 published a dignified autobiography as her perfectly ladylike reply to a storm of ugly and hysterical press coverage about her sex change, which took place in the early fifties. *Christine Jorgensen: A Personal Autobiography* would set the terms of public understanding and debate about transsexuality for decades to come.

The book bears an introduction by Harry Benjamin, M.D., who was one of the first doctors to conclude that psychoanalysis was of no use to transsexuals, since they were not in fact mentally disordered. Benjamin wondered if it wouldn't be more effective to simply give transsexuals what they kept saying they wanted: a chance to live in the gender they preferred. Newly-discovered sex hormones, estrogen and testosterone, made it possible to feminize male bodies and masculinize female bodies. Benjamin was a pioneer in the development of the process of sex reassignment, and the author of a set of standards of care that continue to outline ethical guidelines for the treatment of transsexuals. His 1966 book *The Transsexual Phenomenon* is a classic in the field.

Since the Victorian era, physicians had appropriated a role for themselves as experts on sexual deviance and arbiters of normalcy. Therefore, one of Benjamin's roles in the introduction is to pronounce upon Jorgensen's "true" gender. "Her success as a woman is no longer in doubt," he announces.[10]

His second role is to affirm that the condition of transsexuality is a medical phenomenon, an illness that only modern medical science can cure, and that sex reassignment is the appropriate treatment. In order to accomplish this, he must lift Jorgensen's autobiography out of the realm of titillating tabloids or pornography and into the realm of science. So he writes of Jorgensen being "duty bound to supplement the technical report made by her Danish physicians in the *Journal of the American Medical Association* in 1953 with her own account of the inner and outer events in her still rather young life. Medically, Christine presents an almost classic case of the transsexual phenomenon or, in other words, a striking example of a disturbed gender role orientation."[11]

In order to bolster his medical authority to treat transsexuality, Benjamin must dispute the belief of psychiatrists that "disturbed gender role orientation" was a mental disorder caused by childhood trauma, and could be cured by psychoanalysis. He attacks this belief by describing the Jorgensen family's "warm humanity." Of Christine's childhood, he writes, "This was a little girl, not a boy (in spite of the anatomy) who grew up in this remarkably sound and normal family."[12] Rather than situating the cause of transsexuality in disordered family relations, Benjamin attributes it to hormonal imbalance or genetic abnormalities. However, his honesty compels him to admit that "Absolute scientific proof is as yet lacking that such abnormal events during the mother's pregnancy can produce the gender role disorientation in later life."[13]

He also pleads for family understanding and loving support for transsexual sons and daughters. It is touching to read Benjamin's description of the Jorgensen family's acceptance of Christine. He quotes her father as saying, "She is ours and we love her." He condemns "those who, in their ignorance and prejudice, cruelly reject their unfortunate child just at a time when all their love and understanding was needed."[14] Perhaps in an attempt to retain the sympathy of transsexuals' relatives, he describes their condition as being "inborn, although not hereditary."[15] Benjamin even scolds members of the "theological professions" for being "uninformed and prejudiced" about transsexuality.[16]

In a further attempt to remove transsexuals from the realm of mental illness or sin, Benjamin makes a firm distinction between the desire to change one's sex and homosexuality. "A homosexual relationship can only exist between two men who also feel themselves to be men," he explains. "A homosexual, therefore, does not want to change sex."[17]

Jorgensen was born on May 30, 1926, "a normal baby boy," son of George and Florence Davis [nee Hansen] Jorgensen, and christened George William Jorgensen Jr. Even as a child, Jorgensen felt a keen difference between herself and other children.[18] She preferred to play with girls, hated attending boys' summer camp, refused to skinny dip in the presence of males, and was frequently accused of carrying "his" school books like a girl or being a girl dressed in boys' clothing. An elementary-school teacher who found a piece of needlepoint in George's desk called her mother to school to ask, "Do you think that this is anything for a red-blooded boy to have in his desk as a keepsake? The next thing we know, George will be bringing his knitting to school!"[19]

One of the people who comforted her after these humiliations was her Grandma Jorgensen, who told her after the needlepoint episode, "You mustn't mind if other people can't feel or see a sense of beauty, too." The author adds, "Grandma was always my champion when others laughed at my 'sissified' ways."[20]

By the age of sixteen, Jorgensen was even more alienated from her peers, feeling no interest in sports or dating girls. At the age of seventeen, she developed a friendship with a young man who was four years older than herself, Tom Chaney. When Chaney's revelations about a girlfriend triggered intense feelings of jealousy, Jorgensen realized she was in love with her friend, and suffered intense feelings of guilt.

> Quite accidentally, I came across a book in the library that revealed to me new and incomprehensible facts about human relations. Dealing with the subject of homosexuality, the book was concealed from the general reading public in what were known as the "closed shelves." Between its covers, I found many perplexing statements about sex deviation. I scanned paragraphs and pages of case histories, all of which left me even more bewildered than before.
>
> Question after question raced through my mind. Was this the same thing I felt? Was I one of these people? Was I living half in shadow? Was my feeling for Tom one of love, like the love described in the book?[21]

These troublesome and painful feelings for Tom Chaney were to continue for many years.

Jorgensen developed an interest in photography in her last year of high school and briefly worked in the library of a film company before being drafted in 1945. She had been rejected as a conscript twice before for being underweight. Jorgensen's military career sounds unexceptional (her duties were purely clerical, and she had only one promotion, to Private First Class). However, the intimate contact with other young men and women made her even more poignantly aware of the distance between herself and her peers: "My body was not only slight, but it lacked other development usual in a male. I had no hair on my chest, arms, or legs. My walk could hardly be called a masculine stride, the gestures of my hands were effeminate and my voice also had a feminine quality. The sex organs that determined my classification as 'male' were underdeveloped."[22]

Here we see the beginning of Jorgensen's defining her condition as a medical anomaly rather an affectional disorder like homosexuality. In response to intense emotional distress (and also in response to physical characteristics that she perceived as deficient or different), Jorgensen began to situate her problem within the body.

During this same time period, we see Jorgensen's emphatic decision to distance herself from homosexuals, to reject that as a possible solution to the dilemma of being a failure as a masculine man.

During the months in service, I had seen a few practicing homosexuals, those whom the other men called "queer." I couldn't condemn them, but I also knew that I certainly couldn't become like them. It was a thing deeply alien to my religious attitudes and the highly magnified and immature moralistic views that I entertained at the time. Furthermore, I had seen enough to know that homosexuality brought with it a social segregation and ostracism that I couldn't add to my own deep feeling of not belonging.[23]

It is important to note that, initially at least, Jorgensen's rejection of the homosexual option is based on moral grounds, not on a strong feeling that she wanted to love a man as a woman rather than as another man. Her sexual and romantic attraction to Tom Chaney continued to grow stronger, and while describing a social encounter they had while she was in the military, Jorgensen says, "I knew that I would have to destroy the thing that I had allowed to develop within me, that I must be strong enough to let the desire slip into the past," and also makes a reference to waiting for "a miracle to release me from the growing horror of myself."[24]

After receiving an honorable discharge from the army in 1946, Jorgensen was devastated to discover that her civilian job was no longer available. Through a family friend, she eventually got a job driving a limousine for RKO Studios in New York City. But by 1947, she had left that job to travel to Hollywood, hoping to work as a photographer for the motion-picture industry, following another family friend to Southern California. This friend helped Jorgensen to find lodging, but her attempts to find work were a miserable failure. There was a thriving gay subculture in Hollywood at that time, but Jorgensen spurned the advances of any gay men who tried to befriend or seduce her. Eventually, like many veterans, Jorgensen found herself living on unemployment benefits.

Feeling increasingly like a failure as a man, Jorgensen finally disclosed her discomfort with the male gender to two close women friends, Helen Johnson and June Jensen. "Maybe you'll think I'm insane, but did either of you ever look at me and think that I might not be a man at all, but a…woman?" she asked them with great trepidation.[25] Their first reaction was that perhaps she was a homosexual, which one friend discounted because she had never seen Jorgensen with another man. The other friend, who was from Denmark, suggested that Jorgensen consult a doctor. Although she did not take that advice at once, it was a harbinger of the path she would eventually take to end her confusion and pain. Perhaps it was the relief of this disclosure that enabled her to finally obtain work, albeit as a clerk in a grocery store.

Eventually one of the friends to whom she had made her disclosure got married, and the other returned to Denmark. Jorgensen gave up on a Hollywood career and tried to return home to her parents. But these travel plans were disrupted by a bout of serious illness and high fever, and Jorgensen found herself in Minneapolis, with some vague idea that she ought to visit her great-aunt Augusta. This relative nursed Jorgensen back to health, and eventually she discovered that her aunt was actually the illegitimate child of her grandfather and a woman he had never married. Discovering that another family member had managed to construct a rewarding life despite having a stigmatized identity was another important step forward for Jorgensen.

Back in New York, Jorgensen took her great aunt's advice and enrolled in college. She also returned to church and experienced a deep rekindling of her faith in the loving kindness of God. After reading some endocrinology research by Dr. Harold Grayson, Jorgensen determined to consult with him about her problems. Grayson deeply disappointed her by making a referral to a psychiatrist, Dr. Reznick, who proposed lengthy psychoanalysis to guide Jorgensen away from her "feminine inclinations."[26] Such a course of treatment would have been very expensive, but Jorgensen says, "I would have borrowed the money somehow and paid it willingly…if I thought I could have been helped or, at least, received a credible answer to the eternal question of what was wrong and why."[27]

Despite these discouraging events, Jorgensen continued to study new revelations in the nascent science of endocrinology, to take some classes in medical technology, and to fend off sexual advances from men who were attracted to her apparently male body. She was fascinated with the idea that male hormones could masculinize a female animal, and female hormones could feminize a male animal. (She considered and rejected the idea of simply taking male hormones to make herself more masculine.) Jorgensen finally took the desperate step of conning a pharmacist out of one hundred tablets of ethinyl estradiol, or estrogen. She took the self-administered hormones for a week, and felt the beginnings of breast development, and the lifting of her depression and fatigue. Now Jorgensen was determined to find a medical expert who could supervise her transformation.

Jorgensen had developed a friendship with another student, Genevieve Angelo, and her husband, Joseph, who was a medical doctor.

Once more she had to screw up her courage to disclose her feelings of being in the wrong body to these close friends. "Dr. Joe" made it his business to try to talk Jorgensen out of the idea of a sex change, but he also took on the task of supervising her self-administered female hormones. Then Jorgensen received a letter from Dr. Grayson, who had kept in touch with her after the first visit, suggesting that a sex change might be available in Sweden. Jorgensen made plans to go to Denmark to visit relatives, then to Stockholm to find doctors who could help her. The Angelos supported her in this decision.[28]

By then, Jorgensen had graduated from medical technician training, and took a clerical job at the school to save money for her trip. When she left for Copenhagen in May of 1950, she had only enough money for a one-way ticket, and barely enough extra to live on for a few months. She had no idea where she would seek medical treatment, and she did not know Danish or Swedish. Who could read about this shy, introverted, confused young person without sympathizing with her fear and desperation? Jorgensen says she took this risk because "...how could any future life be worse than the past twenty-three years?"[29]

Jorgensen was met in Copenhagen by Helen Johnson, the friend from Los Angeles who had been one of the first human beings to hear about her gender confusion. She and her husband Olaf befriended Jorgensen and told her she did not need to go to Sweden, that there were endocrinologists who could help her in their city. Johnson took Jorgensen to her own doctor, thus starting her odyssey toward a new identity. Eventually Jorgensen found Dr. Christian Hamburger of the Statens Seruminstitut, who agreed to consider her for a change of sex via female hormones and surgery.

In a letter to the Angelos, Jorgensen compares her doctors to Pasteur and Ehrlich.[30] After sex reassignment, she would take a feminized version of Dr. Hamburger's first name, and call herself Christine. Jorgensen idolized her doctors as the only people who fully understood her dilemma and offered her a solution. Since Jorgensen was serving as a guinea pig for what was at the time a grand experiment on the effects of human sex hormones, her medical care was free. The treatment, which began in August of 1950 at the Seruminstitut, required Jorgensen to collect all of her urine so it could be tested to determine the effects of the hormones she was given, and she nicknamed the ubiquitous black bag that held the specimen container as *yor mor taske* (Danish for "a midwife's bag").[31] A new person was being born, and Jorgensen's doctors were her mother and father.

Jorgensen's first question for Dr. Hamburger was "Am I a homosexual?" The doctor replied that he did not think so:

> I would believe that you are the victim of a problem that usually starts in early childhood, an irresistible feeling that you wish to be regarded by society and by yourself, as belonging to the opposite sex. Nothing is able to change this feeling. ...A psychiatrist couldn't do a great deal for you at present. ...I think the trouble is very deep-rooted in the cells of your body...inwardly, it is quite possible that you are a woman. Your body chemistry and all of your body cells, including your brain cells, may be female. That is only a theory, mind you.[32]

It is ironic, considering Jorgensen's paranoia about being gay, that on her way to Denmark she had read Radclyffe Hall's lesbian novel *The Well of Loneliness*, and mentions it as one of the things that made her "more determined than ever to fight for this victory."[33]

Despite his feeling that psychoanalysis would not affect Jorgensen's condition, Dr. Hamburger required that she see a psychiatrist, just to make sure all possible procedures had been followed to ensure that the sex change was medically valid. So Jorgensen paid several visits to Dr. Georg Stürup, who said to his new patient about the reluctance of American doctors to consider sex reassignment, "You Americans are so childish about sex! ...Operate on the brain, perform a lobotomy, create a whole new personality—but operate on a testicle and everybody explodes!"[34] Nevertheless, Dr. Stürup took a conservative approach to Jorgensen's case and insisted on examining her in depth, although what he was looking for is not clear. Finally, unable to unearth any childhood traumas or emotional aberrations that would cause Jorgensen's conviction that she was meant to be a woman, Dr. Stürup gave his consent, sure that at the very least, the procedure would not leave the young patient in any worse condition than she had been before.

After observing Jorgensen's affect and physiology both with and without female hormones, Dr. Hamburger decided it was time to remove her male "sex glands," i.e., testicles. Before this surgery could be done, an application had to be made to the Medico-Legal Council of the Ministry of Justice. Jorgensen and her medical benefactors hit a snag there when a minor official objected to the application on the grounds that she was not a Danish citizen. Dr. Stürup contacted Helga Pedersen, head of the Justice Ministry and the country's attorney general. Pedersen was a noted feminist who had campaigned for the rights of illegitimate children, psychiatric treatment for sex offenders, and the legalization of artificial insemination. She arranged for Jorgensen to receive permission for surgery. Her commonplace acceptance that this was the humanitarian thing to do stands in contrast with later feminist opposition to the acceptance of male-to-female transsexuals.

So on September 24, 1951, Jorgensen went to the hospital for the first sex-change surgery. There were to be two other operations to remove her penis and create a facsimile of the female genitals. At this point in time, Jorgensen appeared to be quite feminine and was usually called "Miss" or "Mrs." by waiters and clerks in shops. But she was still wearing men's clothing. Before changing her apparel, Jorgensen applied to the American embassy for a new passport and received one in the appropriate gender. As a woman, Jorgensen had more self-confidence in the workplace, and had been selling some color photographs (which were rare in Denmark at that time) to magazines. But this hardly provided an opulent living. Still living on a shoestring budget, Jorgensen had been collecting fabric and patterns, and sewed her own skirts and dresses.

The first family member to know about her transformation was a visiting aunt, Tante Tine, whom Jorgensen met on her first day in female apparel. Tante Tine's attitude was positive and welcoming. She gave Jorgensen flowers and took her for a walk in Tivoli Park, where she was whistled at. Sadly, that lone wolf whistle was to be one of the most erotic moments in Jorgensen's life, if the autobiography is accurate.

On June 8, 1952, Jorgensen finally wrote to her mother and father and to her sister and brother-in-law to inform them of the enormous changes she had undergone. This letter is a touching document, a heartfelt plea for understanding. But once again, Jorgensen raises the specter of homosexuality and vigorously denies it. "I was afraid of a much more horrible illness of the mind. One which, although very common, is not as yet accepted as a true illness, with the necessity for great understanding," she wrote.[35] She enclosed photos of herself so that her family could get some idea of the changes wrought by the female hormones.

By now, Jorgensen's photographic interests had grown to include color cinematography. She had obtained permission from the National Tourist Association to make a color film about Denmark. Her parents had written to communicate their love and acceptance. Her father had told Christine's story to some friends of his at a Danish American social club, and received warm support. Thirteen months after the first surgery, Jorgensen went back to the hospital for a penectomy. Everything seemed to be going well. She did not anticipate how radically her life was about to change.

Shortly after the surgery, Jorgensen woke to find a reporter in her hospital room, holding a telegram that read, "BRONX GI BECOMES A WOMAN. DEAR MOM AND DAD SON WROTE, I HAVE NOW BECOME YOUR DAUGHTER."[36] The reporter informed Jorgensen that someone had leaked the news of her sex change to the New York *Daily News*, and that she was about to make headlines all over the world. Still in pain from the surgery, Jorgensen was too dazed to grant this woman's request for an interview, but she was not allowed to rest. The hospital switchboard lit up with transatlantic calls placed by journalists who demanded interviews. Jorgensen says, somewhat pitifully, "I didn't know it then, but the curtain would never ring down."[37] Her life as a private person was over, and her life as a public spectacle had forcefully begun.

Faced with a barrage of media attention, Jorgensen agreed to grant an exclusive series of interviews to Irmis Johnson, for the Hearst Corporation's *American Weekly* magazine. The Hearst Corporation flew her parents to Copenhagen, and their warm reunion was complicated considerably by the need to dodge the photographers and news hawks who hounded the family.

Jorgensen's first public appearance was on December 15, 1952 at the first showing of her travelogue. Although the Danish audience laughed at some of the mistakes she made in their language, Jorgensen reports that she was on the whole warmly received. If she had known that this was as far as her career as a cinematographer was going to go, the evening perhaps would not have been such a success. "I was unaware of it then," she writes, "but in my long, painful search for a normal life, I had created a paradox; a life that was to be, for me, abnormal and unconventional."[38]

When Jorgensen returned to America, after a five-year absence, on February 13, 1953, she was besieged by the largest assemblage of press reporters in the history of New York International Airport. As she waded through flashbulbs, Jorgensen said, still trying to be polite, "Ladies and gentlemen, thank you for coming, but I think this is really too much."[39] Reporters who could not obtain an interview with her made up sensational items for their scandal-hungry readers. Post-World War II America seems to have had a major case of gender paranoia. During wartime, thousands of women had stepped into "men's work" to keep the economy going, but once their husbands and boyfriends returned, there was an intense campaign to get women back into the kitchen, and men back into the factories. The fact that Jorgensen was so often referred to as an "ex-GI" highlights this hysteria.

Practically everything that could be insinuated about Jorgensen made it into print, including the assertion that she was born female, there had been no sex change, and the whole thing was a hoax.

Jorgensen was especially upset by rumors "that I had been a female impersonator before going to Denmark, and in my private life as 'George,' I doted on wearing feminine clothing. Nothing could have been further from the truth. ...I had never worn, or wanted to wear, feminine clothing while I retained any evidence of masculinity. ...I didn't wear female clothing until my legal status as a woman was established on my passport...."[40]

The Danish government, Jorgensen's doctors, and she herself received a flood of letters from unhappy people who wanted to know how they could get a sex change. According to her autobiography, there had been at least thirty sex changes on record before she went through the process in Denmark.[41] But the Seruminstitut was in no way prepared to cope with this onslaught of misery. Rather than making sex reassignment more accessible, the first impact of the publicity about Jorgensen's case seems to have been that it became harder to obtain. Wary doctors and public officials backed away from anything that would fan the flames of scandal.

Jorgensen was paid very handsomely for the *American Weekly* interview, but even that money had to run out eventually. With working-class practicality, she began to wonder how on earth she was going to make a living. She had many offers from promoters who wanted to book personal appearances, but Jorgensen felt that this would be like being on display in a circus sideshow. At first, she would agree to appear only on behalf of charitable causes, and even so, some television stations banned her from their broadcasts.

A man named Charlie Yates appointed himself Jorgensen's manager, but she did not want to become an entertainer. She wanted to continue to work in film. So Yates arranged for her to show her travelogue at the Orpheum Theater in Los Angeles. The audience came to see something bizarre and fantastical; Jorgensen wanted to do a straightforward presentation of a tourist film about Denmark. The evening was savaged by critics, and Jorgensen realized that the world had left her only one way to make a living. She would have to go on stage.

If she was going to go in front of an audience, she was determined to appear there with wit and dignity. So she took dance lessons and singing lessons and studied acting. In the beginning, Jorgensen performed with a partner, Myles Bell, a comedian. Eventually she took charge of her act and performed alone. The painfully shy boy George

Jorgensen could never have survived this ordeal, but the newly-confident woman, Christine, somehow managed.

This is not to say that her career proceeded without challenges. When she went to Washington, D.C. for an engagement, Jorgensen was met by a vice cop who warned her not to use the women's public toilets in that city.[42] She was banned in Boston. The Licensing Board would not let her appear at the Latin Quarter club until she submitted to a physical exam. Despite protests by some members of the City Council, Jorgensen left Boston without performing.[43] She was also banned from entertaining on military bases, which were a large part of a nightclub entertainer's circuit in those days. When she toured Britain, the press defamed her before she set foot on stage. One reviewer said, "Those who go to see her will not be going to see an act; they will go with the same unhealthy appetites of people who queue up to see murderers." Another critic said she was a spectacle "appealing to the more squalid recesses of the human mind."[44]

In her autobiography, Jorgensen presents these trials and many others with a sort of verbal shrug. Of course she was angry, hurt, and frightened by these events, but she refuses, even when recalling them in her life story, to heap abuse upon her detractors. It is hard to imagine what an effort it was for her to keep her temper in the face of so much bigotry, and record it in her autobiography as if it were no more troublesome than a flat tire. Of course she went on, she had no choice but to go on if she was going to survive, but where did her strength come from? Jorgensen gives us a clue by talking a few times in the book about her close connection to God. She finds it curious that "Never once, in all those acres of newsprint, had I been asked about my faiths and beliefs. ...What I slept in, apparently, was considered more important than what I believed in."[45]

If the reader is not alert for any crumb of information about sex, love, and romance, it would be easy to miss the few pages that mention Jorgensen's unsuccessful attempts to have a normal private life. Toward the end of 1953, Jorgensen appeared at the Hotel Sahara in Las Vegas. A penpal, Pat Flanigan, sent her a bouquet of roses. The flowers were traced by reporters, who promptly publicized his identity. Journalists demanded to know if Christine was engaged to this man, and she refused to say yes or no. Soon the press would have it that she was about to be married. Flanigan lost several jobs because his name had been connected to hers. He continued to send her flowers, small gifts, and letters, but their relationship apparently went no further.

In April of 1959, a man named John Traub proposed to Jorgensen. He was a labor union statistician, and he and Jorgensen had become quite close. She says, "At thirty-three, I'd reached a point where I thought every woman should be married," although she characterizes her feelings for him as deep friendship rather than torrid romance. She tried to explain to Traub what a torrent of publicity he was walking into, but he was determined to apply for a marriage license anyway. After considerable bureaucratic delay, the license was denied on the grounds that Jorgensen's birth certificate said she was male. (All of her other legal identification papers stated that she was female.) In the wake of the inevitable press coverage, Traub lost his job, and marriage plans were abandoned, although Jorgensen says they parted "as warm friends."[46]

The tone of Jorgensen's autobiography is consistently low-key, normal, and even dull. She insists on her right to have a life full of the same trivia and minutiae as anyone else's. She consistently downplays any hint of strong emotion, partly because, it seems, she really did want nothing more than to be an ordinary woman. It is tragic, given her unthinking support for traditional social sex-roles and conventional heterosexuality, that she was denied the opportunity to be some man's wife, a homemaker like her own mother. Of course, it's possible that the story of Jorgensen's real private life never made it to the pages of her staid autobiography. But I doubt there are many skeletons in her closet. Once she was held up to public view as a pornographic scandal and a dirty joke, it seems that Jorgensen was determined to be exemplary in every aspect of her life.

Besides, after having someone close to her family leak the news of her sex change to the tabloids in the early fifties, who could she have trusted in her bed? Newspapers would have been willing to pay exorbitant sums for an exposé by one of her lovers. No tale credible as such ever appeared in print. Jorgensen had her decorum, at the price of intimacy and sensuality. Not until 1966 did she find out that one of the friends her father first told about her sex change at Askov Hall, the Danish-American Beach Club, had gotten two hundred dollars from the *Daily News* for the story about her operation.[47] By then, the exact identity of that person wasn't very important, but Jorgensen had lived with the fact that close acquaintances could sell information about her to the press for years.

It's important to remember what the context was for the news of Jorgensen's sex change. America was in the deep freeze of the Cold War. In 1952, the McCarthy witch hunts were at their height. The Rosenbergs were sitting on death row, awaiting execution for being convicted spies. The nonwar in Korea, ugly harbinger of Vietnam, dragged on and on.

And hydrogen-bomb testing occurred in the South Pacific. Racial discrimination was rampant, and there was little if any political organizing or consciousness among gay men and lesbians. People went to jail for cross-dressing or for being homosexuals.[48] The writings of Sigmund Freud were being popularized in America, and people were speaking more freely (albeit judgmentally) about sexuality and sexual variation. Unfortunately for Jorgensen, her life transition made headlines during a time when public awareness of sexual deviance had increased, but understanding or tolerance for difference had not.

Jorgensen died of cancer on May 3, 1989 at the age of sixty-two. A year before her death, she told the press, "I'm not that recognizable anymore. I can actually go into a supermarket and people don't know who I am, which is just wonderful and suits me just fine. Things don't hurt the way they did then."[49] She lived to see the establishment of the Harry Benjamin Research Foundation, which educated the public about transsexuality and made sex reassignment more acceptable and available. And during her lifetime, Johns Hopkins Hospital in Baltimore began to perform sex-change surgery.[50] Transsexuals would no longer have to become expatriates to get treatment. The last paragraph of her book is a fitting epitaph.

> I suppose the final question to answer is, "Has it been worth it?" I must admit, at certain moments in my life I might have hesitated to answer. I remember times when I lived in a crucible of troubled phantoms, and faltered in the long, painful struggle for identity. But for me there was always a glimmering promise that lay ahead; with the help of God, a promise that has been fulfilled. I found the oldest gift of heaven—to be myself.[51]

This autobiography was not written as a scientific paper or as a political tract. However, at least part of Jorgensen's agenda was to increase public understanding of transsexuality, perhaps in the hope that others who changed their sex would not suffer the agonies of ridicule and harassment that had been inflicted upon her. For many years, this book was virtually the only work in print that a layperson or, for that matter, a medical or mental-health professional, could easily obtain to learn more about the subject of transsexuality. So it's important to examine Jorgensen's assumptions about the nature of transsexuality and what constituted a healthy adjustment to feelings of gender dysphoria.

Jorgensen attempts to normalize transsexuality by disassociating it from perverse pleasure-seeking activities like cross-dressing or homosexuality. This strategy is weakened by her work as an entertainer. No matter how Jorgensen may have wished audiences to view her, her act was perceived by the public and advertised as the ultimate form of female impersonation.[52] Jorgensen makes frequent joking references to her own prudery. Did her lack of lovers or a husband stem as much from her conservative attitudes toward sex as it did from the public outcry that would have resulted? And to what extent did Jorgensen's biases against cross-dressing and homosexuality push her toward a sex change, rather than less radical adjustments which might have afforded some relief from the stress of cognitive dissonance with her body?

Over and over again, transsexuality is presented as a medical phenomenon in her book, not a sexual perversion or a disordered way of seeking erotic gratification. It is the verdict of the doctors that separates transsexuality ("nature's mistake") from sexual minorities who are seen as being more corrupt and willful. Jorgensen's narrative is full of adoration for the doctors. She does more than acknowledge their authority, she practically worships them. While this is understandable given that they validated her deepest feelings and provided her with a solution to a dilemma that was ruining her life, claims that they dealt with her situation scientifically seem questionable now, given how broadly they overstated the case for a genetic or biological basis for gender dysphoria.

Jorgensen never rocks the social sex-role boat. She affiliates herself with normal men and women. She does not consider the problems faced by someone who cannot pass, even after sex reassignment, or the option of forming a third gender or a transsexual community. Indeed, other transsexuals are barely mentioned in this book, partly because they were rare, but also because Jorgensen does not want to be a transsexual; she wants to be a woman. And to do that, she must surround herself with "normal" people. In her flawless and tasteful wardrobe and feminine jewelry, Jorgensen passed perfectly as a woman, at least on a visual level. If it were not for the negative publicity she received, Jorgensen seems to be saying, she would have vanished into some buttercup-yellow kitchen with gingham curtains and never been heard from again. By eschewing feminism or any other political implications of transgenderism, Jorgensen once again attempts to normalize the transsexual.

Despite what we might now view as ideological blind spots, it seems a miracle that in isolation, Jorgensen was able to speak with dignity about her new life. But, perhaps as part of her studied femininity, she refused to take on the role of a social reformer or activist on behalf of other transsexuals. Like kindly fathers, she seems to imply, the doctors would care for the other unfortunate people who shared her affliction.

In the preface to her autobiography, Jorgensen says she is happy if she has made any contribution to medical science, but "it must be admitted that at the time of my transition it was purely an unconscious one. To me, it was a matter of survival. As the object of one of Nature's caprices, I was merely searching for my own personal expression of human dignity, with no thought of what the consequences might turn out to be."[53]

Conundrum, the story of Jan Morris, must also be examined in this chapter, both for the similarities and differences between it and Jorgensen's autobiography. It appeared nearly a decade after Jorgensen's autobiography, in the early seventies when many people were experimenting with new sexual identities and new types of intimate relationships, and it seemed that mores were being permanently liberalized.

Jan Morris was born James Humphry Morris sometime in the early thirties. After a brilliant career as a foreign correspondent and a loving marriage that produced five children, she finally acted (with the support of her wife Elizabeth) on a lifelong conviction that she was meant to be a woman, and changed her body and public identity. Morris was not hounded by the press, at least not to the extent that Jorgensen was, and perhaps because of that and the changing times, her account of her life is considerably more light-hearted, though it does not lack pathos.

Like Jorgensen, Morris reports experiencing the conviction that she was meant to be a girl at a very early age: "I was three or perhaps four years old when I realized that I had been born into the wrong body, and should really be a girl. I remember the moment well, and it is the earliest memory of my life."[54] (When this revelation came she was, by the way, sitting under the piano, clutching her cat, while her mother played Sibelius.) Morris seems to have had a happy childhood with a loving family. She describes the Morrises as a tolerant and somewhat bohemian upper-class English family that permitted its members a high degree of eccentricity as long as they were intelligent.

However, she does not report being a "sissified" boy. "I was James Humphry Morris, male child. ...It is true that my mother had wished me to be a daughter, but I was never treated as one. ...I was not...generally thought effeminate. At kindergarten I was not derided. In the street I was not stared at."[55] But her internal sense of distance from other people made her, she reports, "a solitary child."[56]

In the ten years or so that had elapsed between Jorgensen's sex change and Morris's struggle with her own gender issues, medical science had failed to come up with an ironclad biological or genetic basis for transsexuality. Perhaps this explains Morris's vagueness about the putative cause for her feeling that she had been born with the wrong body. She enumerates various theories about fetal hormones, genes, family dynamics, environment, etcetera, without indicating a preference for any of them. But she is in agreement with Jorgensen on this crucial point: Transsexuality is not to be confused with the other sexual minorities that are often associated with it.

> Both transvestites and homosexuals sometimes suppose they would be happier if they could change their sex, but they are generally mistaken. The transvestite gains his gratification specifically from wearing the clothes of the opposite sex, and would sacrifice his pleasures by *joining* that sex; the homosexual, by definition, prefers to make love with others of his own sort, and would only alienate himself and them by changing. Transsexualism is something different in kind. It is not a sexual mode or preference. It is not an act of sex at all. It is a passionate, lifelong, ineradicable conviction, and no true transsexual has ever been disabused of it.[57]

To underscore the "passionate" and "ineradicable conviction," which Morris situates at the heart of transsexuality, she rejects the concept of gender dysphoria. "It became fashionable to talk of my condition as 'gender confusion,' but I think it a philistine misnomer: I have had no doubt about my gender since that moment of self-realization beneath the piano. Nothing in the world would make me abandon my gender, concealed from everyone though it remained."[58] Several times in the book, Morris tries to explain what she sees as important differences between the way most people think of gender or sexual pleasure, and the way she experiences these things.

> To me, gender is not physical at all, but is altogether insubstantial. It is soul, perhaps, it is talent, it is taste, it is environment, it is how one feels, it is light and shade, it is inner music, it is a spring in one's step or an exchange of glances, it is more truly life and love than any combination of genitals, ovaries, and hormones. It is the essentialness of oneself, the psyche, the fragment of unity. Male and female are sex, masculine and feminine are gender, and though the conceptions obviously overlap, they are far from synonymous.[59]

It's hard to imagine the down-to-earth and prosaic Jorgensen going on a philosophical flight of fancy like this one. And it's equally impossible to imagine Jorgensen frankly describing a number of sexual episodes between "himself" and other boys or young men. Morris does so without shame or apologies. At school, she says:

> I was constantly in trouble, usually for squalid faults of my own, and was beaten more often than any other boy in my house. ...When I thrilled to the touch of a prefect's strong hand surreptitiously under the teashop table, I was able to forget that he had flogged me the week before, and could be my true self with him, not the poor hangdog boy crying over the packing-case, but somebody much more adult, confident, and self-controlled.[60]

Although it "seemed perfectly natural to me to play the girl's role in these transient and generally light-hearted romances, and in their platonic aspects I greatly enjoyed them," sexual activity focused on orgasm was another matter.[61]

> When it came...to more elemental pursuits of pederasty, then I found myself not exactly repelled, but embarrassed. Aesthetically it seemed wrong to me. Nothing fitted...though my body often yearned to give, to yield, to open itself, the machine was wrong. It was made for another function, and I felt myself to be wrongly equipped.[62]

This incapacity for genital sex is a theme throughout the book. As a young adult, she reports, "The actual performance of the sexual act seemed of secondary importance and interest. I suspect this is true for most women, and probably for many men too. ...I felt that my body was not my own, and encouraged myself in pleasures that were neither penile nor vaginal."[63] This did not mean she was completely withdrawn from human society.

> Throughout my young manhood I was in a constant state of emotional entanglement with somebody or other, sometimes men, sometimes women. Though they gave me pleasure at the time, they were unsatisfactory affairs in the long run, for they were necessarily inconclusive. ...I myself did not quite know what I wanted, or what I might allow myself to want, beyond the touch of the hand or lip, the warmth of the body, the long shared confidences at midnight...the laughter and the company.[64]

Morris continued to play the masculine, privileged part that life had given her, joining the Ninth Queen's Royal Lancers and traveling with them to Egypt and then Palestine during the last years of British rule there. In this masculine world, Morris felt like a woman in disguise, being allowed to secretly observe the camaraderie between men. "Far from making a man of me, it only made me feel more profoundly feminine at heart," she wistfully remarks.[65] After her military career, Morris became a journalist and a very successful foreign correspondent. Growing increasingly lonely, she searched for any fragment of evidence that somewhere, someone had shared her feelings. She became a student of history and mythology, discovering the few cases on record of celebrated hermaphrodites or cross-dressers, and the ambisexual deities in Greek and Hindu pantheons.

The closest she came to the validation she craved was a biography of Danish painter Einar Wegener, *Man Into Woman: An Authentic Record of a Change of Sex*. Wegener, convinced he was two people, a man and a woman, underwent surgery in 1930 to have his male genitals removed. Synthetic hormones were not available then, and doctors tried to transplant ovaries into his body. Wegener died a year after the surgery and was buried as Lili Elbe. Morris was upset by the fact that after the surgery, this artist had stopped painting. "Yet astonishingly, you may think," she writes, "the story gave me hope. I was not alone."[66]

She also consulted several expensive doctors, psychiatrists, and sexologists. She says bitterly, "None of them in those days, I now realize, knew anything about the matter at all, though none of them admitted it. ...I can see some of those doctors' faces now, playing helplessly for time and fee as they asked me to describe the symptoms."[67] But this quest did have one positive outcome, it led her to the office of Dr. Harry Benjamin, on Park Avenue in New York City. It was Dr. Benjamin who at last provided some comfort for Morris by suggesting "in mercy, or in common sense, if we cannot alter the conviction [that one is the wrong sex] to fit the body, should we not, in certain circumstances, alter the body to fit the conviction?"[68]

However, Benjamin also counseled Morris that a sex change was "a last resort," and suggested that for a while at least, she try to live as a man, as if she had not already been banging her head against that stone wall for many years. "Stick it out. Do your best. Try to achieve an equilibrium, that's the best way. Take it easy."[69] Despite her resolution to take this advice, Morris also made an appointment with an endocrinologist, who gave her a prescription for estrogen. Morris thought perhaps she could feminize herself enough to relieve her distress without opting for a complete sex change. This doctor warned Morris that there was no telling what impact estrogen might have on her "personality or your talent."[70] After taking the estrogen tablets for a few days, she decided to obey Dr. Benjamin's advice, and threw them away.

Not surprisingly, this strategy intensified Morris's feelings that she was a spectator, perpetually outside the human race, watching them as if they were members of a related but still alien species. Thankfully, this depressing and painful phase of her life ended when she met her soul mate, Elizabeth. Morris says of her, "I have enjoyed one particular love of an intensity so different from all the rest, on a plane of experience so mysterious, and of a texture so rich, that it overrode from the start all my sexual ambiguities, and acted like a key to the latch of my conundrum."[71] It sounds as if part of Elizabeth's charm was the fact that she closely resembled the woman that Morris might have been. "We might have been brother and sister," she writes. "People often thought we were, so absolute was our empathy, and we even looked rather alike."[72]

> It was a marriage that had no right to work, yet it worked like a dream, living testimony, one might say, to the power of mind over matter.... I hid nothing from Elizabeth, explaining to her everything as I had never explained it before: I told her that though each year my every instinct seemed to become more feminine, my entombment within the male physique more terrible to me, still the mechanism of my body was complete and functional, and for what it is worth was hers.[73]

This marriage was to result in five children, three boys and two girls. Morris's drive to have children was intense. In fact, one of the things that most upset Morris about homosexuals was their childlessness. Until her children were older, Morris felt it would not be fair to expose them to the stress of dealing with their father's sex change, and so she did her best to put her gender issues on the shelf for the next fifteen years. In her mid-thirties, shortly after her daughter Virginia was conceived, Morris began taking estrogen again. This child contracted a mysterious virus and died two months after birth. Morris once again abandoned hormones until after the birth of another daughter. "This was the worst period of my life," she says. "...I was tormented by an ever increasing sense of isolation from the world and from myself, and I was plunged into periods of despair that frightened Elizabeth and debilitated me."[74]

These feelings of alienation from her male identity affected Morris's work. She had been a very successful foreign correspondent, working for three major publications. One of the highlights of her career was to be assigned, in 1953, to accompany the first British expedition to climb

Mount Everest. Morris, as always, delighted in being a sort of secret agent in that splendid all-male company and reveled in the way her own body met the intense physical challenges of the climb. But when it was over, she says, "I well understood the masochistic relish of challenge which impelled them, and which stimulated me too, but the blankness of the achievement depressed me. ...This elusive prize, this snatching at air, this nothingness, left me dissatisfied, as I think it would leave most women. Nothing had been discovered, nothing made, nothing improved."[75]

Morris was eventually forced to give up her career as a journalist because her contempt for the male-dominated world she was covering overwhelmed her.

> No life could be more full of disillusionment. No foreign corre-
> spondent of my acquaintance has been either a snob or a syco-
> phant, but few have been optimists, either. They have seen the
> worst too soon in life, and they know the frauds of fame and
> power. ...I instinctively associated these deceits with the male
> condition, since then even more than now the world of affairs
> was dominated by men. It was like stepping from cheap theater
> into reality, to pass from the ludicrous goings-on of minister's
> office or ambassador's study into the private house behind,
> where women were to be found doing real things, like bringing
> up children, painting pictures, or writing home....[76]

And so she took to "writing books, or traveling in my own behalf. I was cultivating impotence."[77] This state of affairs obviously could not continue. Finally, with her wife's "loving help," Morris "abandoned the attempt to live on as a male, and took the first steps towards a physical change of sex."[78]

Morris returned to the care of Dr. Benjamin and began to take estrogen tablets. This treatment was to continue for eight years. It turned her into "something perilously close to a hermaphrodite," she says, and for several years she lived as a gender-ambiguous person, mostly relying on cues from other people to tell her whether she was being perceived as male or female, and adjusting her behavior accordingly.[79]

Her description of what it was like to finally feminize her body is wonderful, to anyone who has ever been curious about what it would be like to experience a transformation into something like the opposite sex.

> The first result was not exactly a feminization of my body, but a
> stripping away of the rough hide in which the male person is

clad. I do not mean merely the body hair, nor even the leather-
iness of the skin, nor all the hard protrusion of muscle; ...there
went with them something less tangible too, which I now know
to be specifically masculine—a kind of unseen layer of accumulated resilience, which provides a shield for the male of the
species, but at the same time deadens the sensations of the
body.[80]

But, of course, this was not enough. Morris and her wife decided
that surgery was the next logical step. But reputable surgeons in
America and Britain would not operate on her until she had "lived for
some years in the role of his [sic] new sex, and proved that socially and
economically it was possible."[81] So Morris began to live a double life.
She moved into a house apart from her wife, and commuted between a
life as Elizabeth's husband and the new female identity.

Morris denies, as did Jorgensen, that there was any erotic reward to
be gained from finally appearing in women's apparel: "The transvestite
gets an unfailing sexual *frisson* from wearing the clothes of the opposite sex, just as the profoundest source of his pleasure is the knowledge
of his hidden phallus, potent and lurking beneath his disguise. But the
true transsexual feels no more than a sense of relief, when she appears
as a woman at last."[82] The phrase "true transsexual" implies that there
are people other than transvestites who might also be aroused by cross-
dressing—"untrue transsexuals"? Since genetic females can become
aroused by dressing up in something slinky, it is very sad that Morris
must give up a claim to pleasure in order to make herself legitimate.

Morris began to obtain new identity papers and inform old friends
about her change. Her relationship with Elizabeth was one of the things
that also had to change. "We did not wish to be merely friends, for that
would deny me any kinship with my children," she writes. "So we set-
tled for sisters-in-law, the nearest to the truth that we could devise. I
had in very truth become my own sister, and as the personality, even
the memory of James began to fade from my life, so I became a kind of
adoring if interfering aunt to my children, and a relative linked neither
by blood nor carnality to Elizabeth."[83]

Morris finally felt ready for surgery in 1972. She credits Jorgensen
with the liberalization of public attitudes toward and medical treatment of transsexuality, and reports that at least six hundred people of
both original sexes had received surgery in the United States, and about
one hundred fifty had been operated on in Britain. But after so many
false starts, it should come as no surprise that Morris hit yet another

snag. The doctor at Charing Cross Hospital refused to perform surgery until Morris and her wife were divorced. Morris acknowledges that she and her wife knew they must eventually dissolve their marriage, but she was also indignant about this intrusion upon their private affairs. So she resolved to return to the African continent, where a fortune-teller had once told "him" that one day "he" would be a woman like her.[84]

In June of 1972, she booked a ticket to Casablanca in Morocco. She went alone. The anonymous "Dr. B____" reportedly performed surgery on hundreds of people from all over the world, without the troublesome psychiatric and social requirements imposed by most Western nations. Her stay in this clinic sounds like a lonely, painful, and frightening ordeal. But Morris was at last home in her own flesh. Of her new body, Morris writes, "Now when I looked down at myself I no longer seemed a hybrid or chimera: I was all of a piece, as proportioned once again, though in a different kind, as I had been so exuberantly on Everest long before. Then I had felt lean and muscular; now I felt above all deliciously *clean*. The protuberances I had grown increasingly to detest had been scoured from me. I was made, by my own lights, normal."[85]

It was also in Dr. B____'s clinic that Morris met, for the first time, other transsexuals. Language barriers made it difficult to communicate with the other patients, but Morris recalls that "we had this in common…that we were all gloriously happy."[86] Despite this euphoria, upon returning home, Morris found that Dr. B____'s work needed some correcting, and so she underwent two more surgeries in England. But "I would have gone through the whole cycle ten times over, if the alternative had been a return to ambiguity or disguise."[87]

Unlike Jorgensen, Morris is keen to track the differences between how she was treated as a man and as a woman. She reports that no aspect of her life was untouched by the change, and although she was happy to accept gallantries and courtesies from men, some of this change in status was galling. "The more preposterous handicaps of the female state, embodied in common law as in business prejudice, are clearly doomed: nobody of sense can support them, and they are mere impertinences left over from the past," she asserts.[88] Elsewhere she refers to herself as a "militant feminist."[89]

Although Morris's treatment of her sexuality post-surgery is daring in comparison to Jorgensen's pallid and sparse anecdotes, it seems that sex change did not make pleasure any more accessible to Morris than it had to her predecessor a decade earlier. The book has one episode that might be called carnal, and is nothing more than a description of an impulsive kiss and a pat on the bottom from a cheeky cabdriver.[90] It is heartbreaking to read this confession:

> Looking back at my old persona, I sadly recognized my own frustrated desires, plain at last, but irretrievably wasted. I saw how deeply I had pined for the arms and the love of a man. I saw how proud and brave a wife I would like to have been, how passionate a mother, how forlornly my poor self had yearned to be released into its full sexuality. ...I am asked sometimes if I plan to marry...but no, the men I have loved are married already, or dead, or far away, or indifferent. Too late![91]

Morris instead consoles herself with the intense love and friendship she shares with Elizabeth, although she is careful to make it clear that the relationship is not a sexual one, and they do not live together full-time. Morris does not say this outright, but it seems that, having braved the stigma of transsexuality, she is not about to trade it for the marginalized status of a lesbian. Morris also asserts that her children have suffered no traumatic effects from her sex change, and remain close with both of their parents.

Perhaps because of her personal connections with members of the press, Morris was able to head off the storm of publicity that had ruined Jorgensen's tranquillity.[92] She describes a happy life which seems that of a kind, busy, unmarried woman of a certain age. After all those years of suffering, it feels as if Morris deserves more of a reward than the right to walk into the village, gossip with the other ladies of the town, and buy a few groceries and some typing paper. Despite the limitations of this life, Morris is unshakable in her conviction that she made the right decision: "If I were trapped in that cage again nothing would keep me from my goal, however fearful its prospect, however hopeless the odds. I would search the earth for surgeons, I would bribe barbers or abortionists, I would take a knife and do it myself, without fear, without qualms, without a second thought."[93]

In the last chapter of the book, Morris reveals a thought that would never have crossed the pages of Jorgensen's autobiography. "I have lived the life of man, I live now the life of woman, and one day perhaps I shall transcend both—if not in person, then perhaps in art, if not here, then somewhere else," she muses.[94] While this is not exactly a description of a two-spirited person, or a statement that transsexuality might, itself, constitute a third and completely valid gender, it points the way to a greater flexibility in our concepts of gender, away from dualism and polarization.

In 1977, just three years after *Conundrum* appeared in print, Mario Martino published *Emergence*. This book was advertised as "the only complete autobiography of a woman who has become a man."[95] Perhaps because transsexuality was no longer such a shocking idea, or perhaps because the public had much less interest in the phenomenon of biological females becoming men than in people who were born male giving up that privilege and allowing themselves to be castrated and relegated to a feminine status, Mario Martino's book never achieved the popularity of Christine Jorgensen's autobiography or Jan Morris's confessional. Even among female-to-male transsexuals today, the book is not well known. Nevertheless, it requires examination as the first text of its kind. From its very obscurity a message can be derived about the noticeably different ways that male-to-female (MTF) and female-to-male (FTM) transsexuals are perceived.

The author of *Emergence* was born Marie Martino in 1938. His Midwestern family were immigrants from Italy. His father seems to have been a brutal and insensitive person, a police officer who wore his gun even when playing poker with his friends. Martino describes several incidents in which he or his mother were beaten by his father. Some of this hostility may have been caused by the fact that Martino closely resembled his father, and from an early age was chided for being too masculine. Martino was strictly reared in the Catholic faith, and the word *sex* was never uttered in the family home or in the parochial schools where he was educated.[96]

This book, like the Jorgensen autobiography, has a foreword by Dr. Harry Benjamin. It is also dedicated to him. Perhaps because Dr. Benjamin was rather elderly by the time *Emergence* was published, the foreword is very brief. Benjamin says, "I have long felt that there is a real need for the detailed autobiography of a female-to-male transsexual," and he hopes the book will "create sympathy" and "dispel a great many wrong ideas—principally the notion that these people could 'change if they want,' and that they can be treated and 'cured' by psychotherapy." He also hopes the book will "clarify the minds of female transsexuals and their families, and help them find themselves."[97]

Like Jorgensen and Morris, Martino reports being convinced from an early age that there was some mistake about his biological sex. "*I was a boy!*" he writes. "I felt like one, I dressed like one, I fought like one. Later, I was to love like one."[98] This last sentence underlines a crucial distinction between early MTF autobiography and the "typical" (if such a thing can exist) life story of FTMs. Sex is central to this narrative, pleasure was something that Martino clearly desired all his life (even though the guilt he felt as a deeply religious Catholic was intense), and making love with a partner is central to Martino's sense of himself as a man. In some ways, the experience of having sex with and gratifying a heterosexual woman is even more important to Martino's gender identity than possession of a virile physique.

Martino began masturbating at the age of eight, excited by mild sexual exploration with a neighborhood playmate. Despite being caught by his mother and rebuked, this activity continued, especially once Martino discovered a douche nozzle. By placing this "between the lips by the clitoris," [99] Martino was able to "make like a man," and especially enjoyed masturbating after looking at a girlie magazine he found in a cousin's bedroom.[100]

Emergence describes puberty as a traumatic time for Martino. In addition to the humiliating experiences of having to purchase and wear a bra, Martino's mother died when he was twelve. Three months later, his father remarried, and this second wife, Lenore, was even less forgiving than Martino's mother had been about his mannish ways. This relationship became especially ugly when Martino began to menstruate. Nobody had warned him about the advent of this physical change. Martino was revolted by the idea of having to wear a dirty pad next to his body, and mortified to hear his stepmother recount their "private" conversation to his father, which caused mutual hilarity.

Finally things became so strained in the family that Martino's father decided to send him away to a school run by nuns. His father told him, "Maybe they can make a lady out of you." Shortly before leaving for this school, Martino heard his stepsister use the term "queer," in reference to a boy he knew, and he asked what it meant. He was told, "A queer is someone who plays with himself or loves another boy. Instead of loving a girl, which is normal." Martino wondered if this insulting term applied to him, since he had crushes on other girls and female teachers.[101]

Another very significant event occurred that year, when Martino was fifteen. The pandemonium about Christine Jorgensen's sex change hit public awareness. Martino recalls the ridicule and dirty jokes that this evoked, but he also says, "At last I had hope. *There were people like me.* And they were doing something about it. Now I had a plan: I must hurry through school, graduate, make a lot of money, go to Denmark. I'd not tell anyone. I'd simply leave this country as Marie, leave this girl-form in Denmark, return to the States as a man with a new name, and lead a new life."[102] It might have eased Jorgensen's suffering to know that news of her courageous action was bringing comfort to gender dysphoric young people like Martino.

The plan to go to Denmark for a sex change was derailed by the deeply religious atmosphere of the boarding school. Martino remembers several crushes on nuns and on other students. He patterned himself after Miss Henderson, the gym teacher, who was rumored to live with her lover, another woman teacher.[103] Martino decided to leave the boarding school his sophomore year, and go to an aspirancy, a convent school for girls who wanted to be nuns.

> The convent would solve all inner conflicts. I said it over and over until it became a prayer. Eventually my religious feelings would master my carnal body and convince me that I was not unlike other girls. I wanted to become a Franciscan and pattern myself after St. Francis, founder of the order. Hadn't he scourged his body and rid it of all sexual urgings? And, in so doing, he had risen above mortal self and become a saint. I would never be a saint—but, with God's help, surely I could purify my soul and consecrate my life to Christ and the world's poor.[104]

Despite these sincere feelings, sexuality won out over self-denial. Martino was caught having a "special friendship" with another student and sent home before the school year was over. (The feminine object of his affections was allowed to remain in school.) Martino completed his studies by correspondence. When summer came, he moved out of his father's house and got a job working as a nurse's aide so he could pay his own tuition to St. Kevin's High School for Girls and finish his senior year on schedule.

Working among older, attractive nurses at the hospital made Martino feel like a spy among innocents, and the plan to go to Denmark for a sex change was revived. However, when Martino went to work at Immaculata Hospital, he received nurse's training from the Catholic nuns there, and one of them, Sister Scholastica, tried to kindle a sense of religious vocation in him. Martino "concentrated more on prayer at daily Mass and asked God for a sign. Was the religious life the answer? Could my mixed emotional feelings be exorcised by holy rituals behind the wall? Would I find peace?"[105]

It was during his first postmortem that Martino made the decision to enter the novitiate. As the pathologist made his first incision and girls fainted around him, Martino stared at the face of death and wondered what he would be able to accomplish by the time he left this life. He worked at two different hospitals to raise three hundred dollars for a dowry and pay for his wardrobe. He wondered if other nuns or priests "had also faced crises of sexual identity" but cut off those questions. "No! Inconceivable. Nuns and priests were selfless individuals. Their reason [for entering religious life] was far loftier than my own. Theirs was dedication to Christ, mine more self-serving. God, help me to become a truly selfless person."[106]

At first, life in the convent alleviated Martino's attraction to women and his conviction that he should really be a man. And for the first time in his life, his family was proud of him. At his investiture, he took the name Sister Mary Dominick, naming himself after his older half-brother.

But disillusion set in when Martino witnessed prejudice against one of his friends, a black nun named Sister Imelda, and favoritism on the part of the head of their chapter, Sister Caritas, toward two novices who were allowed to sit laughing and chatting in her office past the time of the Grand Silence. And sexual need could not be kept at bay forever. Martino dreamed about making love to one of the postulants, exchanged a sexual kiss and caress with a female friend when he went home before his investiture, and continued to agonize about the gender question.

After being informed that a much older nun was leaving the convent, Martino and three other novitiates decided to return to secular life. He was warned that other Catholics would believe he had committed a sin as grave as murder, but the desire to wear trousers and men's shirts again and escape from the nun's habit was just too strong. At home, Martino encountered a great deal of hostility from his father, and distanced himself from his family.

He was still able to call on the nuns at a hospital where he had worked to help him find a job. Martino got a room in a boarding house and made friends with two of the other residents, Louise and Bart. He initiated his first complete sexual relationship with Louise, a relationship which ended because the lovemaking was one-sided, Louise would not tolerate the facsimile of a penis that Martino had made out of a condom and a test tube (or any sort of penetration), and she was jealous and withdrawn whenever Martino spent time with other acquaintances. Louise also rejected Martino's confession about feeling that he really should have been a man, labeling him crazy. Louise insisted that Martino was a lesbian, not a man, and also resisted Martino's attempts to get her to play a domestic role as Martino's wife.

In part because of the confusion generated by this volatile relationship, Martino asked his good friend Bart to try sexual intercourse with him. Bart was willing, despite the fact that they were no more than friends, but the attempt was not successful. Martino was a virgin, and Bart was afraid to penetrate "her" because it would be too painful. Martino was not impressed. "Why had there been no foreplay? It seemed funny now that I'd thought he could teach me a trick or two— why, I could teach him," he says contemptuously.[107] Nevertheless, that experience was a watershed in his life. It "sealed my fate. I knew I could never live as a female, that I should never have been born one. It was all some horrendous mistake."[108]

Martino ended the relationship with Louise by taking a job in another town. There, he went to his first gay bar, escorted by a female coworker who was worried about her own sexual identity. This was the Sandal Bar, and it contained only a few women. Most of the patrons were men. The experience convinced Martino that he was definitely not a lesbian. Furthermore, "I had never wanted—nor was I ever to want—anything other than a straight woman."[109] Martino got his wish when he began a liaison with a heterosexual coworker, Helga, who was pregnant. Martino planned to support this woman and live with her and her child as a family unit. Tragically, Helga died in childbirth, and her daughter was stillborn.

The only reinforcement Martino got for his gender dysphoria during these difficult years was a urine test he conducted at his place of employment, which showed that he had the same level of male hormones as a typical seventeen-year-old boy. He worked in the OB-GYN recovery room for women who had just given birth, and relished the kisses he was given by happy, drowsy patients who mistook him for their husbands. In the aftermath of Helga's death, Martino tried to make a new start, finding a new apartment and applying for more nurse's training, this time to obtain certification as an R.N.

After several rejections, Martino discovered that Irma Matthews, an old coworker to whom he had confided his gender dysphoria, was telling the schools that asked her for a reference that Martino was a lesbian. So instead of R.N. training, Martino went to a school that offered practical nurse training, a lower certification. This school, however, offered scholarships. And it was there that he met Becky, who was to be his lifelong companion.

There is a poignant description of Martino desperately trying to find any pretext to get physically close to Becky. "Friendship with Becky took on new meaning when she shortened my uniforms. I could scarcely thread a needle—how could I sew a hemline? Except for her touch (which stimulated me), I felt like a damn fool: like a man trying on his wife's dress so she can hem it evenly."[110]

During the Thanksgiving holiday, Martino finally lost control and pounced on Becky. Despite being interrupted by other students, they finally managed to consummate a passion that seemed to be quite mutual. Becky had numerous religious objections, which were not quieted by the copy of *The Well of Loneliness* that Martino gave her to read. But Becky eventually came to define their relationship as Martino did, as one between a man and a woman, and began to call him Mario when they were alone together: "Any resemblance to lesbianism on our part was due to my lack of the proper organs. Never did I use my vagina during lovemaking—always, I attached and wore my false penis. Wanting only to be a man, I went to all imaginable lengths to be one: affecting male attire, male mannerisms and figures of speech, having my hair clipped at the men's barbershop, roughing up my bushy brows."[111]

Many lesbians today would probably disagree with Martino's assumption that using a strap-on during lovemaking disqualifies it as lesbian sex. But it is easy to sympathize with this isolated couple, struggling to create a mutual world of shared meaning and plan a future together, when outsiders would invariably see their relationship as something other than a heterosexual bond.

This relationship survived enormous opposition. The two lived in dormitories while going to school, where there was very little privacy. They worked together in a hospital where paranoia about lesbians was high. Finally they acquired an apartment together, where Martino could smoke a pipe (which he hid when they had visitors). There, Becky kept house and Martino did the jobs he thought appropriate for a husband. Becky even agreed to work to put Martino through R.N. school, on the condition that Martino would then take a job to send her to school.

The discrepancy between Martino's physiology and his identity seems to have been much less important to Becky than it was to Martino.

> Through underground papers I located a *dildo*. Shaped like the male phallus, it is a venerable instrument used for intercourse. I was unhappy resorting to this device, it seemed demeaning to me. Strapping such a part to my body was playacting in a way. Hell, I was no actor. I *should* have been born with male anatomy.
>
> So the dildo was a compromise. For now. It assuaged that inner urge that compelled me to accentuate my maleness; it was a step toward matching my body to my gender. Furthermore, *it deepened my determination that my own destiny was not to be set by biological patterns.* I refused to accept such a biological dictum.

Becky and I were happy together. "I love you as you are, Mario," she would say. "But, whatever makes you happy...."[112]

After three years together, the couple decided to tell Martino's family about his decision to seek a sex change. Predictably, Martino's sister Jan and her husband Jim were supportive, while Martino's father refused to even discuss the subject. Christine Jorgensen reemerged as an important figure in Martino's life in 1967, when her autobiography was published. Martino did the same thing that every other gender-confused person of the time did, he called Dr. Harry Benjamin's office in New York. Through a referral from that office, he met Dr. Patterson.

In its treatment of medical authorities, this FTM narrative departs dramatically from the MTF pattern. Jorgensen and Morris had nothing bad to say about the doctors who made their sex changes possible. But Martino seems more able to notice sleazy or unethical behavior in his health-care practitioners, and was more likely to be critical of their treatment. From the beginning, Martino has qualms about Dr. Patterson, who seems affable enough, but insists on performing a mortifying and painful internal exam. He is also dubious about the psychiatrist he is referred to, Dr. Harris, conveniently located across the hall, who approves him for the Gender Identity Program after just one visit. Nevertheless, Martino accepts the expensive hormone injections, which are administered every two weeks.

Further down the road, Martino expresses even more contempt for the doctor who performs his first unsuccessful phalloplasty, and for an unethical attorney who demands hundreds of dollars to change legal documents when it turns out that these documents are routine and inexpensive for transsexuals to change themselves. Instead of idolizing professionals and trusting them to do the right thing in treatment, Martino turns to other FTMs for support, information, and help in changing social policy. This activism seems to be based upon the difference between FTM and MTF self-image. The sex change gives Martino permission to be more socially assertive, and he feels a fraternal bond with other men in his situation, whereas Jorgensen and Morris both reinforce their sense of femininity by avoiding other transsexuals and disappearing into "normal" life.

But Martino had problems at home that were at least as serious as his unsatisfactory doctors and attorneys. Becky, who until then had been supportive of his male identity, withdrew her support when it seemed that surgery was imminent. She even threatened to leave their relationship, and was persuaded to stay only when Martino's sister begged her to remain. The objections that Martino describes are based on a fear of her family's disapproval and religion. "You're interfering with one of God's divine principles in mutilating your God-given body!" Becky tells Martino.[113] But I wonder if part of the problem was not the fact that Becky had come to cherish and love Martino's female body, despite her prejudice against lesbians.

Martino's respect for the doctor is tarnished even further when the physician advises him to dump Becky. Then Martino and another FTM, Nick, discover that Dr. Patterson's bland assurances that it would be easy to find a surgeon to do phalloplasty are not true; no surgeon in the United States was doing phalloplasty at that time. Dr. Patterson was even unable to refer Martino to a physician who would do a mastectomy.

Luckily, Nick is able to help Martino find Dr. Lake, who has his own hospital. Surgery will take place there. Shortly before the surgery happens, Becky decides that she loves Martino and wants to stay with him.

With a great deal of fortitude, Martino braves the surgery despite a nasty reaction to the anesthetic. Once he is healed, he tries to make peace with his father, only to be rejected. The book describes Martino's persistent tackling of obstacle after obstacle—finding jobs despite the female name on his nursing license, getting new identification papers, and enduring the complications of surgery to remove his female reproductive organs.

Exhilarating as it was for Martino to be able to pass more easily as male, this must have been a trying time in Martino and Becky's lives. Their stress was compounded by the rejection of Becky's family, which had religious objections to Martino's transsexuality even though they had apparently supported the relationship when they thought the two of them were living together as women. Another sad event was the death of Martino's father, after a massive stroke and heart attack. Despite rushing to his father's side, Martino was unable to make peace with the old man, and had to content himself with the knowledge that at least he had tried.

But life had its compensations. After a nine-year battle to find a priest or minister who would marry them, Martino and Becky were finally able to celebrate their wedding. They also founded a counseling service for transsexuals with the assistance of Dr. Lake, and a post-operative halfway house for transsexuals undergoing surgery and their partners.

The counseling service and halfway house served FTMs for the most part, and Martino (who was working by then in Dr. Lake's hospital as a nursing supervisor) came to have some strong feelings about the differences he saw between female-to-male and male-to-female transsexuals. These judgments were based on behavior he observed among sex-change patients at the hospital.

> I began to understand why some transsexuals had damaged their own repute. The females-to-males I met seemed to fall into a constructive general pattern: Outwardly, they were more or less like anyone else. They set their life goals, completed their sex reassignments, continued their education, married, built homes and families. Most of these females who came for sex-change surgery made little fuss and, when discharged, quietly left the hospital without incident.

> But the male-to-female patients were another story. Too few of them acted like any other female, either in speech or in manner. The extroverts among them referred to one another as closet queens, shrilled out their demands, showed their newly constructed vaginas to anyone who'd look, and used language I'd never heard from a woman.

> Could I ever accept these exhibitionists as transsexuals?[114]

Martino is especially contemptuous of male-to-female transsexuals who do not have genital surgery. "Living as females, impersonating and working as prostitutes, these transsexuals are the ones who run headlong into the law. These are the ones who give a disreputable tinge to transsexualism," he says darkly.[115] This seems fairly harsh, given his own harrowing experience with one unsuccessful phalloplasty and a second surgery complicated by gangrene. The idea that some transsexuals might reject genital surgery simply because it didn't work very well, or didn't create functional female genitals, does not seem to have occurred to him. Like Jorgensen and Morris, he would probably have rejected two-spirited or third-gender people on the grounds that they are not "true transsexuals."

Furthermore, Martino assumes that all male-to-female transsexuals are heterosexual and want to be married and have children. In a survey of one hundred or so clients of his and Becky's counseling service, he found that "ninety percent wanted to marry 'the old-fashioned girl.' Only five percent of the wives had engaged in a lesbian relationship before meeting the female-to-male transsexual. Only six percent frequented gay bars preoperatively."[116] It would be interesting to see his reaction to the FTMs with gay male identities who are becoming more vocal today.

This view of other FTMs echoes Martino's own life experience. Despite being warned by Dr. Lake not to go through with the first phalloplasty, Martino risks it anyway, so strong is his drive to complete his image of what a male body should look like. When gangrene forces him to shorten the phallus created by the second phalloplasty, Martino is crushed, but Becky tells him, "Mario, I've been looking at your body for almost twenty years now. I'm happy with it. I know you want perfection: a perfect phallus. But be happy with what you have. I will be."[117]

Post-genital surgery, Martino reports a new feeling of completion:

> There is a new part of me—a part I have always conceived of myself possessing. It completes outwardly a picture of myself which I have always carried in my head. By day, whether working, driving, gardening, or relaxing, I sense always the presence of this outward acknowledgment of my maleness. And, by night, my new organ—for all its being less than perfect—is still deeply stimulating to both me and my mate, both psychologically and physically.[118]

Martino feels that other female-to-male transsexuals share his sense of the importance of erotic fulfillment. "I know of no female-to-male who has reported an unsatisfactory sex life in the new gender," he claims. "Even without phalloplasty, each attributes his satisfactory orgasms to the psychological change: now he is at ease with himself—and having his mate respond to him as a male is a dream fulfilled."[119]

This vision of the "good life" for a transsexual after sex reassignment is, to me, much more sympathetic than the picture painted by Jorgensen or Morris. In the two early male-to-female transsexual autobiographies, womanhood is equated with a rather rigid and limited definition of femininity. As long as a person looks like a pretty lady, Jorgensen and Morris seem to be saying, she is a woman. Sex ought not to be that important to a woman anyway, they both imply.

The vigorous and lusty picture Martino paints of a satisfactory adjustment to sex change is one that seems much more realistic and well-rounded. He would never be content to simply be regarded as a man. He wants to prove himself in bed as well as on the street.

Perhaps this simply reflects the difference in the way we all, as men and women, construct our gender identities (or have them constructed for us). In order to be a woman, you simply have to get yourself defined as "not-male." Although there's an enormous amount of effort involved in presenting a feminine image, that energy is not recognized as real work or as an indication of any sort of serious talent or intelligence.

To be recognized as a man, you have to emphatically and publicly reject femininity, but you also have to strive for that recognition. We say "Be a man" in a way that we would never say "Be a woman."

One of the achievements that someone must demonstrate to be recognized as a man is sexual potency, the ability to take or possess a sexual object. Jorgensen and Morris may have felt that by displaying too much of an interest in things erotic, they would convince their readers that they were still trying to fulfill a male agenda. And while there may have been male-to-female transsexuals of their time who were invested in making pleasure an important part of their new lives as women, it's not very likely that reputable publishers would have agreed to circulate their stories.

Gay men and lesbians will recognize these autobiographies as variations on the coming-out story, even though the narrators reject gay identities, and the "happy endings" in these books differ greatly from the rewards that out-of-the-closet, politically aware homosexuals are made to feel they are entitled to receive. For gay men, one of the payoffs of coming out is sexual fulfillment, the opportunity to satisfy himself with as many other gay men as he would like. And for lesbians, one of the payoffs is romantic fulfillment, the greater intimacy, safety, and rapport that one woman is supposed to be able to count on from her female lover. There is also the promise of joining a community of like-minded allies who will strive to ameliorate the bad effects of anti-gay discrimination, violence, and stigma. Only Martino's biography comes close to hinting at the formation of transsexual community.

But then, gay men and lesbians do not have to go to medical doctors or psychiatrists in order to come out. We do not need a prescription for hormones to become fags and dykes, nor do we need surgery before we are comfortable enough in our own bodies to investigate our sexuality. It would be a great mistake to see the shared characteristics of Jorgensen, Morris, and Martino's stories as being due only to the common, innate qualities of transsexuals. The health-care professionals who function as gatekeepers, allowing some transsexuals to receive a sex change and denying those who are not found to be "true transsexuals," had a huge impact on the way transsexuals viewed themselves and the way they presented themselves to each other and to the public.

In the next chapter, we will examine the way the gender scientists served as midwives to the formation of transsexual identity, and in many ways militated against the formation of transsexual community.

Notes

1. Marjorie Garber, *Vested Interests: Cross-Dressing and Cultural Anxiety,* New York: HarperPerennial, 1993, p. 3.
2. Ibid., pp. 259-263.
3. Ibid., p. 264.
4. Ibid., p. 262 and p. 265.
5. Jeffrey Weeks, *Sexuality and Its Discontents: Meanings, Myths and Modern Sexualities,* London, Boston and Henley: Routledge and Kegan Paul, 1985; and Michel Foucault (ed.), *Herculine Barbin: Being the Recently Discovered Memoirs of a Nineteenth Century French Hermaphrodite,* New York: Pantheon, 1980.
6. Vern L. Bullough and Bonnie Bullough, *Cross Dressing, Sex, and Gender,* Philadelphia: University of Pennsylvania Press, 1993, p. 204.
7. Ibid., pp. 207-208.
8. Ibid., pp. 204-207.
9. Ibid., pp. 212-213.
10. Christine Jorgensen, *Christine Jorgensen: A Personal Autobiography,* Paul S. Eriksson, Inc., 1967. Paperback edition, New York: Bantam Books, 1968, p. ix.
11. Ibid.
12. Ibid.
13. Ibid., p. xi.
14. Ibid., p. x.
15. Ibid., p. xi.
16. Ibid., p. x.
17. Ibid., p. xi.
18. Since it is the author's position that transsexual men and women should be viewed as members of their preferred gender, female pronouns will be used for transsexual women and male pronouns for transsexual men, even prior to sex reassignment. If the reader is confused by this, remember how much more painful and confusing it must have been for these individuals to grow up with everyone around them telling them they had to be something they knew perfectly well they were not.
19. Ibid., p. 15.
20. Ibid., p. 16.
21. Ibid., p. 22.
22. Ibid., p. 31.
23. Ibid., p. 33.
24. Ibid., p. 34.
25. Ibid., p. 51.
26. Ibid., p. 66.
27. Ibid., p. 66.
28. Ibid., p. 85.
29. Ibid.
30. Ibid., p. 90.
31. Ibid., p. 96.
32. Ibid., p. 92.
33. Ibid., p. 90.

34. Ibid., p. 102.

35. Ibid., p. 113.

36. Ibid., p. 125.

37. Ibid., p. 134.

38. Ibid., p. 165.

39. Ibid., p. 168.

40. Ibid., p. 157.

41. Ibid., p. xv.

42. Ibid., p. 209.

43. Ibid., p. 221-223.

44. Ibid., p. 230.

45. Ibid., p. xvi.

46. Ibid., p. 260-265.

47. Ibid., p. 291.

48. Leslie Feinberg, *Transgender Liberation: A Movement Whose Time Has Come,* New York: World View Forum, 1992, p. 20.

49. Ibid., pp. 20-21.

50. Jorgensen, op. cit., p. 293.

51. Ibid., p. 300.

52. Lee Mortimer, "Latin Quarter Revue Adds Christine," *Daily Mirror,* January 6, 1954, p. 37. Mortimer says of Jorgensen, "The voice, mannerisms, material and demeanor are reminiscent of impersonators at the Moroccan Village and the old 181, and to anyone who's visited Finocchio's in San Francisco, this is ancient stuff indeed, only there they don't bother going to Copenhagen."

53. Jorgensen, op. cit., pp. xiii-xiv.

54. Jan Morris, *Conundrum: An Extraordinary Narrative of Transsexualism,* New York: Henry Holt and Company, Inc., 1974. Reprinted in 1986 in a paperback edition with a new introduction and epilogue by the author, p. 3.

55. Ibid., p. 4.

56. Ibid., p. 5.

57. Ibid., p. 8.

58. Ibid., pp. 25-26.

59. Ibid., p. 25.

60. Ibid., pp. 22-23.

61. Ibid., p. 23.

62. Ibid., p. 24.

63. Ibid., pp. 54-55.

64. Ibid., p. 55.

65. Ibid., p. 27.

66. Ibid., p. 46.

67. Ibid., pp. 47-48.

68. Ibid., p. 49.

69. Ibid., p. 50.

70. Ibid., p. 52.

71. Ibid., p. 57.

72. Ibid., p. 58.

73. Ibid., p. 59.

74. Ibid., p. 89.
75. Ibid., p. 84.
76. Ibid., p. 91.
77. Ibid., p. 93.
78. Ibid., p. 102.
79. Ibid., p. 105.
80. Ibid., p. 106.
81. Ibid., p. 116.
82. Ibid., p. 118.
83. Ibid., p. 122.
84. Ibid., p. 105.
85. Ibid., p. 141.
86. Ibid., p. 143.
87. Ibid., p. 145.
88. Ibid., p. 151.
89. Ibid., p. 159.
90. Ibid., p. 151.
91. Ibid., pp. 155-156.
92. Ibid., p. 163.
93. Ibid., p. 169.
94. Ibid., p. 174.
95. Mario Martino (with harriet), *Emergence: A Transsexual Autobiography,* New York: Crown Publishers, Inc., 1977, jacket copy.
96. Ibid., p. xi.
97. Ibid., p. ix.
98. Ibid., p. xi.
99. Ibid., p. 24.
100. Ibid., p. 25.
101. Ibid., p. 39.
102. Ibid., p. 40.
103. Ibid., p. 47.
104. Ibid., p. 55.
105. Ibid., p. 76.
106. Ibid., p. 78.
107. Ibid., p. 109.
108. Ibid., p. 109-110.
109. Ibid., p. 113.
110. Ibid., p. 129.
111. Ibid., p. 134.
112. Ibid., p. 144.
113. Ibid., p. 168.
114. Ibid., p. 236.
115. Ibid., p. 239.
116. Ibid., p. 243.
117. Ibid., p. 263.
118. Ibid.
119. Ibid., p. 265.

CHAPTER 2

Father Figures: The Gender Scientists

Harry Benjamin, M.D. has already been mentioned as one of the first medical authorities who advocated sex reassignment as the only appropriate and effective treatment for transsexuality. Indeed, he was one of the popularizers of the term *transsexualism,* mentioning in a lecture he gave at the Society for the Scientific Study of Sex in 1963 that this had been his preferred term for this condition for the past decade.[1] (In 1953, Benjamin had published an article in the *International Journal of Sexology* in which he touted the use of the term *transsexualism.*[2] One of Benjamin's early publications on the topic appeared in 1964 in David Cauldwell's *Transvestism.* In "Trans-sexualism and Transvestism," Benjamin tried to differentiate transsexuality from transvestism by arguing that they were related on a continuum, with transvestites showing milder symptoms, and the transsexual being the most troubled.[3]

Benjamin functioned as a gatekeeper into the transsexual milieu. By the time he published *The Transsexual Phenomenon* in 1966, he had seen two hundred "transvestites," one hundred twenty-five of whom he diagnosed as being transsexuals. This patient population included one hundred eight genetic males and seventeen genetic females. Unlike most other sex researchers, who were determined to craft a theory that would explain the origins of various activities they saw as perversions, Benjamin was honest enough to say that he was baffled by the etiology of transsexuality. He noted that about a third of his patients appeared sexually underdeveloped, but they were chromosomally normal. He could find evidence of "unfavorable conditioning" in only twenty-one percent of his patients, and could identify no causal sequence for at least half of the cases he wrote about. He proposed imprinting as a possible factor that might alter gender identity in a child, and also suggested investigation of the effects of prenatal exposure to hormones.[4]

Doctors, psychiatrists, and psychologists all over the world apparently referred patients to Benjamin, who would evaluate them, give them hormones if it seemed appropriate, and help them to locate a surgeon. This work was supported in part by a grant from the Erickson Foundation, which had been established by an early female-to-male transsexual, Reed Erickson.[5]

The Erickson Foundation also assisted in the establishment of the Johns Hopkins Gender Identity Clinic in 1965, which performed its first sex-reassignment surgery the following year. Gender identity programs with interdisciplinary teams of experts were soon established at the University of Minnesota, Stanford University, the University of Oregon, and Case Western Reserve. Federal grant money to medical schools was at a peak then, and although such monies were never allocated for sex-reassignment surgery, they did support research into issues pertinent to transsexuality.[6]

The Transsexual Phenomenon was, until 1969, when Richard Green and John Money published *Transsexualism and Sex Reassignment*, the classic work in the emerging field of gender science. In the preface, Benjamin credits Christine Jorgensen with focusing attention on "the problem" of transsexuality "as never before. Without her courage and determination, undoubtedly springing from a force deep inside her, transsexualism might be still unknown...and might still be considered to be something barely on the fringe of medical science. ...Without Christine Jorgensen and the unsought publicity of her 'conversion,' this book could hardly have been conceived."[7]

Benjamin also praises the team of Danish physicians who facilitated Jorgensen's sex change. But it is interesting to me that he placed her first in his acknowledgments. It is this attitude, rather than theoretical sophistication or academic ambition, that makes Benjamin unique among the gender scientists. While he is hampered, like all of them, by assumptions that any variation from the norm is pathological—he trots these ideas out almost by rote—what mattered most to Benjamin was the fact that people who were suffering from a painful dilemma came to see him, and he was able to help them by simply giving them what they wanted. This straightforward compassion is unique in the professional literature of the time.

Benjamin suffered from a good deal of stigma and condemnation for championing sex reassignment. He acknowledged that sex reassignment "is often met with raised medical eyebrows, and sometimes even with arrogant rejection and/or condemnation."[8] However, he countered this conservatism with the argument that "the forces of nature...know nothing of this taboo" that aims to protect gender stereotypes. "Facts remain facts," Benjamin writes. "Intersexes exist, in body as well as in mind. I have seen too many transsexual patients to let their picture and their suffering be obscured by uninformed albeit honest opposition. Furthermore, I felt that after fifty years in the practice of medicine, and in the evening of life, I need not be too concerned with a disapproval that touches much more on morals than on science."[9]

At one point, his medical license was threatened. This occurred when one of his patients was convicted for female impersonation. The patient had been carrying a letter from Benjamin, similar to one he gave all his patients, which stated that the individual was under his care as a transsexual, and was not intending to commit a crime or masquerade as a woman. The district attorney in this case complained to the County Medical Society about Benjamin, and attorneys for the state Division of Professional Conduct (to whom the matter had been referred) contacted the doctor and told him to stop providing his patients with these letters. Benjamin was told, for no good reason I can ascertain, that the letters might be judged illegal and thus unethical. He says, with understandable frustration, "And so, one little help for the transsexual's plight was nullified."[10]

Benjamin's relatively humane attitude toward his patients also reveals itself in his condemnation of " 'Behavior' or 'Aversion' therapy." He describes with horror and disgust a treatment process in which the transvestite patient was given an emetic drug. As soon as he became nauseated, he was shown slides of himself dressed as a woman and made to listen to tape recordings describing his cross-dressing. The treatment, according to Benjamin, continued until the patient vomited and acute illness prevented continuation. "Success has been claimed for this rather brutal and humiliating form of brain-washing," Benjamin indignantly writes, "but the time of observation for the 'cure' was, at the time of the report, only three months. And will such violent and undignified interference with an emotional life not again produce other, perhaps more serious substitutional symptoms?" He also condemned a similar form of aversion therapy that employed electrical shock instead of the nauseating drug.[11]

Benjamin's approach to transsexualism was deeply practical. While he did not like the fact that some of his clients worked as prostitutes, he understood that there were few employment opportunities available to them, and he saw it as one of the few ways a transsexual could raise enough money for surgery, which at that time often had to be obtained in Europe or Casablanca.[12] Benjamin says, "The unfortunate fact that a number of [transsexual] patients went into prostitutional activities right after their operations has turned some doctors against its acceptance as a legitimate therapy. As one urologist expressed it: 'I don't want a respectable doctor's clinic to be turned into a whorehouse.' " Benjamin feels that this attitude may "spring from the idea that a doctor is not only there to protect or restore his patient's health but also his morals. A physician with such a concept may enjoy the feeling of being on the side of the angels but he scarcely has ethics or logic for support. …Should a urologist…decline to treat sexual impotence because a cure may induce the patient to start an illicit love affair…?"[13]

The Transsexual Phenomenon seems coy to anyone who has read Money and Anke A. Ehrhardt's *Man & Woman Boy & Girl* and examined their photographs of ambiguous genitalia before and after "corrective surgery." Near the end, Benjamin's book contains a few photographs of transsexuals before, during, and after reassignment. A note in the text indicates that a section of sixteen additional photographs "is available to doctors only," free upon request from the publisher. *Transsexualism and Sex Reassignment* contains graphic material that would never have passed muster with Benjamin's publisher in 1966. Instead of portraits of nude and clothed transsexuals, there are diagrams of the surgery performed upon the genitals, and photos of the forms used to maintain the shape of the new vagina while it heals, as well as foundation garments designed to hold the form in place.

In a prudish and sex-negative time, Benjamin faced the uphill battle of convincing the lay and professional reader, who thought the issue of sex or gender was comparatively simple, to view this important area of human experience in a more complex way. He delineated several kinds of sex: chromosomal, genetic, anatomical, legal, gonadal, germinal, endocrine (hormonal), psychological, and social.[14] If all these different sorts of sex exist, which should hold sway? He also pointed out that maleness or femaleness does not always mean masculinity or femininity.[15] This was heresy in 1966.

From the earliest pages of this work, Benjamin expressed opposition to simplistic theories about the causes of transsexuality. He acknowledged that "early childhood conditioning in an environment unfavorable for a normal healthy development" may cause people to feel " 'trapped' in the wrong bodies," but pointed out that "equally unfavorable childhood influences can be traced back in persons who later grew into perfectly normal adulthood with no apparent split between the psychological and the physical sex." Even today, most sexologists do not seem to realize that conditioning is a two-way street. Benjamin pointed out that a child with an unusual gender identity may "condition" the parents to treat the child as a member of his or her preferred gender.[16]

Benjamin postulated the existence of "a constitutional factor" as the source of gender disturbance.[17] He sarcastically described psychoanalytic theories as "something like a cult, if not a religion" and said they are "often quite incomprehensible to ordinary clinicians. To them, their explanations and analyses many times appear far-fetched, even absurd, in spite of their often intriguing and sometimes poetic quality."[18] He cites a personal visit with Sigmund Freud himself to support his contention that the founder of psychoanalysis would not be averse to a biologically-based explanation of transsexuality, if he were still alive.[19]

Despite this squeamishness about psychoanalytic theories, Benjamin used fairly traditional psychiatric categories to describe his transsexual patients. He reports alcoholism and drug abuse, self-mutilation, suicide, narcissism, asexuality, paranoia, schizophrenia, psychosis, neurosis, and other mental disorders among them.[20] He attributes these problems for the most part to the frustration engendered by not being able to live in the gender of preference. He also concludes that "As a general rule...transsexuals are nonpsychotic."[21]

However, he complains more than once in the text about how difficult this group of people could be to work with. "Another handicap for many transsexuals is their character and their behavior," he says in a section of the book that otherwise addresses physical obstacles to a genetic male passing as female:

> From a so-called "character neurosis" to outspoken hostile, paranoic demands for help from the doctor, all kinds of objectionable traits may exist. Unreliability, deceitfulness, ingratitude, together with an annoying but understandable impatience, have probably ruined their chances for help in more than a few instances. Many transsexuals are utterly self-centered, concerned with their own problems only and unable to consider those of anyone else. ...Still another handicap for transsexuals is their rather frequent immaturity in thinking and acting. Driven by the pleasure of anticipation, they commit the most impractical errors. I have seen grown-up men in their thirties and forties waste their savings on trips abroad to

surgeons they "heard about," without further information or appointments. Others have fallen victim to quacks and fraudulent nostrums and rarely learned by their experiences.[22]

Benjamin, however, balances out this rant with the statement that, "On the other hand, there are also those patients who are touchingly appreciative, grateful, and eager to cooperate. They compensate the doctor for many of his disappointments. Alas, they seem to be in the minority."[23]

Rather than focus on psychosis as a motivation for demanding a sex-change operation, Benjamin outlines four common-sense motives: the sexual motive (the desire of a normal woman to have sex with a normal man, of course), the gender motive (the desire to live in the sex of preference, even if no intimate or romantic relationship is ever possible), the legal motive (to end the constant fear of being exposed or arrested for impersonating a woman), and the social motive (the desire of a genetic male with a feminine physique to end the harassment and embarrassment he experiences from other people who cannot tolerate his difference).[24]

Benjamin's theory of sexual deviation groups transvestites, transsexuals, and homosexuals together as "sex-split personalities."[25] It's not clear why he does this, other than out of the habit of following received wisdom, since he later acknowledges that a male homosexual "is a man and wants to be nothing else. He is merely aroused sexually by another man. Even if he is of the effeminate variety, he is still in harmony with his male sex and his masculine gender."[26] Later, Benjamin tries to escape from this tangle of poor reasoning by asserting, "The transvestite has a social problem. The transsexual has a gender problem. The homosexual has a sex problem."[27] While Benjamin himself places transvestites, transsexuals, and homosexuals on the same continuum, he criticizes doctors who responded to Christine Jorgensen as "just another fairy."[28] It is refreshing to read Benjamin's admission that "If these attempts to define and classify the transvestite and the transsexual appear vague and unsatisfactory, it is because a sharp and scientific separation of the two syndromes is not possible. We have as yet no objective diagnostic methods at our disposal to differentiate between the two."[29]

Many authors do make a sharp distinction between transvestism and transsexuality, classifying the former as a sexual fetish for wearing women's clothing, and the latter as a desire to become the opposite sex that has nothing to do with fetishism (or, perhaps more importantly, masturbation accompanied by enjoyment of fetish objects). This point would perhaps not be so important if it had not been used to deny some applicants, who don't know the appropriate stories to tell, gender reassignment if they confess to getting too much pleasure out of ladies' lingerie. My experience with the gender community mirrors Benjamin's clinical experience of nearly three decades ago: There is so much overlap between the two identities and behaviors that it is often not easy to separate the cross-dresser from the transsexual, and in fact, people in the gender community themselves are often confused on this point, and may think of themselves as transvestites or transsexuals at different points in their lives.

Like virtually every modern medical expert on transsexuality, Benjamin would not define a transgendered person who wished to retain the genitals they were born with as a "true transsexual." In fact, he makes the desire to have the penis removed one of the main diagnostic traits of the "true transsexual."[30] While cross-dressing relieves the distress of the transvestite, true transsexuals "feel that they *belong* to the other sex, they want to *be* and *function* as members of the opposite sex, not only to appear as such. For them, their sex organs, the primary (testes) as well as the secondary (penis and others) are disgusting deformities that must be changed by the surgeon's knife. This attitude appears to be the chief differential diagnostic point between the two syndromes (sets of symptoms)—that is, those of transvestism and transsexualism."[31]

This picture of the transsexual as someone who is "often asexual or masturbates on occasion, imagining himself to be female" continues as a truism in the case literature today.[32] Medical people are unable to countenance castration or penectomy unless the genetic male in question eschews any penile pleasure and utterly rejects his "useless" organ; the belief in transsexual asexuality also sanitizes the transsexual and serves to raise him or her above the rest of sex deviates. The assumption that transsexuals, before sex reassignment, aren't having much sex anyway also serves as a rationalization for the often poor results that surgeons get when they try to create functional genitalia to match the sex of preference.

There was also, of course, a legal reason why many doctors in the sixties and seventies (and even today) were reluctant to perform such surgery. This is the so-called "mayhem statute" that goes back to the days of Henry VIII, a law that was passed to prevent young men from escaping military service by injuring themselves.[33]

Defining the transsexual by "his" compulsion to be rid of the penis is, like so many of the medical and psychiatric theories about transsexuality, a tautology. The argument seems to be, "Transsexuals are people who insist on receiving surgery to alter their bodies, therefore we must provide that surgery." But if transsexuality is merely a variation on the normal gender pattern, it stands to reason that it existed long before surgery was available. Such a definition of transsexuality begs the question. Without the surgical option, it seems to imply, trans-sexuality would not exist. This association of transsexuality with surgery is one of the things that Janice Raymond and other feminist opponents of transsexuality use to bolster their claim that transsexual women are the tools and creations of sexist doctors, part of a backlash against feminism, sent out to undermine the lesbian community and the women's movement.

Benjamin claims that in the absence of surgery, transsexuals will engage in self-mutilation or suicide.[34] This makes it sound as if the surgeon is morally compelled, almost blackmailed, into operating, lest he contribute to self-destruction. In order to justify removal of male sex organs, the doctor must be seen to be as helpless in the face of this "disorder" as the transsexual.

By and large, Benjamin does not recognize differences in sexual orientation among his patients. What he calls the "Sex Orientation Scale," although based on the seven-point continuum developed by Alfred Kinsey,[35] is instead a set of categories based on a progression from pseudo transvestism through fetishistic and true transvestism, on to nonsurgical and true transsexuals. When he reports on the follow-up of fifty-one MTFs, Benjamin's description of an ideal adjustment is that of a young woman who, after surgery, married a slightly older man who "knows only that Joanna as a child had to undergo an operation which prevented her from ever menstruating or having children. They have had a distinctly happy marriage now for seven years. Joanna no longer works but keeps house and they lead the lives of normal, middle-class people."[36]

Benjamin is advocating a form of selective amnesia here, something that would hardly be considered healthy for anyone other than a transsexual. He seems completely unaware of any damage it might do a reassigned transsexual woman to hide her past from intimate partners. The stress of living such a double life seems to me to be almost as great as the stress of living in a body that is inconsistent with one's sex of preference. But Benjamin was not in the business of critiquing social sex-roles or revolutionizing society's concept of womanhood. He was in the business of helping disturbed and upset people fit into society as much as possible, to lead lives that were as contented as possible.

Benjamin's notions of genital reconstruction focus on the goal of creating a vagina that is adequate for heterosexual intercourse. "The creation of the artificial vagina is for many transsexual males (those with a primary sex motive for the conversion) the crucial part of the operation. Its success or failure may spell the success or failure of the entire sex change undertaking," he says.[37] There is no mention in this text of clitoral construction, or any discussion of what the consequences of lacking a clitoris might be for a transsexual woman. Since Masters and Johnson's pioneering work on female sexual response, which established the primacy of the clitoris as the locus of women's pleasure, was published the same year this book appeared, in 1966, it rankles to see women's sexuality reduced to the creation of a hole that is adequate for male use during intercourse.[38]

Benjamin reports that "a climax (orgasm) during sex relations has been reported by most" MTFs postsurgically.[39] Later, when reporting on follow-up results for fifty-one MTFs, Benjamin says, "An absence of an orgasm, if unimportant to the patient, did not necessarily exclude her" from being ranked as having good results. "If this defect, however, was sorely missed by the patient, the result was not considered *good*."[40] Benjamin believes his patients were able to experience orgasm "without a clitoris and a natural vagina" because of the psychological effect of being able to take "the longed-for female role in the sex act" and "the possible retention of sensory nerve endings in the scrotal (now labial) fold and also in the penile (now vaginal) tissue, provided this particular surgical technique was used."[41] However, he also acknowledges that disappointment with sex reassignment "invariably…had to do with the sexual functions."[42] His proposed solution is to encourage the transsexual patient to be conscientious about vaginal dilation, using a plastic or aluminum form to prevent vaginal atrophy or scarring, which will shorten the pouch formed by surgery.

Benjamin typifies "female transsexuals" (FTMs) as "much rarer" than "male transsexuals" (MTFs).[43] His text deals almost exclusively with male-to-female transsexuals, or, as Benjamin calls them, "male transsexuals." To digress—most medical writers are extremely reluctant to grant the transsexual the complete privilege of living in the gender of preference, and retain the sex of birth as long and as often as possible. This leads to such absurdities as a follow-up on transsexual women, in which those in relationships with men are called "homosexual transsexuals," and those in relationships with women are labeled heterosexual.[44] What dignity and validation the medical profession gives the transsexual with one hand, it takes away with the other.

(To be fair, it should be noted that Benjamin specifically addresses this question, and says the male-to-female transsexual who has sex with a man after reassignment is not a homosexual "if the respective patient is treated as an individual and not as a rubber stamp."[45])

By the end of 1964, Benjamin was able to report on only twenty "female transsexuals" (FTMs) as compared to one hundred fifty-two MTFs. Nevertheless, he boldly projected that "sometime in the future she [sic] may merit a book devoted to her [sic] alone." However, Dr. Christian Hamburger, Christine Jorgensen's primary physician, reported that of the hundreds of letters he received from people desiring sex reassignment after they learned of the Jorgensen case, one in three was by a genetic female. Hamburger thought the fact that Jorgensen's was a male-to-female conversion may easily have influenced the sex ratio of his correspondents, as well as perhaps a biological difference that made genetic males more susceptible to transsexuality.[46]

One slightly more modern source estimates that "gender identity disorders" are "quite rare overall. Their incidence in males is estimated to be somewhat less than three per one hundred thousand and in females just under one per one hundred thousand."[47] Transgendered activists today estimate that the proportion of FTMs to MTFs is roughly equal. This is supported by the Bulloughs, who report, "Transsexualism…has an incidence of approximately one per fifty thousand in both men and women, although in societies where male homosexuality is severely stigmatized, some male homosexuals seek reassignment surgery and increase the apparent incidence of male transsexualism."[48]

Benjamin states, "Female transsexuals can be ardent lovers, wooing their women as men do, but not as lesbians, whom they often dislike intensely. They long for a penis, yet mostly understand realistically that the plastic operation of creating a useful organ would be a complicated, difficult, highly uncertain, and most expensive procedure. …In some instances, a prosthesis, an artificial penis made of a plastic material, has been successfully employed. In the United States it is available with difficulty and on a doctor's prescription only."[49] Despite the stated dislike of most FTMs for being perceived as lesbians, Benjamin describes the most desired and "perhaps most frequent" sexual practice as a face-to-face "imitation of the heterosexual coitus, the transsexual female on top, rubbing the clitoris against the partner's genital region. This is accomplished by the TS's closed legs between those of the girl, which are spread apart, or by intertwining the legs, known as 'dyking.' "[50]

Benjamin associates the range of sexual practices available to FTMs with lesbian sex much more closely than he ever associates MTFs with gay-male sexuality. I speculate that it is easier for the experts to see MTFs, even those who still possess a penis, as female, since they have abrogated male privilege, than it is for them to see FTMs as fully male, since they lack the organ that is the primary signifier of manhood.

Benjamin says it's possible that genetic females who are given male hormones may show "thinning of scalp hair...although in practice I have never seen it occur."[51] This reinforces his admission of lack of clinical experience with "female transsexuals," since anyone affiliated with FTMs today is well aware that male pattern baldness is a common sequelae of taking testosterone, and is usually highly valued as an undeniable signal that one is male.

The American psychiatrist Richard Green is another early author in this field. He contributed "Appendix C: Transsexualism: Mythological, Historical, and Cross-Cultural Aspects" to Benjamin's book. Green locates incidents of "cross-gender identity" in Greek and East Indian mythology, the classical history of Greece and Rome, Renaissance Europe, North American Indian tribes, etcetera.[52] Green's point with all this is that "the phenomenon of assuming the role of a member of the opposite sex is neither new nor unique to our culture. ...Appraisal of contemporary clinical material regarding such patients assumes a fuller significance when cast against the backdrop of this historical and anthropological perspective. Ultimately a comprehensive understanding, evaluation and management of transsexualism will take into account the extensively rooted sources of this psychosexual phenomenon."[53] In other words, this is something that has always been with us, and it isn't going away just because twentieth-century Americans, unlike the prehistoric aborigines of Siberia or the Crow Indians, have no third-gender roles. A version of this article also appears in *Transsexualism and Sex Reassignment.*

Given Green's research, which confirms the existence of differently-gendered people throughout human history, it seems odd that he continues to refer to transsexuality as a "disorder." Cultural relativism can only go so far, it seems, to undo the effects of psychiatric training.

Green, with Money, edited the book that was to become the next classic in the new field of gender science, *Transsexualism and Sex Reassignment.* This text was dedicated to Benjamin, "the pioneer of transsexual research," whose "compassion and courage in treatment of the transsexual patient opened a new frontier in the knowledge of human nature." The foreword is by Reed Erickson, the introduction by

Benjamin. Robert Stoller is thanked for critiquing the manuscript. (Stoller, another major figure in psychiatric literature about transsexuality, will be dealt with in chapter three, "The Backlash: Transphobia in Feminism.")

The introduction by Benjamin is of interest because it describes the process by which he came to work with transsexuals. It seems that this began in the early nineteen-twenties when an elderly transvestite patient asked him to prescribe the newly-discovered female hormone Progynon® in hopes that it would stimulate gynecomastia (as "feminine" breast development is called in a genetic male). Benjamin must have been a rare physician, because "with some hesitation," he agreed, and felt the experiment was justified by "the infinite delight of the patient and…emotional improvement"[54] Years later, while working as Consulting Endocrinologist to the College of the City of New York, he met two young students whom he would later think of as transsexuals. Several years after that, Kinsey and his associates introduced Benjamin to his first "more immediately recognizable male transsexual."[55] This transsexual woman was referred to Benjamin for evaluation and possible treatment. She had already been interviewed by two groups of psychiatrists at the University of Wisconsin. One group recommended sex-reassignment surgery (which the patient wanted) to prevent emotional breakdown; the other group advised against surgery, believing it would not solve her underlying psychological problems. Benjamin recommended treatment with estrogen as a compromise.[56]

Benjamin says he met Christine Jorgensen less than a year after her surgery, when she was overwhelmed with letters by other transgendered people, asking for help. Jorgensen and her physician, Dr. Christian Hamburger, began referring some of the people who had written to them to Benjamin for treatment. At the time, he was not able to locate a surgeon in the United States who would help them, so he was limited to providing counseling and hormones. Benjamin was deeply impressed by "the suffering of these tormented people," especially those who attempted genital self-mutilation because surgery was unavailable, and became determined to try to revolutionize the medical profession's attitude toward transsexuals.[57]

After conducting a symposium on transsexuality for the New York Academy of Medicine on December 18, 1953, Benjamin found his list of referrals growing even longer. (The entire symposium was reprinted in the *American Journal of Psychotherapy* in April 1954.)[58]

Benjamin continued his work as an advocate for transsexuals within the medical profession. On December 22, 1964, he reports testifying at a meeting of New York's Health Department to determine whether transsexuals could be issued new birth certificates in their gender of preference. Eventually this idea was vetoed, to Benjamin's discouragement. He says the rationale for denying new birth certificates was "that, although the operated patients admittedly were 'ostensible females,' they were still 'chromosomic males.' The invisible therefore took precedent over the visible. The psychological sex had to yield to the genetic. Common sense, so it seemed to me, was defeated in New York by a technicality."[59]

But Benjamin lived to see surgeons at Stanford welcome a presentation on transsexuality by him in 1967, and to witness reassignment surgery finally performed in the United States in 1967 at Cook County Hospital in Chicago. (The first such surgery had been performed at The Johns Hopkins Hospital in Baltimore in 1966.)[60] It was a great moment of personal triumph for Benjamin when Johns Hopkins' Gender Identity Committee began to assess patients for sex-reassignment surgery. Benjamin credits John Money, a psychologist at Johns Hopkins, who was well-respected for his studies of hermaphroditism and related sexual disorders, for lobbying for provision of these services to transsexuals. He also saw the foundation of a similar unit at the University of Minnesota through its Professor of Psychiatry, Dr. Donald W. Hastings. And early in 1967, the Center for Special Problems was founded in San Francisco, with one of its goals the treatment of gender-role disorientation. [61]

He ends this brief autobiographical work with a statement that could stand as the motto for his entire career: "I am not here to promote any particular operation or treatment. I am here to try to promote scientific objectivity, openmindedness and—a bit of compassion."[62]

Co-editor of *Transsexualism and Sex Reassignment,* Green became interested in transsexuality while working in London at the Maudsley Hospital, while on a Public Health Service Fellowship. He met with several European scientists, some of whom later contributed to *Transsexualism and Sex Reassignment.* In the mid-nineteen-sixties, he interviewed about one hundred people requesting sex-change surgery in New York (patients of Benjamin's) or at the UCLA Gender Identity Research and Treatment Clinic (with Robert Stoller).[63]

His contributions to *Transsexualism and Sex Reassignment* include the aforementioned article on crosscultural evidence of transgenderism; "Childhood Cross-Gender Identification," an article that presages the lengthy study of effeminate boys that became *The "Sissy*

Boy Syndrome," described below; "Attitudes Toward Transsexualism and Sex-Reassignment Procedures"; and "Psychiatric Management of Special Problems in Transsexuals."

The penultimate article is interesting because it investigates the attitudes of doctors rather than transsexuals. Green circulated a questionnaire (designed with the help of Dr. Robert J. Stoller and Dr. Craig MacAndrew) which gave a brief clinical history of a transsexual followed by questions to elicit the respondent's attitude toward such a patient. Psychiatrists, general practitioners, urologists, and gynecologists were polled. About four hundred replied. Four-fifths of the respondents labeled the transsexual "severely neurotic" and fifteen per cent diagnosed her as "psychotic." The majority of the physicians indicated they would refuse a request for sex reassignment, even if the patient was judged nonpsychotic by a psychiatrist, had undergone two years of psychotherapy, had convinced the treating psychiatrist that surgery was indicated, and would probably commit suicide if the request for surgery was denied. Ninety-four per cent of the psychiatrists said they would refuse sex reassignment on "moral and/or religious grounds." Other reasons for denying surgery included fear of a malpractice suit and reluctance to explain their actions to a local medical society. However, if the patient had obtained surgery from some other physician, three-quarters of the respondents were willing to allow her to change legal papers such as a birth certificate and get married in her new gender. One-half said they would allow adoption of a child. Green is caustic, in a genteel way, about the ignorance and prejudice demonstrated here.[64]

In "Psychiatric Management of Special Problems in Transsexualism," Green provides a brief primer for psychiatrists working with transsexual patients. He suggests that treatment should include exploration of the motivation for sex change (which includes weeding out transvestite, homosexual, or psychotic patients who are not appropriate candidates for sex reassignment), informing the patient about what surgery and hormones can and cannot do, helping the patient to live in the gender of preference for a two-year trial period (maintained on hormones to bolster the patient's ability to be perceived as a member of the gender of preference), managing emotional difficulties with family members or sex partners, and promoting realistic expectations of the future (since many transsexuals, according to Green, expect that sex reassignment will quickly solve all of their problems, and they will immediately slip into idyllic married life).[65] Green echoes the practical tone of much of Benjamin's work, focusing on real-life problems like elimination of facial hair through electrolysis or adaptation to the lower wages a working woman makes.

This article contains one of the earliest descriptions of a transsexual who is not heterosexual after sex reassignment. Green says, "An additional complication described by one male seeking sex reassignment was that his erotic attractions are only toward women. Males are not sexually stimulating to him. This patient's primary motive in seeking sex reassignment appeared to be a gender one: that is, he wished to lead the social life of a woman but not the sexual one. He found himself in the rare situation of anticipating a life of lesbianism after surgery."[66] The description of a lesbian as someone who does not lead "the sexual life of a woman" shows that Green, like the physicians he surveyed, has a few strange prejudices of his own.

Today, Green is better known for his book, The "Sissy Boy Syndrome" and the Development of Homosexuality. This fifteen-year study of a group of sixty-six feminine boys and a control group of masculine boys began in 1958 when Green interviewed, with John Money, a family whose son was exhibiting feminine behavior.[67] Green found that the feminine boys were much more likely to become homosexual or bisexual men than the members of the control group. When interviewed in adolescence or young adulthood, three-fourths of the "sissy boys" were classified as homosexual or bisexual.[68] These classifications were based on sexual fantasy and sexual behavior. Only one boy was transsexual.[69] Green states that none became transvestite adults,[70] although elsewhere, Green mentions that three members of the sample continue to cross-dress "periodically."[71] Only one of the control group of masculine boys was bisexual at adulthood; however, one-third of that group was unavailable for follow-up.[72]

This study elicited quite a bit of controversy, especially in the gay press, when it was published. Some gay activists accused Green of "homosexual genocide" for offering treatment to some of the families with feminine boys. In fact, most of the families did not opt for therapy, although they did "try gently to discourage" feminine behavior when it occurred. But for families who desired it, Green made a formal treatment program available for their sons.[73] Treatment options included behavioral modification, group therapy with the boys and their parents, and psychoanalytic therapy with the boy.[74]

It would be difficult to slam Green as a thorough-going sexist or homophobe. He does not advocate that effeminate boys be forced into rough-and-tumble activities; instead, he recommends that they be encouraged to socialize with "non-aggressive male peers" and have more contact with their fathers in groups like "Indian Guides," which features "activities…of a noncompetitive nature."[75] If the transcripts of his clinical interviews are accurate, he seems to be nonjudgmental and supportive of the members of his sample who have become homosexual or transsexual. He tries to increase their self-acceptance and become an ally, to support them in having the happiest, most productive lives possible.

But he is also firmly committed to the idea that, if at all possible, psychiatric intervention during childhood should be attempted to prevent development of a homosexual, transvestite, or transsexual identity in adulthood. To critics of this notion, he says, "The rights of parents to oversee the development of children is a long-established principle. Who is to dictate that parents may not try to raise their children in a manner that maximizes the possibility of a heterosexual outcome? If that prerogative is denied, should parents also be denied the right to raise their children as atheists? Or as priests?"[76]

Despite this position, Green was one of the key people who supported removing homosexuality from the American Psychiatric Association's catalogue of mental disorders in the 1973, and he states in this book that, even though clinical tests reveal differences between homosexual and heterosexual men, "These differences do not paint a picture of mental disorder."[77]

He views heterosexuality as a preferred outcome for his sample in part because homosexuality and transsexuality are so stigmatized. He claims, "The developmental road of the adult transsexual is pocked with psychological potholes. Even if the person eventually obtains sex-change surgery, the long-term outcome remains guarded. And the scars of years of conflict can never be removed. For the child, discontentment with being a male cannot be alleviated by sex-change surgery. Therefore, psychological intervention directed at increasing comfort with being male has a commonsense rationale, for both the short and the long term."[78] It does not seem to have occurred to him that perhaps participation in this study constituted a "psychological pothole," or that easier, quicker access to sex reassignment or greater parental and peer acceptance of feminine boys might reduce "scars of years of conflict."

At least Green is honest enough to admit "the apparent powerlessness of treatment to interrupt the progression from 'feminine' boy to homosexual or bisexual man," because, of the twelve boys who entered therapy during this study, nine emerged as bisexual or homosexual, and this "proportion is comparable to that of the entire group."[79] Green further undermines some of his own conclusions by arguing that psychoanalytic theory may be mistaken when it assumes that boys develop a homosexual orientation because of a feminine identification.[80] Despite these depressing (to him) nonresults of therapy, Green attributes the early intervention of parents with reducing the incidence of transvestism and transsexuality in the sample to only one boy who desires sex reassignment.[81]

Green undertook this prospective study in large part because retrospective data about childhood memories are notoriously unreliable, especially in the case of transsexuals. Green says:

> Accurately tracing a transsexual's life history is highly problematic. Transsexuals come for psychiatric evaluation to utilize the psychiatrist as gatekeeper to the surgical suite. Surgeons are reluctant to operate on a patient requesting sex-change without a "green" light from at least one psychiatrist with whom to share blame if something goes wrong. Knowing this, few preoperative patients report any ambivalence to psychiatrists about their "proper" gender or about any of their conventional sex-typed behaviors beginning with childhood. Nor do they report events from their life history that do not fit the well-publicized autobiographies of "successful" transsexuals. In the circular universe of transsexual autobiographies and clinical evaluations, patients convince physicians of their transsexual nature by repeating the published developmental histories of transsexuals who preceded them. History has a habit of repeating itself.[82]

Green seems to be implying here that transsexuals are inherently deceitful. But if the process of evaluation for sex reassignment is fraught with deception, whose fault is that, the doctors whose clinical picture of transsexuality is so rigid that they will refuse "treatment" to anyone who does not fit their paradigm, or the gender-dysphoric individual who just wants to adapt his or her physical being and get on with making a life? None of the gender scientists seem to realize that they, themselves, are responsible for creating a situation where transsexual people must describe a fixed set of symptoms and recite a history that has been edited in clearly prescribed ways in order to get a doctor's approval for what should be their inalienable right.

Regardless of whose fault it is, the fact that this area of parent/child, doctor/patient, or researcher/respondent communication lacks so much candor should encourage more caution than Green or his colleagues such as Money ever display about their own theories and findings.

Money, perhaps the most influential sexologist doing research and publishing today, contributed four articles to *Transsexualism and Sex Reassignment* (in addition to the preface, which he co-authored with Green).

In "Sex Reassignment as Related to Hermaphroditism and Transsexualism," Money reviews the process by which human beings, beginning at conception, complete "psychosexual differentiation or the establishment of gender identity."[83] He outlines nine separate sequences, beginning with the establishment of chromosomal sex, and ending with gender identity, which Money believes "reaches its full expression with adolescent sexual maturity."[84] He goes on to delineate several "sex-chromosomal errors" such as Turner's Syndrome, Klinefelter's Syndrome (XXY), and the XYY Syndrome; "gonadal errors" such as hypospadias (an incompletely fused or improperly located urethral tract in the male), androgen insensitivity in the XY fetus, and hermaphroditism; "hormonal errors" such as the androgenital syndrome in XX fetuses and gynecomastia; "internal errors" such as male hermaphroditism with uterus and normal penis or hypospadias with uterus differentiated; "external error" such as the masculinization of XX fetuses by administration of hormones to the mother during pregnancy, penile agenesis (in which the XY infant is born with a penis the size of a large clitoris, due to the absence of the spongy tissue of the *corpora cavernosa* in the penile shaft), and penile injury or penectomy; and "gender identity error" such as transsexualism.

For a more complete discussion of all these topics, the interested reader should refer to Money and Anke A. Ehrhardt's 1972 *Man & Woman Boy & Girl*. Money became interested in transsexualism in part because of his work "correcting" what he sees as sex errors of the body in hermaphrodite or transsexual children. At first, it is hard to see the connection between this work and Money's later championing of sex reassignment. One common thread is Money's assumption that this entire area of human experience is primarily a medical problem that ought to be brought under the jurisdiction and treatment of endocrinologists and surgeons. He sees little or no difference between a child born with ambiguous genitalia and an adult who wishes to be rid of an offending appendage, such as a penis or female breasts.

Money is also a firm believer in gender dimorphism and polarization between the sexes, and an upholder of society's definitions of masculinity, femininity, and heterosexuality as the flagship of sexual normalcy. Although he and Ehrhardt include a section in *Man & Woman Boy & Girl* about anthropological studies that found pronounced differences in notions of gender and appropriate sexual conduct for children and adults in the Batak People of Sumatra, an anonymous group in Melanesia, the Pilaga, and the Yolngu of Arnhem Land, he is far from a cultural relativist. The fact that other cultures are able to tolerate some degree of homosexual conduct (and even, in some instances, insist upon it as part of a young man's initiation into adulthood) does not alter Money's view of same-sex behavior as a paraphilia. He is also not swayed by the news that third-gender roles exist for gender-ambiguous people in some more "primitive" societies than our own. Rather than ask if we are not perhaps a pathological culture because we cannot accept the fact that nature has created our species in more than two genders, Money distorts his own medical findings and repeatedly refers to the perfectly natural birth of hermaphrodite children as "Nature's mistakes."[85]

Like Green, Money sees the doctor as a key player in a child's battle for sexual identity. He is firmly opposed to the policies of some doctors who tell the parents of ambiguous children that they may have to wait until adolescence to know what sex their children are. He believes it is up to the attending physician to determine what sex should be assigned to the child, explain that decision to the parents, and enlist their unquestioning and total support for rearing the child in that gender, with no conflict. Time and again he warns that if this procedure is not followed, the child will become transsexual.[86]

It seems odd that someone as sophisticated as Money would allow his gender categories to collapse to two very small boxes, which could be labeled "boy = has a penis" and "girl = has a vagina." While Benjamin might have had some excuse for not emphasizing the clitoris in his study of the postsurgical sexual satisfaction of transsexual women, Money has absolutely no excuse for neglecting Masters and Johnson's discoveries. *Man & Woman Boy & Girl* contains more than one set of photos of little girls whose clitorises were excised lest they fixate on organs that Money or some other "authority" found inappropriately large, and become confused in their gender identities.[87] It is bizarre and disorienting to read Money's self-congratulatory passages about these surgeries, which most intact women with even a shred of feminist consciousness can view only as infant genital mutilation. He clearly sees himself as a benefactor of children who would otherwise have had miserable lives. It is difficult to avoid being swept away by Money's arrogance, and to see underneath this munificent veneer.

One person who has no such delusions is Cheryl Chase, the editor of *Hermaphrodites with Attitude*, a gutsy publication that strives to bring together intersexed people all over the world, including those who were unfortunate enough to lose all hope of functioning sexually as adults when doctors performed "cosmetic surgery" on their ambiguous infant genitalia. She makes it clear that not all of the children Money and his peers "rescued" from gender anomalies feel grateful or well-treated.

At the age of twenty-one, Chase asked her doctor to help her obtain her medical records pertaining to a hospitalization that occurred when she was a year and a half old. The records showed "Diagnosis: true hermaphrodite. Operation: clitorectomy." Chase had been assigned a male gender at birth, and named Charlie. When they thought she was a boy, Chase's patients were deeply ashamed of her small penis. But when doctors decided their child was a daughter, suddenly the small penis became a monstrously huge clitoris that had to be removed.

Chase's parents followed every dictate outlined in Money and Ehrhardt's *Man & Woman Boy & Girl*. They changed her name, burned old baby pictures, got rid of all the blue baby clothes, and consistently began to treat her as and speak of her as a girl and only a girl. According to Money and Ehrhardt, this should have resulted in a feminine little girl growing up to be a heterosexual married woman who could adopt children. Yet, by Money's criteria, Chase's adult gender orientation is far from perfect. (She identifies as a lesbian, and Money sees homosexuality as a disturbance in gender identity.)

Chase is understandably enraged about the fact that functional genitals were removed from her body without her consent. Today, she is unable to have an orgasm. She is also angry about the inability of almost everyone to accept the existence of intersexed people and support her attempts to get doctors and parents to stop authorizing the mutilation of their "different" children's genitals. She asks, "What are genitals for? It is my position that *my* genitals are for *my* pleasure. In a sex-repressive culture with a heavy investment in the fiction of sexual dichotomy, infant genitals are for discriminating male from female infants. It is very difficult to get parents, or even physicians, to consider the infant as a future adult, sexual being."[88]

H. Marty Malin delineates some of the problems with Money and his colleague's bland assumptions that genital surgery is the best solution for an intersexed infant. Malin was formerly the Manager of the Sexual Disorders Clinic at the Johns Hopkins Hospital, so he knows whereof he speaks when he says that so many intersexed children and their families are "lost to follow-up" that research on results is seriously compromised. He concludes, "I don't think we have treated intersex patients particularly well." He also says that "the capacity of genital surgeries to 'normalize' genitals is greatly oversold. ...The worst of these surgeries are simply cosmetically horrendous; functionally they don't seem to be much better. Some individuals experience chronic pain. Few report satisfactory erotosexual functioning."[89]

Given the drastic action he is willing to recommend when intervening in the lives of intersexed people, it would be nice if Money had ironclad data to back up his surgical recommendations. But Money's views about where gender identity comes from are ambiguous. He'd really like to find a genetic, chromosomal, or hormonal source for normal versus a "disturbed" gender identity, and healthy heterosexuality versus homosexuality and other "paraphilias." In the many years since he first began to publish, tantalizing clues, but no definitive proof that such a biological mechanism exists, have come to light. Money very properly points out that it would be unethical to conduct the experiments that might give us more information about these areas of human experience, but he also chafes at these restrictions, referring to ethics committees that protect human subjects as "the watchdogs of anti-research."[90] On the other hand, he has to admit that conditioning, imprinting, social learning, family dynamics, and other environmental factors have a significant impact on the development of gender identity.

Transsexualism and Sex Reassignment includes paired articles coauthored by Money, "Sexual Dimorphism and Dissociation in the Psychology of Male Transsexuals" (with Clay Primrose) and "Sexual Dimorphism in the Psychology of Female Transsexuals" (with John G. Brennan). Samples are very small (fourteen MTFs and six FTMs), but the authors do not qualify their results, or offer any cautions about generalizing from the data.

The Guilford-Zimmerman Temperament Survey was used to evaluate the masculinity and femininity of both groups. MTFs scored lower on masculinity than ninety per cent of the normal male standardization population, and seven out of eleven scored more feminine than sixty per cent of the normal female standardization population. Money and Primrose take this to mean that MTFs are engaging in a "conscious, superficial imitation of female behavior." FTMs scored high for masculine stereotypical behavior, ranking among the least feminine compared with normal women. But compared to normal males, only two patients obtained an average rating for masculinity. Money and Brennan attribute this in part to a flaw in the instrument, saying that some of the items are "doubtful measures of masculinity versus femininity." Money and Brennan see the FTMs, like MTFs, as "conforming to male roles as they perceived them."[91]

MTFs predictably ranked low in measurements of physical aggression, while FTMs ranked high. MTFs recalled being labeled as sissies during childhood; FTMs frequently called themselves tomboys.

As far as "genitopelvic functioning goes," Money and Primrose say, "Love play...including the copulatory act is sexually dimorphic. Males are considered to be alert to sexual conquests, easily aroused, and prone to the initiation of sexual activity. The female stereotype is passive and accepting, more slowly aroused, less prone to the initiation of sexual activity, and able to gain satisfaction from pleasing the partner." They add, "It is not legitimate to generalize too broadly, labeling male sexual behavior aggressive and female behavior passive. The female copulatory role also permits of extremely active participation. The popular notions and stereotypes of behavior are frequently violated in everyday heterosexual relationships."[92]

This study found that the MTF's "conception of sexually dichotomous behavior is defined in conformity with the stereotypes, not their violations." Like Benjamin, Money and Primrose report that MTFs do not enjoy erections or penile stimulation, and "invariably chose the receptor role in sexual relations."[93] Furthermore, "none of the patients expressed any regret at the functional loss of his penis in erection and ejaculation through hormone treatment."[94] Money and Primrose note that "In a large proportion of the cases, the men [sic] had not even the experience of intercourse with a woman on which to base their conceptions of feminine sexuality. They were, therefore, forced to create their own image of the female copulatory role from other more indirect sources of information."[95] Like their doctors, one presumes.

A hatred of breasts was found in FTMs that supposedly correlates with the transsexual woman's dislike of her own penis.[96] However, none of the FTMs reported being sexually aroused by male clothing. Money and Brennan say, "The fetishistic dependency on female clothing...is a common trait in male transvestites and in some, but not all, male transsexuals."[97]

Money and Brennan found that in the FTMs they studied, "much of the style of their reactivity was like that usually expected in the reactivity of the female to the male." Since these FTMs were partnered exclusively with women, this description of their sexuality makes little sense. Although FTMs did respond to visual stimulus, Money and Brennan characterize this arousal as "romantic rather than frankly genitopelvic." After a while, it begins to seem that Money and Brennan are unable to see FTM sexuality as "genitopelvic" because they don't have penises that become erect and ejaculate. FTMs were also described as being like women in their sexuality because when they fantasized about their partners, "no erotic zone of the body was particularly preferred." No data are quoted to demonstrate that all or most men focus in on an "erotic zone of the body" when fantasizing about their partners. [98]

"Though no empirical norms exist," Money and Primrose continue, "it is the generally accepted principle that males, more than females, are responsive to and dependent upon visual and narrative stimulation for genitopelvic arousal. Women...are more dependent than men on the sense of touch for genitopelvic, copulatory arousal."[99] They add later, "Relying on anecdotal evidence, one considers responsivity to visual imagery, either immediate or in the memory, which affects genitopelvic arousal, a male characteristic."[100]

Why should this generalization carry any weight when the very researchers who are making it admit that it has no empirical basis? Even if research could demonstrate that men respond more strongly to visual erotic stimulus than women, that research (to be valid) would have to take into account whether the visual representations were created by and for a male or female audience. Men and women may simply respond to different types of visual stimuli. Good social-science research does not equate "common knowledge" or "truisms," no matter how hoary, with proven fact.

Money and Primrose found that when they questioned the MTFs about sexual imagery during sex or masturbation, the most common response was to imagine the self as a female, with breasts and female genitals. They say this is "a dissociative quality to the male transsexual's disengagement of genitopelvic erotic functioning and his engagement of feminine imagery-content," thus pathologizing something that seems instead to be fairly consistent with gender dysphoria.[101] Wouldn't it be strange if an MTF visualized herself as a man during sexual intercourse? Furthermore, the sample was found to have "a masculine threshold of erotic arousal in response to visual imagery."[102]

FTMs were not found to have this "dissociative" experience with their own bodies during sexual activity. Nor did they alternate between male and female personas, as some MTFs or male transvestites reportedly do.[103]

Finally, Money and Primrose found that only one of their MTF sample had fantasies of pregnancy or wished to have a baby. None of them expressed any envy of pregnant women, but all of the sample wanted to adopt children, usually older toddlers rather than newborns.

They say:

> It appears that the typical male transsexual does not possess the maternalism associated with the female of the species. Pregnancy is not an important goal or desire in their lives. Far more important for the transsexual is the achievement of being accepted as a woman. The desire to adopt children occurs as a reinforcement of the new-found womanhood. The preference for toddlers instead of tiny babies may be interpreted as comparable to owning a fashionable pet as a female status symbol. It is not the same as the compelling urge of the normal female to have her own newborn baby to care for.
>
> A woman may do an excellent job of caring for a fashionable pet. So also a postoperative transsexual, married as a female, may do an excellent job of mothering an adopted or foster child....[104]

The cruel condescension in these paragraphs sets my teeth on edge. Money and Primrose offer no justification for their labeling of a transsexuals woman's desire to raise a child as the equivalent of having a fashionable pet. This denigration of another human being's maternal impulse can only spring from a clinical judgment of transsexual women as narcissistic, shallow, and vain. As far as the desire to be pregnant goes, are the MTF subjects not in a double bind here, just as they were with the question about their sexual fantasies and body image? Since these people know perfectly well it is not possible for them to become pregnant, perhaps they have simply given up on an impossible dream. A transsexual woman who did admit to the desire to bear her own child would run the risk of being labeled delusional or "dissociative," as were the MTFs who admitted to fantasizing about having female bodies during sexual activity.

FTMs fare better on this index of the success of their reassignment, although Money and Brennan acknowledge that most of the members of their sample were too preoccupied with the problem of gender transition to be able to think about parenthood. They say, "Parental feeling toward infants and children, insofar as it could be estimated, was fatherly rather than motherly."[105] What they don't say is that the problem with estimating the fatherly sentiments of FTMs springs in large part from the failure of the researchers to delineate any objective criteria for measuring paternalism, as opposed to their dictum that normal, feminine women have an automatically loving response toward a helpless infant.

fathering urge left out

In his final contribution to *Transsexualism and Sex Reassignment*, "Public Opinion and Social Issues in Transsexualism: A Case Study in Medical Sociology," Money (along with Florence Schwartz) once more emphasizes his belief that opinion about, public policy on, and laws affecting transsexuals should be dictated by medical experts. This article describes a press release that was issued on November 21, 1966 by the new gender-identity clinic at Johns Hopkins Medical Institutions. The press release was issued because journalists had somehow been informed that a sex-change operation, the first in this country, had taken place there, and were threatening to run an exposé. Rather than run from negative publicity, Money and others at the gender-identity clinic consulted with the public relations department of Johns Hopkins and elected to release a statement to the *New York Times*, which published it verbatim. It was their hope that less authoritative newspapers would follow the calm, accepting tone of the *Times*. Money and Schwartz also suggest that rather than going to the law and asking for permission to treat transsexuals, doctors should take the initiative and tell lawmakers what the appropriate treatment should be for gender dysphoria and dictate public policy regarding the issuance of new birth certificates and marriage licenses.

Money and Schwartz say, "Authoritative and respected, physicians are well-qualified to induce liberalization of society's attitudes with respect to transsexualism and related disorders. Yet, the majority neglect their pivotal role in the arena of public education. Themselves conservative and cautious, they underestimate the laymen's comprehension, sophistication, and tolerant willingness to learn about the realm of psychosexual pathology."[106] While it's nice to see laymen lauded for being sophisticated and tolerant, I do not have the same confidence that Money and Schwartz have in "the nonjudgmental tradition of medicine and the judgmental and prosecuting tradition of law."[107] On its own, the law would probably not have come up with the concept of performing lobotomies on or administering chemical castration for sex offenders. It wasn't the law that popularized aversion therapy or electroshock to treat homosexuality.

Money (with his collaborators) is the author of hundreds of scientific papers and more than two dozen books in the field of sexology and psychoendocrinology. He is an enormously influential intellectual and researcher who clearly sees himself as a humanitarian who advocates better treatment for those he views as being less sexually fortunate than normal people. But he does not seem to understand how precarious the scientific basis is for his high-handed division of the world into "normal sexuality" and "paraphilias." Money is essentially a moralist masquerading as a scientist, and he gets away with it because of his medical credentials and his prolific output of technical-sounding publications about sexuality. In fact, it is the sort of attitudes toward sex, gender, and pleasure that he promotes which are the underpinnings of such things as sodomy laws and psychiatric incarceration of "differently-pleasured" people.

Nowhere is this moralism made more clear than in Money and Margaret Lamacz's 1989 *Vandalized Lovemaps: Paraphilic Outcome of Seven Cases in Pediatric Sexology*. Like Green, Money and Lamacz advocate intervention in the lives of sexually different children without conclusive proof that such interventions have any impact on adult sexual orientation, gender identity, or pleasure-seeking behavior. In fact, the dedication of this book is to "Those whose lovemaps will be paraphilia-free in the twenty-first century if this book promotes the founding of pediatric sexology clinics and research centers, worldwide, as we hope."[108] The prospect makes me shudder.

Money says:

> The lovemap is the personal imprint or template of whatever turns a person on. The beginning topography of the lovemap evolves in the womb, where the developing brain is open to the influence of the sex hormones. Spontaneous erections begin in the womb. And throughout childhood erotic play for most youngsters seldom voluntarily stops. The main contours of the lovemap are etched during this childhood sex-rehearsal play; when the lovemap is allowed to grow naturally, the child at puberty matures into a healthy lover. In adulthood an individual seeks to match lovemaps with someone else in a pair-bonding relationship.[109]

This explanation of the genesis of the lovemap has as much to do with objective reality as the fad that swept the country a few years ago for female ejaculation, which supposedly took place because of the G-spot, a mythical organ that no anatomist could ever find in the female body. All Money is really doing is recycling a bunch of very questionable assumptions about the genesis of pleasure-seeking behavior in adults. He moves readily from the "circulating fetal hormones" explanation of the structure of the lovemap to a "traumatic childhood event" explanation, without managing to document that either one is true. This is his "theory" about the etiology of sadomasochism: "The classic example is the kid who gets a hard-on while in a state of abject terror because he's been called down to the principal's office for punishment. ...Suddenly you've got the connection between an erection, sexual feeling, and getting beaten up. So you've got a sadomasochist in the making."[110]

Money, of course, is not troubled by the fact that there are plenty of sadomasochists who had little or no childhood experience with corporal punishment. Nor does it occur to him to ask why the kid who is about to be punished has a hard-on in the first place. Perhaps a predisposition to enjoy exposure, verbal rebukes, and a blow upon the buttocks existed before this make-belief teenager was chastised—or perhaps the potential to respond with arousal to this set of circumstances exists in all of us. The right question to ask may not be, "Why do some people grow up to be perverts?" but "Why doesn't everybody grow up with more sexual diversity and the ability to enjoy polymorphous pleasure?"

Though sexually conservative, Money does not consciously refer to the Bible or English common law to justify his fairly traditional views about what constitutes appropriate sexual conduct. Instead, he makes reference to the secular religion of the West, romantic love. It is the inability to enjoy romantic fulfillment that makes Money's paraphile a sad figure. The paraphiliac, according to Money, has accomplished a triumph in spite of the tragedy of having her or (more often) his lovemap defaced. The paraphiliac rescues lust from total wreckage and obliteration and constructs a new map that gives the erotic side of relationships a new chance. But there is a terrible price to be paid. In Money's world view, paraphiliacs cannot have both love and lust; they sacrifice committed, intimate, romantic partnerships in order to have their strange pleasures.

Having known many people Money would call "paraphiliacs" who do indeed enjoy romance and committed relationships, this generalization seems dubious to me. But Money has a double-bind to cover any exceptions to his rule. He simply pathologizes any relationships that sexually-different people might construct. In an interview, he typified such relationships as "spooky" and added, "I have never really gotten to the bottom of this strange collusional business between a paraphile and the partner. Do they smell each other out at the time of courtship? Does one grow into the paraphilia of the other—or a bit of both? Well, I have to call it a spooky collusional relationship. They know what they're doing. They're not ignorant, but both are powerless to not do it."[111]

As powerless, perhaps, as two heterosexual vanilla people who are deeply in love? When he enters the shadow side of human sexuality, Money leaves Occam's Razor at home.

In case being threatened with the loss of love doesn't convince us that the intense pleasures of the paraphilias are to be shunned, he makes ominous references to epilepsy among paraphiliacs and warns us that it is "terribly dangerous" to have "people who've got too much power" (i.e., politicians) with hidden paraphilias. In an interview, he equated the use of atomic weapons with fetishism and masochism.[112] This, and his attempt to make paraphiliac sex sound radically different from vanilla heterosexual lovemaking, fall rather flat. He says there "must be neurochemical changes" when paraphiliacs "go into a trance-like state and carry out their rituals. ...They have no self-governance over their behavior"—as if neurochemical changes do not take place during all sexual activity![113] Money has absolutely no evidence that a fetishist, sadomasochist, or transsexual is in any more of a "trance," engaging in a "ritual," or lacking self-control than a teenage boy who's getting some at a drive-in movie or a couple of newlyweds during their first night in the honeymoon hotel.

By the way, according to the 1996 edition of *Who's Who*, Money never married and has no children. It seems that what's sauce for the goose is not sauce for the sexologist. I guess it would verge on ad hominem to speculate about what might have happened to *his* lovemap.

Money has gotten big street cred in academia for boldly and calmly confronting dreadful things. He says he made a decision to allow the first sex-change surgery in the United States to take place in February of 1965 at Johns Hopkins because he was interested in the welfare of transsexuals and wanted to change the medical profession's attitude toward people with sexual problems. This kind of talk has made some people see Money as an advocate for positive social change. But the fact is, he wants to get rid of all the weird, scary people who made him so esteemed and famous. When asked by an interviewer if transsexuals would still seek sex reassignment in a "sexual democracy," Money replied, "I have a very strong suspicion that if we had a genuine sexual democracy, we would not create all of these problems in our children."[114] Conformity, not increased tolerance, is Money's recipe for the Sexually Great Society.

Money believes that societies such as an aboriginal community in north central Australia, have no "paraphilias or even bisexual or homosexual stuff either. They had no sexual taboo; the kids were allowed to play sex-rehearsal games without being punished." He continues:

We need a better ethnographic survey of peoples who don't have sexual taboos to find out to what extent we're actually creating these paraphilias by so zealously trying to beat out sex from the development of young children. Perfectly reasonable, nice mothers and fathers go berserk when they encounter the first appearance of normal sexual rehearsal play in their children. If we were truly committed to having our children grow up to be plain, ordinary heterosexuals, we'd treat them exactly as if we wanted them to be athletes—get them practicing and reward them every time we saw them doing it.[115]

It never seems to have occurred to him that small, isolated groups of people are able to do a much better job of controlling and repressing unacceptable sexual conduct than a handful of vice cops and fundamentalist preachers in a big, modern city. Nor has he considered the possibility that the respondents may have lied to whoever was studying them, or not understood the sexual categories used by Westerners. While I can certainly support Money's goal to get parents to stop punishing their children for age-appropriate sex play, it seems intellectually dishonest for him to simply overlook the large amount of such childish "sexual rehearsal" that is unconventional, to say the least. Piaget may not have noticed that, but Freud certainly did. I can't say I relish the prospect of "normal" sexplay being imposed on homosexual or transsexual children as a form of behavioral therapy. Money doesn't prescribe this specifically, but it seems consistent with his philosophy.

In conclusion, I want to be clear that the work of many important people in this field has been left out of this chapter because there simply was no room to cover everything. But I believe the most important themes in gender science have been elucidated, and do not vary significantly among Benjamin, Green, Money, Stoller, and their colleagues. The overwhelming sense that I get from this examination of the history of transsexuality and sex reassignment is that "help" from doctors is truly a double-edged sword for sexual minorities.

Transsexuals became the abused darlings of sexologists and medical doctors because they could be "cured" by using hormones and surgery. Those who see themselves as gender scientists are invested in trying to discover a physiological explanation for human sexual variation. Instead of simply accepting this variation as a normal part of the spectrum of human experience, and seeing its intrinsic worth, these people inappropriately apply a medical model of health versus disease to gender identity and pleasure-seeking behavior.

Once sex hormones were discovered, doctors tried to use them to treat every sex disorder from impotence to homosexuality; in no case were they successful enough to set up a treatment industry. Transsexuality is an exception. By creating a "treatment" process that is intended to churn out feminine heterosexual women and masculine heterosexual men, the gender scientists have turned their backs on the most liberating and revolutionary implications of what they call "gender dysphoria"—the possibility that the categories of "male" and "female" are unrealistic and smothering us all.

It doesn't matter whether sex deviation is caused by social learning or biology; or at least it doesn't matter to the "deviate." If it weren't for loneliness, discrimination, and stigma, most sexual-minority members would never consider giving up or altering their fantasies and pleasures. But it does matter to the doctors and scientists and researchers because these issues give them government grants, publishing contracts, and tenure at universities. We need to question the so-called experts who are too quick to pathologize behavior or self-concepts that are not inherently self-destructive and that don't necessarily interfere with people's ability to love or pleasure one another. We can only do that if we jettison our own guilt and apply the same intellectual standards to sex research that we would apply to a piece of research in the field of astronomy or physics.

Queer activists who believe it would be politically advantageous for us to be able to prove that homosexuality has a genetic basis should consider transsexuals' experience with the father figures of gender science. Doctors have believed that transsexuality is a medical problem with a biological cause for nearly two decades, and the position of transgendered people in society has barely advanced a notch or two. Transsexuals are still perceived as the tragic victims of a delusion that may or may not have a chromosomal or hormonal origin. Not a single recognized authority on this issue has said that transgendered people have intrinsic value and worth, or something important to contribute to the rest of us and our understanding of what it means to be human. Benjamin, Green, and Money would have absolutely no ethical problem with genetically engineering transsexuals out of existence. It would be interesting to see what their recommendations might be if amniocentesis could detect the potential for transgenderism in a fetus.

Gay men, lesbians, and bisexuals would be foolish and deluded if we imagined the gender scientists have a more positive picture of us than they do of transsexuals. To them, we are all manifestations of the same disease, gender identity disorder. As long as we are operating in a social context where sexual or gender difference is seen as a bad thing, the medical model will further stigmatize homosexuals as sick or developmentally flawed people in need of a cure—not equal civil rights. It is very possible that homosexuality does have a biological basis. But the belief that our difference springs from our genes, hormones, or brain chemistry is no guarantee that social policy toward us will be liberalized.

Finally, how very sad it is that even the people who viewed themselves as transsexuals' allies and advocates at the same time saw them as sick, delusional, and inferior people. How much of the hostility that Benjamin notes could be due to the fact that his transgendered patients were not stupid, and understood his essentially negative view of them? And how frustrating it is that all of these lengthy technical texts were constructed to explain gender dysphoria and justify sex reassignment, when the thing that really needs to be explained is our insistence on gender dimorphism, despite all the hard medical evidence that this is not uniformly natural to our species. It is our fear and hatred of people who are differently-gendered that need to be cured, not their synthesis of the qualities we think of as maleness and femaleness, masculinity and femininity.

The next chapter will examine a specific variety of transphobia that exploded in the women's movement as a result of adverse publicity about male-to-female transsexuals entering the lesbian-feminist movement and attempting to participate in lesbian life, love, and politics.

Notes

1. Vern L. Bullough and Bonnie Bullough, *Cross Dressing, Sex, and Gender*, Philadelphia: University of Pennsylvania Press, 1993, p. 256.
2. Harry Benjamin, *The Transsexual Phenomenon*, New York: The Julian Press, Inc., 1966, p. 16.
3. Harry Benjamin, "Trans-sexualism and Transvestism," in David Cauldwell (ed.), *Transvestism: Men in Female Dress*, New York, Sexology Corporation, 1964. Cited in Vern L. Bullough and Bonnie Bullough, op. cit., p. 218.
4. Benjamin, op. cit., pp. 79-80.
5. Vern L. Bullough and Bonnie Bullough, op. cit., p. 259 and p. 368.
6. Ibid., p. 259.
7. Benjamin, op. cit., p. viii.
8. Ibid.
9. Ibid., p. ix.
10. Ibid., p. 67.
11. Ibid., p. 88.
12. Ibid., p. 91.
13. Ibid., p. 131.

14. Ibid., p. 5.
15. Ibid., p. 8.
16. Ibid., p. 152.
17. Ibid., p. 9.
18. Ibid., p. 39.
19. Ibid., p. 41.
20. Ibid., pp. 47, 48, 49, and 51.
21. Ibid., p. 52.
22. Ibid., pp. 67-68.
23. Ibid., p. 68.
24. Ibid., p. 113-114.
25. Ibid., p. 9.
26. Ibid., p. 26.
27. Ibid., p. 28.
28. Ibid., p. 15.
29. Ibid., p. 21.
30. Ibid., p. 54.
31. Ibid., pp. 13-14.
32. Ibid., p. 19.
33. Ibid., pp. 141-142.
34. Ibid., p. 15.
35. Alfred C. Kinsey, Wardell B. Pomeroy, and Clyde E. Martin, *Sexual Behavior in the Human Male,* Philadelphia and London: W. B. Saunders Co., 1948, pp. 638-641.
36. Benjamin, op. cit., p. 126.
37. Ibid., p. 102.
38. William H. Masters and Virginia E. Johnson, *Human Sexual Response*, Boston: Little, Brown & Co., 1966.
39. Benjamin, op. cit., p. 108.
40. Ibid., p. 123.
41. Ibid., p. 129.
42. Ibid., p. 128.
43. Ibid., p. 17.
44. Gunnar Lindemalm, Dag Körlin, and Nils Uddenberg, "Long-Term Follow-Up of 'Sex Change' in 13 Male-to-Female Transsexuals," *Archives of Sexual Behavior*, Vol. 15, No. 3, 1986, pp. 187-210.
45. Benjamin, op. cit., p. 27.
46. Ibid., pp. 147-148.
47. Robert C. Carson and James N. Butcher, *Abnormal Psychology and Modern Life*, Ninth Edition, New York: HarperCollins Publishers Inc., 1992, p. 352, citing J. Walinder, "Transsexualism: Definition, Prevalence, and Sex Distribution," *Acta Psychiatrica Scandinavica*, 203, 1968, p. 255-258.
48. Vern L. Bullough and Bonnie Bullough, op. cit., p. 315, citing Ira B. Pauly, "Gender Identity Disorders: Evaluation and Treatment," *Journal of Sex Education and Therapy* 16, no. 1, 1990, pp. 1-24.
49. Benjamin, op. cit., pp. 150-151.
50. Ibid., p. 151.
51. Ibid., p. 155.

52. Richard Green, "Appendix C: Transsexualism: Mythological, Historical, and Cross-Cultural Aspects," in Benjamin, op. cit., pp. 174-184.

53. Ibid., pp. 184-185.

54. Harry Benjamin, "Introduction," in Richard Green and John Money (eds.), *Transsexualism and Sex Reassignment*, Baltimore: The Johns Hopkins Press, 1969, p. 2.

55. Ibid.

56. Ibid., p. 3.

57. Ibid.

58. Ibid., p. 4.

59. Ibid., p. 6.

60. Ibid., p. 7.

61. Ibid., p. 8.

62. Ibid., p. 10.

63. Richard Green, *The "Sissy Boy Syndrome" and the Development of Homosexuality*, New Haven and London: Yale University Press, 1987, p. 7.

64. Richard Green, "Attitudes Toward Transsexualism and Sex-Reassignment Procedures," in Green and Money, op. cit., pp. 235-242.

65. Richard Green, "Psychiatric Management of Special Problems in Transsexualism," in Green and Money, op. cit., pp. 281-289.

66. Ibid., p. 288.

67. Richard Green, *The "Sissy Boy Syndrome" and the Development of Homosexuality*, op. cit., p. 7.

68. Ibid., p. 99.

69. Ibid., p. 115.

70. Ibid., p. 261.

71. Ibid., p. 258.

72. Ibid., p. 370.

73. Ibid., p. 260.

74. Ibid., p. 263.

75. Ibid., p. 262.

76. Ibid., p. 260.

77. Ibid., p. 258.

78. Ibid., p. 259.

79. Ibid., p. 318.

80. Ibid., p. 319.

81. Ibid., p. 387.

82. Ibid., pp. 7-8.

83. John Money, "Sex Reassignment as Related to Hermaphroditism and Transsexualism," in Green and Money, op. cit., p. 91.

84. Ibid., p. 92.

85. John Money and Anke A. Ehrhardt, *Man & Woman Boy & Girl*, Baltimore: The Johns Hopkins Press, 1972, pp. 6-7, 14, 19, 26, and 186.

86. Ibid., pp. 13, 123, 128, and 159-161.

87. Ibid., pp. 52, 167, and 171.

88. Cheryl Chase, "Affronting Reason," prepared for Dawn Atkins (ed.) *Queer Look*, in press, p. 5.

89. H. Marty Malin, "Treatment Raises Serious Ethical Questions," *Hermaphrodites with Attitude*, Fall/Winter 1995-96, pp. 16, 14, and 15.

90. Kathleen Stein, "Interview: John Money," *Omni*, 8(7), April 1986, p. 131.

91. John Money and John G. Brennan, "Sexual Dimorphism in the Psychology of Female Transsexuals," in Green and Money, op. cit., p. 139.

92. John Money and Clay Primrose, "Sexual Dimorphism and Dissociation in the Psychology of Male Transsexuals," in Green and Money, op. cit., p. 121.

93. Ibid.

94. Ibid., p. 122.

95. Ibid., p. 123.

96. Money and Brennan, op. cit., pp. 145 and 147.

97. Ibid., p. 146.

98. Ibid., p. 142.

99. Money and Primrose, op. cit., p. 124.

100. Ibid., p. 125.

101. Ibid.

102. Ibid., p. 131.

103. Money and Brennan, op. cit., p. 151.

104. Money and Primrose, op. cit., p. 127.

105. Money and Brennan, op. cit., p. 152.

106. John Money and Florence Schwartz, "Public Opinion and Social Issues in Transsexualism: A Case Study in Medical Sociology," in Green and Money, op. cit., p. 264.

107. Ibid., p. 259.

108. John Money and Margaret Lamacz, *Vandalized Lovemaps: Paraphilic Outcome of Seven Cases in Pediatric Sexology*, Buffalo, New York: Prometheus Books, 1989, dedication.

109. Kathleen Stein, op. cit., p. 80.

110. Ibid., p. 128.

111. Ibid., p. 126.

112. Ibid., p. 128.

113. Ibid., pp. 86, 126.

114. Ibid., p. 84.

115. Ibid., p. 86.

CHAPTER 3

The Backlash: Transphobia in Feminism

The 1979 publication of Janice G. Raymond's book *The Transsexual Empire* poured gasoline on the flames of an already fierce debate about the presence of transsexual women in the lesbian community.[1] Actually, it is hardly fair to characterize this controversy as a debate, since the only voices that were given much space in lesbian-feminist media belonged to genetic women who were adamantly opposed to the inclusion of transsexual women, and indeed, did not see them as women, lesbians, or feminists. Raymond painted a gloss of intellectual legitimacy on the anti-transsexual position. Her book remains a classic in the discourse on transsexual lesbians, and has remained in print in part because it continues to represent the opinion of many feminists, especially separatist lesbian feminists. A more recent entry on Raymond's side of the lists is Catherine Millot's *Horsexe*, discussed briefly below.

Raymond's book comes decorated with enthusiastic blurbs from Andrea Dworkin ("Crucial reading"), Robin Morgan ("The definitive exposé... Ground breaking"), and Mary Daly ("A brilliant work of radical feminist scholarship which fuses ethics, philosophy, science, and social criticism... Of enduring value as a development of feminist theory"). It is dedicated to Mary Daly. Adrienne Rich is thanked in the acknowledgments for reading the manuscript and providing "resources, creative criticism, and constant encouragement."[2]

This approbation and Raymond's own rhetoric situate her firmly within the ranks of the feminist fundamentalism that has given us, among other travesties, the "feminist" antiporn movement. Raymond is part of a school of feminist thought that rests on the assumption that men and women are radically different creatures. Sometimes this difference is talked about in ways that make it sound as if it is biologically based; sometimes it is attributed to social learning or conditioning that is so intense as to be ineradicable. Either way, men are assumed to be, by their very nature, oppressors, prone to violence, objectification, insensitivity, sexual perversion, and domination. Thus, the interests of men are seen as always being inimical to women. Women are assumed to be, by their very nature, egalitarian, nurturing, creative, spiritually advanced, nonviolent, and motivated more by love and tenderness than by lust or sexual desire.

This brand of feminism sees women's struggle for freedom as a desperate battle to separate ourselves from the sphere of male influence and control, and rid ourselves of the toxic aspects of maleness and masculinity. Rather than seeing women's liberation as something that could be achieved by redistribution of the privileges and resources that men currently monopolize, this approach sees women as the nearly-perfect half of the human race who need only escape from male power in order to live in peace, justice, and equality. Reallocating the perks that men reserve for themselves is perhaps seen as undesirable because it would entail women acquiring material things, skills, physical attributes, and even behavior patterns that we most often associate with men today. Such an effort would also inevitably require men to change, and under the tenets of feminist fundamentalism and gender essentialism, that is seen as an impossibility.

Thus, this movement tends to focus more on the behavior and attitudes of women, especially women who claim to be feminists, than it does on taking action in the real world to secure equal pay for equal work, reproductive rights, daycare, maternity leave, nonsexist representation in the media, equal protection under the law for homosexuals, decriminalization of prostitution, or any other item that might appear on the agenda of a civil-rights approach to women's liberation. The personal and public lives of women who claim to be feminists are instead examined and policed because if these women fail to excise maleness, they are seen as obstructing the feminist struggle on the only real frontier upon which it can be waged.

Lesbians occupy a privileged position in this view of feminism, because we have ostensibly gone further or done more than other women to purge maleness from our lives. The notion of the lesbian as the ultimate feminist was created, in part, in response to homophobia that was rife in the women's liberation movement of the late sixties and early seventies. During that era, many heterosexual feminists, tired of being dyke-baited, saw lesbians as a public-relations liability. On a personal level, many straight women feared that lesbians would treat them as badly as men had. They saw women's consciousness-raising groups as a refuge from the sexual predation of men. Lesbians were stereotyped as mannish women, as women who wanted to be men. Straight feminists imagined (some would cynically add, and hoped) that once lesbians were admitted to their ranks, there would be no way to escape being objectified and pawed by aggressive butches.

It makes sense that the first response to that was to disassociate lesbianism from masculinity, and promote a view of lesbian feminists as woman-identified women. But in the long run, this has proven to be a tactical error, since it split the lesbian community between old-school "bar dykes," who identified their queerness as the source of their oppression, and New Age lesbian-feminists, who focused on misogyny as the enemy. Very little has been written about the fact that many early lesbian feminists who came out in the context of the women's liberation movement and academe rather than lesbian bars or friendship networks were uncomfortable with their own homosexuality and alienated from the bar-centered, role-playing culture that had helped lesbians to survive in the fifties and sixties. Their attempts to create social change were hampered by the fact that they were ignorant about and ashamed of their own community's history. To some extent, this schism was exacerbated by class differences and differences in education. There were notable exceptions, but most lesbian feminists in the early seventies were middle-class women with college educations, and bar dykes tended to be working class.

The right of lesbians to participate in the women's movement is taken for granted now, but the idea that some lesbians are more feminist (read: more equal) than others continues to interfere with our ability to present a united front. Adrienne Rich's essay "Compulsory Heterosexuality and Lesbian Existence" does a brilliant job of documenting the many brutal or subtle ways that women are coerced into the "natural" mode of heterosexuality.[3] But it is a very problematic document in other regards, imbued with sexual shame. Rich repeatedly denies that lesbian passion is an important component of our identity, and mandates the exclusion of lesbians whose pleasures or haircuts have earned her opprobrium. It's worth noting that Rich specifically excludes female berdaches (female-bodied, cross-dressing Native American warriors and shamans) and by implication all "passing women" from her "lesbian continuum." Something is deeply wrong with a vision of the lesbian community that can include the Beguines, a European lay religious movement, and the trading societies and female sororities of heterosexual women in Africa, while excluding S/M dykes, butch-femme lesbians, and transgendered women. This simply does not make sense.[4]

Belief in illogical or contradictory descriptions of reality requires a leap of faith. It is not surprising that fundamentalist feminism has such a religious cast. It has much in common with other fundamentalist movements, such as the New Christian Right. It is no accident that these groups, which on the surface appear to be opposed to one another, have on more than one occasion formed alliances to further their respective agendas. Both share an obsession with issues of sexual conduct and representation. Although the line of reasoning used to reach a position against pornography, prostitution, gay male sexual license, or sadomasochism may differ, the basic strategy is the same. One side quotes work by Andrea Dworkin or Mary Daly as an authoritative text; the other quotes the Bible. Both have an almost touching belief in the sanctity of woman, or woman as she is meant to be, woman as she could become in a pure, more perfect world. And both are willing to muster the powers of the state against their enemies, even though that state is, according to their own doctrines, hopelessly corrupt (either because it is male-dominated or because it is imbued with secular humanism).

One of the things that makes fundamentalism popular is its digestibility. Fundamentalism offers us reductionist theories about how the world works, what went wrong, and how to fix it. The place that original sin occupies in Christian theology is occupied by the patriarchy in feminist fundamentalism. The rule of men over women is held to be the first cause of all injustice, all oppression, and anything else that makes the feminist fundamentalists uncomfortable. This is why their theories about economic inequity are nonexistent. The only on-the-job issue they are able to address is sexual harassment, and adherents are promised that when pornography is wiped out, female poverty will disappear. Fundamentalist feminists thus tend to be hostile toward Marxism, which places the class struggle at the ideological center of this troubled era, and few New Left feminists are found within their ranks. This wing of the women's movement has paid very little attention to racism, unless it is to critique images of women of color in pornography or their disproportionate appearance in the ranks of sex workers. And it cannot offer an effective or sensible analysis of homosexual oppression, either. Instead, fundamentalist feminists tend to see gay men as just one more evil offshoot of the patriarchy, treating each other the way men treat women, while lesbians who work primarily on gay issues are seen as sellouts, lost to the one true cause.

Fundamentalists of all sorts can brook no dissent. These are positions that are reached instinctively, according to deep-seated, sincere but irrational moral beliefs. They are not reached by experimentation, research, or reasoned debate. And the utopias that are constructed on such a foundation must receive the unquestioning support of every inhabitant, if they are to rise from the ashes of the patriarchy or Sodom and Gomorrah, take your pick. Fundamentalists are driven by such an extreme sense of danger and crisis that they are able to rationalize shocking acts of harassment, libel, vandalism, and violence. They are living in wartime, taking emergency action on behalf of the ignorant masses (male-identified women or those who have not been washed in the blood of the Lamb) who remain oddly ungrateful. Every sign of opposition, every question and criticism, simply fuels a fundamentalist to new zeal. The lack of consensus about the rightfulness and righteousness of their actions becomes just one more proof of the depths to which the world has sunk, one more alarm bell rung to signal that reality is on fire.

In my more cynical moments, I believe that another underpinning of feminist fundamentalism is the fact that it is much easier to harangue and shame women about their sexuality and attack things like prostitution, pornography, and sexual deviation, which the state already sees as dangerous, than it is to dismantle male domination. When I am feeling more patient, I can add other factors to that equation. We've all grown up in a sexist society. Bad as it is, it's all we know of love, comfort, and security, as well as discrimination, stereotyping, and danger. And the current system has its compensations. Counter to what more simplistic feminists have claimed, we do not live in a society where men have all the power and women have none. Men (on average) have more privilege, wealth, freedom, and security, but women also have the power to incite and control male lust, the ability to bear children, and the responsibility for socializing those children and setting a moral tone in society at large.

If we really want to be free, women must realize that at the end of that struggle, we will not be women any more. Or at least we will not be women the way we understand that term today. Nor will men, as a paradigm, emerge unscathed. *But we will have to change at least as much, if not more, than men.* Feminist fundamentalism seems to me like a grand diversion from that awesome and terrifying challenge, a tantrum, a smoke screen. I wonder for how many more centuries women will involve themselves in campaigns for moral purity, which certainly have a major impact on the world we live in, but don't fundamentally alter the concept of woman or propel us into a new battleground. We are *supposed* to be indignant about immorality and vice, dammit. We are supposed to split off from one another along, among other things, sexual lines as well as lines of race and class. We are supposed to view one another with suspicion and mistrust. Feminist fundamentalism, with its "big sister is watching you" attitude, intensifies the divisions and splits between us.

Wandering in the miasma of feminist fundamentalism, no real critique of ourselves is possible. Since we are the sacred martyrs of the patriarchy, the chosen ones who have cast off the artifacts of male domination, we cannot possibly be complicit in our own oppression. I cannot believe in this vision of women as innocent and essentially good beneath a veneer of male hatred. The process of liberating oneself is not like peeling a hard-boiled egg. Certainly we are not to blame for finding ourselves in an unequal world that denies us a complete opportunity to use our talents to better our lives. But we have been damaged by our repression, damaged in ways that feminist fundamentalism, with its recasting of traditional morality, is not equipped to ferret out.

The best way for women to rid ourselves of a subservient, self-defeating mentality is to work with, love, and support one another in every aspect of our daily lives. That is an act of genuine female rebellion. An attempt to divide us into the good girls who deserve freedom and the bad girls who do not smacks more of high school than it does of revolution. It is no accident that since the gender-essentialist school of feminist thought gained political ascendancy, the number of businesses, publications, and institutions owned and operated by feminists and lesbians has declined. The women's culture that seemed about to flower in the early eighties has withered on the vine, and it's not because a handful of S/M dykes, bisexual women, or transgendered women found their way into feminist bookstores and lesbian collectives. It's because too many of us bought into a type of feminism that made us care more about what our sister was thinking about when she had an orgasm than we did about raising money to establish women's centers, lobbying for better healthcare, staffing rape crisis centers, or doing any one of hundreds of more constructive, radical, feminist actions.

Nothing upsets the underpinnings of feminist fundamentalism more than the existence of transsexuals. A being with male chromosomes, a female appearance, a feminist consciousness, and a lesbian identity explodes all of their assumptions about the villainy of men. And someone with female chromosomes who lives as a man strikes at the heart of the notion that all women are sisters, potential feminists, natural allies against the aforementioned villainy. Such people do exist; there's no denying it. But they can't, in the weird world view of Dworkin, Daly, Morgan, and Rich. They just *can't*, they'll spoil it all! Janice Raymond is the Cassandra the goddesses of fundamentalist feminism have appointed to warn the rest of us against taking this Trojan horse into our gates. With such fervor as this, the Roman Catholic Church put Galileo under lifetime house arrest for saying the Earth moved around the sun.

According to Raymond, *The Transsexual Empire* began life as her doctoral dissertation in 1977. Hounding transsexuals out of the lesbian-feminist community has been Raymond's claim to fame for two decades, her raison d'être. She is much more than simply a feminist theorist with an axe to grind about transsexuals. She is also an anti-transsexual crusader who has worked hard to make it more difficult for transsexuals to obtain sex reassignment. This career bears an interesting stylistic resemblance to Anita Bryant's "Save Our Children" antigay crusade in Florida in the late seventies, but unlike Bryant, Raymond hasn't given up campaigning. Her analysis of and position on transsexuality has not changed significantly in twenty years.[5]

It's important to look at Raymond's arguments one by one, unpleasant as that may be to anyone who supports the concept of freedom of choice when it comes to the individual's gender identity, sexual orientation, or political affiliation. These beliefs and attitudes have not gone away, and if they are not actively questioned and dispelled, they will continue to poison the water for transgendered people who feel a principled desire to work with feminists and gay activists. Because Raymond refuses to accept the reality of sex reassignment, she uses such terms as "male-to-constructed-female" and "female-to-constructed-male." She also refers to transgendered women as "he" and transgendered men as "she." I hope the reader will understand, when reading direct quotes, that I am not in any way supporting the derogatory terminology they contain.

Raymond says, "Transsexualism is a recent phenomenon generated by the medical profession."[6] She wants to convince her reader that transsexuality is brand new, something cooked up by the haughty, male-dominated medical establishment and foisted on a gullible world. She says, "As a medical category that enlists many surgical specialties and as a transformed state of being that requires legal validation transsexualism is a relatively new phenomenon. Historical antecedents are found in certain mythological accounts, initiation rites, and certain modes of eunuchism and castration but, strictly speaking, transsexualism has no historical precedents."[7] Raymond wants her readers to see transsexuals as ahistorical and utterly artificial, partly to render them unsympathetic, and partly to bolster her claim that transsexuality is a conspiracy, run by evil doctors and psychiatrists who want to destroy feminism and infiltrate the lesbian-feminist community.

Raymond is a true-blue gender essentialist. She writes, "It is biologically impossible to change *chromosomal* sex. If chromosomal sex is taken to be the fundamental basis for maleness and femaleness, the male who undergoes sex conversion is *not* female."[8] Because Raymond takes the sex chromosomes as the final arbiters of gender, she is able to state categorically, "Transsexuals are *not* women. They are *deviant males*."[9] However, even Raymond realizes that it is rather dangerous to limit her definition of "woman" to the XX chromosomes, because this line of thought leads rapidly down a slippery slope of biological determinism, in which the social sex roles that feminists find so repugnant are taken to be the inalterable results of genetic encoding. It is futile to protest the rule of men over women if it is a tyranny decreed by nature.

So she alternates between the argument that transsexuals cannot be women because they have XY chromosomes and the argument that they cannot be women because they do not share female socialization. She huffs, "Feminists debate and divide, because we keep focusing on patriarchal questions of who is a woman and who is a lesbian-feminist. It is important for us to realize that these may well be non-questions and that the only answer we can give to them is that we know who *we* are. We know that we are women who are born with female chromosomes and anatomy, and that whether or not we were socialized to be so-called normal women, patriarchy has treated and will treat us like women. Transsexuals have not had this same history."[10]

But the fact is that transgendered women do share this history, as soon as they are perceived by society at large to be female. It is not clear why Raymond is unable to give them at least some credit for this experience, given her faith in feminism as a political modality that can allow women to escape from sexist stereotypes. Gender researcher John Money draws fire from Raymond for, in her view, confusing sex roles enforced by the patriarchy with behavior that has been programmed by our hormones, genes, and brain chemistry. In rebuttal to Money, she says, "If women had not been able to alter the nuclear 'core' of our gender programming, we would not be doing many of the things that we are. One of the primary tenets of the women's movement has been that so-called gender identity differences are not natural or immutable. And as such, they are amenable to change."[11]

This would seem to support, not contradict, the possibility of a woman with male sex chromosomes being able to alter the "nuclear core" of her "gender programming." Elsewhere, Raymond takes Money to task for giving more emphasis to the role of fetal androgens in creating sexual differentiation in the male fetus than he does to the fact that all human fetuses swim in a prenatal bath of female hormones, and begin life as morphological females.[12] This also would seem to highlight the possibility that genetic females and transgendered women have many things in common, physiologically, despite their genetic differences. Throughout the chapter "Are Transsexuals Made or Born—or Both?"[13] Raymond aggressively attacks any suggestion that women's identities are biologically determined. Again and again, she comes down on the side of environmental factors or social learning against physiology. But she never seems to realize that, if her arguments are taken to the next logical step, she is actually arguing that *anyone* could learn how to be a woman.

And so Raymond resorts to a sort of biology-*cum*-mysticism to construct the third leg of her definition of genetic females versus transsexuals. She says that males want to become women because of "the male recognition of the power that women have, by virtue of female biology. This power, which is evident in giving birth, cannot be reduced to procreation. Rather birthing is only representative of the many levels of creativity that women have exercised in the history of civilization. Transsexualism may be one way by which men attempt to possess females' creative energies, by possessing artifactual female organs."[14]

Raymond does not explain why, if women who do not choose to give birth or women who cannot have children can still partake of this mystical essence that separates the elevated realm of women from the primeval sludge of masculinity, transsexual women are excluded from the rites simply because they are not fertile. And speaking as a woman who would rather die than have children, I resent any attempt, by either so-called feminists or Christian fundamentalists, to base my creativity, my worth as a person, my politics, or my spirituality on my uterus. The kind of feminism that I support promotes the idea that women have value as individuals, not as incubators or brood mares.

Perhaps aware that her attempt to excommunicate transgendered lesbian feminists because of their chromosomes, socialization, or lack of a womb rests on shaky ground, Raymond liberally sprinkles her text with hostile characterizations of "male-to-*constructed*-females" that are intended to increase the distance between transsexuals and genetic female feminists. Raymond hints that transsexuals are getting away with things that "real women" can't get away with, and have been given benefits that the rest of us are still struggling to receive. Of Renée Richards, she says, "The public recognition and success that it took Billie Jean King and women's tennis years to get, Renee [sic] Richards has achieved in one set. The new bumper stickers might well read: 'It takes castrated balls to play women's tennis.'"[15] Elsewhere, Raymond says that in some cities, sex-change surgery is funded with public monies, whereas abortions are not, and says, "feminists are struck by the inequity of this situation."[16] And she mentions the case of a male-to-constructed-female [sic] prostitute, arrested in New Orleans, who had her case dismissed, reportedly because under Louisiana state law, "only a natural-born woman can be convicted of prostitution."[17]

These isolated incidents hardly form a convincing argument for the existence of transsexual privilege. Since it would not further her position, Raymond does not present data that would create a more realistic picture of a pre- or post-operative transsexual's struggle to survive in a world where access to employment and housing and safety on the street depends upon other people's gender biases. She completely ignores the frequent incidents of harassment and discrimination that transsexuals are subjected to, and makes no attempt to document violent hate crimes against them. Instead she makes it look as if transgendered lesbian feminists are perpetrators of violence. "Loss of a penis...does not mean the loss of an ability to penetrate women—women's identities, women's spirits, women's sexuality. As Mary Daly has noted, their whole presence becomes a 'member' invading women's presence to each other and once more producing horizontal violence."[18] The process of sex reassignment is described as a symbolic form of rape. "All transsexuals rape women's bodies by reducing the real female form to an artifact, appropriating this body for themselves. However, the transsexually constructed lesbian-feminist violates women's sexuality and spirit, as well. Rape, although it is usually done by force, can also be accomplished by deception," Raymond tells us.[19]

In a search for other comparisons that lesbian feminists will find odious, Raymond says things like, "Transsexually constructed lesbian-feminists are in the same tradition as the man-made, made-up 'lesbians' of the *Playboy* centerfolds. ...Men produce 'lesbian' love the way they want it to be and according to their own canons of what they think it should be."[20] Until a transsexual lesbian feminist is actually featured in *Playboy*, I will hold my comment on this. But I believe few things could horrify the editors of that magazine more than someone they would see as a man who had cut his dick off.

Raymond also stoops to this: "Eunuchs were men that other more powerful men used to keep their women in place—i.e., in women's apartments, harems, and the like. In this way, some eunuchs rose to positions of patriarchal power and influence. In a similar way, will transsexually constructed lesbian-feminists be used to keep lesbian-feminists in place?"[21] She asks, "Will every lesbian-feminist space become a harem?"[22] This is hysteric, inflammatory language designed to make lesbians hate and fear transsexuals.

If transsexual women are such evil creatures, the doctors and psychiatrists who are their "male mothers" must of course be even more Satanic.[23] The bulk of Raymond's book is taken up with a determined attempt to paint the medical doctors and therapists who provide the hormones and surgery that make sex reassignment possible as an evil empire of high-tech agents for the patriarchy. She repeatedly attacks gender identity clinics as if they were finishing schools for sexist sex-role conditioning. "To understand how sexual stereotypes are the First Cause of transsexualism," she says, "we should look at how transsexuals think and speak of themselves and how they 'prove' they are 'real' transsexuals by 'passing' as masculine or feminine. In fact, they must prove they are real before they are accepted for treatment. Thus the role of the medical-psychiatric establishment in reinforcing sex-role stereotypes is significant, and one that affects the deepest dimensions of the transsexual issue."[24]

This is a tough argument to counter. It's certainly true that gender identity clinics are guilty of trying to turn out feminine heterosexual women and masculine heterosexual men. But Raymond doesn't see this as an issue that transsexuals themselves might perceive as problematic. While she might be sympathetic with a genetic female who tries to placate a male doctor in order to get more compassionate treatment, she has no sympathy at all for people seeking sex reassignment who have no choice about conforming to the sometimes old-fashioned and excessively orthodox standards of their doctors.

Raymond is closed to any suggestion that gender dysphoria might be caused by something other than the patriarchy. She says emphatically, "A society that produces sex-role stereotyping functions as a primary cause of transsexualism."[25] She goes on to say, "Feminists have described *gender dissatisfaction* in very different terms—i.e., as *sex-role oppression, sexism*, etc."[26] Transsexuals themselves don't understand the nature of their discomfort, Raymond believes. "Once sex-role oppression is given the name of transsexualism, and institutionalized in the gender identity clinics, and realized by hormone and surgical treatment, the 'condition' of transsexualism itself explains *why* one would have the wrong mind in the wrong body. Why? Because one *is* a transsexual. This classification bestows sense on all the disparate and atomic experiences that once seemed so unfathomable. It functions to mask ethical issues and normative statements that raise themselves very pointedly in the case of transsexualism."[27] The only appropriate therapy for gender dysphoria is a feminist revolution. However, as will be seen later on, Raymond also makes it abundantly clear that transgendered women are not welcome to join the army of lovers that cannot fail.

According to Raymond, "the transsexual empire" wants to replace genetic women with transsexuals and ship everybody who opposes sex-role stereotypes to gender identity clinics for behavioral therapy and modification. She warns the reader, "It is not inconceivable that gender identity clinics, again in the name of therapy, could become centers of sex-role control for nontranssexuals. Presently, some of them are 'treating' children who are diagnosed as potential transsexuals."[28]

Raymond says, "As female energy, spirit, and vitality have not proved conquerable, in spite of all the attempts of men to harness them, so too has female flesh been difficult to mold and manipulate according to patriarchal standards. Witness the number and intensity of attempts. Perhaps male flesh will prove much more malleable. Given the historical difficulties of molding both female flesh and energy to patriarchal standards, an alternative is to make the biological woman obsolete by the creation of man-made 'she-males.' "[29] In a weird aside, she also accuses the advertising industry of using subliminal messages to create "covert transsexual appeals,"[30] which supposedly use the mass media to promote the seductive charms of transsexuals.

As Carol Riddell has pointed out in her 1996 article "Divided Sisterhood":

> The fact of the matter is that the gender identity clinics are not regarded with favour by most of the medical patriarchy. They were established and exist in spite of the opposition of the most respectable elements of the medical profession, men who regard transsexualism as an even more disgusting aberration than does Janice Raymond, if that is possible. Their reasons, however, are diametrically opposite to Ms. Raymond's, since for them trans-

sexualism seems to threaten the 'natural order' of things, while she believes it reinforces that order. The clinics developed under the intense and unremitting pressure of transsexuals who would go to any length to obtain an operation and for whom no treatment, other than operation, was satisfactory. The clinics thus came into existence *in spite of* the medical patriarchy, but, like all marginal institutions, they strove to justify themselves by their conformity.[31]

But in Raymond's theoretical universe, this is unthinkable. She is unable to conceive of the existence of sexual minorities whose oppression, although related to and overlapping with the oppression of women, is not identical to it. Nor is she able to make distinctions between medical doctors or sex researchers who, though flawed, are willing to buck the status quo, and professionals who would die to uphold it. "*Transsexualism at this point constitutes a 'sociopolitical program' that is undercutting the movement to eradicate sex-role stereotyping and oppression in this culture. Instead it fosters institutional bases of sexism under the guise of therapy,*" she writes.[32] The italics are hers.

Raymond sees transsexuals as eager co-conspirators in the drive to replace genetic women. She quotes from a letter, allegedly written by a transgendered woman, which says in part:

Genetic women cannot possess the very special courage, brilliance, sensitivity and compassion—and overview—that derives from the transsexual experience. Free from the chains of menstruation and child-bearing, transsexual women are obviously far superior to Gennys in many ways.

Genetic women are becoming quite obsolete, which is obvious, and the future belongs to transsexual women. We know this, and perhaps some of you suspect it. All you have left is your "ability" to bear children, and in a world which will groan to feed 6 billion by the year 2000, that's a negative asset.[33]

This letter is reprinted whenever someone wishes to agitate against transgendered lesbian feminists. It appears, without any critical comment, in Millot's book, more than ten years later. I have not been able to locate Angela Douglas herself, but I have spoken with an acquaintance of hers who describes her as one of the first "out, loud-mouthed" transsexuals in the early seventies. As a highly visible transgendered woman, Douglas reportedly provided information about what resources existed to other transgendered women. Her friendship network provided crucial support. Douglas was apparently an early prostitutes' rights activist who used the colorful tactics that were popular in the counter-culture then—when incarcerated for prostitution, she sat zazen in jail, infuriating the guards.

This letter was reportedly composed in a fit of whimsy and outrage over anti-transsexual articles in the lesbian-feminist press. The author's intention was to create a spoof that was so ridiculous, no one would take it seriously. The reader was meant to read this parody of transphobia, laugh, and get over herself.[34] This backfired, of course, partly because the opponents of transgendered women see nothing funny about their own shrill rhetoric. You can fault Douglas for her lack of common sense, but you can't blame her for being indignant. When people are trashed, sometimes they lash out at random. If this letter in fact represented the misogynist political agenda of transgendered women in general, surely it would not stand in proud isolation as the only published evidence of that agenda.

The existence of female-to-male transsexuals ruins Raymond's paranoid theory that sex reassignment exists only to create artificial, submissive, super-feminine women and undermine lesbian feminism by planting patriarchal moles among us. "How does the female-to-constructed male transsexual fit into such a context?" she asks. "It is my contention that she functions as a token to promote the deception that transsexualism is a supposed *human* problem, instead of a uniquely male problem. The female-to-constructed male transsexual promotes the 'illusion of inclusion.' She is assimilated into the transsexual empire in much the same way that women are assimilated into other male-defined realities—on men's terms."[35]

Usually we think of tokens as an isolated few members of a minority group who are not given any real power, pose no threat to the established order, and exist mostly to promote a false image of tolerance or social change. But the substantial numbers of transsexual men make it clear that they are not tokens in this sense. Raymond trumpets, "Even if the percentage of female-to-constructed-male transsexuals were augmented to the point where they would numerically equal male-to-constructed-females, they would still be tokens because they would be fashioned by a man-made empire, according to male designs."[36]

Lest her readers show any curiosity about or sympathy with transgendered men, Raymond hastens to label them as gender traitors. "Female-to-constructed-male transsexuals divest themselves of the last traces of female identification. Their collusion crosses a critical boundary, from which there is little hope of return. They are truly 'the lost women' to other women," she says.[37] Ignoring the lesbian community's long history of tolerance for "passing women," women who cross-dress as men, and butches whose identity is sometimes male, sometimes female, Raymond makes sure to cast all female-to-male transsexuals out of the Eden of lesbian community. She says in sex reassignment, "the aim would be to assimilate those women who do not conform to male standards of femininity. It is important to understand that assimilation equals elimination. Not being able to assimilate would-be males into the feminine, patriarchy assimilates them into the masculine."[38] She adds, "What is further attempted [in FTM surgery] is to ward off potential lesbianism."[39]

This is a condescending dismissal of the experience of many transgendered men who make an honest attempt to live as dykes and as women who do not conform to sex-role stereotypes, often for many miserable years, before taking a more direct and realistic route toward alleviating their gender dysphoria. When these individuals live and identify as men, they remain men with a lesbian history. If they had a shred of feminist consciousness before beginning to take testosterone, it generally remains after their beards come in and their voices deepen. But Raymond will have it that these people are weaklings who caved in to patriarchal pressure, turned their back on feminism, and bought into the system.

The fact is that transgendered men and women have to do battle with, among other things, sexism before they can live in their gender of preference. They are hardly double agents who retired in luxury behind the castle walls of the robber barons of patriarchy. When transgendered men and women demand their right to define gender for themselves, they are simply taking one of the first lessons of feminism to heart and asking that it be implemented. Raymond's pigheaded refusal to see transsexuals as allies rather than enemies makes me seriously question her commitment to social change.

When Raymond is not portraying gender identity clinics as factories churning out Barbie dolls with XY chromosomes, she is raging against "the transsexual empire" on other grounds. Raymond's attempt to portray sex-reassignment surgery as a medical experiment or an outright atrocity is perhaps the most unsavory aspect of the book. She claims, "There is a substantial amount of evidence that transsexual hormone therapy and surgery cause cancer" and strokes.[40] She says, "The transsexual researchers and clinicians emphasize that persons who desire to change sex seek such treatment eagerly. ...To use another example: Many oppressed people use heroin to make life tolerable in intolerable conditions."[41] In various places, she compares sex reassignment to foot-binding, clitoridectomy and infibulation, "corset mutilation," unnecessary hysterectomies and radical mastectomies,[42] the lobotomies Nobel Prize winner Egas Moniz performed on state mental-hospital inmates, and Nazi medical experiments.[43] In the preface, she says, "Ultimately, female-to-constructed-male transsexuals are the 'final solution' of women perpetrated by the transsexual empire."[44]

Raymond repeatedly tries to smear transvestitism and transsexuality by associating it with the Nazis. She claims that the early gay activist Magnus Hirschfeld's Institute for Sexual Science in Berlin was burned by the Nazis, and Hirschfeld himself forced to flee the country, because, "The Institute's confidential files were said to have contained too many data on prominent Nazis, former patients of Hirschfeld, to allow the constant threat of discovery to persist."[45]

She concedes, "It is not my purpose to directly compare transsexual surgery to what went on in the camps but rather to demonstrate that much of what did go on there can be of value in surveying the ethics of transsexualism."[46] But this is just window-dressing, Raymond's attempt to cover her ass against charges of sensationalism. Later on she says breathlessly, "We know that at least one transsexual operation was done in the camps. ...Some transsexual research and technology may well have been initiated and developed in the camps and that, in the past, as well as now, surgery was not performed for the present professed goal of therapy, but to accumulate medical knowledge."[47]

There is slim evidence indeed for the "one transsexual operation" that was allegedly done in the camps—a second-hand story by Joseph Wechsberg, who attributed it to Simon Wiesenthal, who allegedly met a teenage boy who had been turned into a woman and then back into a man. This is a dubious anecdote given the failure of current medical technology to create a fully-functioning penis.

But Raymond is not deterred by lack of firm evidence, perhaps because she knows that once you accuse someone of being affiliated with Nazis, you've flung mud that can never be washed out. Concentration camp inmates were interred involuntarily. What sort of person volunteers to become the subject of something like a Nazi medical experiment? Raymond has an answer. She says, "It seems that the silence regarding physical pain, on the part of the transsexual, [nota bene: as a result of sex-change surgery] can be explained only by an attitude of masochism ...At least one medical team has recognized this, although in muted and partial form. Categorizing primary clinical types who request sex reassignment, they label one type as masochist (or sadomasochist)."[48]

"What we are witnessing in the transsexual context is a science at the service of a patriarchal ideology of sex-role conformity in the same way that breeding for blond hair and blue eyes became a so-called science at the service of Nordic racial conformity,"[49] she claims. To compare the patients of a gender identity clinic with the millions of people who were herded like cattle into camps by the Nazis and tortured, starved, and murdered is outrageous. Not only is it a ridiculous characterization of transsexuals, it is profoundly insulting to Holocaust survivors and should be most offensive to anyone who is committed to stopping genocide. After reading this part of Raymond's book, I had to put it down for several hours. Although I had no reason to be, I was ashamed on her behalf, ashamed and indignant that feminism, a political cause that is so important to me, should be twisted into this grotesquerie.

These extreme tactics and sloppy thinking are the marks of a fanatic. Although *The Transsexual Empire* is couched in academic language, it is obvious that Raymond is motivated as much by an irrational fear and loathing of transsexuals as she is by the niceties of feminist theory. One of the symptoms of Raymond's transphobia is her refusal to allow transgendered women any way to escape damnation. All through her book, she places them in a double bind. Although Raymond pretends her objection to their presence among lesbian feminists is based on their male chromosomes, lack of feminist consciousness, and submissive adoration of male doctors, she is equally vitriolic about transgendered women who display a feminist consciousness and reject heterosexism.

This comes out in Raymond's description of her so-called "research," interviews with fifteen transsexuals, thirteen of whom she calls "male-to-*constructed*-females." She correctly points out that many commonly-cited studies of transsexuals have samples no bigger than hers, but if she wants to be taken seriously as a social-science researcher, this is hardly anything to emulate or brag about.[50] Careful reading reveals that Raymond, who repeatedly accuses transgendered women of worming their way into the lesbian-feminist community by deceitful means, obtained most of these interviews under false colors. Toward the end of these interviews, Raymond asked her subjects "how they would react to a hypothetical meeting with a feminist who told them they were reinforcing sex-role stereotypes by changing sex. ... In some cases, where I felt I could express my own opinion, I admitted I was the feminist who felt much ambiguity about the rightness of transsexualism because it reinforced sex-role stereotypes."[51]

By labeling herself as someone who "felt much ambiguity about the rightness of transsexualism," Raymond in no way gave her subjects fair warning about her biases or the anti-transsexual agenda of her book. This leaves an especially bad taste coming from someone who talks as much about ethics and morals as Raymond does. One of her objections to sex-reassignment surgery is her belief that transsexuals cannot give informed consent, which is necessary in order for a medical procedure to be ethical. She says, "Discussions on medical experimentation have focused on the question of whether a truly informed consent can ever be obtained from a 'captive population.' As I have shown, transsexuals are just such a captive population within a patriarchal society."[52] It's doubtful that even Raymond would be shameless enough to claim that her own research subjects had the opportunity to give informed consent. It is cruel to make use of unwitting transgendered women to provide "evidence" that justifies Raymond's attempt to dehumanize them.

Undeterred by these sorts of ethical questions, Raymond caustically condemns the thirteen transgendered women she interviews for viewing "themselves as passive, nurturing, emotional, intuitive, and the like. Very often, many expressed a preference for female dress and make-up. Others saw their feminine identification in terms of feminine occupations: housework, secretarial, and stewardess work. Some expressed feminine identification in terms of marriage and motherhood.... One expressed very definite views on child-rearing that were quite ironic in this context: 'I would definitely teach my kids that boys should be boys, and girls should be girls.' "[53] She also says, "For others, prostitution becomes related to their new feminine status."[54]

One can only imagine how Raymond would respond to a transgendered woman who did not present herself in traditionally feminine dress and makeup. Such a woman would be attacked for her obvious maleness and masculinity. Raymond seems callously indifferent to the cosmetic effort that is necessary for someone with a male body, even one that has been somewhat altered by female hormones, to be perceived as and treated as a woman. And would a transgendered woman who did *not* support stereotypical child-rearing practices be stupid enough to imagine that she would ever be allowed to adopt or raise children? Do lesbian mothers tell straight reporters they are raising their kids to be gay?

Perhaps because her own research is so flimsy, Raymond quotes extensively from a 1973 study conducted by Thomas Kando to support her view of transgendered women as dupes of the patriarchy. However, as Riddell points out, none of the women in Kando's study had lived in their gender of preference for more than two years. She says:

> It [nota bene: women's oppression] *is an existential condition, an oppression that is re-created from day to day by the lives that women have to lead, the opportunities open to us, the attitudes presented to us.* This is as true for transsexual women as for any others. Excited by the achievement of something that has involved a lifetime's struggle, [nota bene: sex reasssignment] unaware of the male stereotypes that have formed their idea of femaleness, reinforced in those stereotypes by crudely patriarchal gender identity clinics, it is hardly to be expected that transsexual women who have just come out will present a challenge to male sexist ideology…. The most important thing for transsexuals is ongoing experience. Every woman's history of oppression is re-created in her day-to-day life. …I'd predict that after several years of public female existence, transsexual women would show, on average, just as much uneasiness about social expectations of women's identity as other women round them—no more, no less.[55]

Even Raymond has to admit that some of the "new women" she interviewed have at least a glimmer of feminist consciousness. But she sneers, "the 'equal pay for equal work' ethic was generally subscribed to, not for any feminist reasons but because of the economic straits in which many transsexuals found themselves."[56] This is a ridiculous double standard, especially in a world where so many genetic females would emphatically deny any interest in or identification with feminism. What is the demand of genetic females for equal pay for equal work based on, if not the "economic straits" in which we find ourselves? If transgendered women lack a feminist consciousness, and Raymond thinks they need one, why kick them out of the women's movement? They aren't very likely to acquire a critique of sexism outside that movement!

The fact is, Raymond doesn't really want transgendered women to be feminists. She just wants them to go away. She wants them to not exist at all. This is the kick in the teeth that transgendered lesbian feminists who reject feminine mannerisms and dress receive from Raymond:

> The transexually constructed lesbian-feminist may have renounced femininity but not masculinity and masculinist

behavior (despite deceptive appearances). If, as I have noted earlier, femininity and masculinity are different sides of the same coin, thus making it quite understandable how one could flip from one to the other, then it is important to understand that the transsexually constructed lesbian-feminist, while not exhibiting a feminine identity and role, still exhibits its obverse side—stereotypical masculinity. Thus the assumption that he has renounced patriarchal definitions of selfhood is dubious.

Masculine behavior is notably obtrusive. It is significant that transsexually constructed lesbian-feminists have inserted themselves into positions of importance and/or performance in the feminist community.[57]

Perhaps because she is afraid of being accused of abandoning transsexuals to despair, depression, and, in some cases, suicide, if they cannot get access to sex reassignment, Raymond cynically proposes an alternative form of "treatment." Here's her jolly, fundamentalist feminist program for transsexuals in recovery from gender dysphoria:

> The transsexual is generally no advocate of social criticism and change. ...Consider the possibility of counseling that encouraged the transsexual to break both stereotypes. Here, the transsexual would be encouraged to become the agent of her or his own energies and to strive for more varied modes of being and becoming. In a very real sense, at this point, the transsexual would become a social critic. ...Given a different mode of therapy where "consciousness-raising" is the primary *modus operandi*, the transsexual might not find it as necessary to resort to sex-conversion surgery. ...The medical model and its empire continue to domesticate the revolutionary potential of transsexuals. The potential stance of the transsexual as outsider to the conventional roles of masculinity and femininity is short-circuited. Health values and goals hide the possibility from transsexuals themselves of being "history-bearing individuals" who, instead of conforming to sex roles, are in a unique position to turn their gender agony into an effective protest against the very social structures and roles that spawned the dilemma to begin with.[58]

Exactly what transsexuals would do as "effective protest" against sex roles isn't clear, since Raymond has made it very clear that no alliance or affiliation with feminism is possible. I can't help but be reminded, when reading this smug brush-off, of Roman Catholic support groups for devout homosexuals who believe they must be celibate for the sake of their immortal souls. Or, worse yet, those tearful "cured homosexuals" who appear on talk shows, usually in married pairs, born-again fag in a three-piece suit with baptized dyke whose hair is still not quite long enough or teased enough to let her pass. I am always chilled by the way these tense spouses do not look at each other or touch each other as they preach salvation to the viewing audience at home.

There's no good reason in heaven or on earth why a person who suffered from gender dysphoria would want to subscribe to Raymond's prescription for political correctness. It takes a monumental amount of arrogance for her to seriously suggest such a self-hating and self-destructive program. But her hatred and fear of transsexuals is so great that she would rather have them suffer, even die, as long as she doesn't have to run the risk of seeing them, sitting next to them, talking to them, working with them, or sleeping with them. This is transphobia, pure and simple, and it is as dangerous a social disease as the fear of homosexuality or unapologetic racism. Raymond is a gender supremacist.

The penultimate section of *The Transsexual Empire* is an annoying chapter on ethics that purports to demonstrate that transsexuals violate feminist standards for human health. "Toward the Development of an Ethic of Integrity" is full of dithering recycled Dalyisms that were probably not all that intelligible in their original state. Terms like *integration* and *integrity* are held up in opposition to one another without ever being defined operationally, in terms of human behavior or beliefs. It amounts to a feminist version of predestination: Some of us are born into a state of grace, and will be saved, and some of us won't. After wandering through the highways and byways of Raymond's insular philosophizing, it's almost a relief to come across a blunt statement that summarizes her "ethical" position on transsexuality: "I contend that the problem of transsexualism would best be served by morally mandating it out of existence."[59]

I have some more concrete ethical questions for Raymond and her supporters and promoters. First of all, I'd like to know why women who call themselves feminists think it was a good thing for Raymond to attack a lesbian-feminist business like Olivia Records, simply because Sandy Stone, a transgendered woman, was a member of their collective.[60] Raymond's book intensified a storm of controversy that resulted in threats of a boycott, which would have quickly driven Olivia Records out of business. In its early days, Olivia Records was a hardworking group of women who somehow managed, on a shoestring, to produce live and recorded lesbian music. They enriched lesbian culture enormously by giving us high-quality music that came out of our lives—love songs in which we did not need to change the pronouns, songs that gave us all courage and hope.

For months, "the Olives" suffered from a deluge of hate mail, threats of assault, and death threats triggered by Raymond's book. They become pariahs in a community that should have loved and supported them. The atmosphere of hate became so intense, they conducted a West Coast tour *with bodyguards*. Finally, on the brink of financial ruin, they made the decision to ask Stone to leave the collective. Prior to the publication of *The Transsexual Empire*, these women were happy to work with and live with Stone. They knew she was transgendered before they invited her to join their collective. Was it ethical of Raymond to contribute to the attacks on Stone and Olivia Records, without even giving them advance warning? She did send a draft of one chapter of her book to the collective for review, but Sandy Stone was not mentioned in it by name.[61] How does that show any "integrity"? Does Raymond seriously think it's good for feminism when women threaten each other with physical violence based on the company we keep?

Raymond and her ilk are bullies. Given the lengths to which they are willing to go to keep transgendered women out of "lesbian space," it takes a great deal of courage for any biological female to stand in solidarity with lesbians who did not start their lives with XX chromosomes. Raymond makes it very clear that she includes the supporters of transgendered lesbians in the orbit of her hatred. Under the heading, "The Seduction of Lesbian-Feminists," Raymond writes:

> It is not hard to understand why transsexuals want to become lesbian-feminists. They indeed have discovered where strong female energy exists and want to capture it. It is more difficult to understand why so many feminists are so ready to accept men—in this case, castrated men—into their most intimate circles. Certainly Dionysian confusion about the erasure of all boundaries is one reason that appeals to the liberal mind and masquerades as "sympathy for all oppressed groups." Women who believe this, however, fail to see that such liberalism is repressive, and that it can only favor and fortify the possession of women by men. These women also fail to recognize that accepting transsexuals into the feminist community is only another rather unique variation on the age-old theme of

women nurturing men, providing them with a safe haven, and finally giving them our best energies.[62]

And, finally, "lesbian-feminists who accept transsexually constructed lesbian-feminists as other selves are mutilating their own reality."[63]

Even in 1979, Raymond anticipated charges that she is a bigot and a hate-monger. She sniffs, "This book will, no doubt, be dismissed by many transsexuals and transsexual advocates as intolerant. Tolerance, however, can easily become repressive.... those who take a critical position will be subjected to accusations of dogmatism and intolerance, when in fact those who are unwilling to take a stand are exercising the *dogmatism of openness at any cost*. This time, the cost of openness is the solidification of the medical empire and the multiplying of medical victims."[64] She adds, "Tolerance...fosters a *laissez-faire* attitude to problems—'different strokes for different folks.' Social control flourishes under this ideological umbrella. ...Furthermore, tolerance is essentially a passive position."[65]

Anyone who has tried to get a grip on prejudice, whether it is aimed at gay people, women, people of color, or transsexuals, knows that tolerance is not "a passive position." It is hard work to identify irrational beliefs about people who are different from oneself, understand that these differences don't necessarily mean there's anything wrong or bad about the "other side," say no to hateful stereotypes and struggle to see people as they are rather than weak or inferior, stand up to the terror of difference, and create healthy boundaries between oneself and others, which permit an appreciation of their autonomy and even a love of their unique beauty and strength.

Catherine Millot, author of *Horsexe*, is hardly going to encourage anyone to examine their prejudices about transsexuality. Millot is a psychoanalyst and a professor of psychoanalysis at the University of Paris. While Raymond sees Money and Stoller as suspect because of their sexism, Millot can't get enough of quoting Lacan, Freud, Stoller, even Krafft-Ebing![66] Her book has no footnotes, however, making it difficult to verify any of the material that she cites. Millot's lack of skepticism about Famous Dead White Males makes her political credentials suspect. Not every book by a female academic is informed by feminism.

Millot buys into Raymond's definition of transsexuality as a recent phenomenon, created by the possibility of hormone therapy and surgery. Nevertheless, she devotes many pages of her essay to ancient mythology, focusing on goddesses such as Cybele who have consorts/sons who die or are castrated. Cybele's hierophants were called *gallae*—genetic men who had castrated themselves, and afterward wore female apparel. Millot repeatedly refers to these individuals as "eunuchs" and uses male pronouns and the male word form *galli* to describe them. She also quotes from a satirical version of the gallae's rites in Apuleius's *The Golden Ass* and from early Christian attacks on the cult of the Great Mother. This gives the reader a distorted picture of a dignified, widely esteemed, and very popular religious tradition that survived for thousands of years until it was, with great difficulty, stamped out by Christian prelates. This scurrilous stuff is supposed to somehow support Millot's analysis of male-to-female transsexuality as the result of a pathological relationship between the young boy and his mother, in which he wishes to give up his penis so that he can become, in Stoller's terms, "mother's feminized phallus."[67]

In fact, it is probable that the contemporaries of the gallae viewed them, not as castrated men, but as magically potent individuals who had experienced the miracle of changing their sex. The Roman poet Catallus made a point of calling Cybele's priestesses *gallae*, a feminine form of the noun. Millot does not quote Catallus, or indeed any positive contemporary material about the gallae. According to Margaret Deirdre O'Hartigan, the gallae probably did not identify themselves with Cybele's son and consort Atthis, a mortal who did not survive his castration, but with the goddess herself, who changes sex to become Agdistis in order to impregnate Atthis' mother and so "sire" him. As O'Hartigan points out, "Changing sex is the prerogative of the supernatural; any number of gods and goddesses from all times and places have changed sex when it suited their purposes."[68]

Millot seems obsessed with castration. She has an entire chapter on the Skoptzy, a nineteenth-century Russian sect that practiced mutilation or actual removal of the genitals. All of this stuff is entirely irrelevant, given the fact that the Skoptzy performed castrations, clitoridectomies, ritual cuttings and brandings, and excision of the nipples to remove lust and the possibility of carnal sin from their lives. After surgical mutilation, a Skoptzy attained a higher rank in his or her religious hierarchy, not a change in gender.

But Millot sees sex-reassignment surgery in simplistic Freudian terms, as castration. She focuses on the loss of the penis, without taking into consideration what is gained in the process—female genitals and a female identity. But like many Freudians, Millot cannot quite see that women have genitals of their own; the only sex organ she recognizes is the penis, or in Lacanspeak, "the phallus."

As a gender essentialist, Millot shares Raymond's distaste for sex reassignment. "A young female transsexual once came to see me in the mistaken belief that I would give her the address of a sex-change surgeon," Millot tells us. "When I pressed her to tell me why she so much wanted surgery, she said it was because she had the impression of living a lie in having the appearance of a woman whilst feeling herself to be a man. I objected that surgery would merely exchange one lie for another."[69]

Instead of suggesting "consciousness-raising therapy," however, Millot simply endorses traditional psychoanalysis, which she claims is effective because "transsexuals are sensitive to suggestion."[70] Without citing any research, Millot asserts that after therapy, "they come to question their transsexual identities and their choice of sexual object, and, provisionally at least, give up the idea of hormonal and surgical transformation."[71] In fact, there is very little research that would substantiate this point of view. Instead, it seems that therapy of any kind is not generally successful at budging gender dysphoria. The desire to live in one's gender of preference can only be met by (duh!) allowing transgendered people to live in their gender of preference.

Like Raymond, Millot exploits transsexuals to promote an anti-transsexual ideology. The English edition of her book is packaged with a cover featuring a large photograph of a nude person who has breasts and a penis. The background behind the figure is a psychedelic smear of bright pastels, associating transsexuals (as Raymond does) with delusion and drug addiction. The titillating nudity of a hermaphrodite is used to sell a book that dehumanizes people in gender transition. The presence of the penis also underlines Millot's assertion that changing sex is not really possible. According to her, the person born male remains male, no matter how many female attributes "he" can also display. The text is illustrated with, among other things, photographs of drag queens and Asian transvestite prostitutes. This promotes the idea that transsexuals are exotic and artificial (either because they are performers or because their gender ambiguity has a commercial motive). "The transsexual" is held at a distance from "the reader," and because of that distance, it is of course safe for the narrator to say anything she likes about her remote subject.

Other than Lacan, the chief influence on Millot would seem to be Robert Stoller, a psychoanalyst and a professor of psychiatry at the University of California at Los Angeles School of Medicine. His illustrious career in sex research spanned many decades, and he was an extremely prolific author. Thus, it is difficult to summarize all of his theories about transsexuality, which evolved over the course of his career as a clinician and a researcher.[72] Put in the most general terms, however, it would not be unfair to say that Stoller saw transsexuality as a psychological disorder that was created by traumatic and unhealthy circumstances in the transsexual's family of origin.

His work has the same flaws as any other work based on a medical model of human sexuality. As a clinician, Stoller felt it was his task to delineate what was abnormal and, if possible, bring an aberrant patient back into the fold of normalcy. The medical model has a great deal of respect and authority in the world, partly because it seems very scientific and objective. That may be true when it comes to researching the epidemiology of polio, but when it comes to promoting a clearer understanding of the libido, the medical model has serious weaknesses. First of all, given the enormous variation that has existed from one human culture to another, insofar as we know our own history as a species, how do we define, with any certainty, what is normal and what is abnormal? As therapists, should we accept the norms of whatever culture we find ourselves practicing in? Is it not possible for societies to be sick, wrong, criminal, or deluded, as well as individuals? If we define sexual abnormality as something we should cure, merely because it occurs less frequently than what we think of as normal sexuality, are we also going to wipe out other rare or "aberrant" behaviors like the ability to compose music, mathematical genius, or great artistic ability to wield a paintbrush or a sculptor's chisel?

Stoller never examines his own assumptions about what is normal and what is not. He never defines what it is, aside from sexual difference, that makes his patients "sick." I am dubious about psychological diagnoses that are not based on an inability to function adequately in the real world. Even if Stoller were interested in answering such questions, the population he focused on was far too biased to provide results that we could generalize from. Clinical populations, people who seek therapy, are bound to be people who feel that there is something wrong with them. A patient who does not agree with the therapist's assessment of his "dis-ease" is going to leave treatment. When Stoller runs into a transsexual whose profile doesn't fit his model, he simply dismisses them as "not a true transsexual."

"Authorities" on sexual disorder like Stoller and Millot get away with sweeping generalizations and negative stereotypes of sexual minorities in part because these small, embattled communities are not large enough or self-confident enough to challenge them. One of the first things any sexual minority does, as it develops a political consciousness, is attack the psychiatric establishment for its role in fostering stigma and discrimination. Stoller at least based his disagreeable books and articles on years of solid work with people he was sincerely trying to help and understand. Millot is much more flippant, adopting a sort of yellow journalism approach, taking us on a whirlwind tour of the transsexual milieu.

Her claim that male-to-female transsexuals want to be superstars, more female than genetic women, seems to be based on nothing more rigorous than a few outings to drag bars.[73] Drag performers are simply the transgendered people who are most accessible to her. Would we give any credence to an ethnography of heterosexuality that was based solely on a few hours of watching daytime soap operas? Millot seems completely unaware of the many male-to-female transsexuals who are content to live quiet lives in their gender of preference, who would be appalled at the thought of putting themselves on stage. She makes note of transvestite and transsexual prostitutes and says of their desire to be seen as female, "Perhaps it is the market forces of prostitution—i.e., what the client wants (which is more saleable, a transvestite with or without a penis?)."[74] This is the coarse and sensationalistic voice of an outsider, someone who has no compassion for the economic necessity that drives so many transgendered women into the sex industry.

The interviews she conducts with transsexuals contribute nothing to our understanding of transgendered people because her report of these interviews is so heavily colored by her own prejudice. Millot speaks of finding "hysteria" among her interviewees without ever defining that term. She shamelessly employs circular reasoning. If you assume transsexuals are pathological, and you never define that term objectively, you can find something wrong with any transsexual who will speak to you. She chirps, "The absence of psychotic symptoms does not necessarily exclude the presence of a psychotic structure."[75] Millot has no political analysis, no idea that the stress of living in a gendered world can create havoc even for those of us who are not hampered by gender dysphoria. Of course, she gives the most space in her book to "Gabriel," a female-to-male transsexual who feels that sex-reassignment surgery ruined his life and made him "a monster."[76]

Bad as Raymond's book is, it is a more coherent production than this cobbled-together, shallow essay. Millot seems to have lifted most of Raymond's line of reasoning and used it with very little amendment. There's even a French counterpart to Raymond's chapter about "integration" versus "integrity." Instead of that, Millot natters on about "desire" and "*jouissance*." Use of this jargon masks the fact that both

Raymond and Millot have simply appointed themselves authorities on Good Sex and Bad Sex, and will cheerfully pronounce their verdicts upon the rest of us if we are silly enough to listen to them.

Ironically, my own history contains a period of transphobia as deep as Raymond's or Millot's. When I came to San Francisco in the mid-seventies, I was a separatist. I came out when I was underage, and practically the only dykes who would talk to me were a handful of women who were lesbian-feminist separatists. The rest of the town's dyke community regarded them as crazy bra-burners, by the way, and me as jail-bait. I had absorbed this separatist philosophy because it made sense to me. I loved women, and men tried to prevent me from doing that. Most of the time when I got harassed, it was by straight men. I hated them for that, and I didn't want to be around them. I wanted to be with women.

As I tried to locate myself in San Francisco's much larger and more sophisticated lesbian community, I heard that the Daughters of Bilitis (DOB) had recently purged a male-to-female transsexual who had been an officer in their organization. This event was still a hot topic, and one of the ways I made friends with other dykes was to express my approval of the purge. It made me really angry and unhappy to encounter opposition from a woman I respected, a former bar dyke and diesel butch who liked what she heard about the women's movement and became a feminist. She had actually been present at the stormy meeting where this woman was ousted, unlike most of the rest of us who were talking about it, and she had not liked what she saw.

"This doesn't feel okay to me," she said. "She worked harder than anybody else in DOB. She gave a lot to that organization. There was no good reason to kick her out. She hadn't done anything wrong except be a transsexual. You wouldn't believe some of the vile and vicious things other women said to her. And she just sat and listened to all of it, kept her dignity, and answered them back without losing her temper or calling anybody names."

I didn't know what to think about that. Who cared what happened to some man? Who cared if we had hurt his feelings? Men had hurt my feelings and much worse than that hundreds of times. By kicking out this impostor, I felt we were simply giving the patriarchy back a little of its own shit. But here was a woman I respected, a dyke with good political credentials, older and wiser than me, who was telling me that this was wrong. She called it a witch-hunt. She was brave enough to disagree with me. It didn't change my mind, but I carried this uncomfortable confrontation away with me and thought about it over the course of the next year. I stopped running my mouth about this debate and just listened.

What I heard made me uneasy. I didn't have a lot of leftist political education, but I knew about McCarthyism. I knew that during the fifties this country had been through massive witch-hunts to ferret out queers and Communists. That infamous question, "Have you now or have you ever…" rang in my ears. And what I saw happening began to feel to me like a witch-hunt. It reminded me of all the creeps in school banding together on the playground to beat up a new kid who had not yet acquired any allies or protectors.

This was part of a growing disaffection with separatism in general. I was a volunteer at DOB, answering the mail and staffing the office. The staff in general were separatists, and I began to get annoyed at the way this ideology functioned to divide lesbians from one another. I was attracted to separatism because I wanted to have fun, live with, have sex with, and make things happen with other dykes. If men gave us any shit, I wanted to have a lot of help to resist them. But it was pretty hard to create a lesbian anything if we first had to go through a process of identifying all the women who were male-identified and throwing them out. I got really tired of talking about and looking for men, masculinity, and male identification. I wanted to be talking about women and creating more space for us in the world. But that just wasn't happening.

One day, while I was womaning the desk at the DOB office, a person who looked like a rotund, elderly faggot to me walked in the door and asked for help. Her name was Jewel, she said, and she had just had sex-change surgery in Europe. She said she didn't look like a woman because she hadn't been taking hormones for very long. She wished that she could show me her new genitals, which she swore were perfect, and which no man would ever touch. And she wanted somebody to go shopping for clothes with her, because she was afraid of being beaten up or ridiculed if she tried to buy a dress in her current state.

I was taken aback. I certainly didn't want to look at this person's surgically-constructed crotch, and I hadn't gone shopping to buy *myself* a dress since I'd left home. Some of the other DOB staffers had heard part of this story, and I saw them stomping over to the front desk, getting ready to take care of this male intruder. "You really should leave," I said quickly. "We don't provide any services for transsexuals. There are some women here who would be very angry if they knew you were here. Please go."

Jewel didn't seem to get it. She stood there, looking pathetic, for several more minutes. Didn't I know anybody who could help her? No,

I did not. I could feel my face turning red from shame and aggravation. Why was this weirdo ruining my day? Why did I feel so guilty? Eventually the other DOB staff hustled Jewel out the door and into the elevator. They were happy about it for the rest of the day. I felt terrible.

Eventually it become impossible to ignore the fact that if other separatists knew about my sexual fantasies and the things that at that point I only imagined being able to do with other women, things that involved handcuffs and riding crops, I would be given the bum's rush just as hard and fast as any transsexual. There was no information or any help for me in the lesbian community then, so I went looking outside, first at San Francisco Sex Information (SFSI), a switchboard that trained volunteers to answer questions about all aspects of human sexuality, and later in the gay men's leather community. I came to see sexual shame as one of the things that repress women and keep us from being autonomous human beings. And I began to extend tolerance to people who were not like me, including transsexuals, partly as a way to heal my own sexual shame. If I could learn to accept other people, perhaps I could reach a place of self-acceptance as well.

My consciousness about transsexuality was raised even more when I started exploring my own sexual fantasies about having a cock and being a man. The misery that had motivated me to check out the option of sex reassignment was intense. When I decided to abandon that path, I got a glimmer of how much somebody has to be suffering to be willing to tell the doctors, "Give me those pills. I want to do this. I want to change my sex." And I started to see that transsexuals couldn't do anything about some of the behaviors or visual cues that made them occasionally seem incongruous in their gender of preference.

Prejudice usually can't survive close contact with the people who are supposed to be so despicable, which is why the propagandists for hate always preach separation. Through SFSI and the S/M community, I began to meet more transgendered women. I didn't like all of them, but then, there were a lot of genetic women I didn't like. It became clear that I could take transgendered women on a case-by-case basis. If I liked them and they read as dykes to me, I could invite them to be part of my world. If I didn't trust them or I thought they weren't quite "cooked" yet as women, I could pass. But that didn't mean I had to trash them or hate them. I could support the civil rights of transgendered people *as a class*, without feeling obligated to become intimate with anybody I had not checked out and found attractive. And a lot of them were attractive—smart, sexy, savvy about feminism, strong in their identification and solidarity with other women. No way were these women damaging my community or functioning as eunuch harem-keepers or agents of sexism.

Unraveling prejudice is a lifelong process. Recently, I had a very educational experience. I found out that one of my long-term women acquaintances is transgendered. I had known this person for several years without being aware of that. I was pained by this discovery, since I like to think that my "trans-radar" works as well as my "gaydar." She hadn't intended to deceive me; she thought I already knew. Given how much work I've done to educate myself about transsexuality, I didn't think it would make much of a difference. But I found myself looking at her in a whole different way. Suddenly her hands looked too big, there was something odd about her nose, and didn't she have an Adam's apple? Wasn't her voice kind of deep for a woman? And wasn't she awfully bossy, just like a man? And my God, she had a lot of hair on her forearms.

When I caught myself thinking this way, I had to laugh, although it was a rueful kind of merriment. Transphobia is very difficult to eliminate. Those of us who are not transgendered can hardly ever be trusted to make accurate judgments about transsexuals because we don't see them the way we see each other. We use another set of standards to evaluate them. And those standards are biased, toward uncovering evidence that their chromosomal sex is still affecting their self-presentation, among other things.

I should not end this confessional moment without adding that another thing that made me question my own bigotry about transsexuals was Raymond's book. When it first came out, I read it cover to cover. There were all the things that had been inside my head. But on paper, in black and white, they looked so ugly. No matter how I tried to rationalize it, I couldn't make myself believe that the presence of a transsexual woman ruined a women's event or spoiled a lesbian organization. We were struggling so hard to make women-only things happen, we needed all the help we could get! I didn't want to ally myself with people who were obsessed with hate. I knew what it was like to be hated, to have people call me names and threaten me or assault me, just because they didn't like the way I was dressed and the things I did in bed. I knew how much I needed a community to maintain my mental health and survive in such a hostile world. It felt wrong to me, as a working-class queer who understood oppression on a survival level, on a street level, to yank the rug out from under somebody else's feet.

It still feels wrong to me, which is one of the reasons why it became important to write this book. Gender is not simply an academic or a political issue. It is the most personal of all the "personal is political" topics you could name. A fear of transsexuals is directly traceable to a fear of your own opposite-sex self. I believe that in order to be complete, women need to be able to reach into the black box called "maleness" and take out anything there that they find useful. And until men are able to face, love, learn from, and incorporate the feminine, we will be enemies. It's worth it to spend some time (a lot of time) thinking about how your fear of transsexuality manifests itself, and how your fear of stepping outside the boundaries of "appropriate" gender conduct limits your life.

Unfortunately, gay male academics haven't done much better than feminists at coping with the phenomenon of transsexuality. In an attempt to demonstrate that homosexuality has existed throughout human history, in every human culture, gay male historians and anthropologists have appropriated such people as the Native American berdache and the hijra of India as gay role models. The next chapter, "The Berdache Wars and 'Passing Women' Follies," will present an overview of some of the problems that arise when the gay paradigms of industrialized Western culture are used as lenses through which to view third-gender roles in non-Western societies or preindustrial cultures.

Notes

1. Candace Margulies, "An Open Letter to Olivia Records," *Lesbian Connection*, November 1977. Also see assorted letters in *Lesbian Connection*, May 1978 and November 1979. And see Janice Raymond, "Transsexualism: The Ultimate Homage to Sex-Role Power," *Chrysalis: A Magazine of Woman's Culture*, No. 3, 1978.
2. Janice G. Raymond, *The Transsexual Empire: The Making of the She-Male*, Boston: Beacon Press, 1979, p. xi. This book was reissued by Teachers College Press in 1994, minus the preface, which contains some of Raymond's most extreme statements. I have chosen to use the 1979 edition for citation here because it was in print for far longer than the Teachers College Press edition, and had the greatest influence on the women's movement and lesbian attitudes toward transsexual women.
3. Adrienne Rich, "Compulsory Heterosexuality and Lesbian Existence," *Signs*, vol. 5, no. 4, 1980; reprinted in Adrienne Rich, *Blood, Bread, and Poetry*, New York: W. W. Norton, 1986.
4. For a critique of Rich's essay, see Pat Califia, "Introduction: Or It Is Always Right to Rebel," *Public Sex*, Pittsburgh and San Francisco: Cleis Press, 1994, pp. 11-26.
5. Janice Raymond, "The Politics of Transgenderism," in Richard Ekins and Dave King (eds.), *Blending Genders: Social Aspects of Cross-Dressing and Sex-Changing*, London and New York: Routledge, 1996, pp. 215-223. This article first appeared as part of the introduction to the 1994 New York: Teachers College Press, 2nd edition, of *The Transsexual Empire*.

6. Raymond, *The Transsexual Empire,* op. cit., p. xxvi.

7. Ibid., p. 20.

8. Ibid., p. 10.

9. Ibid., p. 183.

10. Ibid., p. 114.

11. Ibid., p. 64.

12. Ibid., p. 57.

13. Ibid., pp. 43-68.

14. Ibid., p. xvi.

15. Ibid., p. xiii. Renée Richards was a male-to-female transsexual who had to engage in a legal battle to get the right to play professional women's tennis. Far from taking over the field, Richards soon withdrew from tournament competition and, after a brief stint of coaching Martina Navratilova, went back to practicing medicine. For more information, see Renée Richards with John Ames, *Second Serve: The Renée Richards Story,* New York: Stein and Day, 1983, pp. 365-366.

16. Ibid., p. 24.

17. Ibid., p. 79.

18. Ibid., p. xix.

19. Ibid., p. 104.

20. Ibid., p. 118.

21. Ibid., pp. xix-xx.

22. Ibid., p. 105.

23. Ibid., p. 75, note at the bottom of the page.

24. Ibid., p. 70.

25. Ibid., p. xviii.

26. Ibid., p. 9.

27. Ibid., p. 13.

28. Ibid., p. xviii.

29. Ibid., pp. xvi-xvii.

30. Ibid., p. xiv. See also note 1 on page 187.

31. Carol Riddell, "Divided Sisterhood: A Critical Review of Janice Raymond's *The Transsexual Empire,*" in Richard Ekins and Dave King, op. cit., p. 178.

32. Raymond, *The Transsexual Empire,* op. cit., p. 5.

33. Ibid., p. 117. The original letter is attributed to Angela Douglas and was first published in *Sister,* August-September, 1977, p. 7.

34. Interview with Mustang Sally conducted by the author on June 4, 1996. Unpublished.

35. Raymond, *The Transsexual Empire,* op. cit., p. xxi.

36. Ibid., p. xxii.

37. Ibid., p. xxv.

38. Ibid., p. xxiii.

39. Ibid., p. xxiv.

40. Ibid., pp. 33, 140, and 208, footnote 32.

41. Ibid., p. 134.

42. Ibid., p. xvi.

43. Ibid., p. 131.

44. Ibid., p. xxiv.
45. Ibid., p. 152. Raymond is quoting Dr. Harry Benjamin.
46. Ibid., p. 148.
47. Ibid., p. 152.
48. Ibid., pp. 143-144, referring to Jon K. Meyer and John H. Hoopes, "The Gender Dysphoria Syndromes: A Position Statement on So-Called Transsexualism," *Plastic and Reconstructive Surgery*, 54 (October 1977): 448.
49. Ibid., p. 149.
50. Ibid., p. 15.
51. Ibid., p. 191, footnote 13.
52. Ibid., p. 147.
53. Ibid., p. 78.
54. Ibid., p. 79.
55. Riddell, op. cit., pp. 180-181.
56. Raymond, *The Transsexual Empire*, op. cit., p. 82.
57. Ibid., p. 101.
58. Ibid., p. 123-124.
59. Ibid., p. 178.
60. Ibid., pp. 101-103 and 201-202, footnote 1.
61. Interview with Sandy Stone by the author, June 1, 1996. Unpublished.
62. Raymond, *The Transsexual Empire*, op. cit., p. 110.
63. Ibid., p. 119.
64. Ibid., p. 176.
65. Ibid., p. 177.
66. For a critique of Krafft-Ebing's work, see Edward M. Brecher, "Sex as a Loathsome Disease," *The Sex Researchers*, New York: Signet, 1969, pp. 75-86.
67. Catherine Millot, *Horsexe: Essay on Transsexuality*, translated from the French by Kenneth Hylton, Brooklyn: Autonomedia, 1990, p. 52.
68. Margaret Deirdre O'Hartigan, "The Gallae of the Magna Mater," *Chrysalis Quarterly*, vol. 1, no. 6, p. 13.
69. Millot, op. cit., p. 143.
70. Ibid., p. 142.
71. Ibid., pp. 142-143.
72. Robert J. Stoller, M.D., "Parental Influences in Male Transsexualism," in *Transsexualism and Sex Reassignment*, Richard Green, M.D. and John Money, Ph.D. (eds.), Baltimore: The Johns Hopkins Press, 1969; pp. 153-170; "The Transsexual Boy: Mother's Feminized Phallus," *British Journal of Medical Psychology*, 43 (1970), pp. 117-128; "Etiological Factors in Female Transsexualism: A First Approximation," *Archives of Sexual Behavior*, 2 (1972), pp. 47-64; and *Perversion: The Erotic Form of Hatred*, New York: Delta/Dell, 1975, pp. 49, 138-143, and 145-162.
73. Millot, op. cit., pp. 10 and 105.
74. Ibid., p. 12.
75. Ibid., p. 26.
76. Ibid., p. 133.

CHAPTER 4

The Berdache Wars and "Passing Women" Follies: Transphobia in Gay Academia

Antihomosexual ideology is based on a claim that same-sex eroticism and romance is perverse. In other words, it is a rare exception to the "normal" order of things. According to this world view, heterosexuality is natural, and any deviation from that pattern is unnatural (as if anything could exist that truly contradicted the laws of nature). Another common antigay ploy is to claim that homosexuality is an aberration that exists only in decadent or dysfunctional societies. The visible presence of gay men and lesbians or the existence of an above-ground queer culture thus becomes a rallying cry for a return to a more conservative era of traditional values, lest the social contract collapse and chaos reign. In this scenario, the rainbow flag is rung up only to signal that the barbarians are at the very gates of Rome.

Science has frequently been used to justify antihomosexual political positions. Biology is called upon to bolster the notion that sex exists only to facilitate procreation, and to reify the universality of polarized gender roles. Thus, most people are unaware that same-sex activity has been documented in practically all mammals, in many species of birds, and among some reptiles, fishes, and insects. The role of sexual behavior as a marker for dominance or territory is underexamined by researchers in animal behavior, and of course, the notion of pleasure as a motivating factor almost never arises, even when the life cycle of higher primates is studied. The fact that many species of animals on our planet do not have two simple and mutually exclusive sexes is treated as an entertaining piece of trivia, something which certainly has nothing to do with us, here at the top of the food chain.

The social sciences have been used even more heavily than natural sciences to shore up the view of homosexuality as a decadent aberration or a rare act of treason against Nature. In the pages of traditional history, sociology, and anthropology texts, we are paradoxically seen as both evil and nonexistent. We are only allowed to populate the pages of psychology treatises as titillating case histories, "proof" of our mental instability and psychiatric dis-ease.

Thus, the first priority of the gay anthropologists and historians who popularized gay studies in the late seventies was to establish the universality and frequency of same-sex behavior in as many different time periods and human cultures as possible. During that decade, there was a drive to normalize homosexuality by simply documenting its widespread existence. According to this school of thought, gay men and lesbians were not unnatural freaks; we were a normal and universal part of the continuum of human sexuality and relationships. We had always been everywhere, and would always be everywhere. The paucity of documentation for our ancestors was rightly attributed to censorship and active repression of any public expression of homosexuality, rather than any inherent quality of ours that rendered us unspeakably rare and criminally uncommon. If these early gay scholars could also show that homosexuality had not always been held in contempt, so much the better.

The many years of careful academic work that it has taken to construct the wealth of gay history and anthropological data that we now enjoy were a great gift to the lesbian and gay community. But the search for our predecessors sometimes suffered from biases every bit as severe and censorious as the antihomosexual ideology that made it necessary for queer graduate students, professors, and intellectuals outside of academe to start searching for "gay role models." Bisexual activists have already complained, for good reason, that many of the individuals who have been celebrated as queer elders were in fact Kinsey Threes, Fours, or Fives rather than Kinsey Sixes.[1]

If bisexual men and women had been unquestioningly accepted as allies and fellow travelers within gay liberation or lesbian feminism, respectively, this might not have become such a contested topic. But when cheering gay activists carry banners bearing the likeness of bisexual people like Virginia Woolf or Walt Whitman in a pride march, after the organizing committee has voted to exclude the word "bisexual" from the name of the event, well, it rankles. Protests will be lodged, without much foreplay.

Gay and lesbian historians have often fiercely disputed the application of the label "bisexual" to their pet dead famous queers. There was an understandable tendency to deny any importance to the heterosexual aspects of some of our heroes' and heroines' lives, since this research was taking place in a society that smugly emphasized heterosexuality and ruthlessly erased any hint of homosexuality. Gay scholars still view bisexuality as a dilution of the radical potential of homosexuality, as a compromise with or contamination by heterosexuality, rather than as a deviant and defiant identity that has its own potential for engendering social transformation. According to this view of bisexuality, if our gay and lesbian ancestors were tainted with heterosexuality, might it not demonstrate that being straight was, after all, the predominating template, and anyone who thought they could escape from its dictates was deluded?

The most common response to the accusation of fomenting bisexual invisibility or biphobia among gay social-science researchers is to claim that any heterosexual behavior on the part of our long-ago heroes and heroines was made necessary by life in a repressive heterosexual society. Marriages and such functioned, according to this view, to camouflage and protect people who would much rather have been exclusively homosexual. If any of these people lived during a time when homosexuality was not so stigmatized, not so harshly punished, they would no doubt, some gay historians believe, have realized their true natures and cleaved exclusively to members of their own sex.

Condescending as it is, this argument has some merit. None of us know who we might be or what we might do if the social context around us changed radically. Since I am no big fan of the quest for a "gay gene," I'd like to point out here that this view of the apparent flexibility of sexual orientation would seem to contradict the notion that some of us are born homosexual and can't help it. While I think it would be absurd to claim that there is no genetic or physiological component to sexual identity, preference, and behavior, it is equally absurd to overlook the plasticity of so-called "human nature" in the face of religion, economics, race, and the many other powerful institutions that limit our options. If there is a gene that predisposes one to being queer, it may simply be a chromosomal combination that bequeaths one with the courage to be deviant.

But I digress. Ultimately, the attempt to interpret the past according to our own models or our own definitions impoverishes historical research. Rather than combing old documents for evidence of the people who seem most similar to ourselves, why aren't we trying to understand sex roles, gender, and pleasure-seeking behavior *in their own context?* A biography of a bisexual literary figure, for example, would be thin and dishonest if it did not include all aspects of that person's life and times—the marriage and the children, as well as the same-sex flirtations or the devoted same-sex "longtime companion." An attempt to combine "normal" and "abnormal" elements in one life can be as transgressive as a complete dedication to rebellion. While it is vital for those of us who violate the norms of Judeo-Christian morality to understand that we are not alone, not some recent hiccup of the dangerously secular twentieth century and not a putrefying wrinkle in the human libido—once that is established, is it not even more interesting to discover how little is absolute about human sexuality? If anything could bring down the wall of superiority between ourselves and our heterosexual enemies, this would seem to be our biggest weapon.

While bisexual activists have taken gay and lesbian documentarians to task for appropriating famous dead bisexuals and even distorting certain details of their lives, transgendered scholars and activists are just beginning to make some noise about a similar systematic misappropriation of transsexual historical figures.

In his groundbreaking volume, *Gay American History*, Jonathan Katz established the gay-studies paradigm for interpreting the experience of Native American berdaches (genetic males who assumed women's attire, did women's work, and often had sexual relations with biological males who were not berdache) and "passing women" (genetic females who cross-dressed, lived as, and were perceived as men, who often had sexual relationships with women). Katz sees these third-gender or gender ambiguous people as gay role models, as evidence for the existence of lesbians and gay men throughout history, in all human cultures.

In the introduction to the "Native Americans/Gay Americans 1528-1976" chapter, Katz says, "These documents on male and female homosexuality among American Indians present four hundred forty-eight years of testimony from a wide variety of observers: military men, missionaries, explorers, trappers, traders, settlers, and later medical doctors, anthropologists, and homosexual emancipationists; in a few rare instances the voices of Gay Indians are heard."[2] This is a framework that leaves very little room for an interpretation of the sparse data about the berdache that emphasizes cross-gender identity and behavior as well as same-sex eroticism.

The term *berdache* is not based on a word from any Native American language. According to one researcher, this word came originally from a Persian term which spread to the Spanish via Arabic, and from Spain to France. In all its variations, the term refers to the passive male partner in anal intercourse, sometimes with the implication that the person described is a male prostitute.[3] Early European observers in America assumed (usually correctly) that the cross-dressed biological males they saw among many groups of Native Americans were sexually servicing other biological males, men who did not cross-dress. This European definition, based on antihomosexual prejudice, ironically dovetails with the agenda of gay male academics who would like to claim the berdaches as gay ancestral figures.

But when we try to get translations for the terms that Native Americans used (and, in many cases, still use) for these people, it seems that the focus is on gender difference rather than on homosexual activity. The Cheyenne translate *he man he* as "halfman-halfwoman." The Lakota *winktes* are also known as "halfmen-halfwomen."[4] And the Crow translation for *badé* is "not man, not woman."[5] Several other examples from other tribes could be cited. I have been unable to locate a single translation of Native American terms for what white researchers call berdaches that does not focus on gender difference rather than homosexuality as the defining quality of this social role.

The Gay American Indian History Project has published a list of over one hundred thirty Native American tribes that had berdache-like roles for men. Some, but not all, of these tribes also recognized gender-variant roles for women. Not all Native American tribes had third-gender roles, and those that did employed a variety of names for this social category.[6]

In his summation of some early writings about the berdaches, Katz says, "Documents not originally in English are translated, but, when possible, the foreign word referring to *homosexuality* is included."[7] (Italics are mine.) This is a bit of scholarly sleight-of-hand that most readers would take as proof that Native American people saw the berdaches as gay or homosexual. But, in fact, the exact meaning of these terms is controversial. It is probable that each Native American tribe that allocated a third-gender role defined this category in a different way, and attitudes about such people would vary not only from tribe to tribe, but would be affected by many other variables as well, such as the amount or type of contact with disapproving Europeans, or the personality and talents of the berdache herself.

Katz tries to finesse the troublesome issue of transsexuality out of existence in his discussion of the berdaches by saying, "A variety of American Indian homosexualities are documented. That most commonly described involves reversal of the customary sex roles—cross-dressing, cross-working, cross-speaking—as well as homosexual activity."[8] Katz wants the reader to think of the effeminate berdache as just one type of homosexual, similar to a "type" that is commonly recognized today. He notes, "If...uninformed anthropologists today made field trips to New York's Greenwich Village, among the native Gay population they would surely first notice the most obvious 'queens.'" He takes earlier observers to task for "the failure...to discuss the homosexuality of the berdache's non-cross-dressing sexual partners," and claims "tribal attitudes toward and the character of this non-berdache partner are passed over in silence." Furthermore, "Some documents...hint at the existence of homosexual relations between two apparently 'normal' males. These reports refer to 'special friendships' and a 'blood brotherhood'—especially intimate relations between two males, often of a lifelong character, and so often described so as to emphasize their sensual, deeply emotional aspect. Other documents suggest the existence of homosexual relations between adults and youths." [9]

However, this begs the question of how Native Americans themselves perceived the berdache, her sexual partners, "special friendships," and pederasty. If in fact these things were not seen as being related—if, for example, the sexual partner of a berdache was seen as a heterosexual man because the berdache was not socially recognized as fully male; if pairs of male friends were not generally perceived to be deviant because the friendship did not interfere with marriage and procreation, and instead reified the social expectation that men excel as hunters and warriors; or if pederasty was seen as a ceremony that all adult men and youths participated in to assist the boy in making his transition to manhood—it seems important to say that, rather than distort these phenomenon by insisting on seeing them through the paradigm of modern Western male homosexuality.

Later on in this chapter, when discussing the sexual partners of berdache, Katz acknowledges that "such persons would resent being called elxá or kwérhame" (synonyms for berdache), even though coupling with a berdache was "not considered objectionable."[10] If Native American people saw the berdache and her partner as being similar, as being members of the same class of people, why would separate terms exist for one of the members in such couples? And why would one member of that couple insist that he was not like his partner, and be offended by any suggestion that he was like her? This alone seems to demonstrate that Native Americans did not have an umbrella concept like "homosexuality," which would include both the berdache and her partner.

Undeterred by any of these considerations, Katz concludes his introduction to this chapter by denouncing attempts "by the conquerors to eliminate various traditional forms of Indian homosexuality" as "a form of cultural genocide." He connects attempts to suppress the berdache with attempts to "destroy that Native culture which might fuel resistance," thus claiming a status as potential gay and Native American activists for the berdache. "Today, the recovery of the history of Native American homosexuality is a task in which both Gay and Native peoples have a common interest," he concludes.[11]

There is another reason why gay historians, from Katz onward, have shown so much interest in the berdaches. This is because they fulfill the second part of the gay-studies mission statement, which is to demonstrate, if possible, that societies existed which tolerated and even valued their homosexual members. Katz says, "A number of reports suggest that homosexuals often performed religious and ceremonial functions among their people; the exact character and meaning of these roles is not often detailed. Tribal attitudes toward various types of homosexuals apparently varied, although these documents suggest that, before the inroads of Christianity, homosexuals generally occupied an institutionalized, important, and often respected position within many Native groups."[12]

Although it certainly does seem to be true that berdaches sometimes performed in community rituals, Katz has once more overstated his case, this time for acceptance and tolerance. It is not at all clear that Native Americans, even prior to the coming of Christian missionaries, respected or tolerated homosexuality. It is not clear that they would recognize this concept, in the same way that we define it. What is not tolerated, in any society, is conduct that violates that culture's norms and expectations. It seems safe to assume that the berdaches were tolerated, possibly even respected or seen as important, precisely because the people they lived among did not see them as a threat to the common morality, gender roles, and life scripts.

The habit of romanticizing "primitive" cultures is sadly a common error among historians and anthropologists. It is not a certainty that Native American tribal societies offered their members any greater freedom from sex and gender mores than a modern urban environment would, just because those mores differed from ours. Katz himself has to acknowledge "the generally subordinate position of women in Native cultures" and the fact that "Native societies were highly polarized along sexual lines; a strict sexual division of labor seems to have been common, although not universal."[13]

A decade after *Gay American History* appeared, Walter L. Williams published *The Spirit and the Flesh,* in part as a response to Katz's statement that the topic of the berdache deserved a full-length study. Despite the ten years that had elapsed between one work and its successor, Williams shows no inclination to update Katz's reading of the berdaches as gay role models who have absolutely nothing to do with transgenderism.

Williams' analysis of Native American societies and their sex and gender mores rests on the assumption that "American Indians offer some of the world's best examples of gender-egalitarian societies. Anthropologists have debated whether male dominance is universal, and while such dominance clearly exists in many parts of the world, most specialists in North American Indian studies emphasize that at least aboriginally many societies operated on a gender-equal basis."[14] According to Williams, in these societies, "women had a high level of self-esteem for they knew that their family and band economically depended on them as much as or more than it did on men. They were centrally involved in the society's economy, controlling distribution of the food they grew or gathered."[15]

This supposed gender equality is one of the reasons Williams gives for the equally hypothetical revered place of the berdache. "Since women had high status," he reasons, "there was no shame in a male taking on feminine characteristics. He was not giving up male privilege, or 'debasing' himself to become like a woman, simply because the position of women was not inferior. It may be accurate to suggest that the status of berdaches in a society is directly related to the status of women."[16]

Many anthropologists have a tendency to become fond of and to become apologists for the people they study. Among liberal academicians, this can take the form of exaggerated claims for equality between the sexes or tolerance for sexual difference. This is especially true of work by white researchers whose studies of Native American culture are understandably imbued with guilt about the genocidal campaigns that their ancestors carried out against these people. But statements about what Native American societies were like prior to the European invasion, no matter how well-intentioned, are pure speculation. They have absolutely no factual weight whatsoever. A great deal of racist nonsense in the form of colonial propaganda has been disseminated about Native Americans, but fantasy and guesswork make a poor counter to it.

We should be suspicious of any study that claims to describe a group of people who are not male-dominated. Usually it turns out that the social unit in question simply has a different form of male domination than our own society. The rule of men over women is so firmly established that few social scientists have enough imagination to create a paradigm of true gender equality.

As lesbian anthropologist Gayle Rubin has demonstrated, the fact that women produce a great deal of *most* societies' food does not guarantee high social status or political power for women. In fact, such high production rates are usually evidence of the exploitation of women's labor by men, who may control the products of women's work for their own profit and use it to obtain more leisure time for themselves. Rubin makes an elegant argument for the widespread existence of economic oppression of women in preindustrial, noncapitalist societies, and demolishes facile notions of egalitarianism by documenting the many blatant forms that male control over women can take in tribal societies.[17]

At least one woman anthropologist has published work indicating that, of all Native American tribes, only the Iroquois had a power structure that gave women significant control over tribal policy and religion, but even among the Iroquois, women acted through male proxies and all leadership roles were filled by men.[18] This calls into question Williams' link between high status for the berdaches and high status for women, since he himself lists the Iroquois as one of the tribes who are not known to have a third-gender role.[19]

Generalizations are dangerous, especially when there is a paucity of data. Our information about Native American tribal societies before the European invasion is spotty at best. Nevertheless, it seems safe to say that there is, in fact, very little evidence that women in most of these societies had true social, political, or religious equality. There is almost no mention in the historical record of Native American women taking leadership roles in war or peace time, or controlling roles in religious life and ritual. Women usually did not have the right to marry whomever they chose. The father was generally the head of the family. Women did not have reproductive freedom, and as far as we know, few of them had the means to assemble wealth and secure autonomy for themselves. By and large, their lives were controlled by men, who expected their subservience and service. Violence as a form of social control was apparently not absent from Native American society; nor was ridicule.

I am willing to gamble that very few sensible women or gay men would be willing to travel back in time to live out the remainder of their lives in pre-invasion Native American tribal groups, and I include modern Native American women and gay men in that gamble. So much for Williams' idyllic view of them.

Williams follows in Katz's footsteps not only in defining berdaches as gay men. He also believes they were highly regarded by their peers, and in fact were seen as sacred and holy people. "Shamans are not necessarily berdaches," he explains, "but because of their spiritual connection, berdaches in many cultures are often considered to be powerful shamans."[20] This sacred status was reinforced in many tribes by creation myths or other important religious stories that portrayed gender-ambiguous people in a positive light.[21] He believes berdaches were also socially valued because they served as go-betweens between men and women. "They serve a mediating function between women and men, precisely because their character is seen as distinct from either sex," he says.[22] And he cites the importance of their economic contribution to their families, by dint of hard work, as another reason why berdaches remained integrated into their own communities.[23]

Williams seems determined to explain away any evidence that some Native Americans may have viewed the berdaches with ambivalence, or derided them. He attributes most of the derogatory statements about berdaches which have been recorded to "the influence of white people and their Christian religion" or biased reporting by anthropologists, who "themselves have shown prejudicial attitudes toward the berdache." But Williams is forced to admit, "When all these influences are accounted for, there still are some statements in the literature where Indians ridicule or joke about berdaches. To an outsider, this implies a lack of respect for the berdache."[24]

Williams attributes such "teasing" to "joking relationships" which he says exist between some family members. "Joking relatives are properly maligned in public; indeed they expect it and might think something is wrong in its absence," he insists.[25] And furthermore, "Joking relationships often involve sexual themes, so with a berdache it is obvious that the taunting would focus on homosexuality. ...There is no reason to believe...that this taunting denoted a rejection of homosexuality, or that berdaches would have been teased any less if their sexual partners were women instead of men."[26]

Williams even hypothesizes that the baiting of berdaches is actually a marker of their high social status. "Persons of respect and prestige are more subject to ridicule than anyone else," he claims. "While this gossipy aspect of Indian society can be frustrating to someone who takes the initiative, it does function to preserve a basic egalitarianism by taking potentially pretentious persons and reminding them that they had better not overestimate their self-importance. It is one among many mechanisms that Indians use to inhibit social stratification."[27] He concludes, "The literature does not show instances where a berdache was physically attacked because of his differences."[28]

However, we do have a historical record of the murder of a female berdache, or *hwame*, Sahaykwisa, a female-born Mohave who told other Indians that "she" had been turned into a man by white man's magic. Sahaykwisa took several female lovers, many of whom left her after being badgered and publicly humiliated by other Mohaves. Williams glosses over the narrative of this harsh verbal harassment, but it appears in more detail in Katz. It reportedly included comments that sound like classic dyke-baiting to me, such as this gem, addressed to Sahaykwisa's lover: "Why do you want a hwame for a husband? A hwame has no penis; she only pokes you with her finger."[29] One of Sahaykwisa's wives left her for a man, Haq'au. Reluctant to accept her lover's departure, the hwame kept a vigil by her former wife's new campsite. Haq'au is quoted as saying, "Let her come! The next time she comes, I will show her what a real penis can do." And the next time they met, he raped her. After that, Sahaykwisa "ceased to court women."[30] Eventually she was murdered by a group of men who drowned her.

Williams prettifies over this tragic and horrifying tale by claiming that Sahaykwisa was killed "because it was believed that she had killed another person by witchcraft, not because of her gender status or her sexual relations with women." Other Mohave claimed Sahaykwisa wanted to be killed.[31] Well, that's what a murderer would say to justify a killing, isn't it? The magical powers of the berdaches apparently did not protect them from all stigma or violence.

Williams is much more interested in using the ridicule of the hwame's wives to shore up his claim that there is no connection between the berdache and transsexuality. "While the social role of the *hwame* was in some ways like that of men," he says, "the story of Sahaykwisa does not support Blackwood's view of gender *crossing*. The Mohaves did not in fact accept Sahaykwisa as a full-fledged man, and the wife was teased in that regard. She was regarded as a *hwame*, having a distinct gender status that was different than men, women, or *alyha* [nota bene: male berdache]. Mohaves thus had four genders in their society."[32]

An alternative theory would be to suggest that third-gender roles are much less common in Native American societies for female-born people than for biological males because men have relatively greater social mobility, and also because the route to manhood was much more difficult (and thus more susceptible to failure) than the route to womanhood. In such a society, it is much easier for a boy to fall from grace and become girl-like than it is for a mere girl to achieve the high and precarious status of manhood. Thus, we might expect to find that male berdaches, who are perceived as merely being weak and inadequate, would receive somewhat less hostile treatment than presumptuous and overweening female berdaches.

The mere fact that a social role exists does not make it acceptable. It would be hard to find a small town in America that did not have a "town fairy." Such men certainly have a social and sexual role to play in their communities, and while it may be true that they are hardly ever burned out of their houses, they are hardly figures to be envied for their high status. Even Native American people who are clearly viewed as religious leaders and healers, shamans, receive ambivalent treatment from their own communities. They are both valued for their power and feared as outsiders. Few parents would probably choose to have a child they loved take the difficult path of a shaman. Given this, it seems thickheaded indeed for Williams to blithely assume that all berdaches were beloved by their families and communities.

It is central to Williams' view of Native American societies to see the berdache role as one that was adopted voluntarily. Boys grew up to be berdaches, he believes, because of their feminine preferences in work, attire, and mannerisms, and because they believed they were called to do so by spiritual forces. He states categorically, "The assumption of a berdache role was not forced on the boy by others."[33] He describes Mohave, Yuman, Lakota, and Papago rituals that were reportedly used to determine if a boy child would grow up to be a berdache. These rituals all involve the boy voluntarily choosing to do something associated with female identity.[34]

However, he also describes a practice among Aleut and Kodiak Islanders, who sometimes chose to raise one of their sons, from infancy, as a girl, in order to later sell the child, between the ages of ten and fifteen, to a wealthy man who wanted a boy-wife. And he describes a custom among the Lache Indians of Colombia, South America that allowed a woman who had five sons and no daughters to turn one of them into a girl to share her household chores.[35] It is difficult to see any of this as consensual, but Williams insists, "We should not let these sources imply that berdache status would be imposed on any young boy against his will. ...The more likely pattern with the youngsters is that such boys as are 'chosen' by families to be raised as berdaches would already have evidenced an inclination for nonmasculine behavior."[36] Just how an infant evinces femininity is not explicated.

Williams' position on the gender of the berdache is ambiguous. On the one hand, he is forced to admit at the very least that the berdache was differently-gendered, combining male and female qualities, occupying a social role that was "half-man, half-woman" and "not-man, not-woman."[37] Yet he insists, in an amazing series of arguments, that the berdache were not women, transvestites, hermaphrodites, or transsexuals.

"From American Indian perspectives," he says, "berdaches are not women, not even socially defined women. We can understand this by realizing that berdaches do certain things which women do not do, and vice versa." However, his examples are based on immutable biological differences between berdaches and "real women," not on social definitions of gender among Native Americans. While it may be true, as Williams claims, that berdaches did not care for infants because they could not breast feed, in *The Spirit and the Flesh* he has documented berdaches frequently raising older children. "Berdaches have been noted as being physically different from women," he adds. [38] In other words, they are sometimes tall and muscular. There is little a berdache could do about her height or inability to lactate, but it seems fairly clear from evidence that Williams himself cites that berdaches did everything within their power to reject a male identity and align themselves with other women.

Williams raises the point that some berdaches went hunting or went to war or accompanied hunting or raiding parties without actually hunting or raiding.[39] He claims women never would have done this, but in other places in his text, it appears that unmarried women or prostitutes would accompany hunters or warriors to service them sexually. And it was not unheard of for biological females to sometimes become warriors or hunters, counter to what Williams claims here.

Because one of the ways the berdaches marked their female social status was to wear women's clothing, Williams must demolish the notion that they ought to be viewed as transvestites if he is going to preserve his definition of them as gay men. He acknowledges, "In many of the early sources berdaches are referred to as wearing women's clothes, and much of the anthropological writing refers to them as transvestites." However, he says, "This is not an accurate term to use for several reasons. First, there are instances in which men dressing as women were not berdaches."[40] In other words, a few Midwestern tribes forced men who had been cowardly in battle to wear women's clothes as punishment. However, this is a moot point, since it is not clear that these individuals were seen as berdaches.

Williams goes on to say, "If we define transvestism as dressing in the clothes of the opposite sex, then we find (in cases where the dress is explicitly described) that berdaches wore all women's clothing no more often than they wore a mixture of female and male dress."[41] Modern transvestites often don't wear a complete female outfit. It is the presence of even one item of female clothing that defines someone, despite male morphology, as "unmanly." It would be entirely possible for an anthropologist with a different take on gender to read the same evidence that Williams read and come to a very different conclusion about how completely the berdaches in various tribes were garbed as women. Even he admits, "The degree to which a berdache might dress in female clothing would vary. Some dressed completely as women, all the time." But he goes on to try to qualify this admission: "While whites would most likely notice a berdache when he was dressing in women's clothing, we cannot always trust their judgment that he was dressing just like a woman. There may have been subtle differences that whites would not recognize."[42]

Why is Williams so reluctant to simply own the fact that one of the most important defining qualities of a berdache was her donning of female apparel? His line of reasoning here seems based almost entirely on distaste about transvestism, which he dismisses as an embarrassing sexual kink. As any radical faery can tell you, cross-dressing can have spiritual implications for male-bodied people in our culture as well as in Native American tribal societies. I assume that Williams would come down hard on a straight researcher who insisted on interpreting homosexuality solely through the lens of medical or psychiatric pathology, and protest if it was discussed only as a recently-discovered type of sexual abnormality. Why doesn't he reject a similar definition of and treatment of transvestism and transsexuality?

Williams' argument gets even more tenuous when he moves to the present day. "Modern berdaches emphasize that they dress in a way that is distinct from either sex," he says.[43] But the people Williams are calling "modern berdaches" for the most part define themselves as gay men. It seems reasonable to suspect that they were probably socialized into current gay male norms, which are shameful about drag. They are also living in modern communities, both white and Native American, which often have a negative attitude toward cross-dressing. This reads like an attempt to avoid the stigma of wearing women's clothing, and it may or may not be contiguous with the way berdaches saw their garments prior to European invasion.

Williams is so eager to disassociate the berdache from gender ambiguity that he even disputes the label of "hermaphrodite," despite the fact that among the Navajo, the term *nadle* refers both to people with ambiguous genitalia and physiques, and those who would "pretend to be *nadle*."[44] Once again, the evidence contradicts Williams' position and clearly positions the berdache among the ranks of the differently gendered.

It is when Williams specifically addresses the issue of transsexuality that his bias becomes painfully clear. He singles out Harriet Whitehead for criticism because "the analogy she finds for berdachism in our society is the transsexual, which she defines as a person who assumes 'the behavior and public identity of the opposite sex.' "[45] He argues, "While berdaches certainly do women's work and are nonmasculine in character, their social role is not the same as that of women's. In terms of their physical body, lack of involvement with nursing infants, special roles in warfare, participation in dances, status as Go-Betweens for women and men, variable dress, and ability to abandon berdache status, these males need to be seen as something other than the institutional equivalents of females."[46]

Furthermore, Williams says:

The concept of a "transsexual" is a Western one, clearly linked with a medical procedure and based on the notion that there are two "opposite sexes." It is therefore not an apt description of berdaches. Within Western thought, with its numerous dichotomies of paired opposites, there is little tolerance for ambiguities outside of the categories of "women" and "men." As a result, people who are dissatisfied with their gender role will often feel that they have only one alternative, to *trans*fer themselves from one sex to the other. Many transsexuals, as products of our culture, make this transfer completely, by surgical reassignment and hormones. Many lead happier lives, once they do not feel that they are a "female trapped in a male body." But others do not make so happy an adjustment, and may feel no more comfortable as a woman than as a man. Their unhappiness, I would suggest, is the result of a restricted social value, which sees only two opposite possibilities.[47]

It is valid to ask whether all berdaches were happy, post-transition into that role. And it's also valid to ask how much tolerance Native American societies really had for people who were unable to fit themselves into tribal notions of men and women. The berdache role may have been an improvement over twentieth-century homophobia, but it would not have been suitable for everyone who was discontent with gender roles and limitations or for those who wanted to make romantic and erotic same-sex connections without assuming an opposite-sex or third-gender role.

At its root, Williams' attitude toward transsexuality is every bit as negative and prejudicial as that of Raymond or Katz. "It is worth noting that many transsexuals may pass for women because there is no respected alternative to masculinity in this society. *Bodily mutilation is a heavy price to pay for the ideology of biological determinism*," he says.[48] (Italics are mine.)

There is no section in *The Spirit and the Flesh* demonstrating that berdaches were not homosexual. But if transsexuality is a modern Western category, dependent upon medical diagnosis, is not homosexuality also a modern construct of medicine and psychology? If Williams can recognize that desire could exist between males, for one another, throughout human history, why can't he also validate the yearning that some people feel to live in a gender other than the one they were given at birth, even in societies where medically-assisted sex reassignment is not or was not available?

It is almost embarrassing to note the many aspects of berdache life that Williams describes without seeming to realize that they call his restricted notion of the berdache-as-homosexual-man into question. He makes the generalization that in Native American societies, "Physical biological sex is less important in gender classification than a person's desire—one's spirit."[49] He notes that, "In some cultures the berdache might become a wife to a man."[50] And this is how he describes the way that a biological male among the Hidatsa would become a berdache:

> Hidatsa men…believed that when a man looked at a coil of sweetgrass, the female spirit could "cause his mind to weaken so that he would have no relief until he 'changed his sex.' Often a man would tell of his experiences, how everywhere he looked he would see the coiled sweetgrass and how hard he was trying to keep from changing over." Of those who became berdaches, the other Indians would say that since he had been "claimed by a Holy Woman," nothing could be done about it. Such persons might be pitied because of the spiritual responsibilities they held, but they were treated as mysterious and holy, and were respected as benevolent people who assisted others in time of starvation.[51]

Williams says when an Omaha boy sees Moon Being in his vision quest, he can either grasp the man's bow or the woman's pack strap that she holds. If he grabs the pack strap, "in such a case he could not help acting the woman, speaking, dressing, and working just as Indian women used to do."[52] This female frame of reference for berdache identity is cited by Williams as occurring in many different tribes. "A Hupa berdache recalls, 'I was real feminine as a child, from as early as I can remember. Noticing how I liked to do cooking and cleaning, my grandmother said I would grow up as a woman. Within the family, Indians believe you can be whatever you choose.' "[53] And: "In many Native American languages, female and male styles of speech are distinct, in some cases being practically different dialects. Elsie Clews Parsons saw this at Zuni, where she noticed that a boy was using 'the expressions of a girl, their exclamations and turns of speech.' "[54] Also: "Among the Zapotecs, 'Women especially feel close to and trust nonrelated *ira' muxe*. They are often referred to and addressed as "niña" (little girl) by women and seem to enjoy this form of address.' "[55] A Mohave man told Williams that his *alyha* wives wanted their genitals referred to as a cunnus (clitoris) and became violently angry if male terms were used to describe their genitals.[56]

"Among the pre-contact Araucanians, the Mapuche, and probably other peoples, shaman religious leaders were all berdaches. When the Spanish suppressed this religious institution because of its association with male-male sex, the Indians switched to a totally new pattern. Women became the shamans. So strong was the association of femininity with spiritual power...."[57] And later on, he tells the poignant story of a Kwakiutl chief in British Columbia about 1900. A white authority, the Indian agent, forced this chief's berdache lover to dress in men's clothing and cut off her hair. " 'When I saw him again, he was a man. He was no more my sweetheart.' The change from feminine to masculine pronouns indicates that the forced change of clothing and social role could cause the berdache to lose sexual partners as well as social status. Though this chief did not hesitate to detail his love life with the berdache when she was cross-dressing, he did not feel it appropriate to continue the relationship after she took on a man's role."[58]

It is indisputable that the berdaches had sex with other biological males, and for this reason, it makes sense to discuss at least certain aspects of their lives in terms of gay male paradigms. Williams quite properly points out that not all male-male sexuality took place between berdache and nonberdache. "Yet it is on the berdache that Indian male-male sexuality is mainly focused," he admits. His explanation for this? "Because traditional cultures assume that androgynous males are homosexual, berdaches become the most visible practitioners of that behavior." I would argue that sex between berdaches and men may have been socially acceptable to some degree precisely because it was not seen as homosexual behavior. Williams notes that in most tribes, it is not seen as proper behavior for two berdaches to have sex with each other. He explains this in terms of an incest taboo. [59] "Berdaches, with their sense of sisterhood, are in essence a fictive kin group," he claims.[60] Could this not more easily be explained in terms of a taboo on people who occupy the same gender status having sex with one another (in other words, an attitude that homosexuality is not a good thing)? It is the berdache's womanliness that makes her an acceptable sexual partner for a "normal" man. You can't have two women (berdaches) having sex with each other—that's queer. Williams himself says, "The berdache and his male partner do not occupy the same recognized gender status."[61]

His desire to situate the berdache in a homosexual milieu is so intense that he includes a chapter in the book about gay sex in all-male pirate and cowboy cultures.[62] While his suggestion that homosexual men may have been drawn to pirate culture by rumors of buggery or to the American frontier because of tales about the berdache is fascinating, and I'd like to see it included in more American history textbooks, this chapter really has no connection at all to the berdache. It's an attempt to create "guilt by association."

Williams' claim that modern Native Americans make a connection between gay men and berdaches is belied by his own research. He acknowledges that during his field work he could not find out about berdaches by asking tribal elders about "gays" because (according to him) this term "does not account for the aboriginal ceremonial function of berdaches."[63] How about because tribal elders did not see berdache as gay? A Lakota *winkte* even explains to Williams the difference between gay and *winkte*: "Winktes are very spiritual. When Indians say winkte, they mean a male who is effeminate, like a woman. 'Gay' and winkte are different."[64]

Memories of the berdaches do serve as a useful political tool for gay and lesbian Native Americans who want to reclaim space for themselves in their own families and tribal communities. But it is clear that the two roles, that of the berdache and that of the homosexual, are not seen as identical by either gay or straight Native Americans. Harry Hay is an early gay activist who first sparked academic interest in berdache. Williams says of Hay, "With his liberationist values of publicly expressing relationships with other men, Hay reacted against the secretiveness of Pueblo 'straight men who want a woman-substitute.' Despite his awareness that berdaches were respected for their ceremonial roles, Hay understood why younger gay Indians would want to leave the reservation."[65] Later on, Williams admits, "While both berdachism and gayness involve sex with men, there are dissimilarities. Part of the difference between berdache and gay roles is in terms of gender identity. Some homosexually inclined Indians today, especially those who have been exposed to urban gay communities, may not wish to make a choice between being a berdache or a masculine man. They see themselves as gay, not berdache, and do not want social acceptance if it means they will be treated like a halfman-halfwoman. They want to be treated as men."[66]

Ironically, at the end of his book, Williams decries the emphasis upon machismo in modern gay culture. After World War II, he says, "Drag queens, pedophiles, and youths below eighteen were shunted aside politically and socially as a masculine gay community emerged in a number of American cities. With a focus on bars where masculine adult men mixed among themselves, the older forms of gender variance became distinctly second rate."[67] Williams urges the reader to look beyond our current concepts of homosexuality and think about how radically these ideas might change in the future. "How we see other cultures in the past has much to do with our attitudes toward the future," he says. "If we study only the 'modern homosexual,' what about those growing numbers of people who dislike fitting their sexuality into either/or boxes of gay or straight? Homosexual identity will surely change in the future. The modern Western gay role has not been, nor will be, the only role which sees individuals as distinctly different on the basis of same-sex attraction and androgynous character."[68] It's too bad that Williams' transphobia made it impossible for him to use the transsexual paradigm for understanding our past as well as our future.

Another prominent figure in queer cultural studies, Will Roscoe, has also published work that popularizes the berdache as a gay folk hero, at the expense of acknowledging the transsexual and transvestite elements of this Native American role. In "The Zuni Man-Woman," Roscoe describes a well-known, relatively modern Zuni berdache named We'wha, whose life was originally documented by anthropologist Matilda Coxe Stevenson in the late eighteen-hundreds. It took Stevenson a while to find out that We'wha was actually a genetic male in women's clothing, and even after that discovery, she continued to refer to We'wha as the Zuni did, with female pronouns. We'wha made a trip to Washington, DC, in 1886, during which she was accepted and feted as an "Indian maiden." Six years after shaking President Roosevelt's hand, We'wha spent a month in jail for resisting soldiers who had come to arrest a Zuni leader. She was a prominent figure in her community, revered for her skill at weaving and pottery, respected for her hard work, and feared for her apparently sharp tongue. We'wha also had an important role in community ceremonies and rituals, and was often called upon to offer long prayers because of her excellent memory.

The focus of Roscoe's article is, he says, to "describe how I arrived at my interpretation of the Zuni berdache and why, in particular, I have abandoned the cross-gender model. ...I hope to explain why I refer to the Zuni berdache—or *lhamana*—as a 'traditional gay role.'"[69] Roscoe uses male pronouns to refer to We'wha and other berdaches, and justifies this by quoting Stevenson's Zuni informants, who told her (speaking of We'wha), "She is a man." He says, "I use male pronouns in writing of We'wha to convey in English the same understanding a Zuni had: that We'wha was biologically male."[70] But since the Zuni used female, not male, pronouns to refer to their berdaches, it would seem that Roscoe is *not* following their lead here.

Roscoe points out that Zuni berdaches underwent one of two male initiation rites, and participated in all-male societies, which were responsible for portraying the gods (kachinas) in masked dances. He also notes that We'wha's lists of occupations in an 1881 census included two men's activities (farmer and weaver) and two women's activities (potter and housekeeper). We'wha's spirited resistance to white soldiers is also cited as evidence for "his" masculine identity.

Roscoe says, "As my research proceeded, it became clear that We'wha was not crossing genders, but *bridging* or *combining* the social roles of men and women." He cites examples from We'wha's participation in both male and female aspects of the Zuni community's religious, economic, and kinship roles, and also cites his independent, self-assured behavior to support this hypothesis. He concludes, "In short, although We'wha wore a woman's dress, he didn't 'act the part.'"[71] For Roscoe, this analysis is clinched by the fact that We'wha was buried with a pair of men's trousers drawn up under her dress, and was interred on the men's side of the cemetery. Williams also quotes this fact, but since we are not given any data about the burial practices among other Native American tribes who had third-gender roles, it is far from definitive.

Roscoe's explanation for We'wha's ability to bridge or combine genders is based on a belief that the Zuni saw children as raw people who needed to be cooked (socialized) before they acquired adult traits such as gender. It is not clear if this is a Zuni concept or if Roscoe has been bitten by the post-structuralism bug that gives one a case of the twenty-four-hour Lévi-Strauss flu. Roscoe says, "The Zuni berdache, in Zuni terms, is an 'unfinished' male—not an ersatz female."[72] In Zuni society, it may very well be that women were always seen as less "cooked" than men. It took no less than two initiations for a biologically male Zuni child to become recognized as a man by his people. The fact that Zuni berdaches received only one male initiation is, perhaps, proof that their people viewed them as biological males. However, as partially cooked people, it places them closer to the realm of women (who are perpetually raw) rather than affiliating them with men.

Roscoe believes the spiritual value of We'wha and other Zuni berdaches was based on a myth about the kachina Ko'lhamana, who was captured by a warrior woman in a battle between the Zuni and their gods and an enemy people and their deities. When the victory celebration was held, Ko'lhamana was angry and uncooperative, so the warrior woman put him in a dress and told him, "You will now perhaps be less angry."[73] The costume of the dancer representing Ko'lhamana combined male and female elements. The story of this war was acted out in a ceremony held every four years in We'wha's community. From this myth, Roscoe extrapolates a position for the berdache as a go-between who can resolve conflicts between men and women and remind them of their basis for mutual participation in Zuni society. However, he offers no documentation of the *lhamana* functioning as go-betweens in the real world—for example, by mediating conflicts or by acting as agents during courtship.

Roscoe ends up proposing that we see four distinct genders in Native American societies—men, women, berdaches, and biological females who cross gender boundaries. This would seem to support a discussion of the berdache in relation to our modern concept of transsexuality. But Roscoe will have none of it. He objects to the term *transvestite* on the grounds that it was coined in 1910 by German sexologist Magnus Hirschfeld to "refer to men with an erotic desire to wear female clothing—an act usually performed in private by men who, in daily life, fulfilled normal roles. ...Given this definition, we can see that We'wha's perfunctory cross-dressing does not qualify."[74] The fact is, Stevenson never asked We'wha if cross-dressing was erotic for her. Certainly it seems reasonable to suppose that her female clothing was erotic for the men who slept with her. And to call We'wha's cross-dressing "perfunctory" is a gross misstatement of the rules under which We'wha lived, which required female clothing as a public affirmation of the *lhamana* identity.

"Was We'wha a transsexual?" Roscoe asks. "This is an even newer category, introduced in 1948 to refer to individuals who wish to change gender permanently. But if this were the motivation in We'wha's case, why didn't he attempt to act and look more feminine?"[75] The more appropriate question seems to be, exactly what would We'wha have had to do to get Roscoe to recognize her femininity? She could hardly help being tall and physically strong. She used female pronouns to describe herself, wore women's clothing, and arranged her hair like the other women in her tribe. She was content to be treated as a woman when she traveled and met prominent white people. If We'wha had been offered hormones or surgery, it is not at all clear that she would have declined.

With very little factual justification, Roscoe claims that the behavior of nonberdache men who slept with berdaches "was not pseudo-heterosexual, in the sense that berdaches were substitute women, because, as I've shown, the Zunis did not deny the biological gender of the berdaches."[76] Yet his own research has shown that in Zuni society, the biological sex of a male child was not necessarily connected to adult manhood. The Zuni may have recognized We'wha and other berdaches as "not men, not women," but it was precisely the fact that they were more like women than men which made it permissible for otherwise "normal" men to have sex with them.

Even Roscoe has to acknowledge that We'wha cannot properly be called "homosexual," because "there are simply no Zuni equivalents for our single-dimensional categories of homosexual and heterosexual."[77] In other words, Zuni society did not set the berdaches apart from community life, and they were not seen simply in terms of their sexual differences. What Roscoe does not say is that the berdaches were possibly accepted because they were seen as an acceptable variation on heterosexuality, and certainly no threat to it. If the berdaches were perceived as men, it is quite possible that other Zunis would have been scandalized by them seeking sexual pleasure from nonberdache males.

After this convoluted mess of poor reasoning, Roscoe happily settles on the term *gay* as "the closest equivalent in English" to *lhamana* or berdache. But he has to admit, "Some of the individuals who once filled this role might today identify themselves as transsexuals, bisexuals, or transvestites—as well as homosexuals. However, even if the Zunis had had such a thing as transsexual surgery, they still would have had a berdache role, because the social, economic, and religious contributions of berdaches were unique, different from those of either men or women."[78] This is speculative at best. I don't think it takes a great deal of imagination to see a post-operative Native American transsexual performing quite effectively as a berdache.

That's as far as Roscoe is able to go toward including the paradigms of transsexuality and transvestism as useful metaphors that might help white Westerners to understand the berdache role. More important to him is this: "A second reason for my use of gay is the evidence I've found of continuity between traditional berdache roles and contemporary gay American Indians. ...At this juncture, Indian men who might have become berdaches begin to look and act like gay men in today's terms."[79] However, one piece of evidence that Roscoe cites to support this claim seems very dubious. He says that today on the Zuni reservation, Zunis themselves do not use the word *lhamana*. They use the term *lhalha*, which means "homosexual." Does this not instead indicate that Zunis made a distinction between homosexuality and berdachism, since they have different words for each activity? If Zunis saw gay men as berdaches, would they not use the same term for both?

Roscoe makes much of the fact that today, it is more common for homosexual Native Americans to call themselves "gay" than it is for them to use the traditional terms for berdaches. However, once again, this would seem to indicate that the two social statuses are not seen as equivalent or synonymous. If the distinction between the berdache and gayness has been blurred among Native American gay men and lesbians today, Roscoe is partially responsible. He was the coordinating editor for *Living the Spirit: A Gay American Indian Anthology*. And this book repeatedly uses the berdache as an ancestral figure for gay and lesbian Native Americans today, despite such anecdotes as a description of Mohave *alyha* feigning pregnancy, a commonly-performed, months-long charade that included a fake birth and public mourning for the fictive dead child.[80]

Roscoe and others have apparently decided that young gay men and lesbians who are also Native American need the vision of the berdache to reconnect them with their own people, their own spiritual traditions and history, and give them a sense of pride. In a plea to end Native American homophobia, Williams says, "Rather than becoming secretive and defensive about their cultural past, Indian people need to consider the anguish that their defensiveness causes for young people who are struggling to understand themselves in a racist and homophobic society. By redeveloping and adapting the old traditions like those of the berdache, Indian people today can be committed to the preservation of their heritage and the establishment of a new sense of pride."[81] This is very moving, but I wonder about the young Native Americans who are transgendered or who are cross-dressers. Don't they also need a role model and a sense of their own history?

Criticism of this branch of gay scholarship has been scant. Ramón A. Gutiérrez is one of a handful of gay male academics who has objected to the appropriation of the berdache as a gay folk hero. But Gutiérrez does not object to Roscoe's assertion that the berdaches were gay rather than transgendered. Gutiérrez instead objects to what he sees as a romanticization of the berdache and Zuni culture in general, and objects to the use of the berdache as a role model on the grounds that berdaches were actually captives taken in battle who were forced to impersonate women and provide sexual service in order to humiliate them.

"Berdache status," according to Gutiérrez, is "that social arrangement whereby a man or group of men press another male into impersonating a female, forcing him to perform work generally associated with women, offering passive sexual service to men, and donning women's clothes."[82] He says, "Berdache status was one principally ascribed to defeated enemies. Among the insults and humiliations inflicted on prisoners of war were homosexual rape, castration, the wearing of women's clothes, and performing women's work."[83]

Rather than lauding the berdache as a spiritual leader, Gutiérrez sees her role in ritual as a demeaning one. "Berdaches were reported as being under male ownership. They were frequently found in male social spaces performing activities associated with females during male rituals: fellating powerful men or being anally mounted by them." This, according to Gutiérrez, was the origin of berdaches' status as "temple experts or as shamans who fulfilled magical and cosmological functions."[84]

Gutiérrez does not think a lot of Roscoe's positive reading of the berdache as a go-between for men and women, someone who was socially valued for resolving conflicts and binding a gender-polarized community together, and preventing gender polarization from going too far. Instead, he believes the berdache prevented conflict in the sex-segregated society of the Zunis by providing unmarried men with sexual service. Berdaches were not admitted to sacred male space because they were recognized as men; they were there to ease sexual tension and prevent young men from competing with older men for the erotic attentions of women. "So long as bachelors were having sex with the berdaches, their village was not beset with conflicts between men over women," Gutiérrez says.[85]

Williams' and Roscoe's descriptions of berdache roles in Native American societies are based on an assumption that these societies were, for the most part, peaceful and egalitarian. Gutiérrez has no patience with this, and paints a picture of Zuni society, before European interference, as warlike and aggressive. He also sees relations between men and women as essentially hostile. "From men's perspective," he says, "women's capacity to produce, indeed to overproduce, was the problem that threatened to destroy the balance that existed in the cosmos between femininity and masculinity. Only by isolating themselves in ritual and placating the gods would men keep potent femininity from destroying everything. Women constantly sapped men of their energy.... Men got nothing in return from women in this agricultural society, for even if women bore children, until puberty those children belong to their mothers."[86]

But, according to Gutiérrez, a bold warrior could win some compensation for himself in this unequal world. He could obtain a few berdache captives to become his sexual slaves. Gutiérrez paints a grim picture of "these effeminates," claiming "they lost their social standing and family and were at the whim of any man who cared to use them."[87]

Gutiérrez supplies an interesting detail that is missing from Roscoe's description of the dance of thanksgiving in which the berdache kachina appears. Not only does this deity appear in female clothing, Gutiérrez says he also "had blood smeared between his thighs." Gutiérrez does not read this as menstrual blood, since menstruating women had the power to pollute male ritual, and even a surrogate bleeding woman would not have been allowed to be present. He says, "The blood might be explained more adequately as coming from a torn anus due to homosexual rape or castration."[88]

While Gutiérrez cannot make a case for We'wha herself being a captive who was forced to assume berdache status after being taken in battle, he does see her as a stigmatized figure in Zuni society. It is his belief that Zuni families were ashamed to have a *lhamana* among their members, and that such people were frequently ridiculed by other members of the tribe. He points out that "Pueblo Indians are well known for their aloofness toward outsiders, their general unwillingness to talk, and the secrecy with which they guard their esoteric knowledge and religion, even from their own young." He hypothesizes that We'wha was so eager to talk to American anthropologists in the 1890s because berdaches were "...marginalized and low status individuals in the male political world... quite eager to tell their story to anyone willing to listen."[89]

Rather than seeing We'wha's willingness to travel or her initiative in starting a laundry business as proof of a male gender identity, Gutiérrez sees it as evidence for We'wha's discomfort within Zuni society. As a misfit, We'wha was eager to travel among whites who made her feel much more important than her own people ever would. And she was happy to find friendship and make money from whites because these were ways to bolster her self-esteem in a hostile social climate.

such Gutiérrez concludes, "As for gays who seek a less rigid gender hierarchy in which to grow and prosper, the berdache status as a gender representation of power in war is probably not the place to find it. By finding gay models where they do not exist, let us not perpetrate on We'wha…yet another level of humiliation with our pens. For then, the 'conspiracy of silence' about the berdaches which Harry Hay had hoped to shatter will only be shrouded once again in romantic obfuscations."[90]

While Williams' view of Native American societies as idyllic communities full of sexual equality and tolerance seems saccharine, Gutiérrez's view seems harsh. One of the problems with all of the gay male academic writing about Native American culture is the tendency to indulge in sweeping generalizations. Third-gender roles among the Zuni were not identical to, although they may have resembled roles for, deviant people in other Native American tribes. The historical record is frustratingly inadequate to the task of answering our most important questions about who the berdaches were, how they were perceived by their contemporaries, and how they lived their lives. But skimpy though that record is, it does not support Gutiérrez's characterization of all berdaches as war captives. There were more ways to become a berdache than family coercion or outright violence. It seems indisputable that certain individuals became berdaches simply because they believed it was their spiritual calling, or as a way to express what they saw as their innately feminine natures.

Given the spate of published material about berdaches, the comparative silence that exists in gay male academia about the hijra of India is odd, unless you take into account the fact that to be seen as an authentic hijra, the individual must submit to castration. (In fact, we do not know if the berdaches in some tribes practiced a form of genital modification as a token of their serious intent to assume this role. The bloody thighs of Ko'lhamana have more than one possible interpretation.) Williams mentions the hijra briefly, but only to quote the work of one anthropologist who perceives them as suggesting the characteristics of both sexes rather than as biological males who tried to pass as female.[91] Katz, Williams, and Roscoe would probably rather not try to argue that castrated biological males are gay role models, even though the hijra have a somewhat acceptable role in Indian society as singers at weddings and christenings.

In fact, Williams does not acknowledge the rite of castration at all, and says instead, "Androgynous males, usually incorrectly labeled by English writers as eunuchs, were often associated with same-sex desire."[92] If the berdaches are gay, the hijra certainly are. They are biological males who cross-dress as women and often have sex with other males. Other gay male writers such as Arthur Evans[93] and Randy P. Conner[94] have been less cautious in claiming the hijra and the gallae, transsexual priestesses who served the goddess Cybele, as ancestral figures and spiritual role models for gay men today. In a stinging rebuke for this "cultural piracy," transsexual scholar Margaret Deirdre O'Hartigan comments, "Gay men who usurp our societal recognition illustrate a willingness on their part to trade our survival for their own, our acceptance for theirs and claim our history as theirs. If they are so desirous of the history of the Gallae and of transsexuals there is an easy enough remedy: let them resort to the potsherd, the blade or the surgeon's knife, and join us."[95] Since we can no longer study third-gender roles in pre-invasion Native American cultures, the next-best thing is to examine similar social niches that are still extant. These include the hijra of India, the acault of Myanmar (better known as Burma in the West), and the Samoan fa'afafine.

Work by at least one anthropologist has produced an account of an "origin myth" for the hijra, which contradicts a view of them as gay men with no element of transsexuality.[96] The hijra worship their own variant of the Mother Goddess, Bahuchara Mata, and bless babies and married couples in her name. Bahuchara is connected to acts of self-mutilation and sexual abstinence via a myth in which she cuts off her own breast and offers it to a gang of thieves who had threatened to rape her. There is another myth that she will appear to impotent men in their dreams and demand that they emasculate themselves, don female apparel, and become her devotees. (According to Indian mythos, men who have sex with other men become impotent.)

But in the most popular hijra myth, Bahuchara Mata was wedded to a young prince who refused to consummate their marriage. After several months of frustration, the Mata follows him into the forest and discovers him "acting like a hijra," i.e., having sex with other men. To punish him, she cuts off his genitals and transforms him into a hijra.[97] Nanda posits that the loss of the penis transforms the hijra from an impotent man into a new person who is the vehicle of the Mata's power.[98] Post-surgically, hijra are treated both as women who have given birth and as brides.[99]

It would seem that at least one role the hijra play is to provide a socially-sanctioned slot where biological males can be sent to *prevent* them from indulging in homosexuality. Hijra norms dictate that they be celibate, but in fact many of them support themselves by prostitution and even acquire husbands. This sexual conduct between hijra and men is somewhat tolerated in part because it is no longer defined as homosexuality. No wonder gay male academics do not want to draw parallels between the berdaches and the hijra!

The approach taken by Eli Coleman and his associates in a report on the acault of Myanmar (Burma) should be briefly mentioned here as a potentially powerful model for further research on third-gender roles in non-Western cultures. The acault are biological males who cross-dress as women. They are thought to be under the patronage of an animistic spirit or nat called Manguedon who bestows fortune and success. She also intercedes in the lives of some Burmese, whose cross-gender tendencies are powerful evidence of her possession. The acault are considered to be married to Manguedon and seen as taking on "the characteristics of the female spirit."[100] The acault are invited to perform ceremonies that will give the good fortune that is in the keeping of Manguedon, and they also celebrate a three-day festival, which is widely attended, in which the acault perform ceremonial dancing in honor of Manguedon.

The authors observe that "Burmese men may partake in sexual relations with the acault without stigmatization of homosexuality because of the connotation of a connection to Manguedon as well as not seeing the acault as male. In Burmese culture, the thought of a male having sex with another male is socially and morally repugnant. In fact, sex between males is illegal in Burmese society. Having sex with an acault, however, is not viewed as homosexual behavior." Like the husbands of some berdaches described by Williams, the Burmese partners of acaults are "somewhat frowned upon" for being lazy, not for their sexuality. The accusation of laziness springs from the expectation that the accault, like the berdache, will financially provide for her husband or lover. When they asked about acault having sex with one another, the authors' Burmese guides were "totally perplexed, as it apparently suggested lesbianism, an even more foreign concept than male homosexuality."[101]

These researchers suggest that the social category of the acault encompasses aspects of the identities we think of as transsexual, transvestite, and homosexual. They interviewed three acault, some of whom they refer to with female pronouns, and some of whom they use male pronouns to describe. One acault named Toto had lived completely as a woman for five years. She had little or no interest in her own genitalia, preferring to focus on providing oral satisfaction for her partner. She had no knowledge of sex reassignment, but took birth control pills, hoping they would increase breast development and feminization. "When asked about the possibility of surgically changing her body, she became excited about the prospect because she thought it would further her goals of getting married and settling down with one man," they report.[102] A second acault, Maaye, was perceived by the researchers as having a male gender identity because, in their opinion, "his desire to be like a female was restricted to his social sex role." However, their only evidence for this supposed male gender identity is the fact that Maaye reportedly liked "his" penis and enjoyed orgasms. "He" cross-dressed as a woman and supported "his" long-term lover by working as a prostitute. The researchers felt that a third acault, Kothan, also had a male gender identity since he wore his longyi in "typical male style," and engaged in cross-gender behavior only during ceremonies celebrating Manguedon. However, Kothan was reluctant to discuss his sexual behavior with the Westerners, leaving our picture of him incomplete.

If acault were transplanted to a Western context, it seems reasonable to assume that some of them would define themselves as transsexual, some as transvestites, and some as homosexual or bisexual. The authors of this article say:

> It was interesting to see a variety of behavior that we, in the West, would categorize as gender identity disorders, fetishistic behavior, and/or homosexual activity. This cross-cultural observation lends support to the universality of some of these behaviors in mankind, but recognizes that these behaviors become locally interpreted in their own sociocultural and religious context. The Burmese appear to lump male-to-female transsexualism, transvestism, and male homosexuality together in the construct of the acault. It is possible that physical acts do not have as much importance as in Western society. In Burma, greater importance is placed on spiritual or mental phenomena. …Unlike in the Christian tradition, the individual acault bears no personal moral responsibility for being sexually different.[103]

By giving weight to each facet of this third-gender role and also including the spiritual and social significance it bears in its own context, these researchers have created a model that deserves a lot more imitation than it is sure to get within gay academia.

A case study of one Samoan fa'afafine further supports my contention that we cannot understand third-gender roles without making use of the paradigm of transsexuality. According to author Kris Poasa, the word *fa'afafine* means "the way of a woman." The author has interviewed fourteen fa'afafines and states, "Transsexuals appear to make up a large portion of this population, although it has not been established that *fa'afafines* are exclusively transsexual."[104] Poasa believes that the category of fa'afafine "is used as a catch-all for a number of different sexual or gender-mixing behaviors,"[105] including "transsexuals, gynemimetics, and effeminate homosexuals."[106]

Tina, the individual this article is based on, appears to have used the traditional category of fa'afafine as a springboard to the sort of sex reassignment that is available in industrialized Western nations. The people around her may think of her as a third-gender person, as a fa'afafine, but she thinks of herself as a woman.[107] While third-gender identities may serve as roles that can be adopted by people we might label as transsexuals, hermaphrodites, and effeminate homosexuals, I believe that if hormones and surgery were made available to third-gender people in traditional societies, the great majority of them would opt for sex change. And I doubt that even Williams, Roscoe, and Katz could disagree, in all good faith, with that hypothesis.

Gay male and lesbian academics have been equally reluctant to explore the transsexual or transvestite implications for histories of female-born people who depart radically from the feminine social sex-role. Katz presents some fascinating documents about Native American people born female who took on male attire, male roles in hunting or warfare, and married women. But it is in chapter three, "Passing Women 1782-1920," that Katz's bias against including transsexuality in his analytical toolkit shows itself most clearly. The sentiments about transsexuality expressed in this chapter have clearly influenced the entire book, especially the material on berdache.

Katz's definition of a "passing woman" is contradictory. He is eager to claim biological females who lived, as much as possible, as men, for the ranks of lesbian feminism.

> The women whose lives are documented here worked and dressed and lived in what were customarily the occupations and styles of males. Most actually passed as men; the evidence suggests they were also attracted to and had sexual and emotional relations with other women. They both passed as men and passed beyond the restricted traditional roles of women.

...Despite their masculine masquerade, the females considered here can be understood not as imitation men, but as real women, women who refused to accept the traditional, socially assigned fate of their sex, women whose particular revolt took the form of passing as men. ...These passing women can only be understood within the framework of a feminist analysis.[108]

Katz apparently cannot see masculinity as a quality that a female-bodied person might naturally possess, as an aspect of a male gender identity, instead of a "masquerade." Despite his attempt to glorify passing women as proto-feminist heroes, Katz apparently had to conquer some distaste in order to research and write about them. In an astonishing series of paragraphs, he fusses:

> The contradiction between their female gender and "masculine" pose often condemned them to a sense of false identity.
>
> In personal terms, this inauthenticity might mean a life of fantasy, mental confusion and loss of reality possibly leading to madness. Their passing implied an inability to totally accept their own feelings and aspirations as those of women, which their physiological configuration always necessarily reminded them they were. In their hearts and consciences these women knew they were, at least in part, imitations, fakes, frauds. They knew their activity, especially any sexual activity with other women, was, if not legally, then morally condemned. Posing as men might not always help them personally overcome this negative social evaluation and the guilt it could evoke. Appearing to the world as men, they could not but sometimes appear to themselves as immoral impostors.[109]

This is a rather melodramatic projection upon the internal life of the people Katz sees as passing women, people I would rather refer to as transgendered men. The fear of being exposed by hostile doctors, policemen, or others certainly had to engender a good deal of stress for female-bodied people who tried to live in their male gender identity without the benefit of hormones or surgery to help them to pass. But the notion that they would be tormented by a sense of themselves as "immoral impostors" is a long reach. If you feel yourself to be male, living as a man is not a masquerade; it is simply what you must do to get on with the rest of your life. The reference to the "physiological configuration," which Katz believes "always necessarily reminded them they were" women, is a pretty big hint as to why Katz does not see at least some of these people as transgendered men. The presence or absence of a penis is, to Katz as much as it is to John Money, the arbiter of manhood. By holding these people's masculinity hostage in a pair of condescending quotation marks, Katz sadly places himself on the side of the people who jeer when such a "masquerade" is forcibly terminated.

Katz will not even permit the reader to think of "passing women" as "lesbian transvestites." He says this categorization "tends to narrow understanding rather than expand it," but never convincingly shows us why.[110] It is difficult to avoid the conclusion that Katz, like many other students of sexuality, is simply assuming that women cannot be transvestites. Katz argues that we must consider the fact that these women engaged in "cross-work" and "cross-speaking" as being even more important than their "cross-dressing," but does not take the next logical leap, which is to see them, not as women, but as transgendered men.

It is true that many of the cases Katz cites describe women who cross-dressed during only one phase of their lives. But he also presents information on people like Joseph Labdell, who in the eighteen-eighties quite clearly proclaimed a lifelong male gender identity. Like the doctors who eventually gained custody of Labdell and "treated" him for lesbianism and psychosis, Katz refers to him as "she" and "Lucy Ann Labdell," thus denying this man the dignity of choosing his own name and his own identity.[111] He chooses to interpret Labdell's statements about the maleness of his genitals and sexual response as "arising from a desire to justify and explain her Lesbian sexual relations."[112]

Katz consistently refers to the male-identified people in this chapter by their female given names. He discusses the 1908 case of Johann Bürger under the name "Anna Mattersteig." Bürger was working as a typesetter in St. Louis when his life was disrupted by the charge of abducting a woman. (This charge was probably based on a failed seduction or perhaps traveling with his wife across state lines rather than an actual kidnapping.) He was living with his common-law wife, Martha Gammater, when scandal broke. Faced with public exposure of her husband's biological sex, Gammater denied all knowledge of this matter and took refuge in a mental breakdown and an asylum. Bürger told the authorities that he was not attempting to defraud anyone; he felt "wholly like a man" and "would suffer any penalty" rather than wear women's clothes.[113]

A more clear-cut description of female-to-male transsexuality would be difficult to concoct. Even Katz has to acknowledge that "Mattersteig may have actually thought herself to be of the male gender, what today is commonly labeled a transsexual identification."[114]

But he goes on to say:

> The term *transsexual*, however, is so loaded with traditional
> assumptions connecting gender and "masculinity" and "femi-
> ninity" as to render it of the most controversial and doubtful
> character. The solution to the problem of confused gender can
> be of the gravest practical import to those who, seeking help, fall
> into the hands of those doctors claiming to be "experts" on the
> subject, and offering only surgical (or technological) treatment.
> Here, it must suffice to say that to label Anna Mattersteig trans-
> sexual does nothing to explain the complex interrelations
> between her presumable sexual activity with another woman,
> her male identification, and her cross-dressing and passing.[115]

I think it suffices to say that labeling Johann Bürger as a transgendered man does a lot more to explain his sexual activity with his wife,
his male identification, and the way he dressed, than the convoluted
rationalizations one must construct in order to define him as a lesbian.
Katz's position on transsexuality and sex-reassignment surgery is not
that far from Janice Raymond's, although he thankfully lacks her shrill
quality. Like her, he is saying that it is not possible for the individual to
change his or her gender. He views the concept of transsexuality as a
dangerous one, arising from homophobia, and sees transsexuals as
troubled people who have yet to come to grips with their homosexuality. As Raymond does, Katz views transgendered men as women who
are lost to lesbian feminism. He also seems to be implying that sex-
reassignment surgery is dangerous. Like Raymond, he views transsexuals as the product of modern technology, rather than seeing the
technology of sex reassignment as something that arose in response to
the needs of gender dysphoric people.

Katz's hostility toward transsexuality and doctors who are sympathetic to an individual who wants sex reassignment reaches its peak in
his description of the 1918-1920 case of "Alberta Lucile Hart," as
described by Portland, Oregon psychiatrist J. Allen Gilbert. Gilbert
refers to his patient as "H"; Katz's research ferreted out the birth name
of this anonymous case-history subject. This account occupies pages
258 through 279 in the book, by far the longest description of any other
"passing woman."

Gilbert seems to have been an unusually open-minded and compassionate person. He initially saw "H" for treatment of a phobia. But it
became clear that some sort of "sex problem" was also troubling his
patient. Eventually, "H" trusted Gilbert enough to reveal a history of

cross-dressing as a man, identification as a man, and affairs with women. At first, Gilbert attempted to cure "H" with hypnosis, free association, and psychotherapy. "With apologies for the treason to the underlying principles of psychotherapy," he says, this treatment was "a failure."[116]

He says of his patient, "After long consideration, she came to the office with her mind made up to adopt male attire in conformity with her true nature and try to face life under conditions that might make life bearable. Suicide had been repeatedly considered as an avenue of escape from her dilemma."[117] Rather than allow his patient to self-destruct, Gilbert took the extraordinary (for his time) step of deciding to support "H" in his desire to live as a man. This support included obtaining a hysterectomy for "H," which was rationalized in part as a desire to be sterilized (to avoid transmitting sexual abnormality to any offspring), but which also would have had the effect of eliminating the telltale menstrual cycle and greatly reducing the female hormones circulating in "H's" body, thus facilitating his ability to live in his gender of preference.

"Hysterectomy was performed, her hair was cut, a complete male outfit was secured and having previously identified herself with the red cross, she made her exit as a female and started as a male with a new hold on life and ambitions worthy of her high degree of intellectuality."[118] Eventually, Gilbert reports:

> She is now married to a normal woman of high degree of mentality and decided physical attractions. All parties to the deal were fully cognizant of all the facts involved before entering into the contract and they now have a home apparently happy and peaceful based upon psychological attractions with such ministration to the physical as existing conditions can render possible.
>
> She is now practicing her profession in a neighboring state in male garb, making good as a man and known only as a man. *In fact, from a sociological and psychological standpoint she is a man.*
>
> If society will but let her alone, she will fill her niche in the world and leave it better for her bravery in meeting the issue on the merits of the case as best she knew. Instead of criticism and hounding, she needs and deserves the respect and sympathy of society, which is responsible for her existence as she is.[119] [Italics are mine.]

While Gilbert never takes the leap of referring to "H" with male pronouns, he displays a great deal more common sense and empathy with his patient than Katz does in his commentary upon the case. Katz fumes about the "confusion of Dr. Gilbert and 'H' herself about her sexual nature," and declares, " 'H' is clearly a Lesbian, a woman-loving woman." He derides "H's" marriage as "two women, one of whom has had a hysterectomy and passes for a male—two women living and loving together, two Lesbians."[120] He also makes the outrageous comment that "H" "does not identify herself as of the male gender," and claims that "H" covets "the male's socially given power," not "the male's penis."[121] This assertion seems based more on Katz's aversion to transsexuality than it is on any special insight into "H's" self-image. I personally can't imagine "H" declining the opportunity for surgical and hormonal treatment that would bring his body into conformity with his identity. It is my belief that if "H" did not express a desire for a penis or other physical changes that would make him appear more masculine, it is only because in 1920, such things were not possible.

Instead of lauding Gilbert as an advanced and thoughtful mental-health professional, Katz castigates him for ostensibly creating so much shame in "H" that "she" requested a hysterectomy as punishment for "her" lesbianism. He says, " 'H' could only perceive her own situation in the world in heterosexual terms, according to the traditional heterosexual model of male-female husband-wife relations. She found no alternative, no way of transcending this socially dominant model."[122]

The argument that lesbians at the turn of the century chose to live as men because that was the only way they could form partnerships with other women is dubious. Katz is assuming that women in the early nineteen-hundreds were completely ignorant of any alternative to heterosexuality. His own work, which shows at least some level of public awareness of lesbianism and male homosexuality at every stage of American history, casts doubt upon that belief. Other gay historians, such as Caroll Smith-Rosenberg, have documented what appear to be lesbian relationships at the turn of the century between women who were quite clear about their female identities.

Some "passing women," if they were alive today, might very well identify as butch lesbians rather than as men. But to classify all male-identified, female-bodied people who lived as men as self-hating lesbians is simplistic. It is Katz's horror of sex-reassignment surgery, and his denial of the reality of gender dysphoria as a separate experience from "coming out" anxiety, that make him impose such a skewed interpretation upon his own data. *Gay American History* is unfortunately tainted with a heavy dose of transphobia.

It does not further our understanding of human sexuality to press for recognition of homosexuality throughout history at the expense of recognizing other sexual minorities. The history of their oppression is as valid as our own, and if gay male and lesbian scholars deny that history, we are as guilty of censorship and prejudice as any straight anthropologist who chooses not to report homosexual activity when he writes up an ethnography.

Unfortunately, since Katz's work has appeared in print, other gay and lesbian historians have also promoted the myth that all "passing women" are lesbian elders. In 1979, the San Francisco Lesbian and Gay History Project (SFLGHP) began displaying a slide show about passing women entitled "She Even Chewed Tobacco." This slide show was actually created by Alan Berube, and appropriated by some of the women in the SFLGHP who did not feel that it was appropriate for a man to appear as a spokesman for research on lesbian history. Thereafter, it was exhibited with almost no revision, and scant credit to Berube.

Among the figures touted in "She Even Chewed Tobacco" as a prototypical butch dyke was Babe Bean, also known as Jack Bee Garland, whose biography would later be compiled by early FTM activist Louis Sullivan.[123] The lesbian appropriation of Babe Bean has also been noted by Rubin[124] and transgendered scholar C. Jacob Hale.[125] Sullivan, who was a gay man, saw Garland as one of his predecessors. This seems quite reasonable when we read that Garland cross-dressed in part so that he could enjoy the society of other men. Here's what Garland had to say about the women who tried to get his attention: "Well, I have had so many who have asked to call that I have had to form the resolution of receiving no one in petticoats. Somehow, we never were very good friends. Their little deceits, and, I am sorry to say, petty jealousies, always had the effect of making boys my chums."[126] Garland did not support women's suffrage. Upon his arrest in Manila for wearing men's clothes, he was described in a local newspaper as "an effeminate youth, a sort of a 'willy boy,' " who pursued "a queer mode of life."[127] These facts make an interpretation of Garland as a "woman-identified woman" seem rather strained.

The task of sorting out the dykes from the transgendered men, or at least the task of recognizing that both tendencies are present in the histories of "passing women," still remains to be done. An excellent theoretical underpinning for that effort appears in Rubin's cogent essay, "Of Catamites and Kings." Rubin notes the long history during which gay men, lesbians, and transgendered people have shared social space, and delineates "the overlap and kinship between some areas of lesbian and transsexual experience."[128] She calls for an end to the antagonistic "them or us" mentality that has in the past expelled transgendered people from the lesbian community. "Instead of another destructive round of border patrols, surveillance, and expulsion, I would suggest a different strategy. Lesbians should instead relax, wait, and support the individuals involved as they sort out their own identities and decide where they fit socially."[129] She wisely points out, "Lesbian communities and individuals have suffered enough from the assumption that we should all be the same, or that every difference must be justified by a claim of political or moral superiority."[130]

She also notes that the issue of inclusion or exclusion of transgendered people is not limited to the lesbian community. "It is interesting to speculate about how gay men will deal with FTMs who are gay male identified," she says. "Traditionally, gay male communities have dealt relatively well with male-to-female transvestites and transsexuals, while lesbian communities have not. But gay men are now faced with women becoming men, who may or may not have male genitals whose origins are undetectable. I hope gay men will meet the challenge of accepting gay FTMs with balance and good grace."[131]

Well, it's always nice to have hope. But the dialogue about gay FTMs has not even properly begun in the gay men's community. In stark contrast to the many references to FTMs in lesbian political discourse and pornography, I've been able to locate only one reference to FTMs in gay-male literature by biological males, a sexy short story entitled "Bobby's Secret" by Michael Taylor.[132] I attended a May 1995 performance of David Harrison's play *FTM*. After describing how vulnerable he felt when he started answering personal ads placed by gay men, Harrison asked the audience, "Does the penis make the man?" And I swore I could see every gay man in the audience just barely nodding to himself.

Living in an era of safer sex in which dildos or rubber-covered cocks are prescribed seems to have had no effect on the phallocentrism of gay men, and indeed may have reinforced it. FTMs are, like gay men practicing safer sex, quite capable of wielding gloved hands and rubber cocks or offering up their buttholes. But in the gay male sexual culture of the epidemic, the emblems that enable one to have safer sex are most easily eroticized if they are closely associated with genetic males who are able to at least visually display an erect phallus of flesh. These libidinal ties are not easily weakened. Ideologically, gay men in the second decade of the AIDS pandemic continue to cling to a sign that is forbidden to them, both by homophobia and by injunctions against ingesting cum. The thing you desire and yet cannot fully possess without danger easily becomes an obsession. FTMs may be resented by gay men precisely because, on an unconscious level at least, they represent yet another instance in which ejaculation and hard dicks will be withheld from them. While I would like to see gay men embracing and welcoming their transgendered brothers, it is also hard to criticize gay men for insisting upon their right to love and pursue cock.

Of course, gay male misogyny and fear of women's genitals also play an important role in that community's attitude toward the growing number of transsexual men who identify as bisexual or gay. Vulvaphobia is by no means universal among homosexual men, but it is a powerful enough factor to deserve some analysis here. Perhaps because of all the social pressure they experience in adolescence to initiate sexual encounters with girls, many gay men seem to harbor a surprising amount of hatred and resentment toward women. This variety of male homosexuality is rarely labeled gay male separatism, but that is what it amounts to. Thus, we have a certain segment of the gay male community that views its erotic activities as a sort of boys' club, from which it is important to exclude women, who are assumed to be inferior and unattractive. One of the artifacts of gay male separatism is the variety of man-to-man porn that features weird misogynist asides, as if deriding women's bodies were a form of foreplay.

For the gay male separatist, the masculine secondary sexual characteristics of his partner are important not only because they signal unequivocally that he is male, but also because the presence of these characteristics is assumed to blot out, preempt, and otherwise insure the absence of feminine physicality. FTMs have little hope of being accepted by men whose enjoyment of another man's body depends on this dynamic.

Fortunately, there are also gay men who are able to read an FTM's body as male and attractive if certain signifiers, which vary with the individual, are present. These could include baldness, a furry chest, a stout or muscular physique, a boyish appearance, etcetera. Among some gay men in San Francisco, where a comparatively large community of queer FTMs is being established, a fetish for FTMs is being developed. A sexual encounter with a transsexual man has become a badge of erotic courage, outrageousness, and novelty in some quarters. A gay man who views himself as a sexual outlaw or an explorer of the wild frontiers of pleasure is more likely to view a transsexual man's body as a fascinating opportunity to experience something new, rather than a relapse into heterosexuality.

Doctors, therapists, feminist theorists, and gay historians all have their own axes to grind about transsexuality. They are incapable of seeing the world through transgendered eyes or passing on the information that transgendered people need to affirm their own worth and create a place for themselves in our society. Transgendered people are faced with the necessity of uncovering and writing their own history. Unfortunately, the first stage in this task would seem to be the correction or recapitulation of conceptual errors that have been made by lesbian and gay academics whose bias is toward casting as wide a net as possible to obtain evidence of same-sex love throughout human history. Because the validity of gender dysphoria remains controversial, and transsexual experience is seen as something rare, freakish, artificial, and incomprehensible, transsexual autobiography continues to be an invaluable vehicle for education and outreach. Such work both normalizes sex reassignment for people who are not transgendered, and informs people who are unhappy with their biological sex that they have alternatives to misery and self-destruction. Transsexual autobiography has changed a great deal since Christine Jorgensen penned her ladylike and wistful confessional tale. These shifts in the discourse will be addressed in the next chapter.

Notes

1. The Kinsey scale was developed in the nineteen-fifties by Alfred Kinsey and a team of sex researchers to describe the sexual orientation of their respondents. One of the more radical findings of the large-scale Kinsey studies of male and female sexuality was the frequency of homosexual behavior, even among people who self-labeled as heterosexual. The Kinsey scale stood in stark opposition to what was then the accepted view of homosexuality—that it was a rare behavior performed only by a few isolated freaks who were readily identifiable as sexually abnormal. This scale was first presented in *Sexual Behavior in the Human Male,* Alfred C. Kinsey, Wardell B. Pomeroy, and Clyde E. Martin, Philadelphia and London: W. B. Saunders Company, 1948, pp. 638-641. On this scale, 0 denotes a person who is exclusively heterosexual with no homosexuality; 1 denotes a person who predominantly heterosexual, only incidentally homosexual; and 2 is predominantly heterosexual, but more than incidentally homosexual; while 3 denotes someone who is equally heterosexual and homosexual; 4 denotes someone who is predominantly homosexual, but more than incidentally heterosexual; 5 denotes someone who is predominantly homosexual, but incidentally heterosexual; and 6 is exclusively homosexual.

   This scale was revised somewhat in the follow-up volume, *Sexual Behavior in the Human Female,* Alfred C. Kinsey, Wardell B. Pomeroy, Clyde E. Martin, Paul H. Gebhard, and associates, Philadelphia and London: W. B. Saunders

Company, 1953, pp. 468-474. The biggest difference between this version of the Kinsey scale and the one that appeared in 1948 is the inclusion of an eighth category, X, for individuals who do not respond erotically to either heterosexual or homosexual stimuli, and do not have overt physical contact with individuals of either sex. The Kinsey team found very few post-adolescent males who would fit this category, but "...a goodly number of females belong in this category in every age group." (Kinsey et al., *Sexual Behavior in the Human Female*, op. cit., p. 472)

2. Jonathan Katz, *Gay American History: Lesbians and Gay Men in the U.S.A.*, New York: Thomas Y. Crowell Company, 1976, p. 281.
3. Walter L. Williams, *The Spirit and the Flesh: Sexual Diversity in American Indian Culture*, Boston: Beacon Press, 1986, pp. 9-10.
4. Ibid., pp. 76-77.
5. Ibid., p. 81.
6. Will Roscoe (ed.), *Living the Spirit: A Gay American Indian Anthology* (compiled by Gay American Indians), New York: St. Martin's Press, 1988, pp. 217-222.
7. Katz, op. cit., p. 282.
8. Ibid., p. 292.
9. Ibid., p. 282.
10. Ibid., p. 324.
11. Ibid., p. 284.
12. Ibid., p. 282.
13. Ibid., p. 283.
14. Williams, op. cit., p. 65.
15. Ibid., p. 66.
16. Ibid.
17. Gayle Rubin, "The Traffic in Women: Notes on the 'Political Economy' of Sex," in Rayna R. Reiter (ed.), *Toward an Anthropology of Women*, New York and London: Monthly Review Press, 1975, pp. 157-210.
18. Judith K. Brown, "Iroquois Women: An Ethnohistoric Note," in Reiter, op. cit., pp. 235-251.
19. Williams, op. cit., pp. 4 and 39.
20. Ibid., p. 35.
21. Ibid., pp. 18-19.
22. Ibid., p. 2.
23. Ibid., pp. 2-3.
24. Ibid., p. 39.
25. Ibid.
26. Ibid., p. 40.
27. Ibid.
28. Ibid., p. 41.
29. Katz, op. cit., p. 305.
30. Ibid., p. 307.
31. Williams, op. cit., p. 241.
32. Ibid., pp. 241-242.
33. Ibid., p. 24.
34. Ibid., pp. 23-25.
35. Ibid., pp. 45-46.

36. Ibid., p. 46.
37. Ibid., p. 1.
38. Ibid., p. 67.
39. Ibid., pp. 68-69.
40. Ibid., p. 71.
41. Ibid., pp. 71-72.
42. Ibid., p. 73.
43. Ibid., p. 75.
44. Ibid., pp. 77-78.
45. Ibid., p. 79.
46. Ibid., pp. 79-80.
47. Ibid., p. 80.
48. Ibid.
49. Ibid., p. 22.
50. Ibid., p. 2.
51. Ibid., pp. 29-30.
52. Ibid., p. 29.
53. Ibid., p. 50.
54. Ibid., pp. 52-53.
55. Ibid., p. 59.
56. Ibid., p. 97.
57. Ibid., p. 141.
58. Ibid., pp. 180-181.
59. Ibid., p. 93.
60. Ibid., p. 94.
61. Ibid., p. 96.
62. Williams, "Seafarers, Cowboys, and Indians: Male Marriage in Fringe Societies on the Anglo-American Frontier," op. cit., pp. 152-174.
63. Ibid., p. 191.
64. Ibid., p. 217.
65. Ibid., p. 209.
66. Ibid., p. 215.
67. Ibid., p. 270. See also p. 271.
68. Ibid., p. 274.
69. Will Roscoe, "The Zuni Man-Woman," *Outlook*, Summer 1988, p. 57.
70. Ibid., p. 58.
71. Ibid., p. 59.
72. Ibid., p. 63.
73. Ibid.
74. Ibid., p. 64.
75. Ibid.
76. Ibid.
77. Ibid.
78. Ibid., p. 65.
79. Ibid.
80. Midnight Sun, "Sex/Gender Systems in Native North America," in Will Roscoe (ed.), *Living the Spirit*, op. cit., p. 38.

81. Williams, *The Spirit and the Flesh*, op. cit., p. 14.

82. Ramón A. Gutiérrez, "Must We Deracinate Indians to Find Gay Roots?" *Outlook*, Winter 1989, p. 61.

83. Ibid., p. 62.

84. Ibid.

85. Ibid., p. 64.

86. Ibid., p. 63.

87. Ibid.

88. Ibid., p. 65.

89. Ibid., p. 66.

90. Ibid., p. 67.

91. Williams, *The Spirit and the Flesh*, op. cit., p. 259.

92. Ibid.

93. Arthur Evans, *Witchcraft and the Gay Counterculture*, Boston: Fag Rag Books, 1978.

94. Randy P. Conner, *Blossom of Bone*, San Francisco: Harper, 1993.

95. Margaret Deirdre O'Hartigan, "Blossom of Boneheads," *TransSisters: The Journal of Transsexual Feminism*, Issue 5, Summer 1994, p. 43.

96. Serena Nanda, *Neither Man Nor Woman: The Hijras of India*, Belmont, California: Wadsworth Publishing Company, 1990, pp. 2 and 24-26.

97. Ibid., pp. 25-26.

98. Ibid., p. 26.

99. Ibid., pp. 28-29.

100. Eli Coleman, Philip Colgan and Louis Gooren, "Male Cross-Gender Behavior in Myanmar (Burma): A Description of the Acault," *Archives of Sexual Behavior*, vol. 21, no. 3, 1992, p. 315.

101. Ibid., p. 317.

102. Ibid., p. 318.

103. Ibid., p. 320.

104. Kris Poasa, "The Samoan Fa'afafine: One Case Study and Discussion of Transsexualism," *Journal of Psychology and Human Sexuality*, vol. 5(3), 1992, p. 39.

105. Ibid., p. 50.

106. Ibid., p. 40.

107. Ibid., p. 50.

108. Katz, op. cit., pp. 209-210.

109. Ibid., p. 210.

110. Ibid.

111. Ibid., pp. 211 and 221-225.

112. Ibid., p. 211.

113. Ibid., p. 252.

114. Ibid.

115. Ibid.

116. Ibid., p. 275.

117. Ibid., p. 276.

118. Ibid.

119. Ibid., p. 277.

120. Ibid.

121. Ibid.

122. Ibid., p. 278.

123. Louis Sullivan, *From Female to Male: The Life of Jack Bee Garland*, Boston: Alyson Publications, 1990.

124. Gayle Rubin, "Of Catamites and Kings: Reflections on Butch, Gender, and Boundaries," in Joan Nestle (ed.), *The Persistent Desire: A Femme-Butch Reader*, Boston: Alyson Publications, 1992, pp. 466-482.

125. C. Jacob Hale, "Dyke Leatherboys and Their Daddies: How to Have Sex without Men or Women," an unpublished paper presented at the Berkshire Conference on the History of Women, June 8, 1996.

126. Sullivan, op. cit., p. 56.

127. Ibid., p. 131.

128. Rubin, "Of Catamits and Kings," op. cit., p. 474. Footnote 12 in this essay does not credit me with initiating a "fascinating exchange" of letters in the *FTM Newsletter* about the association of FTMs with butch lesbians. Since Rubin is otherwise meticulous in her attributions, I am at a loss to explain this lapse in an otherwise well-researched piece that is a rare voice for common sense and tolerance.

129. Ibid., p. 475.

130. Ibid., p. 477.

131. Ibid., pp. 481-482, Footnote 26.

132. Michael Taylor, "Bobby's Secret," in John Patrick (ed.), *Big Boys, Little Lies: Erotic Tales of Boys Who Have Something to Hide*, Sarasota, FL: STARbooks Press, 1993, pp. 109-116.

CHAPTER 5

Contemporary Transsexual Autobiography

Second Serve: The Renée Richards Story, published in 1983, is a transitional work between transsexual pioneers like Christine Jorgensen and modern transgendered activists such as Kate Bornstein.

Jorgensen and Jan Morris both described childhoods that were free from family violence, sex-role "confusion," or other behavior that might be considered pathological. They were also careful to distinguish their transsexuality from homosexuality or cross-dressing. While this emphasis upon idyllic childhoods and the disassociation from other, closely related sexualities may be accurate reflections of Jorgensen and Morris' experiences, it sometimes lends a flat quality to their narratives. It is difficult to believe that a young person who was burdened with severe gender dysphoria would come to adulthood without bearing some resentment toward his or her parents, or go through sex reassignment without first exploring cross-dressing and homosexuality, to see if they could offer some relief that would not require a shift in public identity or painful and expensive medical treatment.

There is a strong visual link between Richards' autobiography and Jorgensen's. On the back cover of the dust jacket of *Second Serve*, two pieces of identification appear. One shows "Lieutenant Commander Richard H. Raskind, U. S. Naval Reserves," and the other is a Women's Tennis Association card for Renée Richards. The reader who has seen both books cannot help but think of the tabloid headlines that blared "American G.I. Becomes a Woman" when Jorgensen returned to the United States. While it is not the intent of the transgendered narrator to do so, such packaging by publishers plays on the frailty of masculine identity and a callous public's titillating fantasies of humiliation and castration. It reinforces the vigilance that even the most macho of men are encouraged to feel, lest their precious manhood be swept away in one unguarded moment of tenderness, grief, femininity, or homosexual passion. While the male-to-female transsexual's autobiography is an overt plea for tolerance and an attempt to educate the mass-market reader about gender dysphoria, there is also a subtext. In this sotto voce narrative, the male-to-female's life story is a cautionary tale for men's men and the women who love them that way.

When it comes to the text, Richards' book departs in many significant ways from the parameters established by Jorgensen and Morris. Richards, born in August 1934, freely discusses an early family life that is nightmarish. Richards' mother was a psychiatrist who apparently had to struggle to be admitted to the masculine realm of medical practice, and took her frustrations out on her family. According to Richards, S. Muriel Bishop, M.D. ruthlessly dominated her husband, Dr. David Raskind, and refused to take his surname. The family home was full of hostility, which was expressed in daily shouting matches and physical fights. As a small boy, Richards felt great contempt for his father's inability to stand up to his wife, and his inability to protect his son from her bizarre dictates.

Bishop's first child, a daughter, was named Michael (after the maternal grandfather), and raised as a boy. Richards describes growing up in a female-dominated household with a sister who resented, battered, and cross-dressed "him." The cross-dressing sometimes took place in the mother's presence, with her approval. This included a brutal episode in which a shrieking and crying little boy was thrown to the ground and forcibly dressed up as a little girl by "his" mother, who had decided "he" would wear this humiliating costume to a Halloween party. However, most of the time, Richards enjoyed private cross-dressing as it was one of the few times when her mother and sister gave her affection.

Richards' mother also subjected her to weekly enemas. Until she became too strong to physically coerce, she forced her each day to don a sissified outfit of knee socks and short pants with a shirt that buttoned to the shorts. Richards was in the habit of waking up each morning and climbing into bed with Mother. She slept in the nude, and the little boy was allowed to watch her while she dressed each morning. This emotionally incestuous scenario was repeated daily until Richards reached puberty. Richards also says her sister would undress her, push her penis up inside her body to make it disappear, and then say, "See you're not a little boy, you're a little girl."[1] The emotional incest with the mother became physical incest with the sister, who used her little brother to provide herself with sexual gratification when she reached adolescence.

"If I sat down to write a case history of an imaginary transsexual, I could not come up with a more provocative set of circumstances than that of my childhood. ...My early life is strewn with unsubtle touches that beg to be seen as reasons for my sexual confusion. If they aren't the true cause they ought to be," she says ruefully.[2]

Unlike Jorgensen or Morris, Richards details extensive experiences with cross-dressing as an adult. She traces this compulsion back to her childhood, when the family moved into a large mansion and she was finally given a room of her own. These experiments were both ultra-cautious and dangerously bold. Richards would sneak into her sister's room, appropriate certain items of clothing, and return them once the cross-dressing episode was over. But while dressed, she soon began to leave the house—taking walks, window-shopping, and seeing movies. Although she was caught in drag twice by family members, no one ever confronted her about this behavior or tried to interfere with it. Richards says, "Once, when I was fifteen I overheard my sister ask my mother, 'What do you do with men who want to be women?' My mother answered, 'You send them to Scandinavia.'"[3]

This childhood cross-dressing was not accompanied by sexual stimulation or orgasm. Richards writes:

It would be natural to think that this cross-dressing must have been associated with some sexual activity. In fact, it was not. I would sometimes get an erection as I pulled on some silky underthing, but this was pretty much a response to the soft touch of the fabric. It was not associated with the transformation to a girl. The same thing might happen as I dried myself with a soft towel. Then again, there was the prohibition against masturbation which, though not explicitly stated, was understood clearly by every American child of the nineteen-forties. It is peculiar indeed that I could control the desire to masturbate but not the desire to dress in my sister's clothes. I did have wet dreams; so the mechanism was in perfectly good shape.[4]

It was during this period that Richards experienced the development of a female persona called Renée. Her life became an exhausting secret struggle between the acceptable public persona everyone else recognized and called Dick, and the feminine and demanding Renée. Throughout her thirty-plus years of living as a man, Richards repeatedly acquired extensive wardrobes of female clothing, got rid of them in an attempt to "shape up" and exorcise Renée, and then, like an addict, would begin to acquire another woman's wardrobe. This cycle of bingeing and purging on lingerie, dresses, high heels, and fur coats would make Dick Raskind seem to fit the typical profile of a transvestite, not a transsexual, except for one thing—the lack of masturbation. Even as an adult, Richards reports no autoerotic activity associated with wearing feminine garments. It was the assumption of a complete identity as a woman that she craved, not the mere contact with silk stockings, satin and lace petticoats, or other stock transvestite erotic triggers.

Richards would also continue, when Renée was especially strong, to go out dressed as a woman, despite the risk of running into people who knew her only as Dick Raskind, thus beginning a dangerous pattern of self-destructive exhibitionism, which continued lifelong. A reader would have to be charitable to the point of foolishness to see Richards' rash postsurgical decision to abandon a lucrative and successful medical career to become a female tennis pro as anything other than an extension of this exhibitionism, given the fierce opposition of the Women's Tennis Association, the lack of any backing from a civil-rights organization, and the lack of funds for a legal battle or even a clear-cut plan to hire an attorney from the outset.

Although Richards claims this decision was made in response to thousands of letters from transsexuals and members of other minority groups who saw her as a champion, it would be silly to disregard an even more powerful (though perhaps unconscious) motivation, which was to put herself in the public eye at last, after a lifetime of sneaking around and being terrified of discovery. Before sex reassignment, Renée never had to deal with survival issues like earning a living or cope with the consequences of her rash behavior. That was Dick's job. And post-transition, when Dick was no longer supposed to exist, it seems that Renée was still not prepared to think rationally about how she was going to meet her expenses or deal with the consequences of public exposure. At least in the beginning, Renée treated her new life as a woman as one more drag vacation from Dick's drab and repressed reality, and did not take very good care of herself.

Dick was afraid of Renée. "He" experienced her as a dangerous, seductive, and out-of-control personality who became angry when she was not allowed to emerge and have a full life as a woman. "He" blamed an automobile accident which nearly resulted in "his" death on Renée. Every time Richards came close to banishing this succubus, she was afraid Renée would somehow conspire to cause the death of Dick, whose body housed this struggle. It's no wonder Dick was afraid of Renée; she was not exactly kind to the body parts that did not conform to her female identity.

> When I was in the guise of Renée, I hated my genitals; my penis and testicles seemed ugly and abnormal. I recoiled at the cumbersome, embarrassingly external complex of fleshy parts flopping between my legs. I attacked them viciously; with my fingers I pressed the testicles up into my abdomen. ...Once I had done that the problem was to keep them up there. I accomplished this by means of a crosshatching of adhesive tape. To do away with my penis I would stretch it backward between my legs, often using more heavy adhesive tape to secure it in that position. ...The pressures that these delicate structures were never designed to take began to create excruciating pain. Then, too, over the years I became more and more strict in this regard, increasing the strains and inventing new ways to eliminate the hated body parts. ...Believe me, I have great respect for the resiliency of the human penis. Over the years I put thousands of bruises, hemorrhages, and abrasions on mine; in its last days it was literally covered with scars. As for my testicles, they sustained equal damage.[5]

During her medical residency, Richards reports that Renée's "appearances were characterized by increasing violence to the hated male genitals. The techniques of causing them to disappear were the same as they had been, but the violence with which they were carried out was unprecedented. For the first time I began to think of myself (I guess I should say 'my selves') as masochistic."[6] This isolated comment is the tip of an iceberg of discourse in which transsexuality is cathected with sadomasochism. Raymond also attempts to make this connection. This is, of course, one more way in which some "authorities" attempt to pathologize transsexuality, and it also has a bearing upon the screening and selection process for candidates for sex reassignment. It would be extremely unlikely that an avowed masochist would be granted hormones or, especially, surgery, since medical doctors and therapists alike would tend to view this as gratifying the patient's self-destructive fetish for pain and bodily injury.

Unlike Jorgensen, Richards also admits to homosexual experimentation, although, like Morris, she is adamant that she was not a homosexual. "I've been asked many times why I didn't simply live the life of a homosexual," she writes. "This question is asked by those who do not understand that Dick was a heterosexual male and that Renée was a heterosexual female. Dick had no sexual interest in men and, when Renée fantasized, she fantasized the pleasures of sex as a woman with a vagina."[7] However, it seems that Renée opportunistically took advantage of homosexual men since they were much more likely to be willing to engage in sex with her, given her male physique, than any other group of people. The first time this happened was when Renée went to a drag show, the Satin Slipper Revue, at the Apollo Theatre and got herself invited to audition for a role in it by Jimmy, one of the gay men who owned the show. Dick was in "his" freshman year at Yale.

At the audition, which was held in his home, Jimmy proceeded to get Renée drunk and seduce her. As Jimmy removed Renée's clothing, she disappeared "and Dick, who had been sent on a vacation to parts unknown, came snapping back. He didn't like what he found. He was taking a homosexual's penis in his mouth. Renée, however, was not completely gone, and it was she who insisted that Jimmy penetrate her face-to-face as a man would a woman. Jimmy, kindly agreed to this ungainly setup. Dick lay in absolute horror as he felt his anus invaded. There was no satisfaction in it for Renée or for Dick. …It was a stereotypical deflowering: the bloom of romance that had developed during foreplay withered quickly and left a snoring older man flanked by a bleeding youngster who lay quietly sobbing."[8]

This experience made Dick doubly determined to do away with Renée. However, it was apparently not so unpleasant that it could not be repeated. "Being entered anally was still no real fun," Richards tells us, "though I got so I could grin and bear it." Later on in the book, Richards reveals that the first man she had intercourse with postsurgically was a gay male colleague who had enjoyed sexual liaisons with Dick during out-of-town medical conferences. This was apparently acceptable because "I always insisted that he relate to me as if I were a woman."[9]

These same-sex episodes were exceptions rather than the rule. Throughout her life, despite her ambivalence about her gender, Richards attracted a series of women who tried and failed to create lasting relationships with a person they saw as a handsome, if tormented, man, a doctor, a desirable catch. These women had to have certain high qualifications. Richards explains:

My masculine sex drive was low, and my threshold of excitement high. In order for me to function as an ordinary man, all

factors had to be satisfied almost completely. One strong crite-
rion was beauty, but beauty of a particular kind. When I fantasized, like normal boys I used the conventional beauties of the
day as my objects, but unlike normal boys I found it almost
impossible to compromise this standard, especially if I was
looking for a serious relationship. All of the women with whom
I fell seriously in love were beauties. I would accept no less.[10]

Here is one of the least attractive qualities that male-to-female
transsexuals sometimes display, their self-appointed status as critics of
genetic females and experts on femininity. This is one way in which the
pain of being an outsider and fears of being a nonwoman can be transformed into feelings of superiority and super-womanhood. While one
can sympathize with the feelings of failure and alienation that create
this sublimation, it is annoying indeed to see in action. Richards seems
to have taken the presence of these women in her life for granted, and
although she expresses distress as each relationship ends, she evinces
no empathy with the pain of the departing lover. Instead, Richards'
depression at each breakup is focused on the fact that without a woman
to supervise Dick's spare time, the compulsion to become Renée would
return with a vengeance.

Richards' path toward sex reassignment was a difficult one. First
sent into psychoanalysis at age fifteen by her mother, to whom she confessed her transsexuality, for many years Richards' desire to live full-
time as a woman was derailed by Freudian balderdash. One analyst, Dr.
Bak, cunningly interpreted Richards' cross-dressing and longings to
become a member of the opposite sex as a protest against castration
anxiety. It was the fact that "his" penis emerged intact from each
episode of cross-dressing that motivated Richards to continue doing
this, according to Dr. Bak.[11] When his patient inquired about following
the same route that Christine Jorgensen had tread, Dr. Bak told "him"
that getting "his" penis cut off would surely result in psychosis.[12]

This analyst seemed to alternate verbal abuse with prescriptions for
tranquilizers in his attempt to control his unruly and unresponsive
patient. And he certainly seems to have been ill-informed and deeply
judgmental about sexual minorities. When informed that Richards was
considering marriage to a bisexual call girl he was dating, Dr. Bak
reportedly yelled, "A nice Jewish boy from Queens does not step under
the *chupah* with a cunt-lapping lesbian whore...."[13]

Nevertheless, Richards, encouraged and informed by transsexual
and transvestite publications she bought in Manhattan porn shops

(most notably a magazine called *Turnabout*), decided to go to Paris and meet the famous transsexual performer Coccinelle.[14] In Paris, Richards lived for almost a week full-time as Renée. While she did not meet Coccinelle, she met another famous performer, Bambi, who confirmed that sex-change surgery was being performed in Casablanca and furthermore told Richards that although she was tall, her body could plausibly be transformed into that of a woman.[15] However, the other transgendered performers Richards met were less encouraging, and she left Paris in a state of indecision. "I knew that I *could* have the operation, but I still wasn't sure I *should* have it," she says.[16]

Like every other transsexual during that era, it seems, Richards eventually found her way to the office of Dr. Harry Benjamin, despite Dr. Bak's dire proclamations that Benjamin was a scalpel-wielding quack. Initially, Richards was not impressed by Benjamin. He was upset by people in the waiting room who seemed grotesque to him, and Benjamin himself seemed "a likable fussbudget.... He impressed me as kindly and decent but hardly one to inspire unreserved confidence."[17] However, the level of Benjamin's understanding eventually won Richards over, and he accepted a prescription for estrogen. Benjamin cautioned him that it was doubtful that he would be able to continue to practice medicine as a woman.

Richards reports attending Benjamin's first symposium on transsexuality, held to increase the medical community's understanding of that condition. She was accompanied by a woman lover, Patty, and Benjamin went out of his way to warn Patty that she should not expect to marry Dick Raskind and raise children with "him."[18]

Taking female hormones made Richards feel, for the first time in her life, some measure of self-acceptance and peace with her body. Made bold by these changes, she informed her sister Mike about her plans to make a gender transition. Mike did not approve, and apparently called Dr. Benjamin and persuaded him to halt the estrogen therapy. This was devastating for Richards, and set off another war against Renée. Eventually Richards made it to Copenhagen to visit Dr. Christian Hamburger, Christine Jorgensen's physician. Dr. Hamburger gave Richards a new prescription for estrogen, thus freeing him from Benjamin's blockade of the drug.

Richards was understandably afraid of obtaining surgery in Casablanca, because of rumors that the results were sometimes disastrous. So she began a futile and frustrating search for a surgeon in the United States. Again and again, she underwent expensive medical and psychological tests, only to be rejected. And she came to believe, probably accurately, that gender identity programs were rejecting her because she was a physician, and they did not want the notoriety that would result when she began to practice medicine in her gender of preference. Richards says, "I considered this a betrayal by my fellow physicians."[19] Frightened by Renée's angry reaction to these rejections, Richards decided she had no choice but to go to Casablanca.

Prior to this trip, she got plastic surgery for removal of her Adam's apple. Her larynx was damaged during the botched operation, which was obtained under a false identity and pseudonym. (Richards told the doctor she needed the operation because she was a female impersonator, and the Adam's apple was interfering with her performances.) Richards chafed under the perfunctory treatment she received during recovery. "As far as they were concerned, I was an exotic dancer, probably gay, and hardly worth their time," she says sadly.[20] This experience would hardly have filled her with confidence for her adventure in Casablanca. If an American surgeon could treat her this badly, what awaited her abroad, where medical standards were much less stringent?

On her way to Morocco, Richards stopped in Spain, and was accosted in a café by some local toughs who called her a "fucking American queer."[21] When one of the bullies poked her in the chest, Richards erupted in fury and beat him up. She was promptly jailed and charged, among other things, with spying. The American consulate was eventually able to obtain her release, but it was a shaken and physically injured Richards who limped into Casablanca. And, tragically, at the steps of the clinic, Richards was not able to force herself to walk in and pay for her surgery. "I felt that, somehow, I was no longer worthy to be a woman, though I certainly was not a man. I was something horrible—something in between—something like a monster," she says.[22]

It would take a very callous person indeed to read this description of an aborted dream without feeling a rush of compassion and protectiveness. Richards is so alone with her dilemma. After enduring many years of hostility from her psychiatrists, noncomprehension from her lovers, and derision from strangers and friends, Richards was unable to find the strength to take this final step. She does not even seem to have felt compassion for herself. Almost certainly she was suffering from post-traumatic stress disorder as a result of the horribly inept surgery on her larynx and the queer bashing she had recently endured in Spain. But she was not aware of the many overwhelming social pressures that combined to create this intense state of self-hatred and paralysis. Her own pain simply contributed to her self-loathing.

But it is not so easy to feel compassion for Richards in the next phase of her life. Shortly after returning to New York, Richards met and married yet another astonishingly beautiful woman, Meriam. The marriage was motivated in part by yet another rejection from Johns Hopkins in Chicago. The gender identity clinic there contacted Richards' old psychoanalyst Dr. Bak and under his advice refused to treat Richards. It was 1969 and Richards was thirty-five years old. She felt she would soon be too old to make a successful transition to womanhood, and once more resolved to eliminate all traces of Renée from her life and psyche.

Richards and Meriam's relationship began with intense sexual attraction, which quickly fizzled. Richards had breast reduction surgery, even had plastic surgery to close her pierced ears. And she consulted an endocrinologist to see if injections of testosterone would repair the damage done to her male organs by years of estrogen therapy. Despite a low sperm count and infrequent intercourse, Richards' wife conceived, and they had a son.

Despite Andy's birth, Richards and Meriam eventually divorced. Richards went back to Dr. Benjamin's office, found he had retired, and began treatment with his successor, Dr. Allenfield. This physician was appalled by Richards' many rejected applications for surgery and promised to assist her. In spring of 1975, Richards again consulted Dr. Laidlaw, a psychiatrist who years ago had encouraged her to have faith in her own judgment. Dr. Laidlaw seems to have been the only supportive therapist Richards ever met, and it is interesting to wonder why she did not seek to become his patient. These two doctors eventually found a surgeon in New York, Dr. Granato, who finally made Richards' transition possible. Dr. Granato seems to have been something less than a prince of a guy. His greeting to Richards after surgery was, "Let's see what we've got here or, more accurately, what we don't got here."[23]

Richards continued to dress as a man when visiting her son. The idea was to wait to explain the gender reassignment until he was old enough to understand. The photo of Richards in the suit and short wig she wore to visit her son is far from convincing as an image of fatherhood. The book closes with a description of a fishing expedition with her son, who refers to Renée as "Daddy." While the two of them are fishing, Andy asks his father a series of questions about whether "he" has breasts or a woman's sex organs, and whether or not "he" can have children. Richards answers these questions factually. At the end of the expedition, Andy is allowed to steer the boat, and Richards has to suddenly take control to avoid a crash. She asks her son, "You trying to kill us both?" and the boy replies, "You wouldn't let anything happen to me! ...Because I'm the most important thing in your life!"[24]

But it's pretty clear that the most important person in Richards' life has always been Renée. Claims that her son "has never shown any doubt about my ability to fulfill the masculine role," has "no signs of sexual confusion," and "is secure in his masculinity" seem premature and exaggerated. It is difficult to believe that a young boy would not be troubled by the specter of a daddy with breasts and a vagina. Andy is quoted as telling a child psychiatrist, "Mommy told me that my daddy changed into a lady.... But...that's crazy."[25]

Richards' refusal to make a complete gender transition as far as her son is concerned seems symptomatic of the old split between Dick and Renée. The decision to continue to be a daddy despite her female appearance and identity has more to do with Richards' investment in Freudian theories of child development than it has to do with giving her child accurate information. Richards is oblivious to the possibility that she is recreating some of the poor boundaries and contradictory messages about gender that she felt burdened with as a child.

It is not my intention to say here that transsexuals should not have children. The loss of custody or visitation rights with children is one of the many injustices that are sometimes perpetrated upon transgendered men and women. On the other hand, the fact that one is oppressed does not automatically mean that everything one does is above criticism. Granted, Richards was trying to find a solution to a difficult problem in an era when there was no help to be had from experts, and no support from peers. Nevertheless, it seems clear from this narrative that Richards' ambivalence about her gender continued even after sex reassignment, and some of this ambiguity was inflicted upon her son.

Both Jorgensen and Morris shied away from the question of sexuality post-reassignment. Richards breaks ranks here as well, giving the reader graphic descriptions of post-reassignment masturbation and intercourse. Richards describes using a dilator, which "looked like nothing so much as a crudely made dildo," to keep her surgically-created vagina in good working order, but says, "Before you get a picture of me ecstatically working away with this thing, let me say that I never got a second's sexual pleasure out of it. First of all, it's too hard and, even though it's only a bit over an inch in diameter, it always feels uncomfortably big. ...It would often come out stained with pinkish blood."[26] However, clitoral stimulation was another matter.

I could tell right away that there was one big sexual difference between Dick and Renée. Dick had been very inhibited about his body, one might even say a bit prudish. He didn't enjoy touching his sexual parts, and he didn't enjoy having them touched. I conclude that this was a symptom of his ambivalence toward them. Renée, however, had no such ambivalence. She couldn't keep her hands off herself.[27]

Richards' tendency to speak of herself in third person is especially disorienting during her descriptions of sexual pleasure. Throughout this book, Renée remains a persona, an aspect of Richards, not her true or inner self. Renée finally becomes dominant, but Richards never wholly becomes Renée. She describes exploring her surgically-constructed clitoris and newfound female orgasm:

It was slightly higher than where my penis had been located; the one big difference was that there was no sense of projection. The sexy feelings (and by now they were intense) were more associated with the main flesh of my body. The tendency to thrust was lessened. I felt more inclined than ever to receive, to be moved toward rather than to aggress. As I continued to rub myself, the intensity of sensation grew higher. The buildup was slow, and the sensation remained more general, though it definitely strengthened and took shape as if working toward a peak of some kind. I grew more vigorous and occasionally my hand or one of my fingers would slip into direct contact with my clitoris. There was no pain or discomfort when this took place, so I felt less tentative and let it happen more often. As I went higher, I began to perceive a climax. The peculiar awareness of a finish, a final push, a barrier to be broken, loomed ahead. There is no way to adequately describe that moment when I knew for certain that I would make it.

For most people it's a given, but for Renée it was a magic place; it was almost as important as the orgasm itself—that came quickly on the heels of that instant of comprehension. It was not as well-defined as a man's orgasm. The moment of ejaculation…was missing. This climax was more rounded, less intense but longer-lasting, and especially gratifying in the warm sensations that flooded me and that continued to do so for some time.[28]

Richards' first attempt at heterosexual intercourse was not so successful, if sexual success is measured in terms of climaxes. "I didn't have an orgasm myself; in fact, I didn't come near one that time or any other time for several months. Nonetheless, I loved it. I was at last fully capable of the woman's role. I could have been content for the rest of my life with that satisfaction alone."[29] Renée was eventually fortunate enough to meet a bodybuilder named Billy whose combination of physical strength, love of foreplay, and staying power did the trick.

> As the excitement built, I'd feel two impulses; one to push Billy away so that I could move more freely and one to pull him down more closely. Suddenly I had a new perspective on the seemingly irrational actions of some of the women I'd made love to. They hadn't seemed sure of what they wanted, and now I was responding to the same dilemma, not out of perversity but because I was so excited that I didn't know what to do. This divided action terminated at the moment of climax. When I peaked, the wriggling motion that I had been striving for with my torso expressed itself in a free movement of my legs which was almost spasmodic. Everything went out of my mind for those few moments.[30]

Jorgensen and Morris present transsexuality as a medical problem, something that should be left in the hands of compassionate physicians and scientists. They suggest that public policy should conform to the views of the medical experts who administer sex reassignment. Richards outstrips both of them in her harsh view of transsexuality as a disease. "I cannot describe the loneliness and terror that I experienced," she tells the reader. "I wished that I could trade this aberration for any other kind of sickness. If I had had a heart condition at least I would have had some company, and that would have made it more bearable. As it was, I felt that I was the focus for some singular nastiness, the carrier of a germ specific to me and only me."[31] It is difficult to say whether this view of transsexuality as pathological came from the nine years of daily psychoanalysis that Richards endured prior to sex change, or whether it was Richards' self-hatred that made her seek out such a punitive schedule of treatment.

To be fair, there were very few portrayals then of transsexuality as anything other than a loathsome disease. As a fifteen-year-old, Richards was traumatized by discovering a copy of Victorian sexologist Richard von Krafft-Ebing's *Psychopathia Sexualis* in her mother's psychiatric books. This was her reaction:

> Published in the early nineteen-hundreds, this book contained case histories of people described as "lunatics." Most of them

had been studied while they were confined in various mental hospitals. What some of these people had were feelings that matched mine almost point for point. A knot the size of a cantaloupe formed in my stomach as I read this "expert" commentary.... This man kindheartedly consigned these poor wretches into the category of the irredeemably insane. I fought back waves of nausea as I read case after case...some almost exactly like me. What I felt must be like what a terminal patient feels when his doctor tells him there is no hope. ...*Psychopathia Sexualis* went back onto my mother's bookshelf but that day was not the last time I looked at it; I was drawn back again and again like a criminal to the scene of his crime.[32]

Matters were not improved by the teenage boy's discovery of Einar Wegener's life story, *Man Into Woman*. The fact that a biological male had been transformed into a woman via surgery gave Renée new hope, but the fact that this experimental surgery had apparently killed Wegener, who lived for only a year after enduring the operation, filled Dick with dismay.

While Morris makes a few stabs at incorporating a rough sort of feminism into her story, she does not take up cudgels against the women's movement for the simple reason that feminists had not yet begun to agitate against transsexuals' civil rights.

Richards' transsexuality exists in a much more politicized milieu. She confronts the media, other social institutions, and feminism more directly than Jorgensen or Morris ever would, or could. Jorgensen was forced to put herself on display in order to make a living. Morris had independent means and could continue to get by as a writer. Richards refused to give up her medical credentials. She deserves credit as a pioneer for insisting on practicing medicine in her gender of preference. And despite my qualms about the self-serving and exhibitionist quality of Richards' battle for acceptance as a woman tennis player, she has to be admired for her gutsy refusal to back down and accept being pushed out of a sport that had been her lifelong refuge from stress, anger, denial, and pain.

Richards got her dander up when the original news coverage of a tennis tournament she played in claimed she was a man masquerading as a woman, and did not acknowledge her transsexuality and gender transition. Although she received some sympathetic and objective coverage in the press, for the most part she was vilified and treated as a freak. Her dignity under fire and her refusal in *Second Serve* to take pot shots at her feminist opponents is commendable. She is, if anything, a harsher critic of herself than her opponents.

> The ironic thing about this was that I had lived high for most of my life. I'm the first to admit that I'm basically a selfish person. All I want is my Ferrari, my beautiful apartment, and my tennis club. With these I can be happy. I've never even been very political, and here I was getting supportive letters from Black Panthers. In spite of this irony, I was susceptible to this flood of sentiment. Until you have pawed through thirty thousand letters pleading with you to stand up for the rights of the world's downtrodden, you don't know what pressure is. Left to my own devices, I probably would have resolved my personal pique at being summarily barred from competition—but, my god, the whole world seemed to be looking for me to be their Joan of Arc.[33]

Where Jorgensen suffered, for the most part silently, through her ordeal with the media, and Morris sidestepped it by calling in debts from colleagues and asking them to treat her transition as a non-event, Richards met the press head-on and gave reporters her best shot. Because of what she went through, the mere presence of a transgendered woman in any profession would never again engender the blood-in-the-water feeding frenzy that took over Richards' life for months. She speaks of the key differences between herself and Jorgensen:

> I was the heir apparent to Christine Jorgensen, but I possessed an advantage that poor Christine never enjoyed. I had an identity beyond my transsexualism. I was a doctor, a parent, and a tennis player. These dimensions made me a thorny problem for those who liked to think of transsexuals only as perverts dancing in sleazy bars. For those people, I was a puzzle, one that could not be solved by resorting to a stereotype. This was my peculiar value and, no doubt, the source of my surprising popularity.[34]

It's bravado like this which makes it easier to repress a shudder at the news that the attorney who won Richards' case against the Women's Tennis Association was a subordinate of Roy Cohn.[35] This 1977 victory stands as one of the first legal cases in which the civil rights of a transgendered person was recognized by the courts in this country.

The number of male-to-female transsexuals' life stories in print continues to outstrip female-to-male autobiographies. And male-to-female autobiographies tend to receive a lot more promotion and gain wider circulation. It seems the world is still more titillated by "a man who wants to become a woman" than it is by "a woman who wants to become a man." The first is scandalous; the latter is taken for granted. This reflects the very different levels of privilege men and women have in our society. Of course women want to be men, the general attitude seems to be, and of course they can't. And that's that.

Even though it was published quite recently, in 1996, when consciousness about transsexuality was comparatively high, *Dear Sir or Madam: The Autobiography of a Female-to-Male Transsexual* has not been widely reviewed or generally circulated in this country. Still, since printed matter about FTMs is scarce, and because Mark Rees is an important transgendered activist in the United Kingdom, it must be mentioned here. However, it is a depressing narrative in many ways. Rees seems to have taken little joy from his life, and his autobiography is a chronicle of one failure after another—failure at love, failure at building a successful career, and failure as an activist. Unemployed and single, Rees was in his fifties when the book was published. The greatest portion of his melancholy can be chalked up to the intense oppression he endured. However, it is impossible to avoid wondering if negative attitudes toward transgendered people are entirely responsible for the many schools Rees attended, only to fail exams or drop out, and many other poor choices. It is as if his sense of initiative and all self-esteem were burned out of him by the low expectations of his working-class parents, the vicious harassment he was subjected to for being "butch" or "horsey," and the callous treatment he got from medical doctors, who all told the young Rees that sex change was impossible.

Dear Sir or Madam begins, like Jorgensen and Morris's autobiographies, with a foreword written by a medical expert on transsexuality, who pleads for public understanding and tolerance. In this case, the foreword was written by Professor L. J. Gooren of the Free University Hospital in Amsterdam. However, it adds a preface, which would not have appeared in the first wave of transsexual autobiography. This is written by Member of Parliament Alex Carlile, who addresses civil-rights issues. Carlile decries the failure of the British government to allow transsexuals to change their gender on their birth certificate, since this means they cannot legally marry, and also criticizes the lack of protection against discrimination in employment. This plea for social equality is founded in the legitimacy that medical science supposedly grants sex reassignment. "If a person passes the harsh tests set by medical science before gender reassignment can be completed, and functions with total success in the acquired gender, why should they have to suffer the indignity and mental agony of being forced in law to be the opposite of who they really are?" Carlile quite reasonably asks.[36]

Rees was born in 1943, during the Second World War. Many transgendered autobiographies include photographs of the author before and after sex reassignment. In most other cases, the eye is jarred by the contrast between the child and the adult. But the photograph of Rees as a child evokes no dissonance juxtaposed with his adult portrait. Both are indisputably masculine. Rees had an exceptionally unhappy childhood because of his markedly boyish appearance and mannerisms. Wearing girls' clothing and menstruation were especially odious and humiliating for him. As a small child, his choice of toys was masculine, and the pictures he drew of himself were pictures of men.

"I didn't realize until puberty that I'd grow up into a woman," Rees poignantly writes, "it was something so inconceivable that I gave no thought to it."[37] This state of affairs seemed perfectly normal to the young Rees. "I took it for granted that all girls wanted to be boys and would share my masculine interests," he says.[38] However, this attitude was not shared by Rees's mother. "Thirty years later I discovered that my mother had taken me, as a small child, to the family doctor because she was concerned about the size of my clitoris and thought I was changing sex," Rees writes.[39]

Because Rees's gender dysphoria was so pronounced at a very young age, he became a fierce activist on behalf of transgendered young people, and several times in the text appeals to parents to get professional help for their "different" children. "If I had been diagnosed as transsexual, my role change could have started a decade earlier than it did and much needless suffering been avoided, both for me and my family," he asserts.[40] Nowhere does Rees acknowledge that the overwhelming majority of "treatment" for transgendered youth consists of trying to get their behavior and self-image to conform to the sex they were assigned at birth. It would be nice to think that kindly doctors and therapists would have saved Rees and others like him from years of suffocating battles with female clothing and the limited vocational choices open to women, but hardly realistic.

Rees reached puberty later than any of his peers, and began to feel sexual attraction to others. "In common with my schoolfriends, I went through the 'crush' stage, but unlike them did not go on to finding boys attractive. Instead the objects of attraction were young women but I never envisaged having a relationship with a woman as a woman; such an idea was abhorrent. My body was, to me, so repulsive that I didn't want to see it myself, let alone allow anyone else to do so. I realized that what others took for granted—sexual relationships—would be barred from me. Life thus promised to be one of isolation," he says.[41]

The taunting of Rees's peers intensified during adolescence, and he was frequently labeled a lesbian. Rees relates a humorous anecdote of later confronting a boy who had once shouted, "When are you going to change sex, Brenda?" at him across the local High Street. He says, "I met him over thirty years later. He was a very affable middle-aged man. I hoped I was too."[42]

In his late teens, Rees finally consulted a physician, Dr. Gelber, who conducted a humiliating physical exam but spoke nonjudgmentally about hormonal imbalances, and seemed to understand Rees's distress. However, her solution was to refer him to a psychiatrist, Dr. George Bram, who diagnosed Rees as having an inferiority complex and being very depressed. Dr. Bram persuaded Rees and his family to place him in a mental institution for a year. There he saw a female psychiatrist, Dr. Urgup, who belittled Rees's gender identity and attempted to steer him toward becoming more feminine. Rees understandably writes, "My fellow-patients were more helpful than the zealous doctor."[43] One of these patients gave Rees a copy of News of the World that contained the story of a male-to-female transsexual, Georgina Turtle. While this story gave Rees verification that he was not alone, it did not offer any practical help in resolving his gender dilemma.

Rees was to go through several years of education for careers he did not want to pursue and even a period of enlistment in the Women's Royal Naval Service (WRNS) before finally locating an organization that would help him. The public record of the time he spent in Mabledon Hospital resulted in many job and school applications being denied. During this period, he says, "Life would have been simpler had I been lesbian."[44] In time Rees came to think of himself as "some kind of 'deviant' lesbian."[45] "I wasn't even a normal homosexual," he says glumly.[46]

After Rees received a medical discharge from the WRNS, his life seemed stalled in a holding pattern. But hope came in the form of a parish magazine article written by Rees's religious guide and comforter, Father Taylor. Rees had confided his painful problems with his gender identity to this man, who seems to have had more compassion and insight than the typical doctor or therapist that Rees encountered. In the article, Father Taylor "implored the congregation to treat homosexuals with love, not condemnation: they were welcome at church. In 1969 that was a courageous stand to take. He mentioned the work of the Albany Trust, which had been set up to help everyone with any kind of psychosexual problem. I then sent the Trust a donation and asked about their work, but several months passed before I could summon up enough courage to ask directly if they could help me. Probably I was scared of another dose of 'You have to live with it.' "[47]

Rees was also enlightened by a story in *The Times* about an International Symposium on Gender Identity that "told of the condition of transsexualism and the most successful form of treatment which was sexual reassignment therapy, i.e., 'sex-change.' "[48] Eventually, through the Albany Trust, Rees was put in touch with Doctor John Randell, who told Rees, "Just prove to me that you can live as a man and I will do everything I can to help you."[49] But Rees had just begun school to train as a dentist, and it took him a while to gather the courage to ask school administrators if they would allow him to attend as a man and change his records to reflect his new gender. They were cooperative and supportive.

Rees was further encouraged by a television appearance made by Doreen Cordell, director of the Albany Trust, and Philip, an FTM. "Philip was totally convincing as a male, no one would have looked at him twice. Having now seen the results of sexual re-assignment I had no more hesitation and wrote to Dr. Randell to ask if I could begin hormone therapy without delay."

Dr. Randell was happy to oblige, but Rees criticizes the quality of care he was given. For one thing, the doctor told Rees the results of taking the hormones were reversible, when in fact they are not, beyond a certain point. The doctor also did not monitor Rees for side-effects after administering the medication. And he also had an attitude problem. Rees complains, "He continued referring to me in the female pronoun, even years after I had become Mark. Although willing to give me the treatment he made it clear at an early stage that in his eyes I was a female and a lesbian. It angered me but I didn't realize that help could have been available from elsewhere so I tolerated his behaviour. At this stage I saw him as my salvation."[50] It is difficult to imagine Jorgensen or Morris having the nerve to criticize their doctors.

Eventually Rees was to meet Eric, who was so eager to change that he took double the prescribed amount of hormone and had to have part of his liver removed because it became cancerous. "The experience also made me realize that perhaps I was at risk too," Rees says. "Did we really know what the long-term effects of drug therapy were going to be? Was it a risk worth taking? I decided it was."[51] Rees's liver scan was clear, and he was switched to a less toxic form of testosterone. Eventually, he hooked up with the Gender Dysphoria Panel at

Newcastle and finally began to receive monitoring of the levels of testosterone in his blood and quality medical care.[52]

Rees's activism was fueled by anger over on-the-job harassment (while working as a clerk's assistant, he once found a drawing on his desk of a penis and a vagina, bearing the caption, "Which is you, Mark?") and the church's refusal to consider his application to become a priest, since at the time women were not being ordained. He eventually took the British government to the European Court of Human Rights, accusing them of failing to recognize his male status and thus denying him a career and the possibility of marriage.

In 1972, Rees began writing letters to Members of Parliament (MPs) complaining about the shoddy treatment of transsexuals. From 1944 until 1970, British transsexuals had been able to get their birth certificates altered. This changed in a 1970 divorce case, *Cornet v. Corbett*, in which the marriage of April Corbett was declared to be void because she was a transgendered woman. British officials thereafter took the position that "the sex description on the birth certificate was a historical fact and therefore an alteration would allow us to 'deceive others' as to our 'true sex.'"[53] At first, Rees received scant support from other transsexuals for these letter-writing campaigns.

In 1979, he found lawyer David Burgess, who was willing to take his case to the European Court. Rees's application was heard by the European Commission for Human Rights on March 14, 1984. He thus became the first transsexual to take action against the British government. But on October, the commission ruled against Rees's complaint. Rather than give up, Rees founded Press for Change, a group that campaigns for legal recognition for transsexuals in England.

The court failed to keep its promise to protect Rees's identity, and news media in Britain began tracking him down and requesting interviews. He finally agreed to lose his anonymity and became a much more public figure. Of this coming out experience, he says:

> No longer was I looking over my shoulder and wondering "Who knows?"; nor was I afraid of someone passing on my "dreadful secret"...nor could I ever be blackmailed. I lost no friends but made more. The "monster" of revelation had turned out to be a friendly kitten.
>
> It was a liberation. ...I was also made aware of the support of many people, some of whom I didn't even know. By hiding I'd been saying to the world, "This is shameful" and "I cannot believe that you have the capacity to show love."

...I've found a great deal of goodwill amongst ordinary people. As transsexuals we should tap this resource. By hiding we
perpetuate the fallacies about our condition, help no one, and
deny ourselves the very thing we want—to be accepted as part
of society. If all transsexuals (of which there are probably several thousand in the UK) "came out" the press would surely lose
interest?[54]

Rees eventually was asked to speak in Brussels in June of 1989 at a
press conference announcing the European Parliament Committee on
Petitions' demand for legal recognition of transsexuals. Although the
full Parliament passed the motion the following September, the British
government did nothing to implement it, which Rees terms "no surprise."[55] However, despite this anti-transsexual bias on a national level,
Rees was elected to be a Councillor of Tunbridge Wells Borough in May
of 1994.[56] "What my election did say to transsexuals is, if you are open
and get on with living as normal a life as possible then you will be
accepted and integrated into a community. It's up to you," Rees claims.[57]

On a more personal level, Rees's life is less rewarding. Early transsexual autobiography downplays the importance of sexual gratification. It's a dead issue for both Jorgensen and Morris. Richards extolled
her success at sexually performing as a woman, refusing to acknowledge any problems or difficulties. But Rees outlines a difficult struggle
with sexuality, which seems more honest and realistic than any other
account available thus far. His first sexual liaison was with a blond
music student who told Rees she was a lesbian and asked if "she" was
one too. (This was prior to Rees taking testosterone.) "The attraction
was obviously mutual," Rees confesses, "but it shocked me that I should
be drawn to a lesbian."[58] Rees warned the girl that as he became more
masculine she would find him less interesting, but nevertheless began
an affair with her. "Although our relationship was brief and stormy it
gave me my first experience of physical contact, although I refused to
be seen less than fully clothed. It was my first contact ever and I found
it overwhelming—and even more so when I discovered her fickleness. I
can't say it did very much for me, either physically or emotionally. I
hated the idea of being in a lesbian relationship but vainly hoped that
we'd be able to carry on in a heterosexual way once I'd changed roles."[59]

Future contacts were to be even less satisfying. Rees describes several unrequited love affairs with women who were, for one reason or
another, unable to return his affection or passion and engage in a full
relationship with him. One of these infatuations continued for fifteen

years! One exception was Debbie, who seems to have been troubled by emotional and mental difficulties. Nevertheless, she was able to engage in sexual activity with Rees. He writes, "When in a 'good mood' Debbie was very warm and loving, often embarrassingly so. She was a gentle and understanding partner who helped me by her acceptance to come to terms with my own body. What I'd read earlier in Dr. Gelber's *Medical Post* had become demonstrably true: a woman could have a satisfactory sexual relationship with a female-to-male transsexual. For me it was less satisfactory, but that was predictable, given my lack of equipment."[60] Eventually Debbie became convinced Rees was turning people at school against her and left him to return to Australia, leaving him feeling that "the price had been high" for his sexual experiences with her.[61]

By the end of *Dear Sir or Madam*, Rees defines himself as a "forced celibate." He acknowledges that his own fear of rejection, his view of himself as an inferior or undesirable person, and his poor judgment in choosing partners are formidable obstacles to a satisfying relationship. He also says that his problem is not typical: "Amongst female-to-males I am unusual in not having a partner," he says.[62] But he questions whether FTMs find as much pleasure in these liaisons as their partners. He describes his sex life with Debbie as "frustrating and uncomfortable" and says it had "given very little relief." And he criticizes research into transsexuality that inquires only after the satisfaction of their partners. "To my knowledge there have not been questions asked of the female-to-male transsexuals themselves, so I do not know if my discomfort and frustration is limited to me or common amongst us."[63]

Rees is caught in a terrible triple-bind. He does not want to have sex with a partner because he hates his female genitals and does not want them to be seen or stimulated. Yet he rejects phalloplasty. "Eager as I was to have a penis I had no wish to submit myself to perhaps ten operations, great pain, scarring and risk of infection in order to acquire something which was useless, ugly and without sensation," he quite reasonably notes.[64] "Less extreme are those who buy prostheses which are now available," Rees admits. But this solution is not for him either. "I can think of better ways of spending my money especially as I've managed over twenty years without one. I need other things before that, such as some new carpets! I comfort myself with the fact that a penis, whether genuine, constructed or plastic, can at times be an encumbrance, and certainly one needs more than that to attract a woman."[65]

He speaks with envy of "one female-to-male friend" who "was able to cope with his 'undesirable bits' by telling himself that because they

SEX CHANGES

belonged to him they were male. He accepted his body; it was not something alien and despised. Probably he is helped by the fact that he has a very good partner." But Rees refuses to accept this strategy of self-acceptance or working with the parts that are available to achieve a measure of sexual satisfaction. "Generally I think we female-to-males find it hard to feel totally secure in the male role without the right 'bits,'" he writes gloomily. "It is difficult to integrate our female parts. My friend was obviously coping better than most."[66]

And so Rees depicts himself as an embittered man, haunted by his failures in the areas of career and relationships, and so disappointed in God that he has become an agnostic who believes "life is futile and…religion is just wishful thinking."[67] Any joy in his life comes from his relationship with friends and family and choral singing.

As a sex educator, I am of course distressed a great deal by Rees's predicament. His rare candor about his sexual disappointments highlights a rather large area in which sex reassignment is a failure. Very few doctors or therapists are daring enough to challenge society's dictate that people must live out their lives in the gender they were assigned at birth. By the time a mental-health or medical professional has educated himself or herself enough to administer sex reassignment, it seems all energy for challenging other taboos has evaporated. The attitude among the gender scientists seems to be that transsexuals should be grateful for the cosmetic changes that make it possible for them to walk down the street without having their gender of preference called into question. The requirement that candidates for sex reassignment live for an extended period of time in their gender of preference usually forces the candidate to solve any problems he or she might have with making a living. But little or no attempt is made to provide sex education, let alone sex therapy, to this population.

Gender identity programs either assume that sex is irrelevant to the transsexual, or ignore his or her sexual future by assuming that, post-transition, this person will simply become a "normal" heterosexual, just like everyone else. But this is possible for very few transsexuals. Surgically-constructed genitalia may not pass cosmetically for "natural" organs. Function and sexual response tend to be problematic. One obvious solution is to assist transsexuals and their partners to find satisfactory styles of lovemaking that incorporate the existing genitalia. However, this would require the gender scientists to change their own requirement that "true transsexuals" loathe and eschew stimulation of the genitals they were born with. While a transgendered person may very well seek treatment with this attitude, it is questionable whether maintaining it is helpful or necessary for the creation of a new life in the gender of preference.

Rees's orientation is heterosexual, but he briefly mentions gay FTMs in his autobiography, describing "one female-to-male friend" of his who "had a phalloplasty (construction of a phallus) in order to please his man-friend!"[68] And more than once he makes the point that transgendered people come in all sexual orientations. This is in contrast to Jorgensen, Morris, and even Richards (who says she never once met a female-to-male transsexual).

Sadly, there is no autobiography of a gay FTM in print. One such autobiography is missing from this chapter, for the simple reason that Louis Sullivan was always too busy as an activist to write such a thing. Born in 1951, Sullivan began cross-dressing as male and living as a gay man when he was twenty-two. When Sullivan applied to a gender dysphoria clinic, he was rejected because the clinic's guidelines required sexual interest in women. So Sullivan obtained hormones from a doctor in private practice at age twenty-eight, in 1979. The following year, he had a mastectomy. In 1983, the same clinic rejected Sullivan again when he wanted to pursue genital surgery. It was not until age thirty-five that Sullivan managed to obtain a metadoioplasty and testicular implants from a plastic surgeon who was not affiliated with a clinic. In 1987, Sullivan found out that he was HIV-positive.

Sullivan had two long-term relationships with gay men, and never wavered in his sexual-orientation choice, despite the prejudice of the sex-change gatekeepers. Perhaps inspired by early gay liberation, he was determined to make life easier for other men like himself. In 1986, he began holding support group meetings for female-to-male cross-dressers or transsexuals. The group met in private homes. He compiled *Information for the Female to Male Cross Dresser and Transsexual* in the early eighties.[69] This compendium of useful information was a voice of sanity and reassurance for transgendered men and female-to-male cross-dressers who otherwise would have found themselves invisible, even in the literature of the gender community.

In 1987, helped by his friend Ken Horowitz, Sullivan began publishing the *FTM Newsletter*, which today is the oldest publication of its kind. Sullivan firmly believed that if his organization was going to build an FTM community, there had to be respect for diversity. He did his best to make those who were beginning to question their gender identity, or those who simply cross-dressed, as welcome in the group as transgendered men who were taking testosterone and contemplating surgery. During the long years when he was seriously ill with AIDS,

Sullivan devoted himself wholeheartedly to building a community for FTMs and educating medical and mental-health professionals, urging them to update their politics and realize that transgendered people could be gay or bisexual as well as straight. And before he died on March 2, 1991, Sullivan made sure he had turned FTM and the newsletter over to men who would continue the work. Of the disease that would kill him, Sullivan quipped, "I took a certain pleasure in informing the gender clinic that even though their program told me I could not live as a gay man, it looks like I'm going to die like one."[70] Information about Sullivan's life is taken from my personal correspondence with him, remarks made at the 1995 FTM conference in San Francisco by James Green, and an "anonymous" case study of an FTM, which is based on interviews with Sullivan.[71]

Instead of writing his own autobiography, Sullivan left behind his recapitulation of the life of Jack "Bee" Garland, an early role model and hero of his.[72] Perhaps one of the new generation of transgendered scholars will take on the very important task of documenting Sullivan's life and work, so he will not be lost to the history of social change.

Until then, gay-male FTM history will reside in easily misplaced bits and pieces, like the interview with Billy, Mike, Eric, Sky and Shadow, which appeared in *Brat Attack*, a lesbian S/M 'zine, in 1992. [73] Not only does this interview document the formation of a subculture of gay FTMs (and S/M-identified gay male FTMs) in San Francisco, it also validates the existence of female-to-male cross-dressers and establishes a new transgendered category, the two-spirited person who does not wish to be seen as exclusively male or female. Sky says, of the group assembled for this interview:

> Part of the problem that *I* have is clearly exhibited by the group of us gathered here. I think I can safely say that everyone except me is very very male-identified as a primary identity. My dysphoria has to do with my physical body, and not my emotional self. Everybody else in this room is physically much more androgynous than I am. I clearly have very "girly," curvy body parts, and always have. My dysphoria has to do with my body not being the body that lives inside of my head. I get a little annoyed—a lot annoyed—about this process having to be one way. About everyone's assumption that if you start this, "this" is the end result. Because it's different for all of us.
>
> My striving is to be what I really believe lives inside me, and that's a shape shifter individual. That's an individual who can

walk in many different kinds of worlds. That masculine person who has lived inside of me never got validity because I have 38DD tits. No matter what I do, I have those. Even when I bind, even when I would do those things, there are certain physical characteristics that come [only] by using the drugs—the squaring of the jaw, the typical male receding hairline at the temples, the voice—unless you're fortunate enough to have that.

...My process is not to fully identify and realize myself as a man. But neither am I a woman.[74]

Leslie Feinberg's 1993 novel *Stone Butch Blues* affirms the fact that not all transgendered people wish to make a complete transition into a new sex; some straddle the gender line and challenge us to create a new social category that recognizes the dignity and rights of those who blend gender in such a way that they are not easy to label as men or women. Feinberg's hero, Jess, begins the book as a working-class stone butch who struggles to survive in the homophobic and racist atmosphere of nineteen-sixties' Buffalo, New York. The realistic descriptions of the discrimination, stigma, and violence that confront Jess and her friends are chillingly accurate and difficult to relive. When the economy stumbles and the factories where Jess has been able to eke out a living close down and lay off their workers, she decides to take testosterone and pass as a man. The anti-gay violence on the street has escalated sharply. She can see no other way to survive.

"I don't feel like a man trapped in a woman's body. I just feel trapped," she tells another butch who is also considering passing as a man.[75] Jess tries to persuade her lover Theresa that "I'd still be a butch. ...Even on hormones," but Theresa ends the relationship because she does not want to be perceived as a heterosexual woman.[76] Since Jess obtains hormones and breast surgery from profiteering doctors rather than going to a gender identity clinic, she never changes her identification papers. Although passing as male means she no longer suffers the same fear of gaybashing or job discrimination, she is constantly looking over her shoulder, afraid to run into someone who will remember her from her prior life and expose her. She can no longer seek comfort from lesbian femmes, and a sexual encounter with a heterosexual woman is imbued with the fear of being caught impersonating a man and the straight woman's hatred of homosexuals.

Feinberg makes a strong connection between butch identity as a gender apart from male or female. When Theresa tries to convince Jess that feminism is good for butches, because they are women too, Jess retorts, "No I'm not [a woman]...I'm a he-she. That's different."[77] While contemplating taking testosterone, she has a dream about being with "other people who were different like me. ...In the dream it wasn't about being gay. It was about being a man or a woman. ...I always feel like I have to prove I'm like other women, but in the dream I didn't feel that way. I'm not even sure I felt like a woman. ...I didn't feel like a woman or a man, and I liked how I was different."[78] Jess has a traumatic childhood memory of being caught trying on her father's suit, and as a child she is rejected by her parents and harassed and assaulted by peers because of her masculinity. When Jess begins hormones, one of her big questions is, "What happens? Does it just last for a little while? I mean can you go back to being a butch later, when it's safe to come out?"[79]

But she eventually comes to see that she has a vocation to challenge gender stereotypes. While passing, she realizes, "I didn't get to explore being a he-she...I simply became a he—a man without a past."[80] When she stops taking hormones, Jess affiliates with a transgendered woman, Ruth, not a lesbian femme. And it is Ruth who cares for Jess when the lack of testosterone once more makes her gender questionable on the street, and she gets queer-bashed.

Toward the end of a book, she has a dream that confirms this spiritual and political path. In the dream, she enters a hut full of her own kind.

> There were people who were different like me inside. We could all see our reflections in the faces of those who sat in this circle. I looked around. It was hard to say who was a woman, who was a man. Their faces radiated a different kind of beauty than I'd grown up seeing celebrated on television or in magazines. It's a beauty one isn't born with, but must fight to construct at great sacrifice.
>
> I felt proud to sit among them. I was proud to be one of them. ...I felt my whole life coming full circle. Growing up so different, coming out as a butch, passing as a man, and then back to the same question that had shaped my life: woman or man?[81]

Feinberg's book also gives a nod to butch-on-butch relationships, which because of her coding of butches as differently-gendered people can also be seen as an acknowledgment of gay FTMs. Jess has an explosive and negative reaction to the news that her friend Frankie is dating Johnny, another butch. "The more I thought about the two of them being lovers, the more it upset me. I couldn't stop thinking about them kissing each other. It was like two guys. Well, two gay guys would be alright. But two butches? How could they be attracted to each other? Who was the femme in bed?"[82] But by the end of the book, Jess tracks down Frankie to apologize. "I never learned to love myself until I gave in to loving other butches," Frankie tells Jess.[83]

Because of the work of Sullivan and other gay-identified FTMs, the mainstream perception of this sexual minority has become much more inclusive. Although a 1994 article in the *New Yorker* focused more on heterosexual FTMs, the author included a lengthy description of Lou Sullivan's contribution to the separation of gender and sexual orientation in the sex-reassignment process, and includes bisexual and gay-male FTMs among her interviewees. "Male is not gay or straight; it's male," she writes. "We may not know what it is, but we know it's not about whether male or female sexual stimuli inspire your erection."[84]

Few transgendered activists have garnered as much acclaim or charmed as many as the ebullient, gifted, and beautiful Kate Bornstein. In the 1994 work *Gender Outlaw*, Bornstein showcases her "take" on gender. While the book contains some autobiographical detail, Bornstein frustrates the paradigm of transsexual-as-freak-show by insisting that gender is everybody's problem, and by giving more space in her narrative to her many other talents. She insists on her right to be seen as a playwright and feminist theorist, as someone who has much more to tell us than a predictable tale of childhood dis-ease culminating in estrogen, breast implants, and vaginoplasty. Bornstein's work represents the first time a transgendered author has turned the tables on the "normal" reader and insisted that it is gender stereotypes and social sex-role fascism that is pathological, not transsexuality.

Like Feinberg's novel, Bornstein breaks the frame of previous trans-sexual narrative by refusing to write a straightforward autobiography. Feinberg affirms the value of transgendered lives by making them the focus of a serious literary work. In *Stone Butch Blues*, it is the cops who raid gay bars and rape butches, the straight men who beat up or murder queers, and the families who reject their gay or transgendered children whose beliefs and behavior are called into question. Although Feinberg gives us an insider's look at the private lives of he-shes or bulldykes and their lovers, she does not put them on display as freaks or rationalize their passions. Mainstream fiction assumes that the "only" point of view is that of the white, heterosexual, middle-class reader. Feinberg utilizes the radical potential of fiction to create a new point of view. By writing from a transgendered perspective for an audience that is assumed to understand and value her story, she challenges the hegemony of normative gender roles and mandatory heterosexuality.

In Bornstein's book, we learn that she was married three times, had a lengthy flirtation with the Church of Scientology, and finally embarked upon a course of hormones and surgery that make it possible for her to be perceived as a woman. But this is not a traditional autobiography. Bornstein uses fragments of her life story to tease the reader, leading us instead through a complex thicket of gender theory, leavened with bittersweet humor. Rather than being a victim of the media, like Christine Jorgensen, or a combatant, like Renée Richards, Bornstein portrays herself as a fan of talk shows and an able manipulator of the genre. "I love doing television talk shows—I respect the format," she tells the reader. "I'm a child of television, so I'm familiar with the venue, and I've learned the language of sound-bytes. I know now to prepare ahead of time the point I want to get across, so I don't have to think on my feet. ...I can have fun bantering with the host, and parrying questions and answers with the audience. And I can usually get back to the single point I want to make on that show."[85]

By including the script of her play "Hidden: A Gender" in this book, she moves one step beyond the role of transsexual as subject (whether of psychiatric case histories or daytime television talk shows). As a playwright, Bornstein generates her own media, one that is informed in every way by her transgendered life. And in that work, the subject of critical scrutiny is more likely to be "normal" men and women. The transsexual is, through Bornstein's able midwifery, transmuted from an isolated freak whose existence must be examined and explained by experts, into a wise outsider full of wry insight into the freakishness of everyday life and its central organizing principle, polarized, binary gender.

Bornstein adds her voice to the chorus of transgendered activists who are not so sure they want to pass as "normal" men and women, post-reassignment. "I identify as neither male nor female," she says, "and now that my lover is going through his gender change, it turns out I'm neither straight nor gay."[86] Later, she adds, "I know I'm not a man—about that much I'm very clear, and I've come to the conclusion that I'm probably not a woman either, at least not according to a lot of people's rules on this sort of thing."[87] Bornstein challenges the belief that many transgendered people have in the trueness or reality of the gender they assume post-reassignment. "Up until the last few years, all we'd be able to write *and get published* were our autobiographies, tales of women trapped in the bodies of men or men pining away in the bodies of women. Stories by and about brave people who'd lived their lives hiding deep within a false gender—and who, after much soul-searching, decided to change their gender, and spend the rest of their days hiding deep within *another* false gender," she says scornfully.[88]

Because so much of *Gender Outlaw* deals with the politics of transgendered activism and theories about the attribution of gender, this material will be dealt with in more detail in the chapters on activism and the future of gender. But before we move on to these abstract concerns, it's time to take a look at the people who love and support transgendered men, women, and others. The partners of transgendered people have received short shrift from researchers studying this population and from transgendered activists themselves. Until now, medical researchers and sexologists assumed that after sex reassignment, transsexuals would either do without sex and intimacy, or would form "normal" heterosexual relationships with nontransgendered partners. To facilitate this, transsexuals were often encouraged to lie about their pasts and not tell anyone, including a spouse or lover, about their sex change.

In the real world, this advice is difficult or just plain impossible for many transgendered people to put into practice. The need to take hormones on a regular basis is hard to hide, and hard to explain without simply being honest. Surgery often does not create a cosmetically perfect "male" or "female" body, and even if that body passes, there will be scars, numb areas, and possibly a need for special medical follow-up and treatment that cannot be easily concealed from a close partner. The dictum to enter the gender closet in order to find love is a cruel one, reinforcing the idea that a transgendered body is not sexy or lovable; making true intimacy or communication with loved ones impossible; and creating a sort of schizophrenia in otherwise healthy people who should not have to live with the stress of a double life or a hidden past.

More recently, the partners of transgendered people, especially FTMs, have begun to organize, and the idea has been advanced that perhaps there is a new sexual minority emerging, people who find differently-gendered folks especially attractive. In *Stone Butch Blues*, Jess is reunited, while passing as a man, with Edna, an old-fashioned lesbian femme. Jess tells Edna as much about the loneliness and fear of passing as her stone-butch personality will allow. They both decry the death of old-style gay bars and the rise of a lesbian culture that excommunicates butches and femmes. Edna confesses, "I know I'm not a straight woman, and lesbians won't accept me as one of them. I don't know where to go to find the butches I love or the other femmes. I feel completely misunderstood. I feel like a ghost too, Jess."[89]

The next chapter, about the partners of transgendered people, will attempt to bring some of these ghosts back to life.

Notes

1. Renée Richards with John Ames, *Second Serve: The Renée Richards Story*, New York: Stein and Day, 1983, p. 13.
2. Ibid., p. 5.
3. Ibid., pp. 32-33.
4. Ibid., p. 27.
5. Ibid., pp. 56-57.
6. Ibid., p. 127.
7. Ibid., p. 57.
8. Ibid., p. 74.
9. Ibid., p. 294.
10. Ibid., p. 79.
11. Ibid., p. 121.
12. Ibid., p. 139.
13. Ibid., p. 160.
14. Ibid., p. 145.
15. Ibid., p. 148.
16. Ibid., p. 149.
17. Ibid., p. 164.
18. Ibid., p. 176.
19. Ibid., p. 210.
20. Ibid., p. 213.
21. Ibid., p. 239.
22. Ibid., p. 247.
23. Ibid., p. 283.
24. Ibid., p. 373.
25. Ibid., p. 371.
26. Ibid., p. 286.
27. Ibid., p. 287.
28. Ibid., pp. 288-289.
29. Ibid., pp. 295-296.
30. Ibid., pp. 309-310.
31. Ibid., p. 39.
32. Ibid., p. 54.
33. Ibid., p. 325.
34. Ibid., p. 340.
35. Ibid., p. 361-362.
36. Alex Carlile, "Preface," in Mark Rees, *Dear Sir or Madam: The Autobiography of a Female-to-Male Transsexual*, London: Cassell, 1996, pp. xi-xii.
37. Rees, op. cit., p. 6.
38. Ibid., p. 7.
39. Ibid., p. 8.
40. Ibid., p. 9.
41. Ibid., p. 17.
42. Ibid., pp. 18-19.
43. Ibid., p. 35.

44. Ibid., p. 45.

45. Ibid., p. 58.

46. Ibid., p. 73.

47. Ibid., p. 74.

48. Ibid., p. 75.

49. Ibid., p. 77.

50. Ibid., p. 83.

51. Ibid., p. 105.

52. Ibid., p. 148.

53. Ibid., p. 157.

54. Ibid., p. 162.

55. Ibid., p. 170.

56. Ibid., p. 173.

57. Ibid., p. 174.

58. Ibid., p. 82.

59. Ibid.

60. Ibid., p. 131.

61. Ibid., p. 132.

62. Ibid., p. 134.

63. Ibid., p. 135.

64. Ibid., p. 128.

65. Ibid., p. 175.

66. Ibid.

67. Ibid., p. 178.

68. Ibid., p. 59.

69. Louis Sullivan, *Information for the Female to Male Cross Dresser and Transsexual*, Second Edition, San Francisco: L. Sullivan, 1985. The third, revised edition of this work was published in 1990 by Seattle's Ingersoll Center.

70. L. Sullivan, "Sullivan's Travels," *The Advocate*, June 6, 1989, p. 71.

71. Eli Coleman and Walter O. Bockting, " 'Heterosexual' Prior to Sex Reassignment—'Homosexual' Afterwards: A Case Study of a Female-to-Male Transsexual," *Journal of Psychology and Human Sexuality*, vol. 1(2), 1988, pp. 69-82.

72. Louis Sullivan, *From Female to Male: The Life of Jack Bee Garland*, Boston: Alyson Publications, 1990.

73. Deva, "FTM: A Discussion Organized and Facilitated by Deva," *Brat Attack*, no. 3, 1992, pp. 8-12, 15-19.

74. Ibid., p. 11.

75. Leslie Feinberg, *Stone Butch Blues*, Ithaca, New York: Firebrand Books, 1993, pp. 158-159.

76. Ibid., p. 151.

77. Ibid., p. 147.

78. Ibid., p. 143.

79. Ibid., p. 145.

80. Ibid., p. 222.

81. Ibid., pp. 300-301.

82. Ibid., p. 202.

83. Ibid., p. 274.

84. Amy Bloom, "The Body Lies," *The New Yorker*, July 18, 1994, p. 42.
85. Kate Bornstein, *Gender Outlaw: On Men, Women and the Rest of Us*, New York and London: Routledge, 1994, pp. 129-130.
86. Ibid., p. 4.
87. Ibid., p. 8.
88. Ibid., pp. 12-13.
89. Feinberg, op. cit., pp. 214-215.

CHAPTER 6

The Invisible Gender Outlaws: Partners of Transgendered People

When transsexuality first became a topic that could appear, however marginally, in print, advocates for sex reassignment attempted to shift the reader's focus away from prurient questions. The transsexual was presented as a tormented person whose great suffering could only be relieved by hormones and surgery. The foremost issue facing these unfortunate people was gender identification—being accepted as a member of their gender of preference. Questions about how transsexuals might establish ordinary lives for themselves once sex reassignment was accomplished were rarely asked. Indeed, Jorgensen and Morris both seem to be claiming that once their need to be perceived as women was met, they had little or no pressing need for intimate relationships with men or for sexual pleasure.

In the early literature of transsexuality, partners of transgendered people were (when they appeared at all) presented as "normal" individuals. The ordinary manhood of the people who dated (or were merely desired by) Christine Jorgensen, Jan Morris, and Renée Richards validated their female identities. If these men were depicted as anything other than masculine heterosexuals, sex reassignment for male-to-female transsexuals would have been seen as a charade. Transgendered women would have been viewed as homosexuals or extreme transvestites. (This, in fact, continues to be many people's view of transsexuals, no matter how much education or public relations is done on their behalf.) Mario Martino's wife, Rebecca, is also portrayed as an ordinary heterosexual woman, feminine in every way. Martino believes that if Rebecca had not chosen to become his mate, she would have selected a biological male, not a female, as her spouse. He repeatedly makes the point in his autobiography that he and Rebecca are not a lesbian couple. It is Rebecca's femininity and heterosexuality that he advances as the facts which most support his claim to manhood.

While reading these accounts, I was struck by the parallels to early homosexual male and lesbian fiction, in which the sissy or the woman invert, respectively, is portrayed as doomed to pursue the sexual or romantic company of normal, heterosexual men and women, where they can, of course, find no happiness. The queer, effeminate boys in the fiction of Jean Genet would never have sex with each other, and Radclyffe Hall's butch heroine Stephen has a series of unrequited crushes on heterosexual women before finally encountering Mary, who returns her passion. Indeed, without the assumed heterosexuality of Mary, the whole plot of *The Well of Loneliness* would make very little sense. Stephen pretends infidelity and then sends a betrayed and outraged Mary into the arms of a straight man who can give her "real happiness," i.e., a heterosexual marriage and children. These actions would hardly seem noble or tragic if the reader saw Mary as a lesbian who was now doomed to spend a frustrating and unfulfilled life with a man. In Hall's world, there is no such thing as a lesbian femme, only a rare sort of heterosexual women who tolerates a relationship with an invert only because of her manly qualities.

There are many reasons why these parallels between early transsexual autobiography and queer fiction exist. In early gay fiction, homosexual men and lesbians were portrayed as being gender-deviant to a much greater extent than in queer short stories and novels published today. This colored the depiction and understanding of every aspect of homosexual experience, including "coming out." A gay man knew he was gay, according to what people understood from Victorian times until the nineteen-seventies, precisely because he was unmanly, because there was something womanly about him. And a lesbian was a woman who could not "fix herself up," i.e., turn herself into "lady" who was attractive to men. There was no room in this paradigm for the queerness of a pansy's butch gangster boyfriend, or the queerness of a lesbian femme who emphatically chose butch women over straight men. This view of "gay life" shifted dramatically in the mid-seventies, when a "butch-on-butch" paradigm began to govern urban male homosexual life, and feminism stigmatized butch-femme role-playing and redefined the lesbian as a "woman-identified woman."

For a closer look at early twentieth-century attitudes toward gender-defiant people's partners, we must examine *The Transvestite and His Wife*, a 1967 booklet authored by an early activist for the cross-dressing community, Virginia "Charles" Prince. Although *Sex Changes* deals almost exclusively with transsexuals rather than transvestites, cross-dressers are a significant part of the gender community. A lack of space in this volume precludes adequately addressing the role of cross-dressers in shaping current notions of gender. Their cultural history overlaps and is linked with the politics of the transgendered community but is not identical to it.

I have been unable to locate any equivalent work written for the wives, husbands, girlfriends, or boyfriends of transsexuals. It is probable that a self-help booklet of that kind would have been thought to be unnecessary in the fifties and sixties because transsexuals were supposed to become normal men or women. If these new women and new men needed a special manual to help their partners adjust, that would have challenged the sex-change doctors' assurances that sex reassignment could turn troubled people into healthy, happy people who would no longer stand out as odd or different. But the male transvestite cannot hide his difference by becoming a woman. Precisely because he does not wish to go "all the way," he continues to display his sexual difference every time he seeks erotic gratification by cross-dressing. So by examining this text, we will get some inklings about the ways that the partners of differently-gendered people were viewed twenty years ago.

The Transvestite and His Wife was distributed through an organization and magazine founded by its author. (In February of 1960, Prince founded *Transvestia* magazine. He also founded the Society for the Second Self and the Tri Ess Sorority.) This is another critical difference between the two sexual minorities, cross-dressers and transsexuals. Cross-dressers were less able to escape the stigma of being sexual deviants than transsexuals, who through "sex reassignment" supposedly became just like everybody else. Transvestites therefore had more reason to form social organizations for exchanging information and gaining support. During the sixties and seventies, transsexuals had to "piggyback" on cross-dressers' publications and organizations if they wanted these resources. Cross-dressers' media depicted transsexuality as the ultimate form of transvestism, available only to a lucky few, who could now indulge their passion for pretty things on a full-time basis, without having to hide from society's scorn and condemnation. However, as we have seen in the autobiographies of Jorgensen and Morris, male-to-female transsexuals at that time took great pains to distinguish their "condition" from a fetish for women's clothing. The relationship between the community of cross-dressers and the community of transsexuals has always been full of both tension and solidarity, a search for commonality and a need to separate and seek distance from one another.

Ironically, if transsexuals had formed their own organizations, they might very well have undercut all the medical and psychiatric arguments that had made sex reassignment available. A transsexual who retained any consciousness about his or her sexual-minority status after reassignment would not have been seen as a success by the "authorities" who administered the gender clinics. In the beginning, transgendered men and women who had completed the process of sex reassignment were urged to destroy any mementos of their childhoods, create false stories about the past that were consistent with their gender of preference, hide their transsexuality from their partners, and live in a medically-mandated state of duplicity and amnesia. The fear and shame that would have been induced by following this impractical prescription was never acknowledged, nor any help offered to cope with it.

There are many similarities between Prince's book and early transsexual autobiography. The book is dedicated to medical experts in the gender field, a psychiatrist named Dr. Karl Bowman, then-President of the American Psychiatric Association and the first Director of the Langley Porter Clinic, and Dr. Harry Benjamin. Prince encountered Bowman when the author was on the faculty of a medical school and heard that he was studying transvestites. Bowman is quoted as telling Prince, "Stop fighting it, it isn't so terrible. There are thousands of others like you and always have been. Medical science hasn't been able to do much for them, so the best thing to do is to relax and learn to accept yourself. Be happy and adjust to it. Don't be fearful, lonely, or self-condemnatory."[1] Benjamin's work with transsexuals is described in chapter two. Here he is also celebrated as someone who conducted pioneering research on transvestism. Prince says, "Through his education of other doctors, psychologists, and marriage counselors he has helped many hundreds of transvestites." Benjamin is also thanked for providing counseling that assuaged Prince's own "parental and marital problems."[2]

Like Jorgensen and Morris, Prince does his best to disassociate transvestism from deviant sexual pleasure. Rather than *transvestism*, which connotes an erotic fetish often gratified by masturbation, he prefers the term *femmiphilia*, or "love of the feminine." Prince defines *femmiphilia* as "a form of behaviour and personality expression characterized by a desire to wear the clothing of the opposite sex," and says femmiphiles are "persons whose interest is solely in the feminine gender role and not in her sexual activity."[3] Elsewhere, transvestism is referred to, in a letter by "Doctor Charles," as "personality manifestations previously ill understood and confused by serious misconceptions."[4]

Throughout the book, Prince specifically excludes homosexual men from this discourse, despite the fact that there was a well-developed subculture of gay drag queens, of which he was clearly not ignorant. He says, "The femmiphile adopts feminine garb as a matter of personal internal expression—the homosexual 'Queen' does so for external effect—to attract males for sexual purposes and to ease the guilt of both."[5] Prince does not acknowledge that some heterosexual cross-dressers also enjoy receiving sexual attention from men, since this bolsters their sense of femininity. He says, "Practically no femmiphile would advise, induce, or influence another to become a transvestite— he knows the cost too well and has suffered too much to wish it on another. Most homosexuals, however, have no hesitation about indoctrinating and initiating others into the practice."[6] Later on in the book, however, he quotes a letter from a new reader of *Transvestia* who is very excited to discover that there are many other men who share his "love for feminine things."[7] Prince seems naïvely unaware of the fact that his own magazine could easily be seen as a vehicle for "indoctrination" and "initiating others into the practice" of cross-dressing.

By eschewing any reference to or expression of tolerance for homosexuality, Prince probably hoped to make cross-dressing more palatable for wives, whose first reaction to the information that their husbands liked to wear dresses was invariably the assumption that this meant they were homosexual. It also distanced his subject from a stigmatized pleasure-seeking behavior, and kept cross-dressing within the realm of heterosexual romance. Indeed, much of Prince's appeal to wives is based on the stereotype of the female as a nurturing, forgiving, and loving wife. Prince associates acceptance of cross-dressing with the acceptance and compromise that is necessary to keep any marriage strong.[8]

This attempt to normalize male transvestism is ironically furthered by a denial that female-to-male cross-dressers exist. Prince says, "Females can and do wear masculine type clothing so openly and without social disapproval that the desire to do so is not frustrated and does not therefore present a problem."[9] He can perhaps be forgiven for this since historical evidence for the existence of female cross-dressing is routinely censored and its erotic significance misinterpreted or denied altogether. But this putative "difference" between male and female sexuality has more to do with the repression of women's sexuality in general (and, sometimes, women's ignorance of their own sexuality, especially if it takes a minority form) than a shift in couture. I know what I feel when I am in male drag. My conversations with other women who cross-dress as men make it clear that I am not the only woman who gets a sexual rush out of appropriating a masculine image. A whole book could probably be written about the misogyny and homophobia that has led sexologists and other "experts" to frequently state, as Prince does, that women can wear men's clothes without being punished, so they have no need to become transvestites. This is, however, patently false.

After World War II, it became progressively more and more acceptable for women to wear trousers in public. But this change in feminine fashion was made possible by distinguishing certain types of girls' pants from male apparel. A woman who wore a polka-dot pair of Capri pants made out of a lightweight knit fabric and held up with a side zipper could hardly be said to be wearing "men's clothing." Great care is still taken to make business suits for women very different from business suits for men, by choice of fabric, tailoring, cut, and the choice of accessories. You can find photos of women in jeans and oversized, white men's shirts in any fashion magazine today, but the jeans are usually tight enough and the shirt unbuttoned enough to display feminine curves, and the woman in this outfit will usually have long hair and bright red lipstick. The pinstripe suits that are sometimes worn by short-haired waifs hardly count as "men's clothing" in such a magazine, when the cosmetic ads and giggly copy clearly demarcate it as a feminine zone. The boyish gamine is recognized as a certain type of French-flavored feminine beauty.

As any stone butch or passing woman can tell you, the general public continues to be deeply disturbed by a biological female who appears in public in men's clothing. There is no difference between the discrimination, condemnation, and violence that is routinely inflicted upon male and female cross-dressers, if they are exposed as such.

The average heterosexual woman who dons a pastel polyester pantsuit to go to work is not attempting to stimulate herself sexually or take on aspects of the male social role. By identifying male transvestism as the mirror image of any woman who wears pants on the street, Prince is making a bid to desexualize and thereby normalize transvestism in men. He seems to be saying that if men could wear dresses to work, transvestism would cease to exist. But this ignores the fact that, for most cross-dressers, the sensual pleasure and sexual release they obtain from wearing women's clothing is a key part of the experience. The average transvestite might find it pretty frustrating to routinely wear feminine clothing since it's considered lewd and indecent behavior to gratify the arousal triggered by these garments in public view. Prince is also sending a dubious message to a wife who wears trousers, suggesting to her that she is as much a transvestite as her cross-dressing husband.

The Transvestite and His Wife differs dramatically from early male-to-female transsexual autobiography by firmly situating transvestism in the realm of an intimate relationship with another person. Masturbation, a frequent consummation of the cross-dressing experience for men, is not mentioned once in this booklet. Nor are transvestites who have eroticized only certain items of female apparel given any acknowledgment. The author lists "Avis" and "Shirley," wives of transvestites who contributed letters to the book, in the acknowledgment. While it's wonderful to see these women acknowledged for their tolerant and loving attitude toward their different husbands, it also seems important to acknowledge that only one type of transvestism is being justified here, the type that involves dressing from head-to-toe as a woman and socializing with others in a female persona.

This may be because Prince himself prefers to live as much as possible in his female persona, and feels he is motivated much more by a desire to emulate the positive qualities of women than he is by any erotic thrill to be gained from intimate contact with their apparel. Prince has said, in a televised interview, that he feels this transition into a less carnal type of cross-dressing experience is common among older transvestites.[10] Indeed, the uninformed reader might conclude from the jacket photo (which shows Prince in female mode), the author's byline (Virginia "Charles" Prince), and the use of female pronouns to refer to the author, that this booklet was authored by a woman—perhaps even a biological female who cross-dressed as male and used the pseudonym "Charles" for that persona. In 1967, it may have been hoped that a portrayal of Prince as female would make the book more palatable to a confused wife who was desperately looking for a way to hold her marriage together. I've chosen to use male pronouns to refer to Prince to eliminate some potential confusion.

Prince does his best to disengage transvestism from the realm of sexual perversion. He acknowledges various psychiatric theories about the causes of transvestism: "(a) parents wanting a girl and bringing a boy up that way, (b) keeping a boy in dresses and curls to an unusually late age, (c) punishing a boy by making him wear girl's clothes, (d) not having an adequate father figure to emulate; or lastly (e) having a father who demanded so much masculinity of an intellectual, sensitive or artistic child that he took refuge in femininity where he felt more at ease."[11] However, he justly points out that not all transvestites have one of these experiences in their backgrounds, and not all boys who have these experiences become transvestites.

To further depathologize transvestism, Prince outlines four other factors that are reasons for cross-dressing. These include "The Need to Acquire Virtue and Experience Beauty," "The Need for Adornment and Personality Expression," "Relief from the Requirements of Masculinity," and "Relief from Social Expectancy."[12] Prince dismisses psychiatry by quoting experts who believe that any attempt to cure someone of this behavior is doomed to failure.

This returns control of the problem to the private sphere, where Prince suggests that it is just one more problem for a couple to solve, like a fight over the weekly budget or a conflict over how much time to spend with one's in-laws. He wisely attempts to de-escalate hysteria about male cross-dressing by making a mild critique of gender roles. He says, "It is commonly recognized that no man is one hundred per cent masculine and no woman one hundred per cent feminine. Since this is the case, every man has feminine qualities that seek expression, and every female has masculine aggressiveness, domination, etcetera in various activities and allows her to dress to fit the part."[13] However, Prince never really attacks sexism or gender regimentation in a radical or systematic way. He emphasizes that, "Just as a woman bus driver may still be a good wife and mother when off the job and back in her feminine clothes, so the femmiphile does not sacrifice or imperil his masculinity by his transvestic activities. He is still an adequate male, father, and husband."[14] Prince repeatedly distinguishes transvestism from transsexuality. He reprints a letter from a transvestite that contains the statement, "As far as I can see, a homosexual doesn't have much use for women—neither sexually or any other way. Neither do I want to be like Christine and have sex-change surgery. I'm not anxious to give up my manhood or forego the enjoyments of being a man. It's just that I've got a side to my personality that I can't seem to express when I'm in the role of a man."[15]

Indeed, Prince asserts, because he has a feminine personality, the wife of such a person is a lucky woman indeed, because her husband will be more sympathetic to her needs than a man who has not cultivated an appreciation of the feminine.[16] In fact, Prince says, "Femmiphiles (TVs) actually have a higher regard for women than most women do for themselves."[17]

The view of marriage in *The Transvestite and His Wife* seems to be taken straight out of a fifties' television sitcom. Prince assumes that the husband is the breadwinner and the wife is the homemaker. Divorce is something shameful to be avoided at all costs, even if that means putting up with a husband who wears dresses around the house. And it is also taken for granted that the reader has a middle-class standard of living. Despite Prince's assurances that transvestites love and adore women, there are many resentful comments about women in the book that give that "adoration" a bitter edge. The perceived freedom of women to violate gender boundaries is frequently mentioned with a great deal of envy.[18]

One transvestite says, in a letter to his wife:

> It is little wonder that we competitors in the masculine rat-race should seek periods of escape in order to still our unsatisfied souls in the need for calmness and peace, and to allow us contact with pleasing things, little or dainty things, all the enjoyable things that are usually denied us. In some people this need for escape takes the form of transvestism.
>
> Most transvestites feel that you real women have much the best of life, due to your ability to live without the need for intense competition and all the hectic and demanding effort, both mental and physical that such competition requires. No wonder you outlive us![19]

It is difficult to imagine the man who wrote this letter having any sympathy at all with the realities of daily life that most women share, let alone evincing any support for feminist attempts to better those conditions. There is no empathy for the claustrophobia induced by being relegated to a life full of "little" and "dainty things," no sense of how hard most women (even middle-class women) work to keep their families comfortable. The fetishized version of femininity as presented in Prince's book is an ironclad and demanding goddess. There is little or no solidarity with biological women who depart from the perceived demands of Her cult. In a weird twist, one correspondent says, "She [the transvestite's female persona] *does* represent your husband's idealized concept of all that is best in womanhood, and every blow you strike at her sets you farther apart from that ideal."[20] In other words, the wife who opposes feminine behavior on her husband's part is a gender traitor, and actually damages her own femininity.

The book is also tarnished by condescending and sexist promises to explain this difficult subject in terms that women can grasp.[21] I found this comment, in a letter from a transvestite to his wife, especially offensive: "It is inescapable that we transvestites always torture ourselves by marrying or courting the most delightful piece of perfect feminine confectionery we can find, as I did with your lovely self...."[22] It is entertaining to imagine such a husband being asked to validate his wife's masculinity, which Prince insists all women possess, with the same enthusiasm that she is being asked to display for his quest for femininity.

While the book promises TV wives that it's fun to dress your husband up (this process is described as "making your own girlfriend"), and also promises that TV husbands will be less likely to complain about their wives spending money on their wardrobes, few other solid rewards are held out to the wife who elects to remain in such a marriage. Among these dubious promises is the assurance that a man who can cross-dress at home will be very unlikely to cheat on his wife.[23] Prince's focus is on persuading the wife to gratify her husband's need to cross-dress, not on her needs or desires. The wife's fear that she has somehow created her husband's transvestism by not being feminine enough and resentment about competition to be the most feminine or beautiful member of the couple are common problems in such relationships. The blame for both is placed solidly with the wife.[24] Her lack of acceptance is seen as the only really serious problem in the relationship.

A letter from an accepting wife of a transvestite says, "Actually I do not consider TVs unfortunate. Quite the contrary. In themselves they are *fortunate* because they have found a means of expressing ALL of their personality, not just part. The only stumbling block to their fortune is the fact that YOU, someone very dear to them, do not share this understanding and experience."[25] Elsewhere, a distaste for transvestism is termed "immaturity. In a measure this is like the seven-year-old who loves his mother, but when she serves turnips at dinner, he hates her. To love only for what pleases one is to love for selfish reasons."[26] Acceptance of the husband's cross-dressing is seen as a natural extension of the wife's feminine role as the source of love, forgiveness, understanding, and nurturance. Wives are reminded that they promised to love their husbands "for better or worse."[27]

The possibility that a woman might have legitimate reasons for not having an erotic response to a cross-dressing man is never acknowledged. In fact, Prince steers a wide berth away from all questions of sexual expression in such a marriage. This book assumes that the cross-dressing experience is asexual, and that marital sex will be male-dominant and follow the usual pattern for heterosexual intercourse.

The only exception to this is a derogatory comment about a "Level Four Wife," i.e., one who is not really accepting of transvestism: "If he should try to give her a kiss while he's dolled up, she'll freeze. 'Don't you dare kiss me while you are dressed *THAT* way! It gives me the willies. Makes me feel as if I married some WOMAN.' "[28] Elsewhere, Prince assures the reader, "A wife is not being asked to become a lesbian to go along with the transvestism!"[29] But this is in fact not true; fantasies about "lesbian sex" are common among heterosexual cross-dressing men, many of whom wish to be the passive partner in this scenario. Nor does Prince mention domination, bondage, or S/M, other common themes in transvestite fantasy. But this is hardly surprising in a booklet that cannot acknowledge the common use of pornography and masturbation as adjuncts to transvestite pleasure.

Nevertheless, the book is an honest attempt to educate the reader and present a nontoxic view of male cross-dressing. It and *Transvestia* magazine undoubtedly helped many people achieve self-acceptance, and possibly even kept a few loving couples from jettisoning marriages that would otherwise have been wrecked by transphobia. Many of its retro political qualities can be attributed to the times in which it was published. It is impossible to remain unmoved by the letters from exceptional wives who took a common-sense approach to their husbands and gave them love, acceptance, and compassion. Says "Gisele's wife":

> When I realized how much he needed someone who would understand and sympathize with his desires, and accept him as he was, I simply made up my mind that I would be that "someone."
> ...I inspected his wardrobe and found it outmoded. I was determined that if there was to be another "girl" around the house, then I would do all I could to see that "she" was as much a well dressed and well mannered lady as possible.[30]

"Fran's wife," apparently a working-class woman, touchingly describes the big difference it made in her husband's self-esteem when the couple "finally saved up enough to buy a real hair wig."[31] "Barbara's wife" takes her cross-dressing husband out in public, matter-of-factly acknowledging her husband's female persona's need to " 'get out and live a little' from time to time."[32] Some wives apparently used their husband's transvestism as a stepping-stone to expanding their own gender identity. "Gerry's wife" says, "We don't think of each other as male or female but as a combination of both. If we want to, we give each other a manicure or we will go outside and fix the car."[33] And "Pauline's wife" says, "No longer do I want to hide my individuality. I love my TV husband, and two of my dearest friends are homosexuals. It is sad that there are so few people in this world with whom I can discuss my husband and friends openly, honestly, and intelligently...."[34]

Still, the picture of differently-gendered people's intimate relationships as presented in *The Transvestite and His Wife* and as recommended by gender identity clinics in the late seventies have one crucial thing in common: the assumption that the cross-dresser or the transsexual will have to look for a romantic or sexual partner among otherwise "normal" men and women. The transvestite, unlike the transsexual, is not able to hide his sexual difference, but his wife is still seen as an ordinary woman who does not share in her partner's deviance. The idea that cross-dressing a man might give sexual pleasure to some women, who would deliberately seek out such an experience, rarely appears in nonfiction literature about transsexuality or transvestism. But the fact that there is no term for such an identity does not mean that it does not exist. They may be rare, but there are people (male, female, and other) who desire, enjoy, and prefer to be partnered with men or women who cross-dress or who are transgendered. Another notion that does not appear in the academic literature about or journalistic coverage of transgenderism is the possibility of differently-gendered people affiliating romantically or sexually with one another.

Sex reassignment has been available for roughly three decades. And in those three decades, a certain amount of folk wisdom has accumulated in the gender community. Not all of this information is shared with the father figures of gender identity programs. But by now, most transsexuals know perfectly well that the "expert" advice about sex and romance post-gender transition is worthless. For the male-to-female transsexual, medical science is able to produce only a facsimile of female breasts and genitals. The typical MTF needs ongoing monitoring, medical care, and corrective surgery. Few of them emerge from top or bottom surgery with anything approaching the kind of nipple or genital sensitivity that biological females possess. If an MTF is going to have anything other than cursory heterosexual intercourse that is satisfying only for the male partner, her lover or spouse needs to have complete information about her body. *Most* women need to have this kind of intimate exchange of history and needs in order to feel loved or achieve sexual satisfaction.

Although this is rarely acknowledged in the social-science research literature, it is my impression that fewer and fewer MTFs are seeking genital surgery. MTFs talk to one another. They know about the urinary tract infections, poor healing, numbness, lack of lubrication or flexibility, and inorgasmia that commonly accompany vaginoplasty. It seems easier, to many transgendered women, to find a partner who is not disturbed by the notion of making love with a woman who has a penis than it is to find a surgeon who can provide sexually-responsive female genitals with no urinary-tract anomalies. And if an MTF is making her living in the sex industry, losing her penis also often means losing a source of income, since clients tend to be much more interested in "she-males." (This term, which appears frequently in commercial-sex ads, may not reflect the transgendered sex worker's self-image.) Transgendered women who have not had genital surgery are obviously unable to simply blend in with the general female population and pass as genetic females.

The gender doctors' notions of female sexuality are at least three decades out of date. To have a complete life, transgendered women need much more than a pretty face, tits with little or no erotic sensation, and a genital channel suitable for shallow penile penetration. This crude terminology is not intended to demean transgendered women, but to make it clear exactly how crude, inadequate, and deeply sexist the gender clinics' stereotype of womanhood really is. And this critique should not be used to argue against the reality of a transgendered woman's gender preference. Instead, it should be used as the basis for demanding that gender clinics stop making promises to their clients that they cannot keep, adopt a more modern and realistic view of human sexuality, accept responsibility for giving their clients sex education and, when needed, sex therapy or couples counseling.

The situation for the female-to-male post-reassignment is, from a cosmetic standpoint, even less satisfactory, although testosterone does some things for the FTM that estrogen cannot do for the MTF. Male hormones cause beard growth (and male pattern baldness), providing the individual's genetic heritage includes these traits, and drops the voice an octave; female hormones will not eliminate facial hair or make a low voice higher. Chest surgery for FTMs may have fewer undesirable sequelae than breast implants; however, the postsurgical chest may not be completely readable as male due to obvious scarring and (depending on the skill of the surgeon and the client's ability to heal) the size or placement of the nipples. Genital surgery for FTMs is acknowledged to be a painful, dangerous, and outrageously expensive gamble by everyone except the most fanatical (or unethical) plastic surgeons who offer it. It rarely produces an organ that cosmetically resembles a penis, let alone one that functions well as a tool for elimination or sexual plea-sure. The overwhelming majority of FTMs opt for no genital surgery at all or a relatively minor procedure that exposes more of the hormon-ally-enlarged clitoris, lending it the appearance of a micropenis, and converts the labia majora into a scrotum with testicular implants.

Yet FTMs are entitled to have as much intimacy and physical plea-sure in their lives as anyone else. This means that they must find part-ners who are knowledgeable about and supportive of their transgendered bodies. Transgendered men are not content to seek pity or the sort of charitable assistance one would render a disabled person. They want allies and partners who find them attractive, as they are, who will validate their male identities without expecting them to undergo mutilating surgical procedures that are inadequate to the task of creating fully-functioning male genitals.

Another reality the gender identity clinics have been loathe to acknowledge is the fact that many transgendered people are gay or bisexual. Since gay men and lesbians are more aware of transsexuality than the heterosexual majority, a transgendered person is much less likely to be able to keep that a secret in this milieu. A transgendered fag, dyke, or bisexual can't rely on "blending in" as a survival strategy. An ability to question authority, fight discrimination, and resist oppres-sion is crucial, and gender identity clinics do not even try to encourage their gay clients to develop these skills. Even transgendered men and women who identify as heterosexual often choose to be affiliated with the queer community, for the simple reason that they are more likely to find tolerance and support there than any place else. Then there is the fact that, even after hormones and surgery, voice lessons and electroly-sis, body-building and tattoos, some transgendered people are never going to be able to "pass" in their gender of preference. These folks have no choice but to become activists, or self-destruct.

Transgendered political agendas have shifted in the last few years. In its original form, transgendered activism consisted of educating the medical and psychiatric profession, attempting to garner more support for administering the sex-reassignment process. As more and more people went through sex reassignment and had a need for updated legal documents, that activism extended to lobbying public officials and the judicial system, to facilitate complete transition and the cre-ation of new identities that were consistent with the transgendered per-son's gender of preference.

Now, however, more and more transgendered people are saying that it is the binary gender system that is dysfunctional. Rather than pleading for treatment for a medical condition or a mental illness, gender dysphoria, they are asking the rest of society to change the way gender is defined and used in our lives. Rather than striving to blend in and pass, some transgendered activists are touting the view that passing is privilege, and to pass means buying into an oppressive polarized, binary gender system. An ideological connection has been made between being out of the closet as a lesbian or gay man and being visible as a transgendered person, someone who is gender-ambiguous. There are fierce conflicts within the gender community between old-style activists, who prefer to continue lobbying the medical and legal professions for greater tolerance, and an Act Up style of gender activism, which brings transgendered issues into the "queer community," an umbrella group composed of gay men, lesbians, bisexual men and women, and transgendered people. These changes in transgendered activism are tracked in greater detail in the next two chapters.

Concurrent with this change is the emergence of a very new notion, which is that the partners of transgendered people may constitute a sexual minority in their own right. Ray Blanchard and Peter I. Collins coined the tongue-twisting term "gynandromorphophiles" to characterize men who have a sexual interest in transvestites, transsexuals, and she-males.[35] And the female partners of FTMs have begun a dialogue about the differences they perceive between their own sexual identities and the categories of "lesbian" and "heterosexual." Kathy Bobula, the editor of a newsletter for the significant others of FTMs, describes her personal journey toward self-awareness:

> Earlier this year, Silas and I attended a meeting of a local transgender group where three MTFs were going to speak on surgeries. …One of the MTFs was a very "butchy" looking woman with an attitude. I found myself sexually attracted to her and began joking to Silas that maybe I was actually *into* transsexuals. Ha, ha. In August, we attended the First International FTM Conference in San Francisco, and my mind was blown! I had never before in my life been in a room with so many people to whom I was sexually attracted. I *am* attracted to transsexuals— mostly to FTMs, but butch MTFs with a dominant streak are all right too!
>
> …What *is* my sexual orientation, anyway? Do I care?[36]

But Bobula is concerned that these questions might have a negative impact on the credibility of her partner's male identity. Bobula and her partner do not think of his life transition as "sex reassignment." She says:

Gender confirmation is a term that Dr. Toby Melzer uses. He is Silas's plastic surgeon. Gender confirmation is a more valid description of the surgery and ongoing hormone therapy as "treatments" for the condition of gender dysphoria, which Silas was diagnosed as having. The prescribed treatment for this condition of gender dysphoria was a combination of surgery, hormone therapy, and psychotherapy which covered the "condition" from the inside out! Silas is and has always been a man. He never "changed his sex," but he did change the chemical composition of his body and its expression of his sex. His body now conforms to his sex. Seeing Silas in this way has helped a lot with my understanding my own identity. If he had "been a woman" before, I do not think I would be standing by him today. I fell in love with a man. I just didn't know it at the time.[37]

This would seem to put Bobula and her partner firmly in the category of "heterosexual couple." Another reader of the *PF3TM Newsletter* contributes her own description of the ambiguities and tensions of this transformative process.

For many years when I was lesbian I had this weird feeling that I was inauthentic, somehow not as lesbian as my friends and lovers. Many lesbians I met said later that I just didn't "feel like a dyke." I never felt emotionally or physically at home in the lesbian community. I often felt limited in my self-expression, judged for being too feminine-appearing and "behaving" (whatever that means).

…Later, I realized that I had similar feelings of not fitting in when I had dated genetic (non-FTM) males. I ended up in a confused place, responding strongly to masculinity, only not in genetic men. FTMs or stone butches were the only individuals I felt safe, sexual and connected to.

I moved gradually away from my lesbian identity and into a stronger, clearer sense of myself and my desire. …I still feel uncomfortable when asked if I am now "straight," since I feel anything but mainstream. My work as a civil rights attorney for the TS/TG and gay communities reaffirms my outsider status. But I am finally comfortable in my own skin and with my sexuality, and this is a tremendous change.

So for me this was my own transition, maybe not as physically obvious as my partner's, but for me extremely profound. Sometimes I feel reduced to the category of "partner of F-T-M."

I realize there may be no other way to begin the dialogue, but I sometimes feel that my own transition through rage, healing and towards self-respect is lost. It is my own healing that makes it possible for me to be a good, strong partner and I want to honor that and the strengths of other women in this same place.[38]

It seems significant that both of these women have become transgender activists in their own right. As long as transgendered people were admonished to blend in and become just like everyone else, they were prevented from forming any sort of political lobby. Now, it is much easier for both transgendered people and their partners to name the prejudices that make them less-than and work for social change. By affiliating with, loving, and validating transgendered people, partners have become allies and members of their own sexual-minority community.

This change is mirrored in the work of Leslie Feinberg and Minnie Bruce Pratt. Feinberg identifies as a transgendered person rather than a transsexual man. "I'm a woman but I look like a man," she says. "...I don't consider this to be a contradiction. I think there are a lot of ways for women to be. ...I'm defining myself within the transgender community."[39] Pratt has a long history as a lesbian femme, although her definition of that has apparently been altered somewhat by her partnership with Feinberg. The fact that the two of them are lovers as well as authors heightens the experience of reading Feinberg's novel *Stone Butch Blues* and Pratt's *S/he*. The short pieces in Pratt's book are difficult to categorize. They read as essays, short stories, prose poems and snippets of autobiography. *S/he* confounds genres and crosses boundaries as readily and with as much delight as Pratt and her extremely butch lover. The images of the lovers of transgendered people that appear in these two books sometimes merge, sometimes diverge, in a fascinating dialogue of passion, recognition, attraction, and difference.

Jess Goldberg, the stone butch, working-class hero of Feinberg's novel, is attracted to and lovers with lesbian femmes throughout most of the book. Feinberg depicts femmes (prior to the advent of feminism) as women who understand and are attracted to the gender defiance of butches. However, Jess's lover Theresa, a former bar-culture femme who gets involved with the women's movement, gets angry when Jess calls herself a "he-she" and instead tries to get Jess to identify more as a woman. Theresa ends their relationship when Jess decides to take testosterone and pass as a man. She says, "I don't want to be with a man, Jess. I won't do it." Jess replies, "I'd still be a butch...even on hormones," but Theresa doesn't buy it. Later on, she explains, "If I'm not with a butch everyone just assumes I'm straight. It's like I'm passing too, against my will. I'm sick of the world thinking I'm straight. I've worked hard to be discriminated against as a lesbian."[40] In addition to resisting being labeled as a heterosexual woman, Theresa is afraid of taking on the task of sheltering Jess's gender secret: "I can't live as the scared couple in apartment 3G who can't trust people enough to have friends. I can't live like a fugitive with you. I wouldn't be able to survive it...."[41] While Theresa values her stigmatized status as a lesbian, she is not willing to take on even more stigma by maintaining an alliance with a transgendered person. Although Feinberg never says so, this implies a failure on her part (and on the part of lesbian feminism) to develop a higher political consciousness of gender.

Once she begins to pass as a man, Jess has very few sexual options. She has a very brief affair with a femme from the old days and a one-night stand with a heterosexual woman whose virulent homophobia makes Jess too afraid to risk a second encounter. By the end of the book, when Jess has come to see herself as a female-bodied person who is gender-ambiguous, and stops taking testosterone, she does not return to the lesbian community and seek connections with femmes. Instead, Jess courts a transgendered woman, Ruth. This connection does not seem to have a sexual component, although Jess finds Ruth beautiful for her own style of combining and transcending both genders. One of the points that *Stone Butch Blues* seems to be making is that gender outlaws may find some support in the gay community, but not a true home. The book suggests that transgendered people may use the gay community instead as a vehicle through which they can begin to understand their gender defiance, learn how to express it, and eventually find one another, along with the possibility of creating their own tribe.

It takes a femme, of course, to pinpoint the ways in which lesbian femmes are and always have been their own sort of gender outlaws. Pratt's collection of exquisite short pieces adds a crucial layer to the discourse of transgenderism. She carefully documents the ways in which femmes are seen as deviant by both heterosexuals and lesbians.

> I am definitively lesbian to myself, but not in a way recognizable to a heterosexual world that assumes lesbians to be "mannish." Unless I announce myself to be lesbian, which I do often—in my classroom, at poetry readings, to curious taxi drivers—I am usually assumed to be straight. But unless I "butch up" my style,

sometimes I am suspect inside my lesbian world as too feminine to be lesbian. And both inside and outside lesbian space, there is another assumption held by some: No "real" lesbian would be attracted to as much masculinity as I prefer in my lesbian lover.[42]

Instead of portraying the lesbian community as a place where women can be liberated from the constrictions of sexism and gender stereotypes, Pratt (who was married for several years, had two sons, and came out in the early women's movement) weaves a more accurate and troublesome picture of the way lesbian mores interfered with her quest for self-knowledge and shamed her for experiencing femme desire for extremely butch women. And Pratt rescues that component of lesbian experience that has to do with being gender-deviant.

> You in your sports jacket, white shirt and tie; me in a silk skirt, flimsy blouse, sparkling glass jewelry at my neck and ears. In the crowded car when I put my head on your shoulder, with your arm around me, people stared at us. Curious to be so conventional in dress and to draw so much attention. Something too intimate and queer about how we do maleness and femaleness together in public. Perhaps it's easier for you to slip through if you're not with me. One glance and you're a gay man to them, or a slightly ambiguous boy. But when you're with me, I see their eyes flicker: If he's gay, why is he with her? Why is she with him? If they are two women, why do they look so much like a woman and a man? What are they up to?[43]

Unlike Theresa, Pratt knows that being with a passing woman is not the same thing as passing for heterosexual. Nor does she insist that lesbian relationships are restricted to connections between women-identified women.

> Meeting you for the first time over curried chicken and *masala dosa*, she [nota bene: a transgendered woman] is socially appropriate to refer to you as *him*. Meanwhile, you are saying that you are a woman and transgendered, that your masculinity is a range of gender expression that should be available to all women, as femininity should be to men. You insist that you are *him* and also *her*.[44]

During this lunch, Pratt fantasizes the three of them "on the edge of town…a world of those the world casts out, calls freaks, the women-men of the sideshow at the circus, seen as tawdry, pitiful, hidden, wasted, walking their path of reeking sawdust between the tents. Except the people there have lovers, marriages, children, poor-paying jobs. …You live there, and now I live there too, with those who know they are both *man* and *woman*, those who have transmuted one to the other, those who insist they are neither. …I could cross back into that staring crowd and be without question a woman amusing herself, Sunday afternoon at the carnival. But I would rather stay here and talk to you in this in-between place."[45]

Even before becoming a transgendered person's lover, Pratt says, she was a gender outlaw. After separating from her husband, she recalls sleeping "in a motel parking lot for a few hours, to save time and money, to get to my children. They were forbidden to be in my home because I was what a woman shouldn't be. I was too much woman, I was not woman enough. I was too interested in women, in sex, in my own sex."[46]

Pratt fearlessly celebrates the rebellious and outcast nature of her relationship and situates it firmly on the map of queer passion. A friend tells her, "You are not only a lesbian, but very, very queer. You love a woman who is manly, and yet do not want her to be completely man. In fact, you desire her *because* she is both."[47] And she agrees:

> As you take off your men's clothes, I do not secretly want you to be a man so I can be saved from my desire for another woman. And when I unknot your tie and unbutton your shirt, as we lie down together naked, I say with a fearless caress that I love the man I am undressing, and I also know that a woman lies beside me, not a mirror to reflect me. …All those years I was no obedient asexual girl, but a restless lover searching for the lost garden, that place of male woman and female man.[48]

If other lesbians do not recognize Pratt and her lover as homosexuals, homophobic straight men certainly do not have that problem. "The first night we ever went out in your city," Pratt relates, "a carload of white men careened by, screamed at you, 'Faggot!' We were holding hands, I was in a skirt that swirled, but they could see we were somehow queer."[49] Recalling her first drag show, Pratt conjures up a seductive image of "a tall melancholy drag queen" who "lip-synched a love song. She gleamed, copper-skinned under beaded black net. She strolled the edges of the audience. Her gloved hand stretched elegantly out to touch my hand. When she leaned forward, bittersweet gardenia scent drifted across my face, and she looked directly into my eyes. I told myself then: *If she did not have to be the man he was raised to be, I did not have to be the woman.*"[50]

Pratt's position that a femme is also a gender outlaw is stated force-fully in a passage where she describes a fantasy about her butch lover opening a door for her. "She has said to me, 'A butch is not a man.' Now I say, 'A femme is not a woman, at least not the woman people think. It's a case of mistaken identity.' "[51] Through the transgression of loving someone who is differently gendered, she implies, it is possible for someone who does not appear to be a gender outlaw to become one. In subtle and not-so-subtle stories, Pratt makes this deviant status and the invisibility it is usually consigned to painfully clear. It is through liter-ature like this that transgenderism ceases to become a medicalized series of freakish and isolated case histories and becomes instead a liv-ing, breathing, three-dimensional part of the difficult and ecstatic human experience.

Until now, transsexual literature (and by this I mean literature by differently-gendered people, not commentary upon them by outside "experts") has dealt primarily with the individual transsexual's identity conflicts and focused on easing the transition into living in the gender of preference, or living in a perpetual state of ambiguity, in the case of someone who rejects polarized gender categories. The partners and other loved ones of transsexuals are just beginning to create their own culture, including literature and forums where they can explore their own questions of identity and affiliation.

Some of these questions are tied to the nature of transsexual social history during this decade. For example, the lesbian community has historically served as a haven for genetic females with gender conflicts, who have until recently labeled themselves as extreme butches rather than FTMs. As transsexual men become more visible, a growing num-ber of "butches" are rejecting a lesbian and female identity in favor of sex change. This creates a virtually undocumented state of crisis for their partners, who are usually lesbian-identified. The ideology of romance encourages the female partner to remain with the former butch, now FTM, but often this leaves the couple in isolation, rejected by their lesbian extended family and unable to replace it with a hetero-sexual network.

A relationship that changes its label from lesbian to heterosexual can create additional stressors for the nontranssexual partner. For example, one of the things a lesbian relationship offers is an affirma-tion of the worth and value of the female body. The female partners of transsexual men who once identified as lesbians frequently complain that they are negatively affected by the FTM's rejection of his own female morphology. Hormones and cosmetic surgery give the transsexual man a new comfort with his body, but the physical changes he undergoes may negatively impact the female partner's body image.

While the partners of FTMs are just beginning to network at national conferences and create joint solutions to some of their issues, thus far, there are not enough gay male partners of homosexual transsexual men to create a matrix of support. The genetic male half of a gay male relationship may find that other genetic gay males ridicule or reject him. To the extent that he is perceived as bisexual for having a transsexual male partner (who is not accepted as male), this rejection will consist of intertwined biphobia and transphobia—a difficult jungle to hack down.

The genetic female partners of transsexual women have unique issues of their own. If the relationship began before sex reassignment, the genetic female may have great difficulty adjusting to the way public perception of her spouse or lover will change. If she defines as heterosexual, a shift to a lesbian identity may be too discordant, and the relationship will falter. If she is determined to remain in the relationship, sexual and other adjustments will have to be made. Very little exists in print to guide a woman in this situation.

The lesbian-identified partner of an MTF has the opposite problem: at least some portions of her friendship network are guaranteed to label her as someone who has "gone straight." If her partner is a transsexual woman whose strategy for "passing" includes avoiding other transsexual women, the genetic female half of such a couple will be isolated indeed, given the well-nigh universal rejection of MTFs by the lesbian community.

MTFs with genetic male partners often find them in the gay and bisexual men's community. The male partner often has difficulty handling the identity shifts involved in being associated with a woman. A heterosexual male partner of an MTF is, of course, vulnerable to accusations that he is really gay, leveled by people who do not accept the MTF's status as a woman.

More than a few transsexuals have responded to these dilemmas by making romantic and sexual connections with one another. Virtually nothing has been written about this revolutionary strategy, which opposes the assumption that a transsexual needs to have his or her gender identity bolstered by intimate affirmation from someone whose self-image is consistent with his or her genetic sex. This is a risky choice indeed, since it almost always means the couple will be more easily "read" as transsexual. (And, if they are not, they will worry about it more than a "mixed couple.") Much more needs to be said about this relationship configuration, hopefully by individuals who have found it their most viable option.

Ironically, the traditional strategy for creating a new life post-sex reassignment, to blend in and pass as a genetic male or female, may exacerbate the problems faced by transsexuals and their loved ones. Passing in this fashion is always stressful. There is a perpetual fear of being discovered. Even if the charade is perfect, it creates its own tension, a loneliness that is begotten by the inability to be seen, loved, and accepted for what one truly is. The loneliness and isolation of transsexuals and their partners can be alleviated if both heterosexual and gay/bisexual communities update their attitudes toward differently-gendered people. But this will require an educational effort that can only be launched by transsexual people and partners who eschew passing. The formation of a strong transgendered community is also essential. Simply knowing one or two other people who are in a similar life situation can make all the difference between happiness and despair.

Workshops on sexuality are inevitably the most crowded at any FTM or MTF convention. While these live presentations are invaluable, there is an urgent need for more visual art and literature about this aspect of transsexual life. Too many transsexuals still feel that if they are "allowed" to live in their gender of preference, they have won an enormous victory, and ought not to demand or expect anything else. Given the harsh and condemnatory attitudes they face, it is not surprising that MTFs and FTMs by and large wish to protect their sexual privacy. But silence is the enemy of erotic satisfaction. Transsexual women (especially pre-operative MTFs) have long been the alienated objects of pornography produced by "straight" male voyeurs who project their own "freakishness" upon the discordant images of women with phalluses. It is to be hoped that more transsexual artists and their allies will produce sexually explicit material that depicts these communities and individuals in a more realistic way, and gratifies their desire, instead of crudely using them to titillate others. Pleasure is an inalienable right.

Whether they want to or not, the genetic male or female partners of transsexual people find themselves in a unique position to lobby for increased tolerance and awareness of transgenderism. Even the most assimilated heterosexual couple is vulnerable to antigay discrimination if a hostile outsider defines the relationship as one between two people of the same genetic sex. No one in the gender community, no matter how "straight-appearing/straight-acting," can afford to duck the responsibilities of activism. It is a simple matter of self-defense.

Chapter seven documents some of the monumental efforts that transgendered people and their supporters and loved ones have made to force a transphobic society to recognize them and give them more equitable treatment.

Notes

1. Virginia "Charles" Prince, *The Transvestite and His Wife*, Los Angeles, no publisher listed, 1967, pp. 5-6.
2. Ibid., p. 6.
3. Ibid., p. 15.
4. Ibid., p. 60.
5. Ibid., p. 17.
6. Ibid., pp. 16-17.
7. Ibid., p. 26.
8. Ibid., p. 10.
9. Ibid., p. 15.
10. "What Sex Am I?" narrated and directed by Lee Grant, produced by Joseph Feury, 1980 [?], broadcast on Discovery Showcase in 1995.
11. Prince, op. cit., p. 18.
12. Ibid., pp. 18-19.
13. Ibid., pp. 20-21.
14. Ibid., p. 21.
15. Ibid., p. 28.
16. Ibid., p. 46.
17. Ibid., p. 45.
18. Ibid., pp. 28, 29, 51, and 86.
19. Ibid., p. 86.
20. Ibid., p. 89.
21. Ibid., pp. 79 and 81.
22. Ibid., p. 84.
23. Ibid., p. 70.
24. Ibid., pp. 33 and 45.
25. Ibid., pp. 36-37.
26. Ibid., p. 62.
27. Ibid., p. 36.
28. Ibid., p. 73.
29. Ibid., p. 63.
30. Ibid., p. 96.
31. Ibid., p. 105.
32. Ibid., p. 114.
33. Ibid., p. 111.
34. Ibid., p. 118.
35. Ray Blanchard and Peter I. Collins, "Men with Sexual Interest in Transvestites, Transsexuals, and She-Males," *The Journal of Nervous and Mental Disease*, vol. 181, no. 8, 1993, pp. 570-575.

36. Kathy Bobula, "Trying to Figure Out My Sexual Identity," *Partners, Family, and Friends of FTMs Newsletter,* vol. 1, issue 2, December 1995, pp. 4-5.

37. Kathy Bobula, "PF3TM Quotes," October 6, 1996 e-mail to the author. Unpublished.

38. Margo Diesenhouse, "Response to Jean Lingeman's Letter," *Partners, Family, and Friends of FTMs Newsletter,* vol. 1, issue 3, February 1996, pp. 1-2.

39. Kevin Horwitz, "An Interview with Leslie Feinberg," *FTM Newsletter,* issue 23, May 1993, p. 1.

40. Leslie Feinberg, *Stone Butch Blues,* Ithaca, New York: Firebrand Books, 1993, p. 151.

41. Ibid., pp. 151-153.

42. Minnie Bruce Pratt, "Gender Quiz," *S/he,* Ithaca, New York: Firebrand Books, 1995, p. 21.

43. Pratt, "New Year's Eve," *S/he,* op. cit., p. 85.

44. Pratt, "Lunch," *S/he,* op. cit., pp. 88-89.

45. Ibid., pp. 89-90.

46. Pratt, "Paint," *S/he,* op. cit., pp. 92-93.

47. Pratt, "Café Paradiso," *S/he,* op. cit., p. 103.

48. Ibid., p. 104.

49. Pratt, "Fear," *S/he,* op. cit., p. 137.

50. Pratt, "Drag Show," *S/he,* op. cit., p. 160.

51. Pratt, "Closed Door," *S/he,* op. cit., p. 52.

CHAPTER 7

Trashing the Clinic and Burning Down the Beauty Parlor: Activism Transmutes Pitiable Patients into Feisty Gender Radicals

Since the late nineteen-sixties, a growing number of cross-dressers and transsexuals have turned to the political arena to improve conditions for themselves and their communities. The original style of transgender activism focused on such things as laws against female impersonation, policies that made it difficult for transsexuals to obtain identification papers and change other official records so they conformed with their gender of preference, lobbying for greater availability of sex reassignment, forming social groups for cross-dressers and their significant others, educating the general public about transvestism and transsexuality, and doing outreach so that people troubled by gender dysphoria would find it easier to locate the resources they needed to cope with their distress.

This style of transgender activism is still going strong. Today it is exemplified by Virginia "Charles" Prince's Tri-Ess Sorority (which has drawn fire for excluding homosexual men), the International Foundation for Gender Education, Renaissance Education Association, and an annual conference on transsexuality and the law, organized by Houston activist and attorney Phyllis Randolph Frye and sponsored by the International Conference on Transgender Law and Employment Policy, Inc. (ICTLEP). This conference has been held annually since 1992 and typically deals with such issues as insurance law, employment rights, medical law, and international law.

Through ICTLEP, Stephen Whittle, Lecturer in Law at Manchester University in Manchester, England, has provided American activists and lawyers with the latest international case-law statistics and civil-rights strategies that are being used in other countries, particularly the

United Kingdom and Western Europe. But the conference has historically suffered from a lack of full participation by the female-to-male community. ICTLEP organizers have recently taken steps to boost FTM participation by featuring FTM keynote speaker Michael Hernandez in 1994. Writer/activist and president of FTM International Jamison Green received ICTLEP's Transgender Pioneer Award in 1995, and the honor went to Whittle in 1996. The 1996 conference broke new ground by specifically addressing FTMs, transgendered youth, members of the gender community who have not had full sex reassignment, and transgendered people of color.

Like any change, this one will apparently take time. Panelist Jamison Green commented, "It's depressing to think that after five years of transgender community activism, this three-hour session is the first block of time Transgen has devoted to FTM issues. Even sadder is the fact that we could barely scratch the surface of topics pertaining to law—we had to spend the majority of the time explaining the basic reality of FTM existence, so ignorant were the majority of attendees."[1] This state of affairs will hopefully improve with the recent appointment of FTM attorneys Spencer Bergstedt and Shannon Minter as ICTLEP directors. Minter is currently employed as the Staff Attorney for the National Center for Lesbian Rights (NCLR).[2]

ICTLEP founder Frye was instrumental in getting Houston's laws against cross-dressing repealed in the eighties. With Karen Kerin of It's Time America and Riki Wilchins of the Transexual Menace, she coordinated a largely successful effort to have each and every one of over five hundred Senate and House officeholders lobbied by transgender activists on October 4, 1995, National Gender Lobbying Day. Kerry Lobel of the National Gay and Lesbian Task Force (NGLTF) and Nancy Buermeyer of the Human Rights Campaign were on hand to give practical lobbying pointers and encouragement.

One of the organizers of that event recalls her experience:

I remember getting on the underground subway that runs between the House and Senate, and just as we start off toward the House, coming back at us from the other way is an entire carload of cross-dressers, just returning from lobbying the Senate. And of course their driver is trying to keep this totally bored expression like, "Hey, no big deal. I see this every day."

I went into the Rayburn Building cafeteria, which is this block-long thing where many of the Capital Hill staff go to lunch. And I look around, and suddenly notice there are fifty—

maybe sixty—transpeople filling about a third of the tables. And then I notice staffers coming in are doing the same thing. They walk in, start to look around, then really look around, and suddenly notice ohmyfuckinggawd the Rayburn Building cafeteria is filled with men in dresses and transsexuals and who only knows what other kinds of gender-perverts and all of a sudden they're hearing another chorus of "Welcome to Gender Hell!"

The First National Gender Lobbying Day marked a definitive turning point for transpeople. It was the first time genderqueers came in from the shadows of passing and assimilation to the brightest of national lights and said, "No! I'm not going away. I'm not going to hide. I'm not going to be ashamed anymore. I work and pay taxes and vote, and I'm going to live with the same dignity and rights accorded every other U.S. citizen. It was incredibly moving to see one hundred transpeople and friends standing together on the Capital Hill steps with this *visible* determination and pride in all their faces.[3]

The older type of transgender activism closely resembles the "civil rights" approach which characterized the lesbian and gay movement through much of the seventies and eighties. Gay activists in those decades focused on the repeal of sodomy laws; securing First Amendment protection for lesbian and gay male media; passage of local, state, and federal laws banning antigay discrimination; demands that local police departments recognize and take steps to address gay bashing; outreach to young men and women who were "coming out" to make it easier for them to find the gay community; lobbying to remove homosexuality as a diagnostic category from the *Diagnostic and Statistical Manual* of the American Psychiatric Association; and attempts to educate the general public about homosexuality.

Several factors combined in the mid-nineties to produce a change in the tone of transgender activism and its agenda. One was the emergence of a stronger, larger, and more visible FTM community. Another factor was a shift in survival strategies for transsexuals. Rather than attempting to blend in and remain closeted about being transsexual, more and more transgendered people, especially women, began to speak out, write, and work as out transsexual activists. This was a direct result of several nasty transsexual purges committed by many lesbian organizations during the eighties. Transgendered women who attempted to join lesbian organizations were for the most part already politicized by feminism and by confronting antigay discrimination in their daily lives. These vicious purges made it clear that being closeted simply would not work. Transgendered lesbians had few alternatives to becoming radicalized. It was either that, or a retreat to the heterosexual world, a life of complete isolation and silence, or suicide. Lesbian feminists who refused to accept transgendered women as women and tried to drive them away ironically created a generation of determined transgendered women who will do anything but disappear.

The process of sex reassignment itself has also spawned transgender activists. Gender clinics have been operating long enough now in this country to create a significant number of people who are angry about the way these programs are run. Rather than being grateful for any help they are given, transsexuals today are questioning the authority of the medical and mental-health professionals who function as gatekeepers of sex reassignment. While many of them still want access to hormones and surgery, gender dysphoric men and women are uneasy about being labeled as mentally-ill people in need of treatment. The gender community has at this point accumulated a lot of folk wisdom about what you need to tell the doctors to get admitted to a gender-reassignment program. The dangerous side effects of hormones and the shortcomings of surgery are well-known. Transsexuals are becoming informed consumers of medical service, and they want more control over what they receive from their healthcare providers, and more accountability.

Some of this attitude is connected with the growing visibility of the S/M community, particularly the component of sadomasochism that has to do with body modification. One of the basic tenets of S/M is the individual's right to own his or her own body, and make whatever temporary or permanent changes to that body the individual pleases either for sexual gratification or for purposes of adornment. A new sort of transgendered person has emerged, one who approaches sex reassignment with the same mindset that they would obtaining a piercing or a tattoo. This is very different from the old attitude toward hormone therapy and surgery—that it was necessary to receive this treatment because one was a woman trapped in a man's body or vice versa.

There is a growing number of people who are diagnosed as gender dysphoric, but for one reason or another are not deemed to be good candidates for sex reassignment. Gender identity programs can turn down applicants for many reasons—age, a history of psychiatric illnesses, homosexuality, fetishism, sadomasochism, a criminal record, inability to tolerate hormones, a medical history of cancer, possessing a face or body that the surgeon believes will never pass muster as a member of the gender of preference ("somatically inappropriate"), poverty, employment in the sex industry, a refusal to aspire to be a feminine woman or a masculine man, or uppitiness.

Until the mid-nineties, these people had few options. They could try to pay for sex reassignment themselves—an expensive proposition, complicated by the difficulty of finding a doctor in private practice who was knowledgeable enough or willing to supervise such treatment. They could attempt to find a place for themselves on the margins of the cross-dressing community or the gay community. They could try to resign themselves to living in the gender they had been assigned at birth. They could attempt to drown their pain with drug addiction or alcohol, or they could stop living in some more final way.

Today, the growing visibility of the transsexual community has created an alternative: to identify as transgendered rather than female or male, and question the binary gender system that generates these labels. People who cannot "pass" as men or women have little to lose by becoming outspoken gender activists. It feels better to fight oppression, even though it is hard work, than it does to run away from it and try to hide. There's no shame in losing a battle from time to time. All warriors sometimes lose. But it's better to be a warrior, even a defeated one, than a civilian casualty. One can obtain enough pride and dignity from that stance in life to live, even if the conditions of life are frightening and precarious.

Of course, there are also many actively-involved transgender activists who could quite easily turn their backs on their own community and fade into the woodwork. Green comments, "I find that my passability works as a great educational tool in my own activist work. There are quite a few transactivists who…could pass perfectly well. We could do other things with our lives. But we feel strongly about trans oppression and the people whose lives are affected by it, and we want to see it stopped. Instead of 'woodworking,' or disappearing into the mainstream—as we are capable of and qualified to do—we have chosen not to do so."[4]

Outside of the transsexual community, other changes were taking place that made it possible for the new transgender activist to emerge. One was a parallel shift in the strategy of gay activists outraged by lack of effective government intervention and pharmaceutical industry indifference or outright profiteering in dealing with the AIDS pandemic. The rise of a bisexual community that attempted, with mixed results, to affiliate itself with lesbian and gay political goals and social institutions also created a new paradigm for transgender activists.

The increasing visibility of prosex feminism, with its opposition to censorship and emphasis on the value of pleasure and its affirmation of a woman's right to take control over her own body, also had a role to play in the development of a new phase of transgender activism. Prosex feminism's recognition of the contributions communities of sexual-minority women had made to the women's movement created an atmosphere that was much less hostile to transgendered women than the classic radical lesbian feminism of the late seventies and the eighties. This is not to say that prosex feminists have been wholehearted allies of transgendered people; but this more open attitude has created the possibility of more dialogue, and opened a little more space within which "gennies" and transgendered women can encounter one another as something other than enemies.

In fact, however, it would be hard to say which one of these factors "caused" any of the others. Rather than claiming there was a chronological chain of events that led to the formation of groups like the Transexual Menace, it would be more realistic to view all these historical changes as synergistic events, each of which affected and triggered the others, much the same as the breaking shot that opens a game of pool.

In order to give the reader a sense of the flavor of transgender activism in the last few years, it is necessary to describe some of the specific cases or causes around which the gender community has recently rallied, protested, organized, and generally kicked ass. The pathetic, deluded, and self-destructive people portrayed by Harry Benjamin and Richard Green as being in desperate need of rescue by enlightened doctors and therapists could never have created the ruckus that resulted from each of the events outlined below. Nor could these results have been achieved by quiet, well-mannered, closeted transsexuals who politely waited for liberal judges or medical professionals to give them the charitable treatment they needed to eke out a life in the shadows of normal society. Even old-fashioned civil-rights-style transsexual activists are learning that it pays to be rowdy.

Anne Ogborn should be credited as a forerunner of transgender direct action groups. Ogborn's life experiences included a period of living with the hijra in India.[5] Wilchins recalls her surfacing in the summer of 1992 in New York, selling T-shirts that said, "Sex Change: Ask Me How." Ogborn tried to form chapters of a group called Transgender Nation in San Francisco, Washington, DC, and other cities. Wilchins says it took her a whole year to admit that the concept was a good idea, and that it was possible to get enough transpeople together for an effective picket or demonstration. Wilchins modified

Ogborn's concept slightly and formed the Transexual Menace to protest the fact that transsexuals had been left out of the title of Stonewall 25, a New York gay/lesbian/bisexual march that was to commemorate the twenty-fifth anniversary of the Stonewall rebellion in June of 1994. The group's slogan is, "Why should a transsexual be a menace to you?"

The ejection of a transgendered woman from the Michigan Womyn's Music Festival (MWMF) in 1991 is an event that some observers credit with touching off an in-your-face, rabble-rousing style of gender activism that has more in common with Queer Nation and ACT-UP than it has with the Human Rights Campaign Fund. Nancy Jean Burkholder, an electrical engineer from New Hampshire, had attended the Michigan festival in 1990 without a problem. But for some reason, in 1991, another festival-goer asked Burkholder if she was a transsexual, and she told her the truth. Despite the fact that she had yet to enjoy a lesbian relationship, the postoperative Burkholder defined herself as a lesbian feminist. In what must have been a frightening display of force, security guards ejected her from the festival grounds at midnight, without allowing her to contact any of her friends or collect her belongings.[6]

Burkholder did not go away quietly. She and her supporters, including the ubiquitous Wilchins, organized to inform the larger lesbian community and other transgendered women about the shoddy and abusive treatment she had received. But it wasn't until 1994 that enough collective anger had accumulated to result in a visible political action: Camp Trans. Wilchins, one of the key organizers, recalls:

> To my knowledge, Camp Trans was the first time transpeople ever coordinated and pulled off a national event. Not only that, it was the first time that significant numbers of the hard-core lesbian-feminist community backed us. In a sense it was an echo of the Sex Wars in a distant place—off a dirt road in the middle of Michigan—and between our tents and the front gate thirty yards away was as clear a division around issues of hierarchy and legitimacy, diversity and tolerance, as you're likely to find anywhere.
>
> The first year, we had only four or five people (it wasn't even called Camp Trans) and folks were so afraid of being hassled inside that they wouldn't even wear our pro-Nancy buttons back through MWMF's main gate. But at Camp Trans, there were thirty people there continuously. And we drew hundreds

of folks from inside the festival. We knew something was up. But when (in the first two days) I sold every one of the three dozen Transexual Menace T-shirts I'd brought, including the one I was wearing on my back, and these women were wearing them back *inside* the main gate and around the festival—then we knew the prevailing winds had definitely shifted.[7]

Camp Trans consisted of about two dozen transgendered women and their supporters, who simply rented a campsite across the road from the Michigan Womyn's Music Festival, and made their presence known. About one hundred festival-goers left MWMF's grounds to hear a reading by Leslie Feinberg and Minnie Bruce Pratt.

James Green describes his participation at Camp Trans:

I conducted two workshops at Camp Trans on FTM issues—of course these were not so well-attended as Leslie and Minnie Bruce's reading, but a couple dozen people walked out of the festival to attend…. The next day, Leslie, an intersexed person named Cody, Jessica Xavier, Nancy Burkholder, Riki Anne Wilchins, and I had a meeting with the festival security team. The trans women were very quiet and let Leslie, Cody and me do most of the talking. Leslie started by introducing hermself and getting into a bit of an argument about the "womyn-born-womyn" policy. S/he threatened to denounce the festival at all public-speaking events heesh ever did in the future. Next, Cody, who looked like your basic butch dyke but said she had genitals that were indeterminate, asked if she would be welcome in the festival and expressed her reservations about being welcome based on her identity as an intersexed person.

Then I introduced myself and told them first that I did not want to go into the festival. They were visibly relieved at this news. "But," I said, "I'm here in support of my transsexual sisters and there's something I don't understand about your policy. If in fact your policy of exclusion is based on your belief that once a man, always a man, then you must also believe once a woman, always a woman. [pause] And I don't think you want me in your festival." They were shocked. They looked like I had just slapped them in the face. They excused themselves and said they would report back to Lisa and Boo and would return in twenty minutes. They were back much sooner than that with their capitulation that a measure of self-definition was appropriate. At that point, Leslie and Riki led the entire contingent of

Camp Trans (minus myself, a nontranssexual male journalist...and a nontranssexual woman who did not want to go) on a victory march through the festival grounds, accompanied by the Lesbian Avengers.[8]

Lisa Vogel and "Boo" Price, the women who own the for-profit festival, had announced that they would not change their admission policy, which stated that the festival was for "womyn-born-womyn" only. However, they added the somewhat contradictory and chickenshit statement that they would allow festival attendees to decide for themselves whether or not they were "womyn-born-womyn." There was a split among the transactivists at this point, with Davina Anne Gabriel, who is postoperative, reportedly saying that preoperative women should not enter the festival. Wilchins argued against that, using the slogan "passing is privilege. We should not be ashamed of our genitals." So the small contingent she led through the gates of Michigan included pre-, post-, and non-operative transsexual women.[9]

A large contingent of separatist campers reportedly left the event when they heard that transsexuals had been allowed on the land. Their viewpoint was articulated by lesbian-separatist musician and singer Alix Dobkin, who said, "Every lesbian I know supports transsexuals' rights to live their lives. But I support our right to define our own space. I'm very disappointed to learn that they have chosen to support sex-role stereotypes—to be women, which they are not. They're not being who they are. They're trying to be who we are. To me it feels like a male invasion of my sacred space." Dobkin had signed a statement with Wilchins calling for respectful dialogue and "mutually acceptable common ground," but apparently that ground could not be the Michigan Womyn's Music Festival.[10]

Camp Trans was held again in 1995. Three transsexual women led by Davina Anne Gabriel of Kansas City, Missouri reportedly entered the festival and outed themselves. They did not encounter any problems with festival security or staff.[11]

The plight of transsexual lesbians highlights an ideological double-bind. Feminists cannot have it both ways. If we are going to claim that biology is not destiny and present a political analysis of gender as something that is socially constructed, we have to make room in our world view for women who were not born with XX chromosomes. To do otherwise is to subscribe to biological determinism, the regressive belief that our genetic structures determine our potential as human beings, and the notion that biological sex can be used as a justification for placing limits upon the freedom, intellectual abilities, and creative talents of women.

The tragic case of Brandon Teena galvanized transactivists who were energized by their partial victory at Michigan. The brutal and bigoted murder of this young, transgendered man stirred indignation in the heart of any decent or compassionate person. But the way Teena's case was handled by gay organizations, which labeled it anti-lesbian violence, and written about by lesbian journalist Donna Minkowitz, who insisted on calling Teena a woman and referring to him by female pronouns, created a great deal of anger in the gender community, especially among FTMs who recognized Brandon Teena as one of their own. In Donna Minkowitz's 1994 *Village Voice* article about the case, the headline on the first page says, "Brandon Teena Was a Woman Who Lived and Loved as a Man. She Was Killed for Carrying It Off."[12] Yet in her own article, Minkowitz says that, although Teena hung out with gay men, "she" frequently made negative comments about lesbians. Teena repeatedly told anyone he was intimate with that he was a man. The inability of gay media or organizations to process this case as a violation of transsexuals' human rights encouraged many transgendered people to become more outspoken, since it became very clear that the older, larger, and more well-established gay institutions were deeply insensitive to the implications of Teena's murder.

In 1994, Brandon Teena (whose birth name was Teena Brandon) moved to Falls City, Nebraska to live as a man. He may have been planning on eventually seeking out sex-change surgery. He was originally from nearby Lincoln, Nebraska. By all accounts, Teena passed easily as a man, and quickly became something of a local Don Juan. He was discovered to have a female body when cops arrested him on a misdemeanor check-forgery charge two weeks prior to his slaying. The police then outed him by telling the local newspaper, the *Falls City Journal,* about the discrepancy between Teena's gender at birth and his public identity. Teena seems to have been quite a scam artist. By the time he died, he had nearly a score of charges pending for petty crimes like check forgery, credit-card fraud, and auto theft. But what happened to him was way out of proportion to any crime he might have committed. By New Year's Eve, he had been raped and brutally murdered by Tom Nissen and John Lotter, two former friends. Teena was twenty-one when he died.

John Lotter was a former boyfriend of Teena's date for the Christmas party. At that party, Lotter and Nissen held Teena down, forcibly removed his trousers, and insisted that his girlfriend Lana

Tisdale look at his crotch. Afterward, Lotter and Nissen employed a ruse to get Teena alone, and raped him twice. They also beat him severely. Teena escaped when his assailants locked him in a bathroom and ordered him to take a shower to remove forensic evidence. He got out of the house through the bathroom window. Teena reported the attack to police, who refused to make an arrest. Richardson County Sheriff Charles Laux allowed his department to conduct an investigation, which involved interviewing dozens of people and preparing an extensive report, but forbade the arrest of the two men the cops themselves believed to be the culprits. One week later on New Year's Eve of 1993, Teena was shot to death. Two companions, Lisa Lambert and a young black man, Phillip DeVine, were also killed. Lambert's infant son survived the attack on the farmhouse.

Laux seems to be quite a piece of work, the prototype of a redneck lawman who doesn't think the law should protect everyone. He is reported to have told Teena's mother, when she called to ask why no one had been arrested for the rape, "You can call it, 'it' as far as I am concerned."[13] Fortunately, when he ran for reelection shortly after the murders occurred, he was voted out of office. But he has since been elected to the Richardson County Commission.[14] Local law-enforcement people seem to have been a callous and bigoted bunch of bullies who had little regard for the safety of anyone who might be regarded as different. Brandon's mother JoAnn has considered a civil suit against County Attorney Douglas Merz, who told Minkowitz, "I don't know what a hate crime is. I don't know if we have laws against hate crimes in Nebraska."[15] The fact that anyone was ever arrested or tried for this murder seems to be a miracle.

After two days of deliberation, a jury found Marvin Thomas Nissen, twenty-two, guilty of the December 30, 1993 first-degree murder of Brandon Teena and second-degree murder of Teena's two roommates, Lisa Lambert and Phillip DeVine.[16] Nissen agreed to testify against Lotter, who was claiming that he slept in the car outside the farmhouse while Nissen went inside and did the killings. His claims to nonviolence were somewhat strained by the fact that he reportedly ripped the sink off the wall of his jail cell twice while he was in custody awaiting trial. Lotter was found guilty of murder in May 1995. On February 21, 1996, Nissen received a life sentence, and Lotter was given the death penalty.[17] Nissen has since filed an appeal with the Supreme Court, arguing that authorities lacked probable cause to arrest him without a warrant shortly after the bodies were discovered.[18]

In a demonstration called by Wilchins, the Transexual Menace protested the *Village Voice* coverage of Teena's murder, specifically objecting to the use of female pronouns in Minkowitz's article. In fact, they upped the gender ante by referring to Teena as an M2M (male-to-male), a new term that disputes the idea that transgendered men were ever women.[19] Despite the outrage expressed by the transgender community about Minkowitz's use of female pronouns to describe Teena, in October of 1995, a sidebar in an *Out* magazine article about the Sean O'Neill case still referred to Teena as "she."[20]

But gender activists did not stop with attacking defamation in the alternative press. Forty or so gender activists and friends showed up in Falls City, Nebraska for the opening day of Lotter's murder trial, May 15, 1995. A silent vigil was held outside the Richardson County Courthouse. Leslie Feinberg, Minnie Bruce Pratt, and Kate Bornstein were present, among others. Another participant places this event in context:

> In retrospect, there's no doubt this was a turning point for transactivism. It was the first really visible national demonstration we ever pulled off. And it started our practice of doing memorial vigils whenever a transperson is killed in a gender hate crime. After Brandon, we did Tyra Hunter, Chanel Picket, Deborah Forte, and Christian Paige. I got a call from a national news magazine about covering the stories, and they asked, "What is with all the trans-violence lately? Why is it on the increase?" I responded, "Gender activism is very reliable work. About every four or five months, like clockwork, another transperson is killed in a fairly unambiguous hate crime. It's not that there's an increase. It's just that before the vigils, no one was paying attention."
>
> I had called Nancy Nangeroni and said, "Let's call this off. What's the point of going to a town of two thousand people in the middle of nowhere? We'd do more good simply by sending the air fare to his mother." Nancy kept repeating that someone *had* to show up when transpeople were killed. So we kept to our commitment. In the end, forty people flew to the middle of Nebraska to stand that vigil. Almost all were strangers to one another, and almost all of them said the same thing to me when they called to sign up: "I don't know why I'm going. I just know I have to be there."
>
> As Tony [nota bene: Barreto-Neto] has pointed out, Brandon died essentially because the sheriff refused to protect

him, because he couldn't see him as a person. And so after he's murdered, just—what? A year and a half later?—into that same station walks another transsexual man who says to the same cops, "Look, I'm a transsexual man, just like Brandon, and I also carry a badge and a gun, just like you. I'm a brother officer; we *are* you. We are everywhere."[21]

Ending violence against the differently-gendered continues to be one of the most poignant and crucial items on the agenda for the Transexual Menace and similar organizations. During National Gender Lobbying Day in 1995, thirty-five activists from across the United States picketed outside Mayor Marion Barry's office to express their anger over the death of transgendered woman Tyra Hunter, and the ensuing cover-up by District of Columbia Fire Department Chief Otis J. Latin.

On August 7, 1995, Hunter was badly hurt in a hit-and-run automobile accident. An Emergency Medical Service (EMS) technician is reported to have jumped back from her body when he cut her pants off, to enable him to treat one of her injuries, and saw her penis. This EMS technician, whose identity is being protected by the Fire Department, is said to have shouted, "That ain't no bitch!" Treatment of Hunter's injuries came to a halt while other technicians gawked at and ridiculed her. The outraged and frightened cries of bystanders, who are quoted as saying, "It don't make any difference, he's [sic] a human being," finally alerted an EMS supervisor, who treated her. She died in a local hospital shortly after being transported there. Over two thousand people attended her funeral on August 12, a clear sign that, unlike far too many incidents of official abuse of transgendered people, this case was not going to be swept under the rug.

Friends told transgendered activists that Hunter was twenty-four, had lived full-time as a woman since she was fourteen, and worked as a hairdresser. She was well-liked in her neighborhood, a gentle person who had never imagined she would die prematurely while suffering the humiliation of being reviled by the same people who were supposed to rescue and care for her.

An organization called Together in Tyra's Memory (TTM) was formed to protest this terrible incident of neglect. Among the supporters of TTM were Gay Men and Lesbians Opposing Violence; DC Coalition of Black Gay Men, Lesbians and Bisexuals; Gay and Lesbian Alliance Against Defamation of the National Capital Area; Capital City National Organization of Women; Log Cabin Republicans, DC

Chapter; Gay and Lesbian Activists Alliance; Queer Nation; Transgender Nation of Washington, DC, and several other groups.

Despite pressure from TTM, the fire department insisted on its right to conduct an "internal inquiry," and issued nothing more than a one-page press release, which said they could not determine what had occurred despite the availability of at least eight known eye witnesses.[22]

The sad death of Deborah Forte of Haverhill, Massachusetts should also be mentioned here. Ironically, the same day activists were packing up to leave their vigil at John Lotter's trial for murdering Brandon Teena, Forte died. She was found with three very deep stab wounds in her chest, other knife wounds, a smashed nose, multiple severe blows to her head and face, and the marks of partial strangulation. The man who was arrested in connection with her death, Michael J. Thompson, allegedly confessed to a coworker that he killed Forte after he went home with her, began "messing around," and discovered that she had a penis.[23]

Gender ambiguity makes many, if not most, people uncomfortable. But differently-gendered people are no longer taking violence for granted. And they are asking the rest of society to take a stand with them, to acknowledge that this discomfort is the result of ignorance and prejudice, and can no longer be used as a justification for harassment, assault, or murder.

The case of *The People of the State of Colorado vs. Sharon Clark, a.k.a. Sean O'Neill*, a female-bodied person who was charged with several crimes as a result of having sex with teenage girls who believed he was a young man, fortunately had a much happier ending than the Brandon Teena tragedy.

El Paso County prosecutors got four girls to confess that Sharon Clark (living as Sean O'Neill) had had consensual sex with them for months while posing as a boy. Twenty-year-old Clark was charged with one to eight years for each of eleven felony counts (sexual assault, criminal impersonation, and sexual assault on a child). If convicted on all counts, he could have spent thirty-two years in prison. Two of the four complainants were fourteen and O'Neill had been eighteen when some of the sex occurred. The district attorney claimed O'Neill had raped the girls by withholding a crucial piece of sexual information from them.

This situation came to the attention of law enforcement personnel when one of O'Neill's girlfriends filed a harassment complaint against him. O'Neill had told her he was in love with someone else, they quarreled, and he threatened her. Police arrested O'Neill in a shopping mall and found a Colorado ID card in the name of Sharon Clark on his person. O'Neill admitted that he was, legally speaking, Sharon Clark. That night, a pair of policewomen reportedly decided to bring him up on charges of criminal impersonation and sexual assault. The girlfriend who had filed the harassment complaint was so upset by this news that she is said to have thrown her keys in a cop's face.

Gender activists were frightened about the potential consequences of this case in part because of the location where it was being tried. Colorado Springs is the home of over fifty-three Religious Right groups, two Christian colleges, and ten evangelical bookstores. The homophobic Amendment 2 passed here in 1992 by the greatest margin in the state. In 1990, Charles Daugherty, a twenty-six-year-old man, was found guilty of criminal impersonation for enrolling in a local high school as a girl named Cheyen. Daugherty's punishment set a scary precedent for O'Neill. Some of them also recalled the 1991 case of Jennifer Saunders in England. Saunders was given a six-year prison term (which was later reduced, but only after she had spent nine months in custody) for allegedly deceiving another young girl about her true sex. The difference in that case was that Saunders was very emphatic about her lesbian identity, although she admitted to some-times passing as male to deceive the homophobic friends and families of her girlfriends.[24]

Much of the gay and lesbian community's information about O'Neill's case came from Minkowitz. Once again, she downplayed the male gender identity of the key figure in this tale. Minkowitz says, "To me, he [nota bene: Sean O'Neill] looks like a cute dyke, the sort of semibutch woman you can meet on hiking trails all over Colorado Springs."[25] O'Neill reportedly did not use the term *transsexual* or *transgendered* to describe himself, but neither did he call himself a les-bian. Certainly the negative public attitude toward lesbian sex had a bearing on the case. O'Neill was reportedly dyke-bashed frequently in high school, and he was beaten up by a group of teenagers after he appeared on the *Jerry Springer* show. It's possible, because of this, to wonder if O'Neill's cross-dressing and passing as a man was not at least partly motivated by a desire to escape antigay violence, as well as gen-der dysphoria. It seems pretty clear that some of O'Neill's girlfriends kept dating him even after they became aware of his female anatomy. But this is not what they told their parents or the district attorney's office. And it seems improbable that this case would have gone to court if O'Neill had been a genetic male.

Still, it is puzzling to find Minkowitz balking again and again at using the same male pronouns to describe O'Neill that he uses to describe himself. The reader is left with the impression that even if O'Neill had been taking testosterone and was scheduled for chest surgery, Minkowitz might not have been able to bring herself to see him or write about him as a man.

As Minkowitz pointed out, under Colorado law, one is guilty of first-degree sexual assault if one "causes submission of the victim" by violence or threats, and guilty of second-degree sexual assault if one causes submission by "any other means." Sean's lawyer Bill Martinez told Minkowitz that theoretically you could be found guilty under this statute if you falsely told a sex partner, "No, I'm not married" or "Yes, I am independently wealthy."

The other cause for concern was the possible consequences, not just for O'Neill, but for gay men, lesbians, and transgendered people (especially those who were preoperative or non-operative) if O'Neill was convicted. Wilchins commented, "If you look androgynous and someone wants to claim that you're passing yourself off as the other gender, you've just committed a felony." Wilchins wonders why it is the transsexual person's obligation to reveal their gender. "Did Sean's lovers tell him what their gender is?" she asked Minkowitz. Minkowitz connects this to debates about whether HIV-positive people must inform their partners. "Does everyone have an obligation to reveal their gender—or to know it?" she wonders. Robin Kane of NGLTF added, "As we learn more and more about transgendered people, we learn that there is a continuum of gender identification, and that it might actually be impossible for some people to disclose their gender fully."[26]

One of the transactivists who met O'Neill during the course of organizing events to draw attention to the case disputes the characterization of him as a "sexual predator."

> To give you a sense of what a crock the prosecution was, we took Sean to lunch after the sentencing, and while we're all trying to eat lunch his beeper keeps going off with one of the girls who is supposed to be his "victim" calling him. The district attorney kept referring to him as a dangerous and predatory "pedophile." And here's Sean, who weighs about ninety pounds soaking wet. One of his public defenders is a petite woman of about five-four and Sean just about reaches her shoulder.[27]

O'Neill wound up pleading guilty to one count of second degree sexual assault, and all other charges were dropped. On February 16, 1996, a judge gave O'Neill six years of supervised probation, therapy with Dr. Muller (a psychiatrist from Denver who gave testimony on

Sean's behalf) or some other doctor who understood gender disorder, all sexual contact to be reported to a therapist, no unsupervised contact with anybody under eighteen, sex offender counseling, possibly some alcohol issues that needed to be dealt with, and ninety days in El Paso County Jail. The judge stressed that he would find a place for O'Neill to serve his sentence where he would not be harmed. The nervous young man, who had appeared in court with his girlfriend, was visibly relieved.

Gender activists took a large portion of the credit for ameliorating the effects of the criminal case against O'Neill. Their visibility helped to shift the public and judicial view of O'Neill, from predatory lesbian to immature teenage boy burdened by a confused gender identity. In statements before sentencing, District Attorney Schwartz reportedly said, "Sean O'Neill is a predator. She should be removed from the community."[28] Defense attorney Bill Martinez countered, "Sean O'Neill is a troubled young person doing his best to find his way, and to find affection in this world, without role models or appropriate guidance."[29]

While it seems clear that sending O'Neill to prison would have been a great injustice, it is disturbing to see the entire issue of lesbian sex side-stepped here. If O'Neill had been butch- rather than male-identified, it is doubtful that the gay or lesbian community would have sprung into action to provide assistance to the defense attorneys, largely because age-of-consent issues and cross-generational sex are involved.

Transexual Menace had scheduled a press conference and demonstration in support of O'Neill on the courthouse steps preceding the hearing. About seven hundred fifty flyers were distributed that read, "Free Sean O'Neill—Don't Let Colorado Springs Make Gender Non-Conformity a Crime! …The Cops & DA want to waste tens of thousands of dollars of your tax money regulating sex & gender."[30] FTM activists Green and Tony Barreto-Neto, a deputy sheriff from Hillsborough County, Florida, and founder of Transgendered Officers Protect and Serve (TOPS), had testified on his behalf. About twenty people came from all over the country to attend the trial, which then had to be moved to a larger courtroom. One observer reported that transgendered people and their friends made up over half the audience. Wilchins comments, "The Sean O'Neill demonstration was the first time trans-men really came into their own in gender activism. We not only had a great turnout by them, but we also got to see Jamison [nota bene: Green] and Tony [nota bene: Barreto-Neto] testifying on Sean's behalf. A whole new segment of the community was starting to come out, get visible, and be political."[31]

The new, more public and outrageous style of gender activism has not superseded work on more traditional issues, which has proceeded according to the temperate pace of governments and courtrooms. Attempts to gain the same protection for their civil rights that racial minorities and (in some municipalities and states) gay men and lesbians have won have been ongoing among gender activists. In Minnesota, a transsexual World War II veteran lobbied the state legislature to include "gender difference" as a protected civil-rights category. In 1974, Diana Slyter co-wrote the Minneapolis ordinance that was this country's first prohibition of discrimination against transpeople.[32] Early in 1993, Minnesota passed a law that forbids discrimination against people "having or being perceived as having a self-image or identity not traditionally associated with one's biological maleness or femaleness."[33] And in December of 1994, the San Francisco Board of Supervisors outlawed discrimination against transsexuals in schools, housing, public accommodations, and the workplace.

This came only after a careful foundation of hearings and other research had been laid. In 1994, the San Francisco Human Rights Commission organized its first forum on discrimination against transgendered people. On May 12, a four-and-a-half hour hearing took place before the Commission. More than fifty transgendered speakers testified about discrimination. Kiki Whitlock, chair of the Transgender Task Force and a member of the Commission's Gay, Lesbian, Bisexual, and Transgender Advisory Committee, said, "It was a very historic hearing. It's a necessary first step toward legislation so that transgendered people will be a protected class." Among those who testified were Green, photographer Loren Cameron, and San Francisco Police Department Sergeant Stephan Thorn.[34]

In September of 1994, the commission published a groundbreaking paper, "Investigation into Discrimination Against Transgendered People." The principal author was Green, as a contractor to the city, under the supervision of Human Rights Commission staff member Larry Brinkin, who had done much to gain official recognition of the institutionalized oppression transpeople face and to generate moral indignation against that oppression. Out of all these actions, later that year came unanimous passage by the San Francisco Board of Supervisors of an amendment to Article 33 of the Police Code and Chapter 12 of the city's Administrative Code, which add "gender identity" to the list of attributes for which a person may not be discriminated against.

As the author of this report, Green encountered "FTM invisibility" during news coverage of the extension of civil-rights protection to transgendered people.

> The press was all about men in dresses. Mention of FTM presence or issues was absolutely minuscule. Several times at the courthouse, when the press was doing interviews, I stood by and listened as reporters inquired who wrote the report, and when I was pointed out to them as the author I could see them looking right through me, looking past me to find the man in a dress who must have written the report and whom they would want to interview. More than once a reporter asked me incredulously, "You wrote this report?" They assumed because of my "normal" appearance that I wouldn't be newsworthy. ...Does it matter that the world doesn't know we exist, or doesn't take us seriously? You bet it does. ...Invisibility does not equate with acceptance.[35]

When the law was passed, supervisor Tom Ammiano, a gay man, joked, "A guy can't get a pink slip just for wearing one."[36] Ammiano's relatively benign humor took a malignant turn on a national level. Satirical articles in the *Wall Street Journal* and other prominent daily newspapers lambasted San Francisco for what was perceived as a ridiculous and frivolous action. Some of these articles were published in newspapers that no longer feel free to publish similar diatribes against the concept of lesbian and gay rights. Unfortunately, it seems, progress in one area of sexual prejudice does not seem to guarantee progress in another. Transphobia is a separate entity from, although it is related to, homophobia, and activism is the only way to counter its harmful effects.

The Human Welfare and Community Action Commission in Berkeley cast a near-unanimous vote to include transgendered people as a protected group under its anti-discrimination policy on September 20, 1995.[37] But progressive policies on transgender rights still does not sit well in many quarters. Additional backlash against the San Francisco ordinance recently appeared in local media. Transactivists had to picket the *San Francisco Chronicle* after the newspaper ran a story that implied that taxpayers would have to pay thousands of dollars for sex-change surgeries because of the law protecting transsexuals from discrimination. This story was picked up by the Associated Press wire service, which alleged there were six thousand people in San Francisco who might apply for sex-change surgery. It then appeared all over the country. What actually happened was that members of the San

Francisco Transgender Community Task Force and the Human Rights Commission approached Supervisor Tom Ammiano and asked him why transexually-related medical services were excluded from the insurance coverage of city employees. They were asking for the removal of an exclusion from existing insurance coverage, not attempting to impose an additional tax on citizens. And there were only approximately seven transsexual city employees, not six thousand. The later, larger figure may have come from an estimate of the total number of transgendered people in all of San Francisco.[38]

Transsexual activists have won important victories not only in this country, but abroad. On April 30, 1996, the European Court of Justice confirmed the recommendation of Advocate General Tesauro and said that it is against European law to discriminate against a transsexual person in employment. This ruling affects an estimated forty to fifty thousand European transgendered people and four to five thousand in the United Kingdom. This matter began in an unfair-dismissal case brought by a Press for Change activist known only as "P" against her former employers, the Cornwall County Council. The British government was thus placed under pressure to amend the Sex Discrimination Act and the Equal Pay Act to close a loophole that had been used by employers who wanted to dismiss FTM or MTF employees. The European Court decision was especially welcome, since earlier in the year "P" had lost a bid to get the sex on her birth certificate changed. British law continues to make it all but impossible for transsexuals to do this, and since this is their only form of legal identification there, they are outed as transgendered any time they must show their papers.[39]

Sadly, the efforts of transgendered activists to gain basic civil liberties protection for themselves and their community have encountered an obstacle where these efforts should have found allies. In June of 1994, HRC, a venerable gay-rights organization formerly known as the Human Rights Campaign Fund, declined to include transsexual people as a protected class in the Employment Non-Discrimination Act (ENDA), a job discrimination bill it was promoting in Congress to protect lesbians and gay men from being fired for their sexual orientation. ENDA drafter Chai Feldblum was quoted as telling the International Conference on Transgender Law and Employment Policy that HRC "couldn't afford inclusion because it might cost us twenty votes."[40]

Transgender activists were enraged by this news, and quite correctly pointed out that it is often a perceived gender difference that alerts a homophobe to the presence of a gay men or lesbian. A law that did not extend protection to transsexuals and transgendered people might leave effeminate gay men, butch dykes, or anybody who was perceived as violating social sex-role stereotypes vulnerable to unfair termination of employment or other unequal treatment. Trans-activists worked to get themselves mentioned in the bill, and succeeded, but HRC insisted on omitting transpeople again when ENDA was reintroduced on June 16, 1995.

After six months of leafleting and picketing by transactivists, HRC agreed to assist transactivists in drafting an amendment to ENDA and helped them to lobby for its inclusion. This tenuous peace was reached only after the gender community had held demonstrations to educate people about HRC's discriminatory policies in at least eighteen cities.[41] Green feels that "Chai Feldblum has come to a new understanding of the synergy between gay and trans issues. Recently, in a speech at Harvard University she was reported to say that she now believed transpeople should be included in ENDA, and what changed her mind was meeting Shannon Minter, staff attorney for the National Center for Lesbian Rights in San Francisco, who has recently come out as FTM. She was able to have a personal experience of what transgender means through meeting someone she could respect and identify with, and whose gender difference was perceptible to her."[42]

It is never pretty when one disadvantaged group sells out another in an attempt to promote its own interests. Nor is it usually good political strategy. The roots of prejudice against homosexuals and the hatred and fear of transsexuals are so closely woven together that it is not really all that difficult to educate people simultaneously about both communities. No reasonable person at HRC could credibly claim that a significant portion of the gay and lesbian community is not also part of the gender community. Gay lobbyists in Washington often propose legislation that they know has a snowball's chance in hell of passing, but they continue to introduce these bills as a way of maintaining gay visibility and reminding legislators that some Americans are still waiting to be given the protection we need in order to meet our basic survival needs. It would be so easy to include everyone who ought to be protected in the same bill. Why should every single minority have to fight its own separate struggle for recognition and acceptance? I know that some gay men and lesbians believe that we must separate our community from the even more stigmatized realm of cross-dressers and transsexuals, or we will never achieve our political goals. But it seems very important for us to ask ourselves if we will have achieved anything, if we are recognized as a minority group entitled to full civil rights, and differently-gendered people are not. As the Transexual Menace flyer protesting HRC's discriminatory policies vis-à-vis ENDA stated, "A queer movement that's not for ALL of us is good for NONE of us!"[43]

Indeed, it is a lack of an analysis of gender among gay male activists that has created debilitating splits between gay men and lesbians. I believe that we cannot fully understand our own oppression without also understanding the roots of transphobia. If our goal is to create a just society where people are not persecuted for difference in their sexual behavior or personal appearance, among other things, we cannot afford to remain ignorant about every type of sexual prejudice and the ways our society tries to repress and shame us for deviation. As long as the words *sissy* and *bulldagger* remain slurs, gay men and lesbians will have a common cause with the transgendered community. It would be better to acknowledge it and move ahead with a new group of solid allies and supporters than it would be to engage in yet another exhausting and stupid attempt to jettison "undesirables" from the Lavender Freedom Train.

As Riki Wilchins, editrix of *In Your Face*, says:

> The fight against gender oppression has been joined for centuries, perhaps millennia. What's new today, is that it's moving into the arena of open political activism. And nope, this is not just one more civil rights struggle for one more narrowly-defined minority. It's about all of us who are genderqueer: diesel dykes and stone butches, leatherqueens and radical fairies, nelly fags, crossdressers, intersexed, transexuals, transvestites, transgendered, transgressively gendered, intersexed, and those of us whose gender expressions are so complex they haven't even been named yet. More than that, it's about the gender oppression which affects everyone: the college sweetheart who develops life-threatening anorexia nervosa trying to look "feminine," the Joe Sixpack dead at forty-five from cirrhosis of the liver because "real men" are hard drinkers. But maybe we genderqueers feel it most keenly, because it hits us each time we walk out the front door openly and proudly. …We're not invisible anymore. We're not well behaved. And we're not going away. Political activism is here to stay.
>
> So get out. Get active. Picket someone's transphobic ass. Get in someone's genderphobic face. And while you're at it, pass the word: the gendeRevolution has begun, and we're going to win.[44]

In a personal communiqué, she adds:

I am not personally interested in being a transgender activist—
even less a transsexual activist. What I am interested in is fighting a liberatory struggle against gender-based oppression—all
the ways in which culture seeks to regulate, confine, and punish
bodies, gender, and desire.[45]

In the next chapter, the future of gender activism and gender itself
will be examined.

Notes

1. Vicky Kolakowski, "Fifth International Transgender Law Conference Held in
Houston," *Bay Area Reporter,* July 11, 1996, pp. 25-26.
2. Phyllis Frye, "ICTLEP Appoints Another FTM to Board of Directors," December
12, 1996 press release from ICTLEP.
3. Riki Anne Wilchins, "Quotes, Quotes, Quotes," e-mail to the author, December
13, 1996, p. 1. Unpublished.
4. Jamison Green, "Chapter 7," December 21, 1996 e-mail to the author, p. 2.
Unpublished.
5. Anne Ogborn, "Going Home," pp. 2-3, and "Hijras and Intersexuals," p. 3,
Hermaphrodites with Attitudes, vol. 1, no. 1, Winter 1994.
6. John Taylor, "The Third Sex," *Esquire,* April 1995, pp. 102-114.
7. Wilchins, "Quotes, Quotes, Quotes," op. cit., pp. 2-3.
8. Green, op. cit., pp. 2-3.
9. Interview with Riki Anne Wilchins by the author, December 12, 1996.
Unpublished.
10. Fish, "Moshing with Michigan Womyn (& Transsexuals!)," *San Francisco Bay
Times,* August 25, 1994, p. 53.
11. Riki Anne Wilchins, "Michigan Womyn's Music Festival Controversy Grinds
On," *In Your Face,* Fall 1995, page 6.
12. Donna Minkowitz, "Love Hurts," *Village Voice,* April 19, 1994, p. 24.
13. Ibid., p. 25.
14. Riki Anne Wilchins, "Brandon Teena Revisited," GenderPAC press release,
December 6, 1996.
15. Minkowitz, op. cit.
16. Mindy Ridgway, "Nebraska Man Guilty of Brandon Teena's Murder," *San
Francisco Bay Times,* March 23, 1995, p. 4.
17. Green, op. cit., p. 3.
18. Riki Anne Wilchins, "Seeking A New Trial," GenderPAC press release, December 6,
1996.
19. Riki Anne Wilchins, "New York Citaaay," *In Your Face,* Spring 1995, p. 3.
20. Dorothy Atcheson, "Culture Vultures in Nebraska," *Out,* October 1995, p. 100.
Sidebar to Donna Minkowitz, "On Trial: Gay? Straight? Boy? Girl? Sex? Rape?,"
Out, October 1995, pp. 99-101, 140-146.

21. Wilchins, "Quotes, Quotes, Quotes," op. cit., pp. 3-4.
22. Riki Anne Wilchins, "Another One, It Just Doesn't Stop: Tyra Hunter," *In Your Face*, Fall 1995, pp. 2-3.
23. Riki Anne Wilchins, "The Murder of Deborah Forte," *In Your Face*, Fall 1995, p. 2.
24. Anna Marie Smith, "The Regulation of Lesbian Sexuality through Erasure: The Case of Jennifer Saunders," in Karla Jay (ed.), *Lesbian Erotics*, New York: New York University, 1995, pp. 164-179.
25. Donna Minkowitz, "On Trial: Gay? Straight? Boy? Girl? Sex? Rape?," *Out*, October 1995, p. 100.
26. Ibid., p. 146.
27. Wilchins, "Quotes, Quotes, Quotes," op. cit., p. 4.
28. Jamison Green, "Predator?" *San Francisco Bay Times*, vol. 17, no. 9, February 22, 1996, p. 3. Reprinted in *FTM Newsletter*, issue 34, May 1996, pp. 2-6. Page numbers in text refer to the *Bay Times* original printing.
29. Ibid., p. 29.
30. Ibid., p. 2.
31. Wilchins, "Quotes, Quotes, Quotes," op. cit., pp. 4-5.
32. Margaret Deirdre O'Hartigan, "Stealing Our History," an unpublished review of Leslie Feinberg's *Transgender Warriors*, p. 4.
33. Dan Levy and David Tuller, "Opening Up the World of Drag," *San Francisco Chronicle*, May 28, 1993, pp. A-1 and A-17.
34. Dennis Conkin, "Human Rights Commission Addresses Transgender Issues," Bay Area Reporter, May 19, 1994, p. 1.
35. James Green, "Keynote Address for the FTM Conference," August 18, 1995, pp. 11-12. Unpublished.
36. Jeff Stryker, "Bigotry and Ignorance vs. the 'Transgendered', " *San Francisco Examiner*, December 13, 1995, p. A-33.
37. Mary Ann Swissler, "Berkeley Adopts Transgender Rights," *Bay Area Reporter*, October 12, 1995, p. 5.
38. Riki Anne Wilchins, "SF Chronicle Has Transphobia Attack," GenderPAC press release, October 18, 1996. The article "Move to Cover City Worker's Sex Changes" appeared in the *San Francisco Chronicle* on September 23, 1996.
39. Christine Burns, "Victory in the European Court of Justice," April 30, 1996, press release by Press for Change.
40. Transexual Menace flyer headed "HRCF to Transpeople: Drop Dead!", undated.
41. Riki Anne Wilchins, "1995: A Breakout Year in Review," *In Your Face*, Fall 1995, p. 1.
42. Green, "Chapter 7," op. cit., pp. 4-5.
43. Transexual Menace flyer headed "Hey HRCF: Can You Spell I-N-C-L-U-S-I-O-N?, undated.
44. Riki Anne Wilchins, "A Note from Your Editrix," *In Your Face*, Spring 1995, p. 4.
45. Interview with Riki Anne Wilchins by the author, op. cit.

CHAPTER 8

The Future of Gender and Transgenderism

Until the latter part of this decade, transsexual activism focused on gaining social acceptance for post-reassignment transsexuals. The goal of this activism, which focused on medical and mental-health professionals and the judicial system rather than laypeople, was to allow transsexuals to receive sex reassignment as quickly and easily as possible, and live in their gender of preference as if they had been assigned that sex at birth. More recently, transgendered activists have been questioning the entire system of binary and polarized gender. Some leaders of the gender community have called for transsexuals to direct their political efforts toward eliminating the notions of "men" and "women," rather than working to be perceived by nontranssexuals as a member of either gender. This has coincided with an increase in the numbers of people who label themselves as third-gender, two-spirit, both genders, neither gender, or intersexed, and insist on their right to live without or outside of the gender categories that our society has attempted to make compulsory and universal.

One of the most visible and articulate proponents of this view is Kate Bornstein. In her book *Gender Outlaw: On Men, Women and the Rest of Us*, Bornstein labels her own gender as follows: "I know I'm not a man—about that much I'm very clear, and I've come to the conclusion that I'm probably not a woman either, at least not according to a lot of people's rules on this sort of thing. The trouble is, we're living in a world that insists we be one or the other—a world that doesn't bother to tell us exactly what one or the other *is*."[1]

Despite her statement that "after thirty-seven years of trying to be male and over eight years of trying to be female, I've come to the conclusion that neither is really worth all the trouble,"[2] she acknowledges that she tries to pass in public as female, if only to protect herself from danger. "I still make an effort to walk down the street and pass on a very private level. I do this because I don't want to get beaten up. I do this because all my life it's been something I've wanted—to live as a woman—and by walking through the world looking like one, I have that last handhold on the illusion, the fantasy, the dream of it all. Passing is seductive—people don't look at you like you're some kind of freak."[3]

With great courage, clarity, and humor, Bornstein rejects the traditional narrative of the "typical" transsexual experience—that of being trapped in the wrong body. She says frankly, "I've no idea what 'a woman' feels like. I never did feel like a girl or a woman; rather, it was my unshakable conviction that I was not a boy or a man. It was the absence of a feeling, rather than its presence, that convinced me to change my gender."[4] Later on in the book, she says, "Of all the options I've got, I like being girl the best."[5] Given this statement and the fact that she does not suggest an alternative, gender-neutral pronoun in her book, female pronouns will be used to refer to her here.

Bornstein calls the idea that "we are trapped in the wrong body" a myth, and counters, "I'll bet that's more likely an unfortunate metaphor that conveniently conforms to cultural expectations, rather than an honest reflection of our transgendered feelings."[6] She also rejects the idea that transsexuals must, of necessity, hate their unaltered bodies, including the genitals they were born with: "I never hated my penis; I hated that it made me a man—in my own eyes, and in the eyes of others. For my comfort, I needed a vagina—I was convinced that the only way I could live out what I thought to be my true gender was to have genital surgery to construct a vagina from my penis. Fortunately, I don't regret having done this."[7]

This may be one of the first public acknowledgments by a transsexual that the outcome one can expect from genital surgery is often less than satisfactory. Prior to this decade, the overwhelming majority of transsexuals expressed nothing but gratitude for such surgery, even if the results were not cosmetically pleasing or functional for urination or sexual activity. This comment by Bornstein is the result of the gender community reaching and exceeding a "critical mass," which seems necessary before sexual minorities can view themselves as a minority, share histories and accumulate a common agenda of grievances, and begin to demand accountability from individuals and institutions outside of their own subculture.

Bornstein clearly implies that it ought not be necessary for transsexuals to go under the knife, risking loss of sensation and sexual pleasure, to achieve comfort in their bodies. This is an extension of her belief that gender is well-nigh mythical, something invented and enforced by the culture. In this text, gender is seen as purely and entirely a social construct, with no significant biological or physiological content.

> But rather than look at some underlying reasons for inequality [nota bene: between men and women], most people keep going on about the differences between the genders. *The differences are only what we decide they are.* By focusing on so-called "inherent differences" between men and women, we ignore and deny the existence of the gender system itself, and so we in fact hold it in place. But it's the gender system itself—the idea of gender itself—that needs to be done away with. *The differences will then fall aside of their own accord.*[8]

On its face, this will seem absurd to most readers. Bornstein seems unwilling to acknowledge the physical facts upon which gender is based. There really are XX and XY sex chromosomes, penises and clits, prostate glands and vaginas, sperm and eggs, testicles and uteruses, testosterone and estrogen, a sex that impregnates and another that bears children. Few feminists would argue with her contention that our society has assigned meanings to these differences that go way beyond what pure biology would dictate. But it's probable that few people, feminist or not, are prepared to agree with her when she dismisses the physiological and genetic realities that really do divide most of the human race into two very different groups of people.

Bornstein is the opposite of a biological determinist. Furthermore, she is not willing to see anything positive about male/female differences. At various points in her book, she compares binary gender to drug addiction,[9] religious cults,[10] and racism.[11]

In Bornstein's opinion, transgendered people are not born into the wrong bodies; they are people who bridge male/female categories or combine them in new ways. Thus, it is not really possible for a transsexual to become a man or a woman. Bornstein claims that the medicalization of transsexuality and the sex-reassignment process, which encourage transsexuals to try to shoehorn themselves into the same gender categories that most people take for granted, has actually created a great deal of pain and suffering for transgendered people, and distorted their sense of their own life histories and desires. While acknowledging the bravery of her transsexual forebears, she begs to differ with the assumptions on which their medicalized autobiographies were written: "Up until the last few years, all we'd be able to write *and get published* were our autobiographies, tales of women trapped in the bodies of men or men pining away in the bodies of women. Stories by and about brave people who'd lived their lives hiding deep within a false gender—and who, after much soul-searching, decided to change their gender, and spent the rest of their days hiding deep within *another* false gender."[12] For the doctors and therapists who have urged transsexuals to blend in, fit in, and hide, Bornstein has nothing but contempt:

> A less visible reason for the silence of the transgendered hinges on the fact that transsexuality in this culture is considered an illness, and an illness that can only be cured by silence. …We're taught that we are literally sick, that we have an illness that can be diagnosed and maybe cured. As a result of the medicalization of our condition, transsexuals must see therapists in order to receive the medical seal of approval required to proceed with any gender reassignment surgery. Now, once we get to the doctor, we're told we'll be cured if we become members of one gender or another. We're told not to divulge our transsexual status, except in select cases requiring intimacy…. Transsexuality is the only condition for which the therapy is to lie.[13]

And later, she emphasizes again, "It's the therapeutic lie that eventually causes us to go mad: it's hiding, passing, and being silent that makes us crazy."[14] Bornstein's rage echoes earlier efforts to question the prescription of the closet to postsurgical transsexuals.

> In follow-up studies of "reassigned" transsexuals, one of the criteria for mental health is how well they have "passed." A transsexual in a heterosexual relationship who has no contact with other transsexuals is "normal," a success. Transsexuals who spend time in the gay community, acknowledge their transsexual identity, and maybe even think it's a political issue are failures. How can schizophrenia or amnesia be mentally healthy? Transsexuals have strong feelings of yearning to change their biological sex; no matter how many people eventually come to accept them as members of their preferred sex, that history cannot be erased.[15]

Bornstein sees transsexuals as the unwitting inheritors of the gender dis-ease of their doctors and therapists—the transsexual's desire for sex reassignment as an iatrogenic illness.

Rather than educating the general public to accept transgendered men and women and support their attempts to live in their gender of preference, Bornstein encourages transsexuals to attack the binary gender system, which she sees as responsible for creating virtually every form of human misery and oppression. But this will not happen, she believes, until transsexuals begin questioning their own sense of themselves as men or women: "We talk casually…about *trans*-gender without ever clearly stating, and rarely if ever asking, what one gender or the other really is. We're so sure of our ability to categorize people as either men or women that we neglect to ask ourselves some very basic questions: what is a man? and what is a woman? and why do we need to be one or the other?"[16] And later on: "The correct target for any successful transsexual rebellion would be the gender system itself. But transsexuals won't attack that system until they themselves are free of the need to participate in it."[17]

Transsexuals who continue to cling to outmoded notions of their own gender are, in this view, counter-revolutionaries. Bornstein does not exempt herself from fierce self-criticism: "When, for example, I lived my life saying I was a man or a woman, I was tacitly supporting all the rules of the gender system that defines those two identities. I supported those rules in order to belong, or rather to *not* be an outsider, a non-belonger."[18] The goals of such a radical movement for social change remain somewhat vague, perhaps because it would require such a dramatic rethinking of our most basic paradigms. On this point, Bornstein says, "We haven't dared to name a goal: probably something like 'a society free from the constraints of non-consensual gender.'"[19]

Such a movement obviously has no chance of success if it is supported only by a handful of transgendered people who share Bornstein's conviction that it is a grave error to ally with either gender camp. She makes a spirited appeal to other feminists, the majority of whom have historically been hostile to transsexual women and sex reassignment in general, and asks them to rethink theories about the origins of misogyny and dismantle gender itself, rather than lobbying for equality between the sexes. "The trap for women is the system itself: it's not men who are the foe so much as it is the bipolar gender system that keeps men in place as more privileged," she claims.[20]

Bornstein attributes the fact that feminism has been able to win only limited victories for women to the failure to dismantle gender. She says, "Gender struggles have historically failed to reach their goals, whereas class conflicts have historically had some degree of success."[21]

While it is true that any progressive social change can be reversed, Bornstein's contention that women's rights are especially susceptible to repeal is dubious. Her belief in a triumph over class conflicts would probably be news to anyone who has worked in the American trade union movement for the last three decades, and watched the relentless erosion of the rights of workers in this country and elsewhere. And the recent passage of Proposition 209 in California, which revokes affirmative action, confirms that people of color are as likely to be the victims of a conservative backlash as women or working-class people.

Despite its eloquence, Bornstein's view of the power dynamics between men and women is simplistic as well.

> In the either/or gender class system that we call male and female, the structure of one-up, one-down fulfills the requisite for a power imbalance. It became clear that the reason that the bipolar gender system continues to exist, and is actively and tenaciously held in place, is that the bi-polar gender system is primarily a venue for the playing out of a power game. It's an arena in which roughly half the people in the world can have power over the other half.
>
> Without the structure of the bi-polar gender system, the power dynamic between men and women shatters. People would not have gender to use as a hierarchical framework, and nearly half the members of the bipolar gender system would probably be at quite a loss. ...I think that male privilege is the glue that holds the system together.[22]

Bornstein borrows a key concept from Marjorie Garber, author of *Vested Interests,* that of the third. "The 'third,'" Bornstein says, quoting Garber, "is that which questions binary thinking and introduces crisis."[23] Garber's book is a comprehensive analysis of the many ways that cross-dressing, as it is depicted in history, literature, film, photography, and other products of mass and popular culture, serves to highlight the artificial aspects of "natural" gender categories, among other effects. It seems that in Bornstein's view, transsexuals occupy a privileged position as "the third," because she explicitly rejects both bisexuality and androgyny as destabilizing, politically radical categories.[24]

> Straights and gays alike demand the need for an orderly gender system: they're two sides of the same coin, each holding the other in place, neither willing to dismantle the gender system that serves as a matrix for their (sexual) identity. Because of the

bi-polar nature of both sexual orientation and gender, one system strengthens the other. Bisexuality and androgyny also hold two sides in place by defining themselves as somewhere in the middle of two given polar opposites.[25]

Bisexuality may not challenge our adherence to the concept of "men" and "women," but it certainly challenges a very influential gender-based dichotomy, that of heterosexuality versus homosexuality. The concept that one can lust after or fall in love with members of both biological sexes certainly has the potential to alter the way people think about pleasure and gender, and change the way these categories affect their personal and public lives. It seems reasonable to ask if Bornstein perhaps brushes aside bisexuality as another type of Third because gender dysphoric people are often counseled to become bisexual, rather than change their own sex.

Bornstein's dismissal of androgyny is even more confusing, since this quality is frequently associated with someone who is, as Bornstein describes herself, not clearly committed to being a man or a woman. It seems reasonable to wonder if Bornstein's aggravation with androgynes is not in part due to her personal choice to dress, speak, walk, and present herself as a feminine woman in her daily life. She confesses to making a conscious effort to "pass"; someone who is androgynous cannot or will not. Few of us have escaped witnessing the calumny that is heaped upon androgynous folks precisely because they upset the gender binary. If such people are not members of the Third, a transsexual who passes perfectly as a member of his or her preferred sex can hardly qualify.

Bornstein's reading of gender as a simple one up, one down system, composed only of men and women, leaves out an often-ignored "third class" in this gender binary—the class of children, over whom women have great power, which they often abuse. I would argue that Western notions of childhood "question binary thinking and introduce crisis." The intense social conditioning directed at children to enforce social sex-roles is a powerful indicator that infants and toddlers are believed to arrive in a genderless state, and are in danger of remaining there if adult intervention is not successful. What adults perceive as gender-inappropriate behavior in childhood is so common that child-development experts carefully label each "phase" of this subversive activity, thus ensuring that it is not seen as a critique of our current gender system or an alternative to it that should be allowed to find full expression in adulthood. What Freud called the polymorphous perverse sexuality of infancy is another potentially gender-destabilizing condition that cannot be allowed to persist. Children are much more visible than cross-dressers, but the existence of this particular Third has not altered our beliefs about the nature of male and female identity. Simple recognition of exceptions to a rule do not automatically lead to the rule being questioned or revised.

Bornstein's précis of the war between the sexes ignores the fact that men and women both have power, albeit of different sorts. While men wield more economic power and find it easier to manipulate events in the public sphere, women continue to exercise considerable authority over private life and our notions of morality. One might also argue that oppression is not inherent to all binary systems, or at least that its inevitability has not been fully demonstrated in Bornstein's text. Paired systems can be based on cooperation and mutually beneficial exchange instead of exploitation or violence. And there can certainly be oppression in three-way systems too. In a system where third-gender roles were acceptable, men might continue to oppress women and differently-gendered people. Also, a monopoly on public political power need not inhere merely to classes based on gender. In a society that had dismantled or discounted gender, it would still be possible to base privilege upon ownership of property, profession, skin color, height, religion, sexual proclivities, membership in a certain family, etcetera.

Nevertheless, Bornstein is passionately dedicated to her position that it is the gender binary that is responsible for women's oppression, which can only be ended by getting rid of gender. She says, "Gender could be seen as a class system. By having gender around, there are these two classes—male and female. As in any binary, one side will always have more power than the other. One will always oppress the other. The value of a two-gender system is nothing more than the value of keeping the power imbalance, and all that depends on that, intact."[26] To feminists who advocate a fight for equality between men and women, she says, "Fight rather for the deconstruction of gender—it would get to the same place much faster."[27]

In Bornstein's brand of feminism, gender is seen as the most insidious artifact of the patriarchy. She explains, "After all, men couldn't have male privilege if there were no males. And women couldn't be oppressed if there was no such thing as 'women'. ...Doing away with gender is key to doing away with the patriarchy, as well as ending the many injustices perpetrated in the name of gender inequity. ...Gender inequities include sexism, homophobia, and misogyny."[28]

This overlooks the ways that gender serves many fundamental needs for women as well as men. Bornstein does not elucidate the fierce opposition she would encounter from most women to this vision of a genderless world. Most women admittedly can accumulate only limited power by wielding feminine wiles, youth, physical beauty, sex, or maternal skills. (We can't all be Madonna.) But this remains practically the only route that women have to achieve self-esteem, close relationships with others, economic security, pleasure, a sense of purpose in their lives—in short, happiness. If gender is purely an artifact of the patriarchy, what are we to make of women who are among its most enthusiastic defenders and enforcers? It is simplistic to merely dismiss them as cat's paws of male dominance. Feminism, I suspect, will continue to experience limited gains until we have a sophisticated and widely accepted analysis of women's complicity in and perpetuation of their own oppression. Giving up power, even if it is circumscribed, is hard to do when it isn't clear what, if anything, will take its place.

Bornstein's appeals to the women's movement are bolstered by a spirited attack on male privilege, which she believes survives in some transgendered women.

> I've seen some examples of what [nota bene: Janice] Raymond fears: male-to-female transsexuals entering "women-only" spaces, and attempting to assume a position of control and power.... I can empathize with her anger. My contention, however, is that it is not the transsexual person or even the issue of transsexuality that is bad for feminism. I think that what's bad for the future of feminism is male privilege, and I think that occasionally a male-to-female transsexual will carry more than a small degree of that over into their newly gendered life. A better solution to this situation would be to point out what's going on, and to talk it through. I don't think male privilege has a place *anywhere*, and I think it would best be processed out of *any* environment.[29]

But many feminists have struggled to escape the trap of being expected to educate sexist men or argue them into less chauvinistic ways. This has freed feminists from wasting significant amounts of energy on people who are not really interested in changing their view or treatment of women, and allowed us to create a discourse with one another that goes far beyond "Feminism 101." Bornstein ignores this history, and doesn't explain why a feminist would want to fight male privilege or residual sexism in a transgendered woman. Having attempted a few of the sorts of conversations that Bornstein suggests take place between feminists and transgendered women who have

sexist definitions of womanhood and an exaggerated level of entitle-
ment left over from their lives as men, I can vouch for the fact that it is
no easy task. Any rewards to be gained on the part of the educator in
such an arrangement are limited and ephemeral. Bornstein does a less
than thorough job of pointing out the many ways traditional gender
clinics reinforce sexism among male-to-female clients, or of holding
transsexual organizations responsible for the lack of feminist consciousness they not infrequently display. Transsexual women will have
little credibility as feminists until they clean their own house.

Bornstein also attempts to sidestep conflicts between lesbian separatists and transsexuals by pointing out that lesbians are not powerful
enough to be the biggest enemies of transsexuals or the prime enforcers
of gender taboos. She encourages everyone to engage in mutually
respectful dialogue, without specifying what outcome might be desirable or possible.

> Some transsexuals take exclusion by lesbian separatists as
> oppression, but I don't think so. Lesbian oppression at the
> hands of the dominant ideology is not the same as the exclusion
> experienced by the transgendered at the hands of the lesbian
> separatists—lesbians just don't have the same economic and
> social resources with which to oppress the transgendered. I
> think both sides need to sit down and talk with one another and
> I think both sides need to do some serious listening.[30]

Sadly, this well-meaning approach does not address the real and
deep ideological differences that prevent many lesbians from accepting
transgendered women as women, let alone taking on the mission of
eliminating gender itself. If Bornstein is really taking the position that
she (and other transsexuals) are neither male nor female, why should
such individuals feel entitled to a place in the lesbian community,
which is a women-only club? Bornstein's approach to reconciling
transsexuals and lesbians seems even more doomed to failure than
efforts I and a few other genetic women have made to validate the
female and lesbian identities of some transgendered women.

By defining homophobia as a form of gender oppression, Bornstein
attempts to draw lesbians and gay men into political action against
bipolar gender.

> The reason for exclusion by the dominant culture of both
> homosexuality and gender ambiguity has less to do, I think,
> with sexual orientation than it does with gender role. When a

gay man is bashed on the street, it's unlikely that the bashers are thinking of the gay man butt-fucking anyone or in fact being butt-fucked. It has little to do with imagining that man sucking cock. It has a lot to do with seeing that man violate the rules of gender in this culture.[31]

This hypothesis is contradicted by my own experience of being queer-bashed, something that has unfortunately happened to me more than once. On more than half of these occasions, the men or boys who assaulted me referred specifically to lesbian sexual practices as a rationalization for the attack. While our violation of gender norms is certainly one of the reasons why some gay men and lesbians are discriminated against or victimized by violence, we are also targeted because we pursue sexual pleasure and romantic affiliation with members of our own sex. Gay or bisexual people who don't conform to masculine or feminine stereotypes are probably more vulnerable to violence on the street, but queers who "pass" gender muster are still vulnerable to discrimination *solely* on the basis of their sexual activities. In fact, the reaction to such a person, who is viewed as a mole and a deceiver, a traitor and a liar, is sometimes much more intense than attempts to punish feminine gay men or butch dykes.

Bornstein's attempts to corral gay men and lesbians under a transgendered banner of liberation are further hampered by the fact that such an alliance would, to her way of thinking, require homosexuals to abandon the very categories that inspire their desire and love. Bornstein is well aware of the can of worms she's opening here. But she is a persuasive advocate for her vision of unity:

> So let's reclaim the word *transgendered* so as to be more inclusive. Let's let it mean "transgressively gendered." Then, we have a group of people who break the rules, codes, and shackles of gender. Then we have a healthy-sized contingent! It's the transgendered who need to embrace the lesbians and gays, because it's the transgendered who are in fact the more inclusive category.
>
> Of course, this will offend everyone. It will seem to negate and belittle the hard-won gains of lesbians and gay men. It will tend to make invisible the bisexuals. It will seem to dilute a supposedly unique transgender struggle. But it's the only point all these groups have in common, it's the only flag around which they all could rally. Failing one great big happy family under one great big happy name, we need to at least stop attacking each other.

It's going to be difficult. For lesbians and gays to include transgendered people, or indeed be included by them, it would require that gays and lesbians admit to what amounts to their own transgender status. It would require that they question their definition of their sexual identity, which is currently based solely on the gender of their desired partners. That's a lot to ask, but I think that competent and compassionate negotiators from the sexual and gender minority camps could get together and come up with some umbrella name that would be more inclusive, and acceptable to the majority. Lesbians and gay men today stand at a crossroads with bisexuals and transgendered people, says Leslie Feinberg. Further down the road, we're going to need all the community we can muster when it comes time to stand at the crossroads against patriarchal oppression. Only our bonding will permit a true revolution of sex and gender.[32]

This utopian vision begs the question of whether gay men, lesbians, and transsexuals do in fact share identical political goals. When these agendas are compared point for point, I doubt they will perfectly mirror one another. Asking gay men and lesbians to give up the very qualities they are struggling to defend, qualities that are key to their individual and communal identities, is taking a very long road indeed to making a political alliance. It would be a lot easier and more efficient to simply agree to work together on the goals that we have in common. I can't imagine how a law could be worded that would effectively protect the civil rights of homosexuals and exclude transsexuals, which would not leave a large portion of the gay/lesbian/bi community twisting in the wind. Straight culture reads much of the public expression of gay identity as gender transgression. To them, we're all part of the same garbage heap of sex-and-gender trash. It is practical points like this that can most easily draw queer and trans activists together.

Bornstein places the onus for marching under the banner of the Third upon gay men and lesbians, as if the entire transgender community waits to greet an alliance with us with open arms. This ignores the homophobia that is rampant in much of the heterosexually-identified gender community. There are many heterosexual transvestite males who have based their whole argument for social and spousal acceptance on distinguishing themselves from homosexuals. Most of these guys won't even tolerate the presence of gay transvestites at their conferences and socials. Similar conditions make many postoperative transsexuals unwilling to identify with any movement that advocates same-sex expression. These people want to put as much distance as possible between themselves and homosexuality. Their notion of the good life is to find a partner of the opposite sex and be accepted as just one more heterosexual couple next door. I've even met MTFs who are still living with the women they married pre-transition, who insist that they are not having a lesbian relationship! Some of this homophobia is the result of the fact that transsexuals are often falsely accused of being homosexual prior to sex reassignment. And some of it is just plain old bigotry.

I would argue that we cannot realistically expect to end sex- or gender-based discrimination or stigma by simply eliminating identities that are the loci of abusive power or disenfranchisement. Indeed, eliminating such identities would *be* a form of oppression. I cannot imagine Bornstein seriously suggesting, for example, that we eliminate racial or ethnic categories as a way to combat racism. Human xenophobia—our fear of difference—cannot be placated so easily. We need to learn to celebrate our differences, not "morally mandate them out of existence."

Even if it were possible to get rid of homophobia by eliminating the concept of homosexuals or combat sexism by eradicating the biological sexes, there is no reason to believe that oppression, however one chooses to define that, would not continue in some other guise. Of course, it is possible that we could create a system where power, privilege, or leadership became the kind of dirty secret that sexuality, particularly deviant sexuality, is today—something that everyone knew about, but did not discuss or acknowledge; something that many people did, but no one owned publicly; a quality that would be severely punished if its external manifestations became impossible to ignore. But that would make it even more difficult to hold powerful people or institutions accountable for their destructive actions.

The need to form hierarchies and find one's own place within them may be hardwired into us, part of our primate heritage. Or it may be a powerful piece of social conditioning that persists simply because we need some way to organize our social lives and understand our positions relative to others. The tendency for hierarchies to become systems of nonconsensual domination, and structures for funneling resources away from some groups and disproportionately toward others, is well-nigh universal in human societies. No one group, simply by virtue of its identity, is free of the potential to exploit others, not even disenfranchised groups like women, young people, racial minorities, and transsexuals. The will to make use of, control, and deprive others has to be addressed apart from the guises or personas we currently recognize as masks for the privileged and the victimized. Changing or getting rid of those roles is not, I think, an adequate strategy for eliminating "isms." If we need to hate, if we need to believe there is somebody out there who is inferior to us, or groups of people who owe us things we are not in fact entitled to receive, that desire will always find a target.

Bornstein doesn't stop with looking for allies in the women's movement and the gay/lesbian/bisexual community. She attempts to define anyone who might be dissatisfied with gender as a transgendered person and therefore a potential activist dedicated to opposing polarized systems of "opposite" sexes. She believes this point of view has widespread appeal because of the damage that the binary gender system does to almost everyone. She says, "Eventually the gender system lets everyone down. It seems to be rigged that way. Sometimes, even with all the time and effort we put into obeying the rules, we get hurt. We can get badly hurt by being a real man or a real woman."[33]

While this certainly sounds good, the paucity of examples makes it a less than convincing statement. Most people attribute feelings of inadequacy about their personal appearance, sexual experiences, or intimate relationships to an individual failure to achieve feminine or masculine ideals, among other things. A failure in these realms is more likely to be experienced or felt as a need to be more of a masculine man, more of a feminine woman, rather than discomfort with either role or biological sex. Teasing out the inadequacies of social sex roles in a way that will resonate for people who do not consciously experience gender dysphoria is, to be fair, a task that exceeds the scope of Bornstein's book, or this one, for that matter.

Her attempt to blur the boundary between transsexuals and "normal" people is a bid to eliminate the stigma that arises from the minority status of transgendered people. She explains:

> There's a myth in our culture that defines transsexuality as rare, and transsexuals as oddities. But nearly everyone has some sort of bone to pick with their own gender status, be it gender role, gender assignment, or gender identity. And when this dissatisfaction can no longer be glossed over with good manners, or cured by purchasing enough gender-specific products or services—and when this dissatisfaction cannot be silenced by the authority of the state, the medical profession, the church, or one's own peers—then the dissatisfaction is called transsexuality, or gender dysphoria. We're most of us—whether "transsexual" or not—dissatisfied. Some of us have less tolerance for the

dissatisfaction, that's all. I accept the label transsexual as meaning only that I was dissatisfied with my given gender, and I acted to change it. I am transsexual by choice, not by pathology.[34]

Bornstein isn't buying into the sorts of definitions of transsexuality touted by John Money and other gender scientists. She says cheerfully, "One answer to the question, 'Who is a transsexual?' might well be, 'Anyone who admits it.' A more political answer might be, 'Anyone whose performance of gender calls into question the construct of gender itself.' "[35] Thus, her vision of this new movement for social change is a rainbow of diversity: "Rather than wallow in self-pity or boil in some cauldron of rage and injustice, I think it's time for transgendered people to come together under our own banner: a banner that would include anyone who cares to admit their own gender ambiguities, a banner that includes all sexualities, races and ethnicities, ages, classes, and states of body, a banner of the Third."[36]

Since Bornstein's entire theoretical edifice is constructed on the foundation of eschewing self-identification as a "man" or a "woman," it seems only fair to critically examine that piece of this text. Bornstein has included images of herself in the book, as a child and as an actor, which make her look male. But the author's photo is not readable as anything other than the image of a beautiful, feminine woman. *Gender Outlaw* includes an anecdote in which a supposedly transsexual-supportive man calls Bornstein "he."[37] Her resulting anguish and anger are detailed. Granted, this episode may have taken place during a time in Bornstein's life when she was identifying as a woman, but it undermines her claim to living without gender. It is impossible to avoid wondering if Bornstein's proud rejection of both sexes is not in part based on a fait accompli, being overwhelmed by the level of resistance she has experienced from ignorant and bigoted people who refuse to accept her as a woman.

Bornstein, like most other male-to-female transsexuals, has gone to a lot of trouble, pain, and expense to acquire a body that reads as a woman's body. In the narrative of her life, Bornstein makes it clear that she did not come to a place of being neither male nor female until she had done considerable growth and soul-searching. But still, the reader is left with a sense of skepticism. Why go through years of taking hormones, expensive and painful surgery, and a difficult transition period if the end result is to dispense with any clear gender identification?

In 1983, I published an article that reads as if it could be the source for Bornstein's disaffection with bipolar gender. It says, in part:

Why does our society allow only two genders and keep them polarized? Why don't we have a social role for hermaphrodites? Berdaches? Why do transsexuals have to become "real women" or "real men" instead of just being transsexual? After all, aren't there some advantages to being a man with a vagina or a woman with a penis, if only because of the unique perspective it would give? And why can't people go back and forth if they want to?[38]

While one cannot fault Bornstein for having the guts to talk frankly about such difficult issues and come to controversial conclusions, it is worrisome to see her echoing positions taken by transphobic feminist Janice Raymond, who firmly believes the proper response to gender dysphoria is to refuse sex reassignment, refrain from identifying as a member of one's gender of preference, and compensate for the resulting frustration by becoming a sort of feminist male missionary preaching against sexism.

The availability of sex reassignment is by no means something that transsexuals and their loved ones can take for granted. It remains a controversial treatment modality that is viewed with suspicion and outright hostility by the majority of mental-health professionals and medical people. Although Bornstein says that sex reassignment should continue to be available for those who need it to reach a comfort level with themselves,[39] she presents another option:

Now there's a new generation of transsexuals who are assessing their journey not as either/or, but as an integration, as a whole. In bypassing the either/or construct...these new transsexuals are slipping out from under the control of the culture. And a *whole* new sub-culture is being born.

Many people divide transsexuals into preoperative and postoperative, referring to genital conversion surgery. I want to include the option of a "non-operative" transsexual—someone who doesn't opt for the genital surgery.[40]

Bornstein is well aware of the problems that could result from the growing visibility of non-operative transsexuals. She says:

The demedicalization of transsexualism is a dilemma. There is a demand for genital surgery, largely as a result of the cultural genital imperative. Due to financial requirements, the fulfillment of the surgical dream is subject to cultural and class constraints; cosmetic and genital conversion surgery is available primarily to the middle and upper classes. Transsexuals, especially middle-class pre-operative transsexuals, are heavily invested in maintaining their status as "diseased" people. The demedicalization of transsexuality would further limit surgery in this culture, as it would remove the label of "illness" and so prohibit insurance companies from footing the bill.[41]

But she does not dedicate much space to suggesting how transsexuals might protect their access to hormones and surgery without accepting a label of themselves as "diseased people." Her genderless and anti-gender stance is not a strong platform from which to argue with transphobes who'd like to keep gender dysphoric people firmly in the bodies and identities they were born with.

It's important to note that Bornstein's theories are controversial within the transsexual community as well as outside it. Activist and scholar Margaret Deirdre O'Hartigan objects to the use of the term *transgendered*. She says:

Naming is power…. The beginning or end of freedom lies in the power to name ourselves—or others.

There are names for people such as I—transsexual, galla, changeling, male-to-female, sex-change. These names describe us: what we've done, what we do…what we've done is change sex; we shapeshift; we transform ourselves from one form of humanity to another.

This power of ours to transcend the human form we were given is too much for some people to bear contemplating; they would deny us our power, they would deny us our names. …These people would pin their own labels onto our bodies. These people would have us be eunuchs, or freaks, or simply men—or transgender.

Every application of the term *transgender* to me is an attempt to mask what I've done and as such co-opts my life, denies my experience, violates my very soul. I changed my sex. Like the hijra of India and the gallae of Rome I took cold steel to myself and proved that anatomy is not destiny. Like the Siberian Chukchee shaman I have died and been taken apart, reassembled, changed sex, and come back with new powers. Like the inkte of the Mdewakanton Siouxs I grew up amongst, I have had my visions.

I am not transgender.[42]

O'Hartigan vigorously denies the idea that she changed gender (rather than sex), since gender is a social construct "and as such changes from society to society and over periods of time." She also specifically objects to the idea that gay men and lesbians are transgendered, and criticizes organizations that add the term *transgendered* (rather than *transsexual*) to their names in an attempt to be "inclusive."[43]

O'Hartigan states what is probably the majority transsexual position on sex-reassignment surgery. In 1978, she won a lawsuit that forced the state of Minnesota to pay for medically necessary sex-change surgery. At the time, O'Hartigan was on welfare, and she makes a powerful case for the surgery being instrumental in allowing her to get off government assistance. In a 1995 article which opposed an attempt to cut off public funds in similar cases, she says, of that surgery:

> Few people can imagine the disgust and self-loathing transsexuals feel for their genitals, nor do they understand the impossible obstacle to even a semblance of a normal life that having the "wrong" genitals means for us. It is not necessary to understand, however, to appreciate the depths of despair that drive some of us to attempt, as I did, to cut off the horrors ourselves. I nearly bled to death in the process. Such desperation to acquire a normal body was one of the facts that led legal, medical and psychiatric professionals to offer their considered opinions that sex-reassignment surgery was, for me, a medical necessity.
>
> ...Receiving surgery allowed me to aspire to what most Minnesotans take for granted—a normal life. I never again attempted suicide.... I also obtained what I never dared hope for in the days before my last surgery—a relationship that has lasted ten years now.
>
> ...Medical researchers themselves are divided as to whether transsexualism is a mental disorder or biologically based. What matters is that sex-reassignment surgery succeeds.[44]

Elsewhere, O'Hartigan speaks of "the desperate desire to escape life in an alienating body which epitomizes the transsexual experience."[45] Since the desire for surgery is, for O'Hartigan, the common experience that defines all transsexuals, it seems doubtful that she would classify Bornstein, who questions the necessity of the surgery, as a transsexual despite her postoperative status. Postoperative transgendered women are more likely to reject pre- or non-operative transsexuals as being like themselves than accept them, as Bornstein does, under a common umbrella of shared identity. Transsexual and transgendered women have at least as much power to damage one another's female identities as the lesbian community or the larger society. The lack of agreement among transsexual women about who "counts" as female can only confuse nontranssexuals and delay the time when the larger society will not balk at validating a self-selected gender identity.

This issue may be the most important one that faces transsexual activists today. It will determine both how transgendered people define themselves and how they are perceived by others. Mental-health professionals currently use three broad diagnostic categories to label gender dysphoric patients. Under the heading of Sexual and Gender Identity Disorders, there are the categories of Gender Identity Disorders (GID) which includes Gender Identity Disorder (with subtypes "in Children" and "in Adolescents or Adults"); Gender Identity Disorder Not Otherwise Specified (NOS); and Sexual Disorder NOS.[46] These labels appear in a book published by the American Psychiatric Association called the *Diagnostic and Statistical Manual*, known colloquially as the *DSM-IV* because it is in its fourth edition.

The *DSM-IV* is the mental-health industry standard for defining client concerns, and serves as the official source book for the names of disorders that insurance companies will recognize and offer reimbursement to treat. This latter function is actually its most important, since many mental-health professionals do not agree with the conceptual framework of the *DSM-IV*. It is telling that this volume, which is supposed to be the bible of therapists everywhere, has little or nothing to say about various treatment modalities or their efficacy. Little or no objective evidence is offered to support the existence of these categories, and the book also sidesteps the issue of the supposed etiology of various forms of mental illness.

DSM-IV categories impact on transsexuals because sex-reassignment surgery (SRS) is very expensive. Some insurance companies will cover SRS provided the individual is being treated by licensed medical and psychiatric professionals who describe his or her condition in terms of GID. Of course, many transsexuals have no private health insurance, and despite the fact that SRS has been performed for three decades, most insurance companies and HMOs classify it as an experimental procedure, and will not cover it. This should be compared to the response to organ transplants, which have been performed only since the nineteen-seventies. Transplants are almost universally reimbursed.[47]

To qualify for a diagnosis of GID, the individual must present evidence of "a strong and persistent cross-gender identification" as well as "evidence of persistent discomfort about one's assigned sex or a sense of inappropriateness in the gender role of that sex." The cross-gender identification "must not merely be a desire for any perceived cultural advantages of being the other sex."[48] This "disorder" is described as occurring among children as well as adolescents and adults. Rather than attempt to classify the person with GID as heterosexual, homosexual, or bisexual (which confuses clinicians who do not know whether to use the sex at birth or the gender of preference as the point of reference for determining sexual orientation), "sexually mature individuals" may be labeled as "Sexually Attracted to Males," "Sexually Attracted to Females," "Sexually Attracted to Both," and "Sexually Attracted to Neither."[49] GID is distinguished from Transvestic Fetishism (cross-dressing), although the DSM-IV acknowledges the possibility of some individuals displaying both conditions.[50] Transvestic Fetishism is considered to be a Paraphilia.[51]

Despite the fact that the DSM-IV states, "Only a very small number of children with Gender Identity Disorder will continue to have symptoms that meet criteria for Gender Identity Disorder in later adolescence or adulthood,"[52] there is a well-established and lucrative industry that metes out sometimes brutal treatment and incarceration to young people who do not conform to social sex-role stereotypes or heterosexual social patterns. This industry has a homophobic as well as transphobic bias. As the DSM-IV states, "By late adolescence or adulthood, about three-quarters of boys who had a childhood history of Gender Identity Disorder report a homosexual or bisexual orientation, but without concurrent Gender Identity Disorder. Most of the remainder report a heterosexual orientation, also without concurrent Gender Identity Disorder. The corresponding percentages for sexual orientation in girls are not known."[53]

Among the gender activists educating the public about the impact of GID on queer youth is artist Daphne Scholinski. She was institutionalized between the ages of fourteen and eighteen because she stopped going to school. This was in response to being tormented by other teens who didn't like the fact that "I wasn't concerned with my appearance. I was not out to impress the boys and have that be my obsession." Shortly after being incarcerated, Scholinski attempted suicide. She spent four years in three different mental institutions in Illinois and Minnesota before being discharged. Now she has a bachelor's and master's degree in fine arts, is writing a book about her experiences, and paints.

She says, "I find it incredibly disturbing that it's evolved [nota bene: GID diagnosis for queer youth] and no one's taking notice. When it hits the gay community, they have a hard time believing it and can sometimes resist it. When I'm speaking, people will say, 'Aren't people using this therapy in a positive way?' and I'll say, 'no way.' ...The target is gay and trans-gender youth." Scholinski points out the economic motivation for such policies: Her parents maxed out a one-million-dollar insurance policy for her "treatment."[54]

Further documentation of these abuses is provided by Phyllis Burke, author of a recent book that documents the barbarous treatment of children and teens diagnosed with GID and the unnecessary surgery given to intersexed infants. Burke was able to document at least one and a half million dollars in National Institute of Mental Health grants to research "treatment" of GID in young people, and questions the rationale behind this allocation of resources.[55]

Ironically, despite the fact that Burke's book is being used to justify lobbying to get gender identity disorders out of the *DSM-IV*, other transsexual activists condemn Burke as a dangerous transphobe. Margaret Deirdre O'Hartigan feels that Burke doesn't believe that children or teens can be transsexual. O'Hartigan is afraid that elimination of a psychiatric diagnosis will make it impossible for young people to receive supportive services. Of course, such services are not available now. Treatment for gender dysphoric youth consists of attempts to cure them, not assist them with sex change. But O'Hartigan feels that simple elimination of the diagnosis will destroy any chance of making sex reassignment more available to young people.[56]

Gender activists have made several attempts in this decade to address the problems created by transphobia and homophobia among mental-health professionals and doctors. This is a delicate task, given the fact that if the GID diagnosis is simply removed from the *DSM-IV*, no officially-recognized rationale for SRS will exist.

In 1993, the APA, at its annual conference in San Francisco, proposed that well-adjusted transsexuals should not automatically be considered to have a mental disorder.[57] This action was taken after the APA was picketed by Transgender Nation, a direct-action group organized by Anne Ogborn. Picketers included Christine Beatty, Christine Tayleur, Susan Stryker, Carol Kleinmaier, and others.[58]

On May 5, 1996, over a dozen gender activists from the queer community, Transsexual Menace Connecticut, Transsexual Menace New York, Transsexual Menace Men, and Transsexual Officers Protect and Serve (TOPS) demonstrated outside the annual meeting of the APA and called for an end to diagnosing transpeople as mentally disordered. Activists handed out over one thousand leaflets. Picket signs included the message, "Gender Euphoria NOT Gender Dysphoria." The presence of TOPS was key to the demonstration being able to proceed, since New York State Police attempted to move demonstrators from their site in front of the Jacob Javits Center. They relented after a lengthy negotiation with TOPS members Deputy Sheriff Tony Barreto-Neto and Lt. Janet Aiello.[59]

A press release about the event acknowledges that the GID diagnosis was useful to some transsexuals to obtain insurance reimbursement for SRS, and further acknowledged that most of the demonstrators who identified as transsexual were also postoperative. However:

> Other activists...have compared "GID" to "homosexuality" when it was a disorder: more a political than a medical category. Since they show no symptoms of mental impairment or disorder, they state they resent the diagnosis.... They point out intersexed "corrective" [sic] surgery is routinely reimbursed without question, although it is often exclusively and openly cosmetic. In addition, they note that childbirth is also reimbursed but is not a disease or a disorder.[60]

As a result of this demonstration, Dr. Wynelle Snow, MD, a psychiatrist and a member of Transexual Menace Connecticut, and Riki Anne Wilchins of Transexual Menace New York City met with members of the Association of Gay, Lesbian and Bisexual Psychiatrists and aired gender activists' concerns. Snow formally requested that the group add *transgender* to its title.[61]

In July, transactivists made plans to demonstrate outside the APA annual meeting in Chicago. Once again, they planned to draw attention to GID. The APA was now being accused of "GenderPathoPhilia" ("an abnormal need or desire to pathologize any gender behavior which makes you uncomfortable"). An anonymous Transexual Menace spokesperson was quoted as saying:

> Yes, it's important that people get their surgery and insurance reimbursement. But it's also crucial we do so without pathologizing millions of gender variant and transgendered teens, adults, and kids. GID isn't about dysfunction. It's about punishing gender difference and enforcing gender norms in the guise of practicing medicine. Just like the earlier disease of "homosexuality," GID is inevitably used against the most vulnerable among us—our genderqueer kids.[62]

Before this demonstration took place, Hermaphrodites with Attitude (HWA) called for picketing at the American Academy of Pediatrics (AAP) annual meeting, held in Boston during the last week of

October 1996. AAP was criticized for allowing the genital mutilation of intersexed infants. HWA spokesherm Cheryl Chase said, "No other patient group is cut up as we are without even a hint of consent." Chase estimated that about one in two thousand babies are born with anomalous genitals, "and the response of American doctors is to cut them off, simply because they judge a clitoris to be 'too large' or a penis to be 'too small.' ...Cutting infant genitals to fit heterosexist norms is *not* medicine; it's mutilation in every sense of the word and it's got to stop."[63]

On October 19, four dozen demonstrators held an hour-long meeting with representatives of the APA. Some of the flyers about GenderPathoPhilia somehow wound up in hundreds of APA program guides so they were the first thing attendees saw when they registered for the conference. Wilchins told APA representatives, "If I want my nose done, it's a 'nose job.' If I want my breasts done, it's a 'boob job.' But if I want my groin done, suddenly I have a mental disease." The process of confronting the APA gathered enough steam at this point for Transexual Menace, the National Gay and Lesbian Task Force, Hermaphrodites with Attitude, and the International Gay and Lesbian Human Rights Commission to jointly call for picketing the APA's national office in Washington, DC as part of the NGLTF's annual conference in November.[64]

The NGLTF issued a statement on Gender Identity Disorder and Transgender People that documented their work with transgender rights organizations and compared their efforts to the struggle of gay and lesbian people in the early seventies when the then-NGTF backed efforts to eliminate homosexuality as a mental disorder. This statement calls for GID reform rather than "wholesale eradication."

> Reform means another diagnosis—possibly medical—that does not pathologize transgender people or gender-variant youth and children. Reform also means increased funding for research on transgenderism and full participation by transgender people in policy decisions that affect their lives. We are particularly concerned with the use of GID against children. Gender-variant youth, whether they grow up to be gay, lesbian, bisexual, transgendered or not, should not be stigmatized or mistreated because of a GID diagnosis.[65]

About forty activists held a demonstration outside the national offices of the American Psychiatric Association in downtown Washington, D.C. on November 8, 1996. The effort was jointly sponsored by the Transexual Menace, the NGLTF, HWA, Bi-Net USA, and the International Gay and Lesbian Human Rights Commission (IGLHRC). While these picketers were waving signs that said, "Keep Your Diagnoses Off Our Bodies!" other picketers from a group called Transgender Nation were holding up signs that said, "Keep Your Hands OFF Our Diagnoses." A Menace spokesperson countered these objections by pointing out that the civil-rights protection that has been extended to transgendered people is not dependent on a diagnosis, and asked, "Is mental illness a sound foundation on which to build a national movement for gender rights?"[66]

The desire to be free from the stigma of having been diagnosed with a mental disorder is understandable. But if sex-change surgery is going to continue to be available to transsexuals, what rationale will exist for a doctor to prescribe hormones or for a surgeon to operate? Physicians might accept hard evidence that transsexuality is the result of a genetic disorder or a fetal hormone imbalance, but research on the possible biological basis of transsexuality is sparse. The transactivists who are trying to eliminate Gender Identity Disorder from the *DSM-IV* have not come up with any credible replacement for the diagnosis, which is the prerequisite for sex reassignment. They are not lobbying doctors to ensure that sex-change surgery will continue to be available. Most preoperative transsexuals desperately want sex reassignment and (for good reason) believe that it is necessary before they can expect to lead any sort of normal life. This may be one instance in which transactivists have taken their ideology to the point of logical absurdity and left the majority of their own community in the lurch.

If transgender activists can succeed in getting doctors and therapists to authorize SRS without first forcing them to submit to a pathologizing diagnosis, perhaps they can also succeed in establishing higher standards for surgery outcomes. An informal 1996 survey of surgeons offering SRS found that "none of the surgeons offered anything of substance regarding orgasm: 'a sensitive clitoris'; 'a small surviving flap carries erotic sensation'; and 'the results are very good both cosmetically and functionally' don't say much."[67]

Outcome studies by recognized authorities in the field show even worse results. A 1987 study evaluated surgical outcomes for male-to-female transsexuals by measuring the depth of surgically-constructed vaginas. The average depth was only eight and three-tenths centimeters. Researchers were puzzled by the fact that "only a minority of subjects...complained that the neovagina was inadequate for coitus. It is possible that transsexuals accomplish coitus, despite short vaginas, by assuming positions that limit the depth of their partners' thrusting."[68]

Even in 1987, it seems obtuse for a group of sex researchers to define women's sexuality in terms of possessing a hole that is adequate to provide a male partner with pleasure during intercourse. Researchers seem oblivious to the possibility that their respondents may have been having (gasp!) anal sex. Nor do they take into account the natural tendency of a group of people who have undergone a painful and expensive experience to avoid evaluating that experience negatively. No attempt was made to evaluate the respondents' knowledge about how genetic females experience sexual pleasure.

A 1986 study which found that "overall sexual adjustment is often unchanged by genital surgery" was widely quoted by opponents of SRS, despite the fact that it was based on a sample of only thirteen male-to-female transsexuals. At least this article mentions orgasms, albeit in insulting terms. ("More than half of these castrated and estrogen-treated former males experienced orgasm, but only one-third were judged as having a fair or good sexual adjustment after sex reassignment.") The authors of this study still focused on vaginoplasty as the yardstick of female sexuality, reporting that "surgical outcome was disappointing, and only one-third of the patients where a vaginal construction was carried out had a functioning vagina."[69]

A 1990 survey of research conducted prior to that year on transsexual surgery follow-up complained of a lack of standardized criteria for SRS or follow-up studies. The authors of this article argue that adoption of such standardized values would be useful in persuading insurance companies to stop classifying SRS as cosmetic or experimental surgery, and provide reimbursement for it. The authors are forced to acknowledge, however, that most of the people receiving SRS do not do so through medical centers involved in research on transsexuals, and have the grace to wonder if the sample of gender dysphoric people that is available to such clinics is representative of the larger group. They seem ignorant of the hostility that many transsexuals feel toward researchers, who put the purity of their data ahead of the well-being of their transsexual patients. Instead, they call for greater control over SRS, envisioning a joint effort between American and European centers to standardize patient evaluations and correlate follow-up studies.[70] To date, it would seem that this was a vain hope, since the trend is clearly toward SRS being provided by private physicians rather than data-gathering gender identity clinics.

A 1993 study took a great leap forward by including female-to-male transsexuals as well as male-to-female. But sample sizes were still minuscule (fourteen transsexual women and nine transsexual men). These researchers found that "orgastic capacity declined in the M-F group and increased in the F-M group." However, "satisfaction with sex and general satisfaction with the results of surgery were high in both groups.... A phalloplasty does not appear to be a critical factor in orgasm or in sexual satisfaction. The general conclusion is reached that it is possible to change one's body image and sexual identity and be sexually satisfied despite inadequate sexual functioning."[71]

I think it's reasonable to ask whether acceptance of inadequate sexual functioning represents "sexual satisfaction" or oppression that runs so deep, the people affected by it cannot question or rebel against the awful circumstances that are imposed upon them. If a necrotizing bacteria appeared that made men's genitals fall off, you can be damn sure that phalloplasty would suddenly take a great leap forward in terms of funding, and the results would improve dramatically and quickly. The improvements that are currently being made in SRS are usually the innovations of individual surgeons in private practice who are not motivated to share their techniques with colleagues, since these improvements have assumed the form of trade secrets that can provide any given doctor with a lucrative edge over his competition.

I was unable to locate a single sexologist who seemed aware of the possibility that his respondents were alert to the ways that their answers might be used either to support further access to SRS or shut it down. Transsexuals who have survived the medical and psychiatric system's sex-changing authorization process are quite sophisticated about how that system works. They know that negative answers to surveys about their postsurgical quality of life will hurt the transsexuals who come after them. Until there are excellent alternatives to the current treatment modality, among which transsexuals are truly free to pick and choose, follow-up studies will be hopelessly skewed.

If the quality of inquiry into the impact that SRS has on the sex lives of postoperative transsexuals seems shoddy, at best, it is hard to know what term of contempt might best be used to describe the almost complete lack of research on possible medical sequelae. For example, we still don't know if long-term use of opposite-sex hormones increases a transsexual's risk of contracting cancer or sustaining other physiological damage. Research on the partners and children of transsexuals is practically nonexistent. This situation is not likely to improve until transsexual social scientists, therapists, and medical professionals take it upon themselves to frame the questions their community needs to have answered, and go in quest of those data.

Given the many shortcomings of SRS, it becomes much easier to empathize with Bornstein's insistence that our notions of transsexuality be expanded to include those who refuse to alter their genitalia. Surely the right to have an orgasm is at least as important as the right to choose one's own gender. If gender-ambiguous people become more visible, and significant numbers of people become conscientious objectors to the gender binary, everyone's notions of gender will be forced to shift—transsexuals as well as "gennies."

Some of the most interesting parts of *Gender Outlaw* deal with the question, what might replace gender? If we convict the two sexes we currently believe in of being inherently oppressive, and stop categorizing people that way, how will we organize desire or close relationships? Will we lose the important things that gender (according to Bornstein) falsely promises to give us? This includes, but is not limited to, passion, romance, beauty, and fun. Bornstein complains, "Some people think I want a world without gender, something bland and colorless: that's so far from how I live! I love playing with genders, and I love watching other people play with all the shades and flavors that gender can come in."[72]

She lists many alternatives to the gender binary as systems for organizing pleasure and intimacy: the butch/femme model, top/bottom model, butch/butch, femme/femme, triad (or more), human/animal, adult/child, same-aged, parent/child, multiple partners, able-bodied/differently-abled, reproductive, owner/slave, monogamous/non-monogamous.[73] Elsewhere, she suggests sexual preference could be based on genital preference, on the kind of sex acts one prefers, and mentions Samois' handkerchief code as an example of a way to code desire without making reference to polarized gender.[74] I wouldn't want to argue with these lists, partly because they closely resemble a similar list of concepts I once suggested:

> It is very odd that sexual orientation is defined solely in terms of the sex of one's partners. I don't think I can assume anything about another person simply because I've been told she or he is bisexual, heterosexual, or homosexual. A person's politics may be conservative, liberal, radical, or nonexistent, regardless of sexual orientation. In fact, a sexual orientation label tells you nothing about her or his sex life, for God's sake. There are lots of "heterosexual" men who have plenty of anonymous sex with other men. There are celibate faggots and dykes. There are lesbians who've been married for thirty years and have six children. There are heterosexual women who frequently have sex with other women at swing parties. For many people, if a

partner or a sexual situation has other desirable qualities it is possible to overlook the partner's sex. Some examples: a preference for group sex, for a particular socioeconomic background, for paid sex, for S/M, for a specific age group, for a physical type or race, for anal or oral sex.[75]

However, I do want to point out that many of the systems that Bornstein proposes as replacements for gender would be every bit as offensive and oppressive as the sexist, homophobic, and transphobic standards that are currently inflicted upon us—*if they were administered in the same fashion as gender.* For example, I don't have much trouble imagining a society in which doctors or child psychologists would decide, using their own mysterious and probably arbitrary set of standards, which infants or toddlers are bottoms and which are tops. Such a society would mandate different sorts of treatment for these two "natural" types of children. This system could easily be used to justify preferential treatment for one role or the other. And people who were uppity enough to think they really belonged in a different role could be severely punished. As for switches, well, let's pass a bond initiative and build another prison—or incarcerate these dangerous loonies and give them electroshock therapy. That'll teach 'em.

Bornstein does not make a distinction between the sexist system of differential privilege and the potentially innocuous male and female categories on which that system is based. While I'd love to live in a society where I got to emphasize other aspects of my personality more than gender, or could move back and forth between gender identities, I don't think we're going to get there by trying to erase the dividing line between male and female.

Bornstein's attack on gender as an organizing principle for close relationships is reminiscent of some arguments made by early feminist author Shulamith Firestone, who thought women could not be liberated until artificial reproduction broke the connection between women and childbearing. Firestone envisioned a world in which humans would use technology to drastically alter the nature of their bodies, and thus make our current notions of gender obsolete. Her theories have fallen into obscurity, perhaps in part because she also attacked romantic love, had no patience with the family, and advocated the eradication of twentieth-century Western notions of childhood, with its imposition of economic dependence and sexual innocence upon the young.[76]

Bornstein's vision of the future of gender is likely to have a greater impact on how transgendered people see themselves than on the stereotypes that most of us accept with blindness and comfort. The differences between old and new styles of transsexual activism are fiercely felt in that nascent movement. Sadly, there is a strong possibility that the transgendered movement will be embroiled in identity issues like lesbian feminism in the seventies and eighties. So much energy was wasted during those decades on the so-called "feminist sex wars"! Bornstein seems to be agitating for exactly this kind of split.

> Any revolution in deconstructing gender should look for *no* support among communities of people whose identities depend on the existence of this bi-polar gender system. This would include, but most certainly is not limited to, the fundamentalist right wing, purists in the lesbian and gay communities who believe in the ultimate goal of assimilation into the dominant culture, and some cultural or radical feminists. Nonsupporters of any movement to deconstruct gender would also, unfortunately, include those transgendered people who subscribe fully to the culture's definitions of gender, and seek to embody those definitions within themselves.[77]

At the same time, she dismisses the possibility of this new and relatively fragile movement being damaged beyond repair by internal conflict over whether to make eliminating gender a priority: "Setting about to do away with gender could itself turn into a frighteningly fanatical mission. Fanatics are distinguishable by the fact that they can't laugh at themselves. Camp is the safety valve that can keep any gender activism from becoming fanaticism."[78]

This strikes me as the equivalent of someone hoping, in 1981, that lesbian music would save leather dykes from being trashed by antiporn feminists. Rather than dealing with more concrete items that should appear on a political agenda for transsexual activists, Bornstein makes a case for alternative gender identities as a spiritual path: "I think anyone who regularly walks along a forbidden boundary or border (gay/straight, sober/drunk, female/male, black/white, etc.) has the potential to attain some degree of spiritual awareness. The task for those who take that road is, usually, to point a way out of struggle and suffering for as many people as possible, and that can best be accomplished by raising questions and implicating people."[79]

In keeping with her theme that only humor can save us from fanaticism, Bornstein asserts:

> Cross-culturally, the individuals who have freed themselves from the fear of humiliation are clowns, fools, jesters, and tricksters.

This can be Coyote, Uncle Tolpa, Br'er Rabbit, Raccoon Dog, or any number of documented practitioners of what Scoop Nisker calls *crazy wisdom* in cultures around the world. ...What do fools have in common? Well, they don't play by the rules, they laugh at most rules, and they encourage us to laugh at ourselves. Their pranks of substituting one thing for another create instability and uncertainty, making visible the lies imbedded in a culture. Fools demonstrate the wisdom of simplicity and innocence. These are valuable crafts, these are skills we could use in our problem-laden world. ...Any healthy civilization would certainly have people performing these fool skills at every level of the culture. In our civilization, the only people doing these things are considered trouble-makers, whatever their line of work.[80]

Over the next decade, it will be interesting to see whether other transgendered activists will follow Bornstein's lead, or adhere to a more traditional civil-rights approach. If transsexuals and other members of the gender community abandon the medicalized goal of becoming "normal" men and women, their only recourse may be to create their own community, parallel to and sometimes overlapping with the gay community, where gender norms are safely blurred. Creating such a subculture would take an enormous commitment of time and energy, but perhaps it is the only way to change the rest of society, by modeling a way of life that does not involve gender polarization.

I suspect that such a genderless culture- and community-building effort may be most attractive to transgendered people who either cannot or will not accept a transition from a special, if stigmatized, identity to a more boring and ordinary one. Most transsexuals will probably continue to obtain sex reassignment with as little fuss as possible, and then gratefully blend into the madding crowd. This more traditional group of transsexuals may be in the majority, but since relatively fewer of them will choose to become activists, their impact on transsexual politics may be lighter. After all, the fact that someone is different does not make him or her or shim a candidate for radical political work. And the further any individual is away from what's considered to be typical or average, the more highly motivated that person will be to argue with the way that mean is determined.

Just as there is tension within the gay and lesbian community between assimilationists, who seem to want nothing more than accessibility to middle-class American notions of the good life, and more radical queers who see little desirable in such a lifestyle, there will probably continue to be conflict between transsexuals who see the sex-reassignment process as confirming their true gender, and transgendered people who believe that their only hope for liberation lies in dismantling biological sex itself.

Although it would seem that the goals of these two aspects of trans-activism are mutually exclusive, in fact, both are important components of the struggle for a gender-sane society. If the concept of gender freedom is to have any meaning, it must be possible for some of us to cling to our biological sex and the gender we were assigned at birth while others wish to adapt the body to their gender of preference, and still others choose to question the very concept of polarized sexes.

Unfortunately, the hope that advocates of each of these positions will be able to recognize the validity in the others is probably a dim one. Difference is always the most difficult thing to tolerate; and competition is such a deeply-ingrained behavior that even the most radical among us have what amounts to a reflex to work at cross-purposes to anyone without an identical agenda. The resulting conflicts and debates will be fierce, but I do not believe they will derail the gender community's politicization. And that's fortunate, because if transgender activism makes significant gains, it offers the rest of us many benefits.

Some people who are not differently gendered will support trans-activism because they would support any minority group that was struggling for more visibility and basic civil rights. But many more nontranssexuals and noncross-dressers will find it too difficult to empathize with members of the gender community. There's also the fear, among gay and bisexual activists, that making common cause with transgendered people will slow us down, embarrass us, and damage our credibility. This fear is based on a denial that the gender community and the gay community overlap to a great extent. But acknowledging some transgendered people as members of the gay/bisexual community doesn't automatically lead to a willingness to add their needs to the list of things we are lobbying for.

The strategy of jettisoning the more stigmatized members of the gay and bisexual community has become quite popular. But, if we can make any predictions based on the gay movement's successfully ditching and disavowal of boy-lovers and sexual minority youth, this strategy will not give us a leg up. Instead, it weakens us, by turning us against one another. It also narrows our vision of social change and damages our ability to think critically about the kind of society we would really like to build. The larger culture will always be happy to give the more mainstream members of the gay/bisexual community the responsibility for disowning and keeping down drag queens, sadomasochists, pedophiles, transsexuals, and other "undesirables." But that's a far cry from freedom. Do we really want to become the sex police for a morally bankrupt and hypocritical heterosexual majority?

I suspect there is a deeper psychological dynamic at work here, something irrational that has nothing to do with getting pragmatic about what's possible for us in the contemporary arena of American politics. People who have succeeded at the gender game and formed an identity as a man or a woman prize that accomplishment. If the achievement of a traditional gender identity ceases to be an ordeal, the worth of that accomplishment diminishes. If the standards of gender performance change significantly, or if the "losers" refuse to accept their less-than status, the "winners" won't be able to justify the suffering and hard work that was necessary to become men or women. Of course, it's not supposed to be hard work to be accepted as a man or a woman; it's supposed to be a natural and effortless process. Few of us are even aware of the pervasive rewards and punishments that shaped our gender identities—unless that process was not successful. I suspect that much of the hatred and fear of transsexuals is based on the discomfort that others experience when they are forced to recall the pain of involuntary gender conditioning. It is easier to believe we never had a choice about something so fundamental than to process and accept the fact that the choice was taken away from us and ruthlessly suppressed.

But it is time for all of us to begin to uncover that history and consider it as carefully as nascent feminists once did in consciousness-raising groups. What was done to us in the name of manhood and womanhood, and why? What doors were closed to us? What selves were murdered? What pleasures and possibilities were stilled? And why was it so important for the entire process to exist in the first place? Whose interests did it serve? Certainly not the needs of the individual child, the adolescent, the adult.

Because the barriers to acceptance of transgendered people and alliance with them are so powerful, I want to end this chapter with a few questions that might shed some light on how the movement for gender freedom could have a positive impact for us all. Gender tyranny is virtually invisible. We have to learn to see it in action if we are going to understand it and put a stop to it. Who would you be if you had never been punished for gender-inappropriate behavior, or seen another child punished for deviation from masculine or feminine norms, or participated in dishing out such punishment? What would it be like to grow up in a society where gender was truly consensual? If the rite of passage was to name your own gender at adolescence, or upon your transition into adulthood?

What would it be like to walk down the street, go to work, or attend a party and take it for granted that the gender of the people you met would not be the first thing you ascertained about them? What impact would that have on how you treated them? Or on how they treated you? What if gender was no longer a marker for privilege, certain personality traits, or roles in the family? If gender was a sexual fetish or a symbol of your ability to provide certain types of erotic or spiritual experiences, how would you put your public persona together? What would you want other people to know about you first? Would it be more important to identify your totem animal, astrological sign, career goals, dietary needs, religion, allergies, or degree of sexual availability to passing strangers than it would be to identify your gender?

If you could change your sex as effortlessly in reality as you can in virtual reality, and change it back again, wouldn't you like to try it at least once? Who do you think you might become? What is that person able to do that you don't think you can do now? What would you have to give up to become oppositely sexed? What would change about your politics, clothing, food preferences, sexual desires, social habits, driving style, job, body language, behavior on the street? Are you able to imagine becoming a hybrid of your male and female self, keeping the traits that you value and abandoning the ones that are harmful?

What would it be like to live in a society where you could take a vacation from gender? Or (even more importantly) from *other* people's gender. Imagine the creation of Gender Free Zones. These retreat centers could be maintained by a new class of rude (as opposed to civil) servants. And what would it be like to live in a society where nobody was punished for dressing up in drag? What if it was taken for granted that cross-dressing was a normal developmental phase? Let's expand the definition of drag so that it applies to any other fantasy role that someone needs to act out so they can obtain nourishment or hidden knowledge. What if we all helped each other to manifest our most beautiful, sexy, intelligent, creative, and adventurous inner selves, instead of cooperating to suppress them? What if cross-dressing and other forms of gender blending became markers for wise people, healers, and visionaries instead of a signifier of sexual perversion and shame? What drag is hiding in your personal closet, kept there by the threat of violence or ridicule?

If these questions frighten, offend, or annoy you, you are one of the people who stand to benefit from transactivism—although it probably doesn't feel like your benefactor. And if these questions amuse, engage, and challenge you, you're probably a transactivist already. Welcome to the genderevolution, indeed.

Notes

l. Kate Bornstein, *Gender Outlaw: On Men, Women and the Rest of Us*, New York and London: Routledge, 1994, p. 8.
2. Ibid., p. 234.
3. Ibid., pp. 125-126.
4. Ibid., p. 24.
5. Ibid., p. 233.
6. Ibid., p. 66.
7. Ibid., p. 47. See also p. 119.
8. Ibid., p. 114. Italics are mine. See also pp. 12 and 115.
9. Ibid., p. 45.
10. Ibid., pp. 103-104.
11. Ibid., p. 105.
12. Ibid., pp. 12-13.
13. Ibid., p. 62.
14. Ibid., p. 94.
15. Pat Califia, "Genderbending: Playing with Roles and Reversals," *The Advocate*, 1983, reprinted in *Public Sex: The Culture of Radical Sex*, Pittsburgh and San Francisco: Cleis Press, 1994, pp. 181-182. See also Pat Califia, *Sapphistry: The Book of Lesbian Sexuality*, Tallahassee: Naiad Press, 1980, pp. 134-135.
16. Bornstein, op. cit., p. 55.
17. Ibid., p. 83.
18. Ibid., p. 101.
19. Ibid., p. 111.
20. Ibid., p. 106.
21. Ibid.
22. Ibid., pp. 107-108. See also p. 106.
23. Ibid., p. 118. See also Marjorie Garber, *Vested Interests: Cross-Dressing and Cultural Anxiety*, New York: Harper Perennial, 1993; original hard-cover edition from Routledge, 1992, p. 11.
24. Bornstein, op. cit., p. 113.
25. Ibid., p. 133.
26. Ibid, p. 133
27. Ibid.
28. Ibid, p. 115.
29. Ibid., p. 76.
30. Ibid., p. 83.
31. Ibid., p. 104.
32. Ibid., pp. 134-135.
33. Ibid., p. 80.
34. Ibid., p. 118.
35. Ibid., p. 121.
36. Ibid., p. 98.
37. Ibid., p. 126.
38. Pat Califia, "Genderbending: Playing with Roles and Reversals," op. cit.
39. Bornstein, op. cit., p. 120.

40. Ibid., pp. 120-121.

41. Ibid, p. 119.

42. Margaret Deirdre O'Hartigan, "Changing Sex Is Not Changing Gender," *Sound Out*, May 1993, p. 20.

43. Ibid.

44. Margaret Deirdre O'Hartigan, "In Long Run My Sex-Change Surgery Saved Tax Dollars," *Minneapolis Star/Tribune*, February 4, 1995, p. 17A.

45. Margaret O'Hartigan, "A Surgery Sampler," *The Transsexual News Telegraph*, Spring 1996, p. 15.

46. American Psychiatric Association (APA), *Diagnostic and Statistical Manual of Mental Disorders*, Fourth Edition, Washington, DC: APA, 1994, p. 22. See also pp. 532-538.

47. Margaret O'Hartigan, "A Surgery Sampler," op. cit.

48. APA, op. cit., pp. 532-533.

49. Ibid., p. 534.

50. Ibid., pp. 536-537.

51. Ibid., pp. 530-531.

52. Ibid., p. 536.

53. Ibid.

54. Eric Burney, "The Art of Survival," Vallejo, California *Times-Herald,* June 23, 1995, pp. B1 and B6.

55. Phyllis Burke, *Gender Shock: Exploding the Myths of Male and Female,* New York: Anchor, 1996.

56. Conversation between Margaret Deirdre O'Hartigan and the author, January 25, 1997. Unpublished.

57. Dan Levy and David Tuller, " 'Transgender' People Coming Out," *San Francisco Chronicle*, May 28, 1993, pp. A-1 and A-17.

58. Lori Olszewski, "Transsexuals Protest at Psychiatry Meeting," *San Francisco Chronicle*, May 24, 1993, p. A-13.

59. Riki Wilchins, "Transactivists Protest APA—Call for End to 'Gender Identity Disorder,' " *In Your Face* on-line press release, May 5, 1996.

60. Ibid.

61. Ibid.

62. Riki Wilchins, "APA Target of 2nd National Demonstration by Transactivists," *In Your Face* on-line press release, July 20, 1996.

63. Riki Wilchins, "Hermaphrodites with Attitude Calls for Unprecedented Demonstration," *In Your Face* on-line press release, October 17, 1996.

64. Riki Wilchins, "Protesters Meet with APA," *In Your Face* on-line press release, October 19, 1996.

65. Phyllis R. Frye, "NGLTF Statement on Gender Identity Disorder and Transgender People," GenderPAC on-line press release, December 11, 1996.

66. Riki Anne Wilchins, "Top Psychiatrists Picketed at Creating Change," GenderPAC press release, November 12, 1996.

67. Margaret O'Hartigan, "A Surgery Sampler," op. cit., p. 17.

68. Ray Blanchard, Suzanne Legault, and William R. N. Lindsay, "Vaginoplasty Outcome in Male-to-Female Transsexuals," *Journal of Sex and Marital Therapy*, vol. 13, no. 4, Winter 1987, pp. 265-275.

69. Gunnar Lindemalm, Dag Korlin, and Nils Uddenberg, "Long-Term Follow-Up of 'Sex Change' in 13 Male-to-Female Transsexuals," *Archives of Sexual Behavior,* vol. 15, no. 3, 1986, pp. 187-210.

70. Richard Green and Davis T. Fleming, "Transsexual Surgery Follow-Up: Status in the 1990s," *Annual Review of Sex Research,* 1990, pp. 163-174. For a scorching indictment of sex researchers at gender identity clinics, see Margaret Deirdre O'Hartigan, "Like Coals Beneath Ashes," *Sound Out,* December 1994, pp. 13-14.

71. Harold I. Lief and Lynn Hubschman, "Orgasm in the Postoperative Transsexual," *Archives of Sexual Behavior,* vol. 22, no. 2, 1993, p. 145.

72. Bornstein, op. cit., p. 58.

73. Ibid., pp. 33-35.

74. Ibid., p. 36.

75. Pat Califia, "Gay Men, Lesbians, and Sex: Doing It Together," *The Advocate,* 1983, reprinted in *Public Sex,* op. cit., pp. 186-187. Also see Pat Califia, "Genderbending," op. cit., p. 179, for a discussion of Amber Hollibaugh's concept of butch/femme as "gay gender."

76. Shulamith Firestone, *The Dialectic of Sex: The Case for Feminist Revolution,* New York: William Morrow and Co., Inc., 1970, paperback edition by Toronto, New York and London: Bantam Books, 1971.

77. Bornstein, op. cit., p. 132.

78. Ibid., p. 138.

79. Ibid., p. 97.

80. Ibid., pp. 89-90.

Works Cited

American Psychiatric Association (APA). *Diagnostic and Statistical Manual of Mental Disorders*, Fourth Edition. Washington, D.C.: APA, 1994.

Atcheson, Dorothy. "Culture Vultures in Nebraska." *Out*, October 1995, p. 100. Sidebar to Donna Minkowitz, "On Trial: Gay? Straight? Boy? Girl? Sex? Rape?" *Out*, October 1995, pp. 99-101, 140-146.

Benjamin, Harry. "Introduction." *Transsexualism and Sex Reassignment*, Richard Green and John Money, eds. Baltimore: The Johns Hopkins Press, 1969.

———. *The Transsexual Phenomenon*. New York: The Julian Press, Inc., 1966.

———. "Trans-sexualism and Transvestism." *Transvestism: Men in Female Dress*, David Cauldwell, ed. New York: Sexology Corporation, 1964.

Blanchard, Ray, and Peter I. Collins. "Men with Sexual Interest in Transvestites, Transsexuals, and She-Males." *The Journal of Nervous and Mental Disease*, Vol. 181, No. 9, 1993, pp. 570-575.

Blanchard, Ray, Suzanne Legault, and William R. N. Lindsay. "Vaginoplasty Outcome in Male-to-Female Transsexuals." *Journal of Sex and Marital Therapy*, Vol. 13, No. 4, Winter 1987, pp. 265-275.

Bloom, Amy. "The Body Lies." *The New Yorker*, July 18, 1994, pp. 38-44, 46-49.

Bobula, Kathy. "Trying to Figure Out My Sexual Identity." *Partners, Family, and Friends of FTMs Newsletter*, Vol. 1, Issue 2, December 1995, pp. 4-5.

———. "PF3TM Quotes." October 6, 1996 e-mail to the author. Unpublished.

Bornstein, Kate. *Gender Outlaw: On Men, Women and the Rest of Us*. New York and London: Routledge, 1994.

Brecher, Edward M. "Sex as a Loathsome Disease." *The Sex Researchers.* New York: Signet, 1969.

Brown, Judith K. "Iroquois Women: An Ethnohistoric Note." *Toward an Anthropology of Women,* Rayna R. Reiter, ed. New York and London: Monthly Review Press, 1975.

Bullough, Vern L., and Bonnie Bullough. *Cross Dressing, Sex, and Gender.* Philadelphia: University of Pennsylvania Press, 1993.

Burke, Phyllis. *Gender Shock: Exploding the Myths of Male and Female.* New York: Anchor, 1996.

Burney, Eric. "The Art of Survival." Vallejo, California *Times-Herald,* June 23, 1995, pp. B1 and B6.

Burns, Christine. "Victory in the European Court of Justice." Press for Change press release, April 30, 1996.

Califia, Pat. "Gay Men, Lesbians and Sex: Doing it Together." *The Advocate,* 1983, reprinted in *Public Sex: The Culture of Radical Sex.* San Francisco: Cleis Press, 1994.

———. "Introduction: Or It Is Always Right to Rebel." *Public Sex.* Pittsburgh and San Francisco: Cleis Press, 1994, pp. 11-26.

———. *Sapphistry: The Book of Lesbian Sexuality.* Tallahassee: Naiad Press, 1980.

Carlile, Alex. "Preface." *Dear Sir or Madam: The Autobiography of a Female-to-Male Transsexual,* Mark Rees. London: Cassell, 1996, pp. xi-xiii.

Carson, Robert C., and James N. Butcher. *Abnormal Psychology and Modern Life,* Ninth Edition. New York: HarperCollins Publishers Inc., 1992, p. 352, citing J. Walinder, "Transsexualism: Definition, Prevalence, and Sex Distribution," *Acta Psychiatrica Scandinavica, 203,* 1968, p. 255-258.

Chase, Cheryl. "Affronting Reason." *Queer Look,* Dawn Atkins, ed. In press.

Coleman, Eli, and Walter O. Bockting. " 'Heterosexual' Prior to Sex Reassignment—'Homosexual' Afterwards: A Case Study of a Female-to-Male Transsexual." *Journal of Psychology and Human Sexuality*, Vol. 1(2), 1988, pp. 69-82.

Coleman, Eli, Philip Colgan and Louis Gooren. "Male Cross-Gender Behavior in Myanmar (Burma): A Description of the Acault." *Archives of Sexual Behavior*, Vol. 21, No. 3, 1992, pp. 313-321.

Conkin, Dennis. "Human Rights Commission Addresses Transgender Issues." *Bay Area Reporter*, May 19, 1994, p. 1.

Conner, Randy P. *Blossom of Bone*. San Francisco: Harper, 1993.

Deva. "FTM: A Discussion Organized and Facilitated by Deva." *Brat Attack*, No. 3, 1992, pp. 8-12, 15-19.

Diesenhouse, Margo. "Response to Jean Lingeman's Letter." *Partners, Family, and Friends of FTMs Newsletter*, Vol. 1, Issue 3, February 1996, pp. 1-2.

Douglas, Angela. *Sister*. August-September, 1977, p. 7.

Evans, Arthur. *Witchcraft and the Gay Counterculture*. Boston: Fag Rag Books, 1978.

Feinberg, Leslie. *Stone Butch Blues*. Ithaca, New York: Firebrand Books, 1993.

————. *Transgender Liberation: A Movement Whose Time Has Come*. New York: World View Forum, 1992.

Firestone, Shulamith. *The Dialectic of Sex: The Case for Feminist Revolution*. New York: William Morrow and Co., Inc., 1970, paperback edition by Toronto, New York and London: Bantam Books, 1971.

Fish. "Moshing with Michigan Womyn (& Transsexuals!)." *San Francisco Bay Times*, August 25, 1994, pp. 27 and 52-53.

Foucault, Michel, ed. *Herculine Barbin: Being the Recently Discovered Memoirs of a Nineteenth Century French Hermaphrodite.* New York: Pantheon, 1980.

Frye, Phyllis, R. "ICTLEP Appoints Another FTM to Board of Directors." International Conference on Transgender Law and Employment Policy, Inc. press release, December 12, 1996.

———. "NGLTF Statement on Gender Identity Disorder and Transgender People." GenderPAC on-line press release, December 11, 1996.

Garber, Marjorie. *Vested Interests: Cross-Dressing and Cultural Anxiety.* New York: HarperPerennial, 1993. First published in 1992 by Routledge.

Green, James. "Keynote Address for the FTM Conference." August 18, 1995. Unpublished.

Green, Jamison. "Chapter 7." December 21, 1996 e-mail to the author, p. 2. Unpublished.

———. "Predator?" *San Francisco Bay Times*, Vol. 17, No. 9, February 22, 1996, pp. 2-3, 29. Reprinted in *FTM Newsletter*, Issue 34, May 1996, pp. 2 and 6. Page numbers in text refer to the *Bay Times* original printing.

Green, Richard. "Appendix C: Transsexualism: Mythological, Historical, and Cross-Cultural Aspects." *The Transsexual Phenomenon*, Harry Benjamin. New York: The Julian Press, Inc., 1966.

———. "Attitudes Toward Transsexualism and Sex-Reassignment Procedures." *Transsexualism and Sex Reassignment*, Richard Green and John Money, eds. Baltimore: The Johns Hopkins Press, 1969.

———. "Psychiatric Management of Special Problems in Transsexualism." *Transsexualism and Sex Reassignment*, Richard Green and John Money, eds. Baltimore: The Johns Hopkins Press, 1969.

———. *The "Sissy Boy Syndrome" and the Development of Homosexuality.* New Haven and London: Yale University Press, 1987.

Green, Richard, and Davis T. Fleming. "Transsexual Surgery Follow-Up: Status in the 1990s." *Annual Review of Sex Research*, 1990, pp. 163-174.

Green, Richard, and John Money, eds. *Transsexualism and Sex Reassignment*. Baltimore: The Johns Hopkins Press, 1969.

Gutiérrez, Ramón A. "Must We Deracinate Indians to Find Gay Roots?" *Outlook*, Winter 1989, pp. 61-67.

Hale, C. Jacob. "Dyke Leatherboys and Their Daddies: How to Have Sex without Men or Women." Paper presented at the Berkshire Conference on the History of Women, June 8, 1996. Unpublished.

Horwitz, Kevin. "An Interview with Leslie Feinberg." *FTM Newsletter*, Issue 23, May 1993, pp. 1-3.

Jorgensen, Christine. *Christine Jorgensen: A Personal Autobiography*. Paul S. Eriksson, Inc., 1967. Paperback edition, New York: Bantam Books, 1968.

Katz, Jonathan. *Gay American History: Lesbians and Gay Men in the U.S.A.* New York: Thomas Y. Crowell Company, 1976.

Kinsey, Alfred C., Wardell B. Pomeroy, Clyde E. Martin, Paul H. Gebhard, and associates. *Sexual Behavior in the Human Female*. Philadelphia and London: W. B. Saunders Company, 1953.

Kinsey, Alfred C., Wardell B. Pomeroy, and Clyde E. Martin. *Sexual Behavior in the Human Male*. Philadelphia and London: W. B. Saunders Co., 1948.

Kolakowski, Vicky. "Fifth International Transgender Law Conference Held in Houston." *Bay Area Reporter*, July 11, 1996, pp. 14 and 25.

Levy, Dan and David Tuller. "Opening Up the World of Drag," *San Francisco Chronicle*, May 28, 1993, pp. A-1 and A-17.

———. " 'Transgender' People Coming Out." San Francisco *Chronicle*, May 28, 1993, pp. A-1 and A-17.

Lief, Harold I. and Lynn Hubschman. "Orgasm in the Postoperative Transsexual." *Archives of Sexual Behavior*, Vol. 22, No. 2, 1993, pp. 145-155.

Lindemalm, Gunnar, Dag Körlin, and Nils Uddenberg. "Long-Term Follow-Up of 'Sex Change' in 13 Male-to-Female Transsexuals." *Archives of Sexual Behavior*, Vol. 15, No. 3, 1986, pp. 187-210.

Malin, H. Marty. "Treatment Raises Serious Ethical Questions." *Hermaphrodites with Attitude*, Fall/Winter 1995-96, pp. 14-16.

Margulies, Candace. "An Open Letter to Olivia Records." *Lesbian Connection*, November 1977. Also see assorted letters in *Lesbian Connection*, May 1978 and November 1979.

Martino, Mario (with harriet). *Emergence: A Transsexual Autobiography*. New York: Crown Publishers, Inc., 1977.

Masters, William H., and Virginia E. Johnson. *Human Sexual Response*. Boston: Little, Brown & Co., 1966.

Meyer, Jon K. and John H. Hoopes. "The Gender Dysphoria Syndromes: A Position Statement on So-Called Transsexualism." *Plastic and Reconstructive Surgery*, 54 (October 1977).

Midnight Sun. "Sex/Gender Systems in Native North America." *Living the Spirit: A Gay American Indian Anthology*, Will Roscoe, ed. Compiled by Gay American Indians. New York: St. Martin's Press, 1988.

Millot, Catherine. *Horsexe: Essay on Transsexuality*, Kenneth Hylton, trans. Brooklyn: Autonomedia, 1990.

Minkowitz, Donna. "Love Hurts." *Village Voice*, April 19, 1994, pp. 24-30.

———. "On Trial: Gay? Straight? Boy? Girl? Sex? Rape?" *Out*, October 1995, pp. 99-101, 140-146.

Money, John. "Sex Reassignment as Related to Hermaphroditism and Transsexualism." *Transsexualism and Sex Reassignment*, Richard Green and John Money, eds. Baltimore: The Johns Hopkins Press, 1969.

Money, John, and John G. Brennan. "Sexual Dimorphism in the Psychology of Female Transsexuals." *Transsexualism and Sex Reassignment*, Richard Green and John Money, eds. Baltimore: The Johns Hopkins Press, 1969.

Money, John, and Anke A. Ehrhardt, *Man & Woman Boy & Girl*. Baltimore: The Johns Hopkins Press, 1972.

Money, John, and Margaret Lamacz. *Vandalized Lovemaps: Paraphilic Outcome of Seven Cases in Pediatric Sexology*. Buffalo, New York: Prometheus Books, 1989.

Money, John, and Clay Primrose. "Sexual Dimorphism and Dissociation in the Psychology of Male Transsexuals." *Transsexualism and Sex Reassignment*, Richard Green and John Money, eds. Baltimore: The Johns Hopkins Press, 1969.

Money, John, and Florence Schwartz. "Public Opinion and Social Issues in Transsexualism: A Case Study in Medical Sociology." *Transsexualism and Sex Reassignment*, Richard Green and John Money, eds. Baltimore: The Johns Hopkins Press, 1969.

Morris, Jan. *Conundrum: An Extraordinary Narrative of Transsexualism*. New York: Henry Holt and Company, Inc., 1974. Reprinted in 1986 in a paperback edition with a new introduction and epilogue by the author.

Mortimer, Lee. "Latin Quarter Revue Adds Christine." *Daily Mirror*, January 6, 1954, p. 37.

Nanda, Serena. *Neither Man Nor Woman: The Hijras of India*. Belmont, California: Wadsworth Publishing Company, 1990.

Ogborn, Anne. "Going Home" and "Hijras and Intersexuals." *Hermaphrodites with Attitudes*, Vol. 1, No. 1, Winter 1994, pp. 2-3.

O'Hartigan, Margaret Deirdre. "Blossom of Boneheads." *TransSisters: The Journal of Transsexual Feminism*, Issue 5, Summer 1994, pp. 42-44.

———. "Changing Sex Is Not Changing Gender." *Sound Out*, May 1993, p. 20.

———. "The Gallae of the Magna Mater." *Chrysalis Quarterly*, Vol. 1, No. 6, pp. 11-13.

———. "In Long Run My Sex-Change Surgery Saved Tax Dollars." *Minneapolis Star/Tribune*, February 4, 1995, p. 17A.

———. "Like Coals Beneath Ashes." *Sound Out*, December 1994, pp. 13-14.

———. "Stealing Our History." Review of Leslie Fineberg's *Transgender Warriors*. Unpublished.

———. "A Surgery Sampler." *The Transsexual News Telegraph*, Spring 1996, pp. 15-17.

Olszewski, Lori. "Transsexuals Protest at Psychiatry Meeting." *San Francisco Chronicle*, May 24, 1993, p. A-13.

Pauly, Ira B. "Gender Identity Disorders: Evaluation and Treatment." *Journal of Sex Education and Therapy* Vol. 16, No. 1, 1990.

Poasa, Kris. "The Samoan Fa'afafine: One Case Study and Discussion of Transsexualism." *Journal of Psychology and Human Sexuality*, Vol. 5(3), 1992, pp. 39-51.

Pratt, Minnie Bruce. *S/he*. Ithaca, New York: Firebrand Books, 1995.

Prince, Virginia "Charles." *The Transvestite and His Wife*. Los Angeles: no publisher listed, 1967.

Raymond, Janice. "The Politics of Transgenderism." *Blending Genders: Social Aspects of Cross-Dressing and Sex-Changing*, Richard Ekins and Dave King, eds. London and New York: Routledge, 1996.

———. "Transsexualism: The Ultimate Homage to Sex-Role Power." *Chrysalis: A Magazine of Woman's Culture*, No. 3, 1978.

———. *The Transsexual Empire: The Making of the She-Male*. Boston: Beacon Press, 1979. Second edition by New York: Teachers College Press, 1994.

Rich, Adrienne. "Compulsory Heterosexuality and Lesbian Existence." *Signs*, Vol. 5, No. 4, 1980. Reprinted in *Blood, Bread, and Poetry*. New York: W. W. Norton, 1986.

Richards, Renée with John Ames. *Second Serve: The Renée Richards Story*. New York: Stein and Day, 1983.

Riddell, Carol. "Divided Sisterhood: A Critical Review of Janice Raymond's *The Transsexual Empire*." *Blending Genders: Social Aspects of Cross-Dressing and Sex-Changing*, Richard Ekins and Dave King, eds. London and New York: Routledge, 1996.

Ridgway, Mindy. "Nebraska Man Guilty of Brandon Teena's Murder." *San Francisco Bay Times*, March 23, 1995, p. 4.

Roscoe, Will. "Living the Spirit: A Gay American Indian Anthology." (compiled by gay American Indians). New York: St. Martin's Press, 1988.

———. "The Zuni Man-Woman." *Outlook*, Summer 1988, p. 57.

Rubin, Gayle. "Of Catamites and Kings: Reflections on Butch, Gender, and Boundaries." *The Persistent Desire: A Femme-Butch Reader*, Joan Nestle, ed. Boston: Alyson Publications, 1992, pp. 466-482.

———. "The Traffic in Women: Notes on the 'Political Economy' of Sex." *Toward an Anthropology of Women*, Rayna R. Reiter, ed. New York and London: Monthly Review Press, 1975, pp. 157-210.

Smith, Anna Marie. "The Regulation of Lesbian Sexuality Through Erasure: The Case of Jennifer Saunders." *Lesbian Erotics*, Karla Jay, ed. New York: New York University Press, 1995, pp. 164-179.

Stein, Kathleen. "Interview: John Money." *Omni*, 8(7), April 1986.

Stoller, Robert J. "Etiological Factors in Female Transsexualism: A First Approximation." *Archives of Sexual Behavior*, 2 (1972), pp. 47-64.

———. "Parental Influences in Male Transsexualism." *Transsexualism and Sex Reassignment*, Richard Green and John Money, eds. Baltimore: The Johns Hopkins Press, 1969.

———. *Perversion: The Erotic Form of Hatred.* New York: Delta/Dell, 1975.

———. "The Transsexual Boy: Mother's Feminized Phallus." *British Journal of Medical Psychology*, 43 (1970), pp. 117-128.

Stryker, Jeff. "Bigotry and Ignorance vs. the 'Transgendered'. " *San Francisco Examiner*, December 13, 1995, p. A-33.

Sullivan, L. "Sullivan's Travels." *The Advocate*, June 6, 1989, pp. 68-71.

Sullivan, Louis. *From Female to Male: The Life of Jack Bee Garland.* Boston: Alyson Publications, 1990.

———. *Information for the Female-to-Male Crossdresser and Transsexual*, Second Edition. San Francisco: L. Sullivan, 1985. The third, revised edition was published in 1990 by Seattle's Ingersoll Gender Center.

Swissler, Mary Ann. "Berkeley Adopts Transgender Rights." *Bay Area Reporter*, October 12, 1995, p. 5.

Taylor, John. "The Third Sex." *Esquire*, April 1995, pp. 102-114.

Taylor, Michael. "Bobby's Secret." *Big Boys, Little Lies: Erotic Tales of Boys Who Have Something to Hide*, John Patrick, ed. Sarasota, FL: STARbooks Press, 1993, pp. 109-116.

Transexual Menace. Flyer headed "Hey HRCF: Can You Spell I-N-C-L-U-S-I-O-N?" Undated.

———. Flyer headed "HRCF to Transpeople: Drop Dead!" Undated.

Williams, Walter L. *The Spirit and the Flesh: Sexual Diversity in American Indian Culture.* Boston: Beacon Press, 1986.

Weeks, Jeffrey. *Sexuality and Its Discontents: Meanings, Myths and Modern Sexualities.* London, Boston and Henley: Routledge and Kegan Paul, 1985.

SEX CHANGES

"What Sex Am I?" narrated and directed by Lee Grant, produced by Joseph Feury, 1980 [?], broadcast on Discovery Showcase in 1995.

Wilchins, Riki Anne. "A Note from Your Editrix." *In Your Face*, Spring 1995, p. 4.

———. "Another One, It Just Doesn't Stop: Tyra Hunter." *In Your Face*, Fall 1995, pp. 2-3.

———. "APA Target of 2nd National Demonstration by Transactivists." *In Your Face* on-line press release, July 20, 1996.

———. "Brandon Teena Revisited." GenderPAC press release, December 6, 1996.

———. "Hermaphrodites with Attitude Calls for Unprecedented Demonstration." *In Your Face* on-line press release, October 17, 1996.

———. Interview by the author. December 12, 1996. Unpublished.

———. "Michigan Womyn's Music Festival Controversy Grinds On." *In Your Face*, Fall 1995, page 6.

———. "New York Citaaay." *In Your Face*, Spring 1995, p. 3

———. "1995: A Breakout Year in Review." *In Your Face*, Fall 1995, p. 1.

———. "Protesters Meet with APA." *In Your Face* on-line press release, October 19, 1996.

———. "Quotes, Quotes, Quotes." E-mail to the author, December 13, 1996, p. 1. Unpublished.

———. "Seeking A New Trial." GenderPAC press release, December 6, 1996.

———. "SF Chronicle Has Transphobia Attack." GenderPAC press release, October 18, 1996. The article "Move to Cover City Worker's Sex Changes" appeared in the *Chronicle* on September 23, 1996.

———. "The Murder of Deborah Forte." *In Your Face*, Fall 1995, p. 2.

———. "Top Psychiatrists Picketed at Creating Change." GenderPAC press release, November 12, 1996.

———. "Transactivists Protest APA—Call for End to 'Gender Identity Disorder.'" *In Your Face* on-line press release, May 5, 1996.

Additional Reading

Below is a list of work that provides additional information about transsexuality and cross-dressing. Given the enormous amount of material published on this topic, this bibliography is far from exhaustive, but it is hoped that the reader will find this material useful in and of itself, and as a jumping-off point for further research, reading, and discussion.

Books

Ackroyd, Peter. *Dressing Up: Transvestism and Drag: The History of an Obsession*, New York: Simon and Schuster, 1979.

Allen, Mariette Pathy. *Transformations: Crossdressers and Those Who Love Them*. New York: E. P. Dutton, 1989.

Beatty, Christine. *Misery Loves Company*. San Francisco: Glamazon Press, P. O. Box 423602, San Francisco, CA 94142, 1993.

Cameron, Loren. *Body Alchemy: Transsexual Portraits*. Pittsburgh and San Francisco: Cleis Press, 1996.

Denny, Dallas. *Identity Management in Transsexualism: A Practical Guide to Managing Identity on Paper*. King of Prussia, Pennsylvania: Creative Design Services, P. O. Box 61263, King of Prussia, PA 19406, 1994.

Dickens, Homer. *What a Drag: Men as Women and Women as Men in the Movies*. New York: Quill, 1984.

Feinbloom, Deborah Heller. *Transvestites and Transsexuals*. New York: A Delta Book, 1976.

Fiedler, Leslie. *Freaks: Myths and Images of the Secret Self*. New York, London, Toronto, Sydney, Auckland: Anchor Books/Doubleday, 1993. Originally published in hard-cover by Simon & Schuster in 1978.

Gagnon, John H. *Human Sexualities*. Glenview, Illinois: Scott, Foresman and Company, 1977.

Gosselin, Chris, and Glenn Wilson. *Sexual Variations: Fetishism, Transvestism and Sado-masochism*. London and Bostom: Faber and Faber, 1980.

Green, Jamison with Larry Brinkin. *Investigation into Discrimination Against Transgendered People*. Human Rights Commission, City and County of San Francisco, 25 Van Ness Avenue, Suite 800, San Francisco, CA 94102-6033, (415) 252-2500. September, 1994.

Heilbrun, Carolyn G. *Toward a Recognition of Androgyny*. New York, Evanston, San Francisco, London: Harper Colophon Books, Harper & Row, Publishers, 1974 First hard-cover edition by Alfred A. Knopf in 1973.

Kennedy, Elizabeth Lapovsky, and Madeline D. Davis. *Boots of Leather, Slippers of Gold: The History of a Lesbian Community*. New York: Penguin Books, 1993.

Kessler, Suzanne J., and Wendy McKenna. *Gender: An Ethnomethodological Approach*. New York, Chichester, Brisbane, Toronto: John Wiley & Sons, 1978.

Maitland, Sara. *Vesta Tilley*. London: Virago Press Ltd., 1986.

Maricevic, Vivienne (photos), and Vicki Goldberg (text). *La Cage aux Folles: Male to Female*. Zurich: Edition Stemmle, 1995.

Nataf, Zachary I. *Lesbians Talk Transgender*. London: Scarlet Press, 1996.

Newton, Esther. *Mother Camp: Female Impersonators in America*. Chicago and London: The University of Chicago Press, 1972.

Salem, Michael. *How to Impersonate a Woman*. New York City: Michael Salem Enterprises, 1973.

Scott, R. H. F., trans. and ed. *The Transvestite Memoirs of the Abbé de Choisy*. London: Peter Owen Limited, 1973.

Thompson, Mark. *Gay Spirit: Myth and Meaning*. New York: St. Martin's Press, 1987.

Vidal, Gore. *Myra Breckinridge*. Boston: Little, Brown, 1968.

————. *Myron*. New York: Ballantine Books, 1975.

Magazines

Please contact the publishers below for information about the current price of a sample issue or subscription. Some of the organizations mentioned in the resource list also publish newsletters or magazines.

Chrysalis: The Journal of Transgressive Gender Identities
    P. O. Box 33724
    Decatur, GA 30033
    (404) 939-0244
    Published by AEGIS

Hermaphrodites with Attitude
    The Intersex Society of North America, ISNA
    P. O. Box 31791
    San Francisco, CA 94131
    e-mail: info@isna.org.

Holy Tit Clamps
    Larry-bob
    P. O. Box 590488
    San Francisco, CA 94159-0488
    e-mail: lroberts@bellahs.com
    A yearly (more or less) directory of queer 'zines. A good place to look for homegrown transgender publications.

In Your Face
    Riki Anne Wilchins
    274 W. 11th Street
    New York, NY 10014
    e-mail: Riki@pipeline.com
    A newsletter about political activism against gender oppression.

The Transsexual News Telegraph
   41 Sutter Street, No. 1124
   San Francisco, CA 94104-4903
   (415) 703-7161
   e-mail: GailTNT@aol.com
   Make checks payable to TNT.

TV/TS Tapestry Journal
   The International Foundation for Gender Education, Inc.
   P. O. Box 229
   Waltham, MA 02154-0229
   (617) 899-2212 or 894-8340
   Contains a comprehensive directory of organizations for cross-dressers and transsexuals.

Resources

Aegis Information Center
American Education Gender Information Service
P. O. Box 33724
Decator, GA 30033
(770) 939-2128
Helpline: (770) 939-0244 answered after 6 p.m.
FAX: (770) 939-1770
e-mail: aegis@mindspring.com

The American Boyz
P. O. Box 1118
Elkton, MD 21922-1118
e-mail: majordomo@netgsi.com (with "info amboyz" in message)
A mailing list for gender variant people of any orientation and those who support them, including but not limited to tomboys, butches, f2ms, transmen, drag kings, intersexuals, with our Sos, friends, family, and allies.

Davina Anne Gabriel
4004 Troost Avenue
Kansas City, MO 64110
Back issues of TransSisters are available from her. Order form sent on request.

East Coast Female-to-Male Group (ECFTMG)
P. O. Box 60585
Florence Station
Northampton, MA 01060

The Filisa Vistima Memorial Foundation
P. O. Box 82447
Portland, OR 97282
(503) 231-9554
Founded in honor of the memory of a twenty-two-year-old Seattle transsexual who committed suicide, in part because sex reassignment was not available to her, this foundation works to make surgery and hormone therapy accessible to all transsexuals. It also challenges state laws that refuse funding for transsexuals' health care needs. It is a nonprofit corporation.

FTM International
5337 College Avenue #142
Oakland, CA 94618
http://www.ftm-intl.org/intro.html

GenderPAC
Riki Anne Wilchins, Executive Director
284 West 11th Street, No. 4R
New York, NY 10014
(212) 645-1753
Riki@Pipeline.com

GenderPAC
123 Moody Street
Waltham, MA 02156
(617) 642-8575
e-mail: GPac@GPac.Org.

Ingersoll Gender Center
1812 E. Madison Street
Seattle, WA 98122-2843
(206) 329-6651
ingersol@halcyon.com
http://www.halcyon.com/ingersol/about.html

International Conference on Transgender Law and Employment
Policy, Inc.
P. O. Drawer 35477
Houston, TX 77235-5477
(713) 777-8452
e-mail: ictlep@aol.com

International Foundation for Gender Education
P. O. Box 229
Waltham, MA 02154-0229
(617) 894-8340
(617) 899-2212
FAX (617) 899-5703
e-mail: ifge@world.std.com
http://www.transgender.org/tg/ifge

Kathy Bobula
PF3TM Newsletter
4623 N. Mississippi Ave.
Portland, OR 97217-3138
e-mail: crowbob@aol.com
Send your name and address to receive a hard copy of the newsletter;
send e-mail to get an electronic issue.

Miss Vera's Finishing School (for boys who want to be girls)
P. O. Box 1331
Old Chelsea Station
New York, NY 10011
(212) 242-6449
FAX (212) 242-2273

Partners list
e-mail: request-partners@starwars.com
For the significant others of transgendered, transsexual, and cross-
dressing people. Last time I checked, this resource was primarily for
partners of male-to-females.

The Transexual Menace
http://www.echonyc.com/~degrey/Menace.html

Transgender Forum
http://www.tgforum.com

Transgender support group listings
http://www.tgfmall.com/info/nagrp.html
wwwgrp.html

Index

SEX CHANGES

About the Author

Pat Califia is a sex radical and a feminist whose fiction and nonfiction work addresses issues such as censorship, violence, sexual variation, state regulation of pleasure, and the sex industry. In *Sex Changes,* she analyzes the history and politics of transgenderism in popular culture, medical and psychiatric discourse, literature, gay liberation, feminism, and differently-gendered communities.

Books from Cleis Press

SEXUAL POLITICS

Forbidden Passages: Writings Banned in Canada, introductions by Pat Califia and Janine Fuller.
ISBN: 1-57344-019-1 $14.95 paper.

Public Sex: The Culture of Radical Sex by Pat Califia.
ISBN: 0-939416-89-1 $12.95 paper.

Real Live Nude Girl: Chronicles of Sex-Positive Culture by Carol Queen.
ISBN: 1-57344-073-6. $14.95 paper.

Sex Work: Writings by Women in the Sex Industry, edited by Frédérique Delacoste and Priscilla Alexander.
ISBN: 0-939416-11-5 $16.95 paper.

Susie Bright's Sexual Reality: A Virtual Sex World Reader by Susie Bright.
ISBN: 0-939416-59-X $9.95 paper.

Susie Bright's Sexwise by Susie Bright.
ISBN: 1-57344-002-7 $10.95 paper.

Susie Sexpert's Lesbian Sex World by Susie Bright.
ISBN: 0-939416-35-2 $9.95 paper.

EROTIC LITERATURE

Best Gay Erotica 1997, selected by Douglas Sadownick, edited by Richard Labonté.
ISBN: 1-57344-067-1 $14.95 paper.

Best Gay Erotica 1996, selected by Scott Heim, edited by Michael Ford.
ISBN: 1-57344-052-3 $12.95 paper.

Best Lesbian Erotica 1997, selected by Jewelle Gomez, edited by Tristan Taormino.
ISBN: 1-57344-065-5 $14.95 paper.

Best Lesbian Erotica 1996, selected by Heather Lewis, edited by Tristan Taormino.
ISBN: 1-57344-054-X $12.95 paper.

Serious Pleasure: Lesbian Erotic Stories and Poetry, edited by the Sheba Collective.
ISBN: 0-939416-45-X $9.95 paper.

Switch Hitters: Lesbians Write Gay Male Erotica and Gay Men Write Lesbian Erotica, edited by Carol Queen and Lawrence Schimel.
ISBN: 1-57344-021-3 $12.95 paper.

GENDER TRANSGRESSION

Body Alchemy: Transsexual Portraits by Loren Cameron.
ISBN: 1-57344-062-0 $24.95 paper.

Dagger: On Butch Women, edited by Roxxie, Lily Burana, Linnea Due.
ISBN: 0-939416-82-4 $14.95 paper.

I Am My Own Woman: The Outlaw Life of Charlotte von Mahlsdorf, translated by Jean Hollander.
ISBN: 1-57344-010-8 $12.95 paper.

Sex Changes: The Politics of Transgenderism by Pat Califia
ISBN: 1-57344-072-8 $16.95 paper.

SEX GUIDES

Good Sex: Real Stories from Real People, second edition, by Julia Hutton.
ISBN: 1-57344-000-0 $14.95 paper.

The New Good Vibrations Guide to Sex by Cathy Winks and Anne Semans.
ISBN: 1-57344-069-8 $21.95 paper.

POLITICS OF HEALTH

The Absence of the Dead Is Their Way of Appearing by Mary Winfrey Trautmann.
ISBN: 0-939416-04-2 $8.95 paper.

Don't: A Woman's Word by Elly Danica.
ISBN: 0-939416-22-0 $8.95 paper

Voices in the Night: Women Speaking About Incest, edited by Toni A.H. McNaron and Yarrow Morgan.
ISBN: 0-939416-02-6 $9.95 paper.

With the Power of Each Breath: A Disabled Women's Anthology, edited by Susan Browne, Debra Connors and Nanci Stern.
ISBN: 0-939416-06-9 $10.95 paper.

LESBIAN AND GAY STUDIES

The Case of the Good-For-Nothing Girlfriend by Mabel Maney.
ISBN: 0-939416-91-3 $10.95 paper.

The Case of the Not-So-Nice Nurse by Mabel Maney.
ISBN: 0-939416-76-X $9.95 paper.

Nancy Clue and the Hardly Boys in A Ghost in the Closet by Mabel Maney.
ISBN: 1-57344-012-4 $10.95 paper.

Different Daughters: A Book by Mothers of Lesbians, second edition, edited by Louise Rafkin.
ISBN: 1-57344-050-7 $12.95 paper.

Different Mothers: Sons & Daughters of Lesbians Talk about Their Lives, edited by Louise Rafkin.
ISBN: 0-939416-41-7 $9.95 paper.

A Lesbian Love Advisor by Celeste West.
ISBN: 0-939416-26-3 $9.95 paper.

On the Rails: A Memoir, second edition, by Linda Niemann. Introduction by Leslie Marmon Silko.
ISBN: 1-57344-064-7. $14.95 paper.

Queer Dog: Homo Pup Poetry, edited by Gerry Gomez Pearlberg.
ISBN: 1-57344-071-X $12.95. paper.

WRITER'S REFERENCE

Putting Out: The Essential Publishing Resource Guide For Gay and Lesbian Writers, third edition, by Edisol W. Dotson.
ISBN: 0-939416-87-5 $12.95 paper.

Women & Honor: Some Notes on Lying by Adrienne Rich.
ISBN: 0-939416-44-1 $3.95 paper.

THRILLERS & DYSTOPIAS

Another Love by Erzsébet Galgóczi.
ISBN: 0-939416-51-4 $8.95 paper.

Dirty Weekend: A Novel of Revenge by Helen Zahavi.
ISBN: 0-939416-85-9 $10.95 paper.

Only Lawyers Dancing by Jan McKemmish.
ISBN: 0-939416-69-7 $9.95 paper.

The Wall by Marlen Haushofer.
ISBN: 0-939416-54-9 $9.95 paper.

TRAVEL & COOKING

Betty and Pansy's Severe Queer Review of New York by Betty Pearl and Pansy.
ISBN: 1-57344-070-1 $10.95 paper.

Betty and Pansy's Severe Queer Review of San Francisco by Betty Pearl and Pansy.
ISBN: 1-57344-056-6 $10.95 paper.

Food for Life & Other Dish, edited by Lawrence Schimel.
ISBN: 1-57344-061-2 $14.95 paper.

Since 1980, Cleis Press publishes provocative books by women (and a few men) in the United States and Canada. We welcome your order and will ship your books as quickly as possible. Individual orders must be prepaid (U.S. dollars only). Please add 15% shipping. CA residents please add 8.5% sales tax.

Mail orders: Cleis Press, PO Box 14684, San Francisco, CA 94114.

MasterCard and Visa orders: include account number, exp. date, and signature.

FAX your credit card order: (415) 575-4705.

Or, phone us Mon-Fri, 9 am - 5 pm PST: (415) 575-4700.

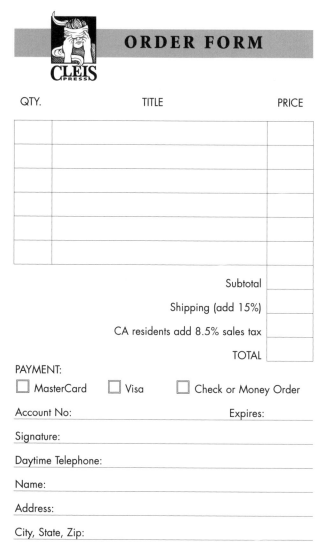

ORDER FORM

CLEIS PRESS

QTY.	TITLE	PRICE
	Subtotal	
	Shipping (add 15%)	
	CA residents add 8.5% sales tax	
	TOTAL	

PAYMENT:

☐ MasterCard   ☐ Visa   ☐ Check or Money Order

Account No: _____   Expires: _____

Signature: _____

Daytime Telephone: _____

Name: _____

Address: _____

City, State, Zip: _____